Teach Yourself
DYNAMIC HTML
in a Week

Bruce Campbell
Rick Darnell

201 West 103rd Street
Indianapolis, Indiana 46290

President, Sams Publishing   Richard K. Swadley
Publishing Manager   Mark Taber
Acquisitions Manager   Beverly M. Eppink
Managing Editor   Jodi Jensen
Indexing Manager   Johnna L. VanHoose
Director of Marketing   Kelli S. Spencer
Product Marketing Manager   Wendy Gilbride
Marketing Coordinator   Linda B. Beckwith

Acquisitions Editor
Randi Roger

Development Editor
Bob Correll

Production Editor
Tonya R. Simpson

Copy Editor
Kristen Ivanetich

Indexer
Erika Millen

Technical Reviewer
Brett Bonenberger

Editorial Coordinators
Mandie Rowell
Katie Wise

Technical Edit Coordinator
Lorraine E. Schaffer

Resource Coordinator
Deborah Frisby

Editorial Assistants
Carol Ackerman
Andi Richter
Rhonda Tinch-Mize
Karen Williams

Cover Designer
Tim Amrhein

Book Designer
Gary Adair

Copy Writer
David Reichwein

Production Team Supervisor
Brad Chinn

Production
Jennifer Dierdorff
Brad Lenser
Paula Lowell
Ian A. Smith

Overview

Contents

Contents

To Jane, Margaret, and Elizabeth.
—Rick Darnell

To my nuclear family in the information age.
—Bruce Campbell

Acknowledgments

Of all the projects I've worked on for Macmillan, this has been one of the most intriguing, even more so than the many pages I've churned out about Java and JavaScript. Dynamic HTML is an interesting concept with a rather nebulous implementation. Writing about it is like trying to pack shaving cream into a tight ball—the harder you push, the more it pops out through your fingers.

Bruce and I have tried the best we can to put a handle on this new technology. It's an exciting technology that holds a lot of promise for Web developers and authors. While making page authoring a bit more complicated by uniting scripts, style sheets, and other elements, it also simplifies life by reducing the need for server programs and other specialty items.

Even as exciting as this stuff is, I do need to take a moment and stand on my soapbox. The Internet is only technology. Life is what happens on the outside of the computer, not inside it. Don't forget to take a break and go pull some weeds, walk in the wind, or just sit and watch the sun move across the sky for a few minutes.

For the last several years I've had this thing I call a writing career. There are two really neat aspects about getting paid for putting words on paper. The first is seeing your name in print. I know it's vain, but I get great satisfaction from seeing my name attached to a work like this.

The second is the people you meet along the way, who make the whole process possible and enjoyable. We writers are pretty pointless without editors, and vice versa. It's one of those dichotomies that results in a certain tension, but also holds incredible satisfaction when both sides reach the end of the process and another book is born.

With that preamble, I send a big thanks to Bruce Campbell, the co-author on this project. His technical knowledge and easygoing manner made this book very enjoyable. I learned a great deal in our exchanges about the content, style, and structure of the book. For having never met the man before the first draft was completed, I think we turned out a fine book. We hope you agree.

Our Acquisitions Editor, Randi Roger, was a great coordinator and cheerleader. She's been there since the beginning, working on outlines, recruiting Bruce and me to work on the project, and making sure we delivered the goods. Bob Correll was the Development Editor, and worked hard to make sure we knew what we were talking about and communicated it clearly to you.

Many other folks at Macmillan Computer Publishing make these projects happen, from the Publisher and lawyers, to technical and copy editors, production editors, designers, lawyers, secretaries, custodians, and many others. Although I don't know everyone's name, they all make a contribution to the finished product. Many thanks to you all.

I also extend thanks to Battalion Chief Jess Mickelson of the Missoula (Montana) Rural Fire District, the head of our regional hazardous materials team. He's been very supportive when I've had to miss training for deadlines, and he continues to offer me the chance to use the HazMat team as lab rats for my ideas in utilizing emerging technology to develop the team's capabilities and efficiency.

And then there are the many people who have fostered me along the way, giving me the needed guidance so I could learn how to put the right words in the right order. This list includes Bonnie Montgall, David MacFarland, John Braden, and influences such as Edward Abbey, Kenneth Grahame, and A.A. Milne.

Last in this list of acknowledgments, but certainly not least, is you, the reader. I hope you find this book useful and worth the money you shelled out for it. If it makes your job easier or gives you the tools to develop new ways of communicating with your fellow humans, then Bruce and I have done our jobs. Thank you.

—*Rick Darnell*

I would like to acknowledge the folks at Sams, Microsoft, Netscape, and the Web community in a fashion similar to Rick as well as Rick himself.

Personally, I would like to acknowledge my fellow researchers at the HIT Lab who took the time to provide valuable feedback for the examples in this book. I especially wish to thank Mark Billinghurst, Suzanne Weghorst, and Susan Tanney who kept my enthusiasm going throughout this project. I must also show appreciation for the district staff at Catapult who have provided me often with the opportunity to teach HTML courses and keep my skills up-to-date through interaction with such wonderful students.

—*Bruce Campbell*

About the Authors

Bruce Campbell

Bruce Campbell (bdc@hitl.washington.edu) lives in Seattle, WA and works with technologies related to Web-based 3D collaboration, such as VRML. When he is not writing, he is either teaching for Catapult training centers or Central Seattle Community College, performing VR-related research at the Human Interface Technology Laboratory at the University of Washington, or running around somewhere in North America. His home page URL is http://www.hitl.washington.edu/people/bdc/.

Rick Darnell

Rick Darnell (darnell@montana.com) is a flatlander by nature, currently living with his wife and two daughters in the middle of a bunch of mountains in Montana. He began his print career at a small weekly newspaper after graduating from Kansas State University with a degree in broadcasting. While spending time as a freelance journalist and writer, Rick has seen the full gamut of personal computers since starting out with a Radio Shack Model I in the late 1970s. When not in front of his computer, he serves as a volunteer firefighter/EMT and member of a regional hazardous materials response team. Rick has authored and contributed to many books for Sams.net Publishing and Que, including *HTML 4 Unleashed*.

Tell Us What You Think!

As a reader, you are the most important critic and commentator of our books. We value your opinion and want to know what we're doing right, what we could do better, what areas you'd like to see us publish in, and any other words of wisdom you're willing to pass our way. You can help us make strong books that meet your needs and give you the computer guidance you require.

Do you have access to the World Wide Web? Then check out our site on the World Wide Web at `http://www.mcp.com/sams`.

 NOTE

> If you have a technical question about this book, call the technical support line at 317-581-3833, or send e-mail to `support@mcp.com`.

As the team leader of the group that created this book, I welcome your comments. You can fax, e-mail, or write me directly to let me know what you did or didn't like about this book—as well as what we can do to make our books stronger. Here's the information:

Fax: 317-581-4669

E-mail: `newtech_mgr@sams.mcp.com`

Mail: Mark Taber
          Comments Department
          Sams Publishing
          201 W. 103rd Street
          Indianapolis, IN 46290

Introduction

Welcome to the dawn of the point-and-click, drag-and-drop, interactive Web. Welcome to Dynamic HTML.

What is Dynamic HTML? It's an emerging Web standard that revolutionizes how Web authors add interactive, dynamic features to their Web pages. At the same time, Dynamic HTML relieves a Web server's load by shifting the processing demands for animation, data processing, and other interactive features to the client machine.

So the question remains, what is Dynamic HTML? Dynamic HTML is a combination of technologies, including HTML, scripting, and object-oriented programming combined to create individual Web pages. It's not a new version of HTML, it's not a new scripting language, it's not a new way of structuring documents. It's a new way of tying all of those pieces together to make pages that cross the traditional static Web page boundary.

Why Dynamic HTML? Both Netscape and Microsoft hear the market screaming for easy-to-use Web page tools and easy-to-add features. Both companies have created a dynamic Web page object model for you to use to extend your HTML tags within a context that has a reasonable learning curve for an HTML aficionado. You can learn Dynamic HTML in a week.

At the same time, both Netscape and Microsoft have heard the cries of the electronic publishers of the world. Some electronic documents just have not looked the same when converted to HTML files. Dynamic HTML makes extensive use of new style sheet specifications to give a Web author more control over the exact placement and appearance of elements on the Web page. In fact, Netscape and Microsoft extend the style sheet concept to Web readers. You, as a Web surfer, can specify your own style sheets to use when browsing the Web.

The features of Dynamic HTML are working their way into the HTML standard through the primary standards maker for the Web—the World Wide Web Consortium. Do the features of Dynamic HTML deserve such recognition? Yes. Absolutely. Without a doubt. Tools are already in development to author Web pages that include Dynamic HTML's features and hide the messy details of coding from an author. But, even with new tools on the horizon, a strong understanding of the technical details will go a long way in helping you understand what's happening to your pages when the finished product hits the Web server. Staying on the edge has always required putting in the extra effort.

Do you have to know anything about Dynamic HTML to read this book? No. A solid knowledge of HTML is needed, and we'll supply the rest. Over the next seven days, you'll work your way through the building blocks of Dynamic HTML and into the details, including building Web pages that can change themselves without the help of the Web server, and tables that can receive data from databases without CGI scripts.

Aaahhhh. The wonders of the information age. Hope you enjoy the wonders of the Web. Hope you enjoy Dynamic HTML and the interactive features it adds to the world's Web-surfing citizens. And, in the spirit of the Web:

Have Fun!

Who Should Read This Book?

We wrote this book for the vast numbers of people who have spent the time to understand HTML and are chomping at the bit for new features. Perhaps, at the same time, we have written this book for people who have been using technology for a long time and are quick learners as well. Because we provide the complete HTML file listing for each example and Web page authoring is so visual (what you see is what you get), you could probably get through this book without understanding anything about HTML.

Still, our primary audience is those readers who have read the *Teach Yourself Web Publishing with HTML in a Week* book and enjoy its style. We have worked hard not to disappoint the Sams *Teach Yourself* series fans. If you have not read a technical book on HTML (standards 1.0, 2.0, or 3.2), you might want to read one first. Even for readers who think HTML is straightforward technically, understanding the philosophy of its intent makes sense. We've included a bit of DHTML philosophy and rationale along with the lessons and examples.

What This Book Is

This book is a do-it-yourself primer on Dynamic HTML. Because Dynamic HTML means different things to Netscape, Microsoft, and the W3C, there is a lot of philosophy mixed in with the examples you create and follow in each chapter. This book covers every major feature of Dynamic HTML we have found through Web surfing, discussions, and electronic mail messages from Microsoft and Netscape.

By following examples that build on one another, you learn how to add features to Web pages in order to let your readership interact with a Web page. You add dynamically changing text, styles, and graphics, provide interactive access to a data source, and add animations to your Web pages, all of which readers can access through mouse- and keyboard-based events. You learn how to place text and graphics more precisely on a Web page as well as define a region on a Web page where your readers can drag and drop graphics themselves. We cover competing technologies at appropriate places within the text in order to round out your knowledge of interactive Web pages.

What You Need Before You Start

Because Dynamic HTML is a way of integrating existing HTML technologies, all you need to create Dynamic HTML files is a simple text editor (such as the Notepad application accessory provided with either the Windows or NT operating systems). You can use a word processor as well or a more sophisticated Integrated Development Environment (IDE) that comes with many of today's visual programming applications.

To see the Web pages you create in an interactive mode, you need either the Netscape Communicator or Microsoft Internet Explorer 4.0 Web browser. To see all the examples in this book perform their dynamic features, you need both Communicator and Internet Explorer 4.0. Both are available on the Web for download. Because Dynamic HTML is not implemented as a standard, Netscape and Microsoft present different implementations. We provide examples of each implementation.

A live Internet connection is not necessary except for one ActiveX example in Chapter 13, "Integrating Other Languages and Objects into Dynamic HTML." Yet, having access to the Web will let you look up the many Web pages referenced throughout the text in this book.

Your Week At a Glance

The week begins on Day 1, "Introducing Dynamic HTML," with an introduction to Dynamic HTML concepts, including a more complete definition of DHTML and an overview of where it lies within the standards process.

Day 2, "The Building Blocks of Dynamic HTML," continues to build the foundations with a look at the Document Object Model, which serves as the foundation of virtually everything that DHTML can accomplish. It also includes a course in Cascading Style Sheets, which become critical to changing the appearance of your Web pages.

Day 3, "The Role of Scripting in Dynamic HTML," moves to the next step with a look at scripting and its role in creating DHTML. This includes an overview of JavaScript style sheets and how to detect and respond to user events.

Day 4, "Dynamically Changing Text and Styles," and Day 5, "Dynamically Changing Content and Placement," is where all the pieces start to come together. You'll learn how to change the appearance and content of Web pages using a combination of scripting and style sheets.

Day 6, "Creating Data-Aware Documents," moves to one powerful use of DHTML—data-aware documents. New attributes associated with DHTML enable you to create connections to databases without the need to use server-side scripting. The result is a major breakthrough in creating Web pages that can interact with data, by placing all the data functions within familiar HTML tags.

Day 7, "Advanced Issues," is a wrap-up and review of the week, with a look at using other scripting languages such as VBScript to create Dynamic HTML pages. You'll also take a look at using your new knowledge and abilities in a responsible manner. When you're finished, we want you to create pages that are going to help your users, not drive them to distraction.

Last is the set of appendixes. We know you'll have questions while you're working your way through the week. Instead of keeping another three or four books open at your side to look up information on HTML, style sheets, and scripting, we've provided a set of quick reference chapters that cover all the technologies we've implemented.

After you're finished, the rest is up to you. Dynamic HTML offers new and exciting ways to enable your Web pages to communicate with your audience. And, isn't that what you're looking for? You've come to the right place—read on!

Conventions Used in This Book

This book contains several conventions to aid you in your learning process.

 A *new term* is highlighted with italics or with this icon to clarify its meaning.

 Note boxes highlight important or explanatory information in the surrounding text.

 These helpful nuggets offer insight or shortcuts to programming puzzles.

Pay special attention to warnings. They may save you time and money!

INPUT This icon appears next to a listing that you should enter to follow along with the lesson.

➥ This arrow at the beginning of a line of code means that a single line of code requires multiple lines on the page. Many lines of code contain a large number of characters, which might normally wrap on your screen. However, printing limitations require a break when lines reach a maximum number of characters. Continue to type all characters after the ➥ as though they are part of the previous line.

Introducing Dynamic HTML

Chapter 1

What Is Dynamic HTML?

It's Day 1 of your week with Dynamic HTML (DHTML). You've chosen to embark on a voyage to learn what Dynamic HTML (DHTML) is, and more importantly, to learn to develop your own Web pages using the Dynamic HTML techniques presented in this book. You might not have any idea what DHTML is, but that's OK; it's so new that no one is an expert yet. But here's the good news: You don't need to be an expert. All you need is a basic grounding in Web development and a desire to learn some scripting.

This book goes beyond the hype about DHTML on the Web and in the numerous trade magazines. It looks at the theory, concepts, and implementations, and separates heads from tails on this new way to look at Web pages.

As you get started, it helps to have a common terminology and frame of reference. That's what this chapter is for. DHTML is a moving target—everybody says DHTML is exciting, but not everyone is talking about the same technologies or capabilities. So take some time here to put a handle on it so that you can get an idea of what you're in for.

This chapter introduces the concepts and possibilities that DHTML brings to the World Wide Web, including the following:

- ☐ What Dynamic HTML is
- ☐ Different ways to implement Dynamic HTML
- ☐ How you're going to learn to implement Dynamic HTML on your Web pages

The examples in this chapter illustrate the basics of some important ideas. Don't worry too much about understanding how the examples work; those details are handled later in the week. We're just giving you a "sneak peek" at what a DHTML page looks like under the hood. In the meantime, sit back and take a look at the next generation of Web publishing.

What Is Dynamic HTML?

Dynamic HTML is a big term that can encompass a lot of ground or very little—it all depends on who's using it. For the next seven days, you will learn the definition of the term and some different ways to implement DHTML in a variety of ways for a variety of uses.

NEW TERM *Dynamic* as it's used in *Dynamic HTML* doesn't follow the traditional dictionary definition of the word. Like most good followers of grand ideas, users and devotees to the World Wide Web take existing words and shift them around to mean something else. In the context of HTML, *dynamic* means subject to change at any time. In the real world, it means continual change. I hope my former high school English teacher, Mrs. Montgall, will forgive the impropriety.

NEW TERM *HTML* stands for *HyperText Markup Language*, and consists of a set of tags that define how a page should be displayed on the browser. In the early days of the Web, these tags were based on structure and content, which meant that the user's machine could interpret the tags in the best way it could. With the massive rush of new users onto the Web, designers sought to achieve greater control over the appearance of pages to attract as many people to their site as possible. Software developers responded with many new tags to control the physical appearance of the Web page and leave fewer decisions to the browser.

Traditional HTML is static. After it's loaded onto a browser, it just sits there like a good dog. You can look all you want at it, but it's not going to change. You can click on a hyperlink and then return to the starting page, but the page isn't going to change. You can stand on your head in a corner while moving the computer mouse, but the page isn't going to change. Do you get the point?

The HTML tags used to create a Web page are interpreted by the browser as the page is loaded. The tags tell the browser what kind of headings to use, where to place new paragraphs, which addresses to associate with hyperlinks, where to put images, and so on. When the browser is finished, the page is displayed and all processing stops until the browser sends a new request to the Web server.

HTML has advanced a lot from its early days. One of the latest and most useful developments is called a *style sheet*. A style sheet basically is an extension of HTML that allows a much finer degree of control over how the browser interprets elements, resulting in more control over the appearance and placement of text and other objects on a Web page. However, the Web page still is a static creature. After all the style rules are defined and interpreted, the browser displays the page and there it sits, just like a good dog.

So far, HTML has done everything expected of it. That's all well and good, but a discerning public demands more from their good dogs and HTML. After all, they've paid a lot of money to buy a computer and hook up to the Internet, and they expect to see a little more than an electronic rendition of a book page. This type of expectation leads us to Dynamic HTML— a page that can change after the server is finished delivering the page to the browser.

This is the concept you're going to spend your time with over the next seven days. The Dynamic HTML you will learn about means a Web page can react to the user *without relying on the server or depending on an embedded program*. This is very important, so I'll say it again. *Dynamic HTML can change itself.* This is a pretty big leap for the static Web page you started with at the beginning of this section.

Does this mean radically changing the old HTML we all know and love—the <H1> and the <STRONG> and the <A HREF>? No, it means adding a way to control whether an element is displayed. This also includes how and where the element is displayed. To accomplish these tasks requires a couple of things: a way to get a handle on any element on the page, and a way to control those elements with scripts.

The Document Object Model

First, DHTML needs a way to look at the document. When you work with static HTML, the browser looks at the entire document, interprets it, displays it, and is finished with it. It begins and ends life as a text file filled with display instructions. With Dynamic HTML, the document takes on a structure of its own, which is called the Document Object Model (DOM).

The DOM works something like this: Although the page still exists as a text file, the browser now handles it differently. As the browser encounters each element on the page, it notes what the element is and where it is and places it in a stack with similar elements. In this way, it can keep track of everything on the page, from the smallest <H6> heading and <HR> horizontal rule, to all of the elements on a form. In essence, the browser creates a database each time a page is loaded, and each tag becomes a record in the database.

It's kind of like looking at a chessboard. Think of the board as the page, and each of the pieces are elements on the page. There is a variety of pieces, and some duplication among all of them. However, each is handled and moved individually.

Controlling the Document with Scripts

Next, DHTML needs a way to control how the different elements of the document are controlled. This is accomplished through scripting languages, such as JavaScript or Visual Basic Scripting Edition (VBScript). The scripting language is equipped with the knowledge to tap into the various elements on the page, look at their settings, and make the wanted changes.

NEW TERM   *Scripting languages* are specialized programming languages that are inserted on a Web page to control different elements of the page, including elements, frames, and the browser interface. They have fairly limited power, because they can run only within a Web page on a browser compatible with a scripting language, such as Internet Explorer or Navigator.

In short, Dynamic HTML is not about server-side scripts, Java applets, or animated GIF images. All of these can accomplish nifty things on their own, except for changing the content of the Web page without a return trip to the server.

Dynamic HTML is about grabbing hold of any element on the page, at any time after the page has downloaded, and changing its appearance, content, or location on the page. This includes a lot of neat things, such as dragging images from one place to another or expanding and collapsing documents that provide instant results to a user.

Although Dynamic HTML is just one more step in the natural evolution of the World Wide Web, it's a very important one. It enables Web pages to act much more like computer programs and interactive CD-ROMs rather than as the static book pages they've been limited to for so long.

Some Features of Dynamic HTML

Dynamic HTML isn't an official term on the Web—at least it hasn't yet been blessed by the World Wide Web Consortium (referred to as W3C—see the next chapter for more information about its work). However, the term is growing in use by some vendors to describe the combination of HTML, style sheets, and scripts that let documents grow beyond their traditional lifeless behavior and appearance.

W3C has received several submissions from member companies on the ways in which an HTML document can attain dynamic behavior. The submissions to the W3C include offerings from both Netscape and Microsoft, which increases the importance and difficulty of the role of W3C as arbiter to make sure interoperable and scripting-language neutral solutions are the best for everyone, and not just one of the software developers' products.

With all of that preamble out of the way, it's time to take a closer look at some of the basic features of DHTML that have been identified by one or more of the players developing the standards.

Changing Tags and Content

This is the bit I was harping on just a few minutes ago. The capability to change tags and their content utilizes the Document Object Model, which uncovers everything for change, including all tags and style sheet attributes. Figure 1.1 is a shot from Microsoft's overview of its version of DHTML. Note that it's just a bunch of headings.

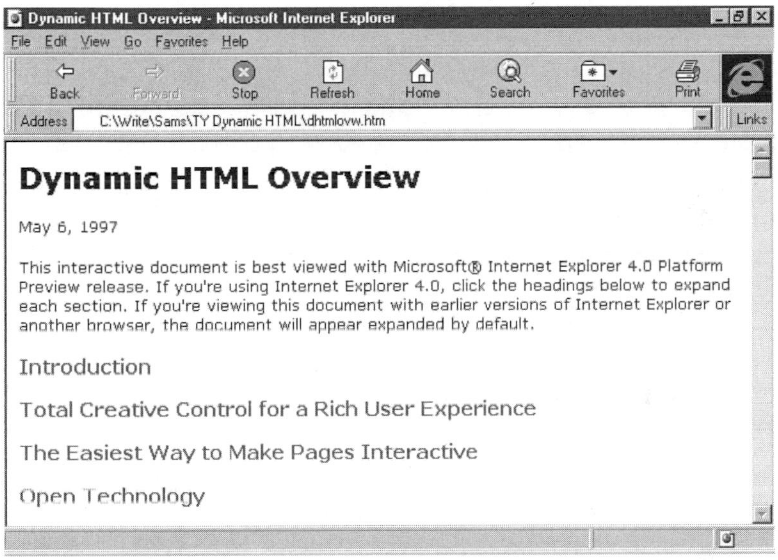

Figure 1.1.

A Dynamic HTML Web page by Microsoft initially displays as a set of headings without much text.

Here's the neat part. Each of the headings is a special hyperlink that runs a script instead of loading another page. If you click on one of the headings, voilá! Without any browser-server gyrations, the page is changed. Figure 1.2 shows the same page, which now displays a paragraph of text to read under the heading. This is a pretty slick trick, and it's all accomplished with a little bit of JavaScript and an extra style tag or two.

In a nutshell, this is how this particular DHTML page works: The headings are hyperlinks with the names of JavaScript functions as their URLs. The paragraph under each heading is marked with an inline style that indicates that its contents should not be displayed. When the user clicks on the heading, the JavaScript routine changes the no-show to show, and the browser updates the page to reflect the new status. It's really that simple.

Are you excited yet? Read on.

Figure 1.2.
Clicking on a heading reveals the text hidden underneath without any additional server interaction.

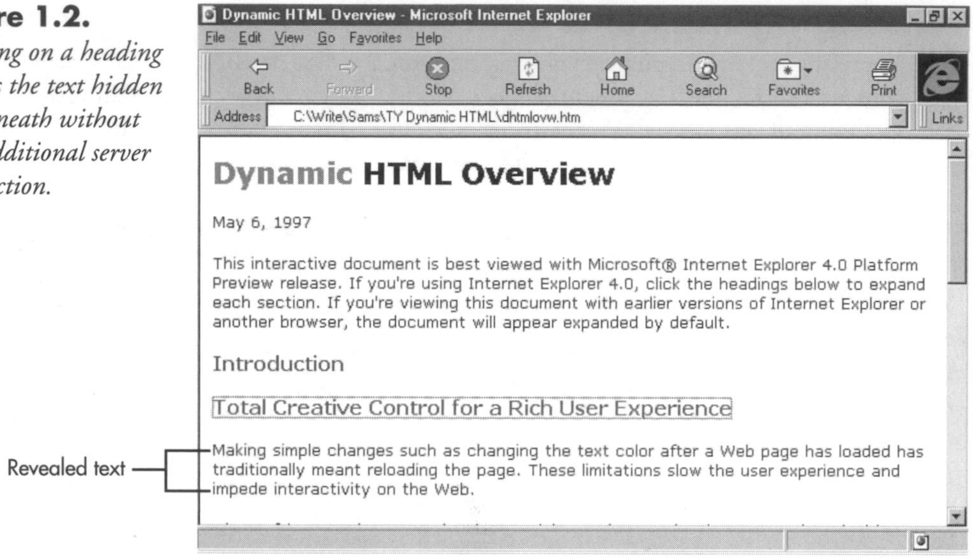

Dynamic HTML Overview - Microsoft Internet Explorer

File Edit View Go Favorites Help

Back Forward Stop Refresh Home Search Favorites Print

Address C:\Write\Sams\TY Dynamic HTML\dhtmlovw.htm   Links

Dynamic HTML Overview

May 6, 1997

This interactive document is best viewed with Microsoft® Internet Explorer 4.0 Platform Preview release. If you're using Internet Explorer 4.0, click the headings below to expand each section. If you're viewing this document with earlier versions of Internet Explorer or another browser, the document will appear expanded by default.

Introduction

Total Creative Control for a Rich User Experience

Revealed text —— Making simple changes such as changing the text color after a Web page has loaded has traditionally meant reloading the page. These limitations slow the user experience and impede interactivity on the Web.

Live Positioning of Elements

Live element positioning can turn Web pages into an interactive playground. The term *interactive* once meant that the user was interacting with some embedded program or plug-in, or he or she was filling out a form and clicking a submit button.

Both Microsoft and Netscape include this capability with their implementations of DHTML, although they accomplish it in different ways. Microsoft uses the style sheet <DIV> tag, whereas Netscape can use <DIV> or its own <LAYER> invention (layers are covered in more detail later in the book).

Between the two companies, there are several ways to move things around on the page after the page is loaded into the browser. First, the movement can happen automatically. Examples of this are illustrated with Netscape's layers, which make it possible to incorporate slides, fades, and other animated effects (see Figures 1.3 and 1.4). This is accomplished by hiding or moving each layer independently of the others to any position on the screen. They can overlap, let other layers show through, or hide everything underneath.

The process of layering, also referred to as *z-ordering*, makes it possible to download an entire site or section of a site at one time. Each layer represents one page, and because all the layers are loaded into the user's browser to begin with, no additional requests to the server are needed. As the user requests additional pages, the browser simply passes the requested pages to the top of the stack for viewing. It's a lot like dealing from the bottom of the deck, except the recipient is on the winning side instead of the losing side.

Figure 1.3.

The initial appearance of this page looks rather simple.

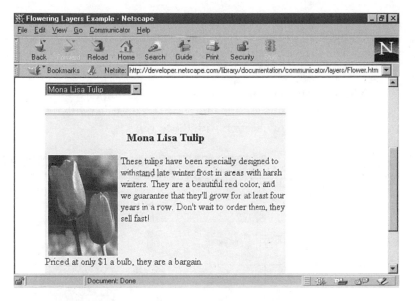

Figure 1.4.

Using the <LAYER> tag and a form element, another set of text and graphics replaces the original picture.

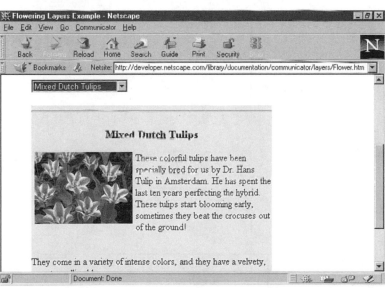

NEW TERM *z-ordering* comes from the old *x* and *y* coordinate system you learned in high school geometry. Where *x* and *y* describe two dimensions (height and width), the *z* element describes the third dimension (depth).

The Microsoft approach is capable of the same types of effects, plus the movement of specific elements on the screen. Instead of moving a section of the Web page, the user can click on a single element, such as a graphic or plug-in, and drag it to a new location on the page (see Figures 1.5 and 1.6).

The best part about these changes is that they don't require additional software, such as Java applets. The animation and movement are provided within the Web page itself and without additional communication with the server.

Figure 1.5.
Watch what happens to the "live" image selected with the mouse pointer.

Select this graphic

Figure 1.6.
The image is now relocated to the bottom of the screen after it was moved manually by the user.

Moving the graphic

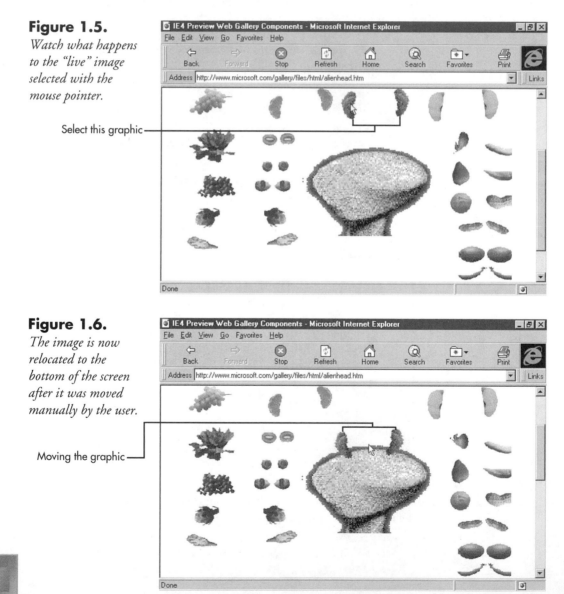

Dynamic Fonts

Netscape developed the idea of dynamic fonts, and it hopefully will catch on with other browsers. If you've worked with style sheets or the <FONT> command, you've probably become aware of a severe limitation: just because you specify a font doesn't mean that the user has it on his or her machine. The end result is that the page developer just doesn't know how the page is going to appear.

You can try to work around the problem with style sheets or the <FONT> tag by providing a list of fonts in order of preference, followed by a general type such as sans-serif. This works, but not very elegantly. Netscape's way around this uses TrueDoc technology from BitStream. The result is font information in a highly compressed format that is downloaded with the page. The details of the font are stored in vector format, which is assembled on-the-fly using common information from a library on the user's machine.

NEW TERM   A *vector format* describes a picture—which includes individual letters—as a series of shapes. This includes all the curves, lines, and other attributes of the shape, which is stored in a much smaller space than a similar image in a bitmapped format.

Data Binding

Data binding is one of the features Microsoft has worked hard to develop. Data binding enables page elements such as table cells to "attach" themselves to database records. This might not seem like a big deal, but this feature is a big leap forward for page authors.

Displaying database records currently requires advanced programming in a language such as C or Perl to access the database across a network connection and retrieve the desired information, which is virtually identical to using a CGI script for dynamic content (see the next section, "Other Approaches to Dynamic Web Pages"). Other programs, such as Backstage, have made this connection easier to create and manipulate. However, even using special authoring software requires the use of a special server and complicated instructions embedded on the page. In short, you can't just slap a database connection on a page and expect it to work.

With direct data binding, this middle ground of database processing is passed over. Changes to a record are updated on-screen, while user modification of information is passed back to the database for updating. This is accomplished with a new attribute for the <TABLE> tag, which names the database to use for the contents of the table. By using the functions supported by Microsoft, authors now can connect to virtually any database, including comma-delimited, SQL, ODBC, and JDBC.

NEW TERM   *Comma-delimited, SQL, ODBC,* and *JDBC* are all types of databases. A comma-delimited database usually is represented by a text file, in which each field is separated by a comma and each record is separated by a carriage return. SQL stands for Structured Query Language and is the favorite choice of network programmers. It defines a common set of commands used for a variety of databases. ODBC and JDBC stand for Open Database Connectivity and Java Database Connectivity, respectively. These two standards are similar to SQL in that they define common ground for a program to access a database without resorting to a bunch of commands that are specific to one database.

By allowing users to channel input directly back and forth between the browser and a database, the amount of time it takes to complete the interaction is shortened dramatically because only the data or its display is changing, not the entire page.

Other Approaches to Dynamic Web Pages

O.K., you've heard all the fanfare and hoopla about Dynamic HTML and the wondrous things it does for Web pages. So what, right? There are lots of ways to add dynamic features to a Web page without installing a new browser and tacking on a scripting language to bring the electronic page to life.

NEW TERM *O.K.* began life as a printer's mark for *all correct*. I just hope it wasn't the printer doing the proofreading. What does this have to do with DHTML? Nothing, but it might gain you an extra $3,000 in *You Don't Know Jack*.

Just to be fair, here's a quick survey of some other ways to add dynamic capability to a Web page. Understand that because we're writing this book and want it to sell like hotcakes, we're leaning toward DHTML as the quicker and easier way to implement these new features on a Web page. However, there are other methods mentioned earlier in this chapter, and here's a quick survey of how they fit into the equation.

CGI Scripts

Still a favorite method for many Web developers, CGI scripts offer a lot of power and flexibility in their operation. To change a page, the user clicks on a hyperlink or submits a form to connect the browser with the server, which contains a script that evaluates what happened and generates a new page in response. The new page might be a revised version of the current one, or a completely new creation.

NEW TERM *CGI* stands for Common Gateway Interface. It is a standard that describes how Web servers should connect to external programs, which in turn generate new Web pages. CGI programs are called scripts, and they usually describe how to handle input submitted by a Web form.

There are a lot of interesting things you can do with a CGI script, such as interact with databases or create Web pages with user-specific content. Other possibilities include creating sites that depend on various forms of information management, such as order processing or access to archives.

Although CGI scripts are powerful tools, they're still slow. In addition to the client-server transactions required for the original page, it requires an additional interchange for the subsequent page, plus the additional processing time required to run the script. This probably is the biggest drawback to CGI scripts. The browser must send the input for the script, which is received by the Web server, evaluated, and processed, and then a new page is sent back to the browser. It's like browsing to a whole new page, except there's some additional processing time thrown in.

If only one user is connected to the server, then server processing time probably isn't an issue. However, if the server is dealing with a lot of requests for other pages and script processing, the server's host computer can start to become bogged down with all the demands. This slows the process for the user that much more.

The other problem with CGI scripts is the time it takes to put one together. It involves writing a small program in one of the common scripting languages such as Perl, testing it with a variety of input, and then posting it to the Web site. The development process is long when compared with the time required to put together a Web page.

Java Applets

CGI scripts are neat, but using them requires some knowledge of client-server relations. Therefore, some bright people at Sun Microsystems developed a way to embed Web pages with programs that could run on any computer. This was accomplished with applets written in languages such as Java. A Java applet has the capability to interact with the user and in some cases look at or modify various elements of the Web page.

NEW TERM *Java* is a programming language developed by Sun Microsystems. It has found an enthusiastic audience with its "write once, run anywhere" capability. The same piece of Java code can run on any computer equipped with the Java Virtual Machine.

NEW TERM An *applet* is like an application such as a spreadsheet, except it needs a host program (such as a browser) to run. For example, the little Microsoft Graph program packaged with Word or Excel works only within those programs. In turn, its output is displayed only within documents created by the parent program.

Applets offer a way for you to build applications customized to a Web page or site (see Figure 1.7). An applet can also be extended to recognize various elements on the Web page, such as the contents of form elements.

The clnet applet in Figure 1.7 is designed to gather information from the user, which is then passed along to a CGI script that generates the final results. This is typical of some of the more advanced Java applets. At some level, most require another connection with the server to generate a new page with updated information.

Figure 1.7.

This Java applet from c\net develops a shopping list for building a home computer network.

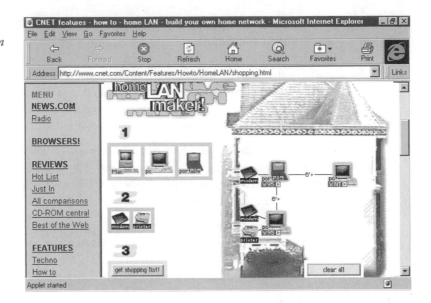

This applet shows some of the power of Java. After all, Java is a full-featured programming language capable of great things. Take HotJava, for example, which is a not-too-bad Web browser written entirely in Java.

Because applets behave just like programs, they're capable of a great deal. However, they still have some critical drawbacks. First, you must know how to program in Java. Java isn't the hardest language in the world to learn, but you still need to know about Web-based programming, and that's a level beyond most HTML authors. Then, like a CGI script, Java applets aren't able to update a Web page without reloading the entire page or referring back to a CGI script on the server.

Although designing the applet itself to interact with the user is a fairly simple and straightforward task, actually doing anything with the Web page in which the applet is located is more complicated. You can use scripting languages to help control the applet's behavior, and Netscape has provided an additional set of tools to help the applet look at the Web page. If the applet is going to start working with the contents of a form or other page elements, it is typically written for that specific page. You can probably start to see rather quickly the implications of customizing a program to fit every page where you want interaction with the Web page.

One other drawback to applets is the same as for other external content to a Web page—the download time for the page is increased because one more element on the page has to be loaded, initialized, and started. By the same token, the applet chews up some additional resources when you leave the host page. While you're waiting for a page to load, the Java

Virtual Machine in the browser stops the applet's execution and releases all of the resources it sucked up.

If the applet uses any images or other support files, the download times are extended that much more. Although Java transports well across computer platforms, it still has the big drawback of requiring additional bandwidth to copy a Java-powered page.

Plug-Ins and ActiveX Controls

There are some very important differences between plug-ins and ActiveX controls, but their purpose on the page is basically the same. Like an applet, they add additional features and functionality to a Web page without directly affecting the host page. And, again like applets, creating interaction between the user and the plug-in is easier.

Plug-ins were initially developed by Netscape, and ActiveX controls are a Microsoft invention. The basic principle of both is that the controlling software is loaded onto the user's computer, and then the Web page contains another file that contains the specific instructions or content. This type of interactive software can do all sorts of things, such as provide an interface to look at different types of graphic files (including movies and animations), listen to special sound files, view and edit spreadsheet and word processing files, or even play games.

However, like the applets, plug-ins and ActiveX controls also add to the download burden of a page. In addition to the time it takes to download and install the actual plug-in or control, there's also the extra time to download the content files. It also is virtually impossible to get a plug-in or control to interact with other elements on the page. Some ActiveX controls are used to provide features such as tooltips or pop-up menus, but, like plug-ins, these items are operated directly by the control, and their reach doesn't extend beyond the features itself.

Client-Pull

Client-pull is how the vast majority of users get their content on the Web. They type a URL, or click a hyperlink, which sends a request (the pull) for a page. There are other methods to implement this as dynamic behavior. One is to use a special tag called <META> in the header. Used with the HTTP-EQUIV=REFRESH attribute, the <META> tag causes the browser to reload the page from the server after a predetermined number of seconds, specified with CONTENT=seconds. If you wanted the browser to reload the current page in four seconds, you would add this tag to your HTML page:

```
<META HTTP-EQUIV="Refresh" CONTENT=4>
```

This starts a process called client-pull.

NEW TERM   *Client-pull* usually refers to a mechanism for pages to automatically reload after a certain amount of time has passed, or for a series of pages to automatically load themselves with a pause between them.

If the value of CONTENT is 0, the page is refreshed as fast as the browser can retrieve it, which can be rather slow if the user has a slow or poor-quality connection. It's definitely not fast enough for any type of quality animation.

When you add the REFRESH attribute to a page, the browser will reload it *ad infinitum.* To stop the process, you need to provide a hyperlink to another page without a client-pull tag.

In order to be a dynamic process, client-pull needs something to change the page on the server in between downloads. There are special programs designed to do this, usually from a database that is updated. This type of strategy is used by sites providing "live" updates of sports scores, stock quotes, and other information that changes on a steady basis.

However, client-pull is also used to load a different page. Continuing the process of loading a new page enables you to automatically lead a user through a series of slides or instructions, similar to a PowerPoint presentation. Modify the CONTENT attribute to provide this capability.

```
<META HTTP-EQUIV="Refresh"
CONTENT="8;URL=http://www.mrfd.com/safety/tip2.html">
```

Inside another <META> tag on the target page, you can include a pointer to the next page, and so on. This technique allows any number of pages to load in sequence.

Server-Push

The server-push technology, as you might have guessed from the name, is the opposite of client-pull. With push technology, the server doesn't wait for the request. When the content is ready, the server shoves it down the line to the user's browser so he or she can read it at his or her leisure.

The most common analogy of server-push is to television. Broadcasters send out their signals to their viewers, who turn on their TV sets to receive the signals. The TV set doesn't request a program from the broadcaster, it only receives what's already out there.

Actually, push technology bears a closer resemblance to customized cable channels. The users are allowed to select the channels or specific programs that really interest them instead of surfing through the entire gamut of information. The other part of the analogy is the storage aspect. Your TV can't store the broadcast signal as it passes through the air—that's the job of a VCR.

With server-push technology, you and your computer become the center of the process. You decide which portions of which channels you want to subscribe to, and the computer stands ready to receive the content and store it for future viewing when the material is broadcast.

Creating a Dynamic Web Page

Now that you've had a glimpse of the capabilities everyone is raving about, you'd like to jump right in and make a Web page that sings, dances, and stands on its little pointed head, right? Creating a flashy new page with Dynamic HTML is a four-step process.

1. Plan your page. This step shouldn't be any different whether you're working with static HTML or dynamic content. If you don't know what you want to say or why you're saying it, you'll end up creating one of those "all-flash-and-no-substance" pages.

2. Create the HTML for the basic content. In essence, you begin with the lowest common denominator. Everyone is going to be able to process the basic HTML, right? Then build the page as if the user didn't have Dynamic HTML capability (which most won't for a while, until the number of users of Internet Explorer 4 and Navigator 4 starts to increase dramatically).

3. Add the style sheet information. This includes special color and font information, layers and divisions, and anything else you're doing to make the page stand out from a crowd.

4. Make the page dynamic. This is where you add the scripts and attributes to make the content dance. Remember that it should have a purpose in your plan at step 1. Playing with a lot of nifty effects is fun, but if their only purpose is to show off your talent and the user's browser, there's not much point.

Except for all the details, that's about all there is to it. You'll walk through an easy example at the end of this chapter so you can get a feel for what's going on and get your feet just a bit wet.

Summary

Dynamic HTML is one of the best things to happen to HTML since HTML was blessed by the World Wide Consortium. With DHTML, Web designers and authors can make their pages do the sing-and-dance without relying on click-and-sit. DHTML enables a page to change itself after it is loaded on the browser without any further input or guidance from the Web server.

Remember, HTML has never been interactive. It has hosted a great number of things that have been interactive, including plug-ins, applets, VRML, and other assorted adornments. DHTML makes the page itself interactive—a lot like some of those cool CD-ROMs you can buy that show you the cost of tea on Uranus or how to sweat a pipe while crammed under a crawl space.

DHTML might seem like smoke and mirrors, but it's really like old friends—the interaction of two features (documents and scripting) already available in rudimentary forms. By making every tag of a page identifiable (Document Object Model), the page developer can access and change virtually everything in reaction to the user's behavior (scripting).

You will look at a simple example at the end of this chapter. Then, you'll take a step back and work your way into more complicated examples by beginning with style sheets and JavaScript.

Q&A

Q You've talked about a lot of capabilities, Microsoft, Netscape, and the World Wide Web Consortium. Just who's running the Dynamic HTML show, anyway?

A Good question. Unfortunately, there's no answer yet. Microsoft and Netscape are busy posturing to try and advance their ideas of how DHTML should look, and W3C is sitting in the middle, fielding comments, suggestions, and trying to strike some kind of balance. In the meantime, you'll have some choices to make. See Chapter 2, "In Search of a Standard," for more information about the battle for a DHTML definition.

Q Isn't DHTML just another way of implementing superfluous effects like `<BLINK>` and `<MARQUEE>`?

A Although these effects give the appearance of animation and interactivity, they're really just static items like the most mundane `<H3>` tag. Dynamic HTML enables you to change the blinking message or cause the marquee to scroll in the opposite direction from its original path.

Workshop

Are you ready to take DHTML for a spin after all of the hype? Here's your chance. You're going to build a small page that doesn't serve much purpose, other than to react to the user. You won't learn much of the details about what's happening, but you can at least see some real DHTML and how it looks on a browser.

Begin with a basic HTML document as in Listing 1.1. As you can see, you're going to skip the first step in creating a DHTML document—this page is designed exclusively to give a little taste of what it looks like, and serves no other useful purpose. Planning is moot. You're going to jump right in to creating the base of the page in plain vanilla HTML.

INPUT **Listing 1.1. The basic HTML page, sans dynamic features.**

```
<HTML>
<HEAD>
<TITLE>A Dynamic HTML Page</TITLE>
</HEAD>
<BODY>
<H1>An introduction to Dynamic HTML</H1>
<P>Duis autem vel eum iriure dolor in hendrerit in vulputate velit esse
molestie consequat, vel illum dolore eu feugiat nulla facilisis at vero
eros et accumsan et iusto odio dignissim qui blandit praesent luptatum
zzril delenit augue duis dolore te feugait nulla facilisi. Nam liber
tempor cum soluta nobis eleifend option congue nihil imperdiet doming id
quod mazim placerat facer possim assum. Accumsan et iusto odio dignissim
qui blandit praesent luptatum zzril delenit augue duis dolore te feugait
nulla facilisi.</P>
</BODY>
</HTML>
```

There's not a whole lot going on here; it's just a basic page that appears without any fanfare (see Figure 1.8).

Figure 1.8.

Your dynamic page begins with a standard lifeless HTML page.

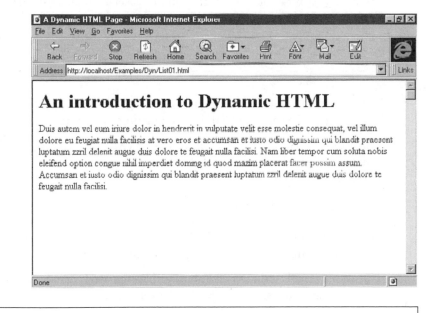

NOTE

No, I didn't take Latin in high school, college, or anywhere else. The text you see for the content is called "greeking." It's a bunch of non-sense highbrow-sounding words used by some graphic designers during the design stage in place of real textual content, which might not exist yet.

Next, we'll add some style to the page so that you can see something happen when you implement the rest of the DHTML into the Web page (see Listing 1.2).

Listing 1.2. Two styles have been added to the heading tag so you'll have something to compare when the last step of DHTML is implemented.

INPUT

```
<HTML>
<HEAD>
<TITLE>A Dynamic HTML Page</TITLE>
</HEAD>
<STYLE>
H1.italic {font-style:italic; text-decoration:none}
H1.underline {font-style:normal; text-decoration:underline}
</STYLE>
<BODY>
<H1 class="italic">An introduction to Dynamic HTML</H1>
<P>Duis autem vel eum iriure dolor in hendrerit in vulputate velit esse
molestie consequat, vel illum dolore eu feugiat nulla facilisis at vero
eros et accumsan et iusto odio dignissim qui blandit praesent luptatum
zzril delenit augue duis dolore te feugait nulla facilisi. Nam liber
tempor cum soluta nobis eleifend option congue nihil imperdiet doming id
quod mazim placerat facer possim assum. Accumsan et iusto odio dignissim
qui blandit praesent luptatum zzril delenit augue duis dolore te feugait
nulla facilisi.</P>
</BODY>
</HTML>
```

With the styles in place, the page now has a slight artistic touch to it (see Figure 1.9). The biggest part of Dynamic HTML is manipulating styles in response to the user.

When the first two elements are in place—HTML and style sheets—it's time to add the dynamic activity to the page. This happens in three ways, implemented in two places (see Listing 1.3).

The first place you make additions is within the <H1> tag. Add an id attribute to identify the specific tag. Then, add event attributes to detect user activity. Use two for this example—onmouseover and onmouseout. The first is triggered when the user passes the pointer over the top of the heading. The second is triggered when the pointer leaves the area over the heading.

The second place is at the top of the body, where the two JavaScript routines are added. These routines change the style class for the heading tag, referenced using the heading tag's id attribute.

Figure 1.9.

The heading has been cast in italics through the use of an embedded style sheet.

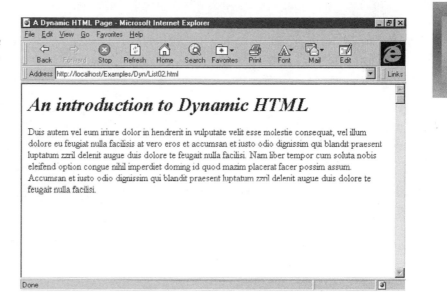

Listing 1.3. The scripts and events are added to the page, which is now ready for dynamic interaction with the user.

```html
<HTML>
<HEAD>
<TITLE>A Dynamic HTML Page</TITLE>
</HEAD>
<STYLE>
H1.italic {font-style:italic; text-decoration:none}
H1.underline {font-style:normal; text-decoration:underline}
</STYLE>
<BODY>
<SCRIPT language="JavaScript">
function changeHead() {
  if (H1_1.className == "underline") {
    H1_1.className = "italic"; }
  else {
    H1_1.className = "underline"; }
}
</SCRIPT>
<H1 id="H1_1" class="italic" onmouseover="changeHead()"
➥onmouseout="changeHead()">An introduction to Dynamic HTML</H1>
<P>Duis autem vel eum iriure dolor in hendrerit in vulputate velit esse
molestie consequat, vel illum dolore eu feugiat nulla facilisis at vero
eros et accumsan et iusto odio dignissim qui blandit praesent luptatum
zzril delenit augue duis dolore te feugait nulla facilisi. Nam liber
tempor cum soluta nobis eleifend option congue nihil imperdiet doming id
quod mazim placerat facer possim assum. Accumsan et iusto odio dignissim
qui blandit praesent luptatum zzril delenit augue duis dolore te feugait
nulla facilisi.</P>
</BODY>
</HTML>
```

Whenever the user passes the pointer over the heading, it adds an underline and loses the italics (see Figure 1.10). When the pointer leaves the heading, it changes back to its original appearance when the page was loaded (refer to Figure 1.9). Both of these actions happen without any additional communication between the browser and the server.

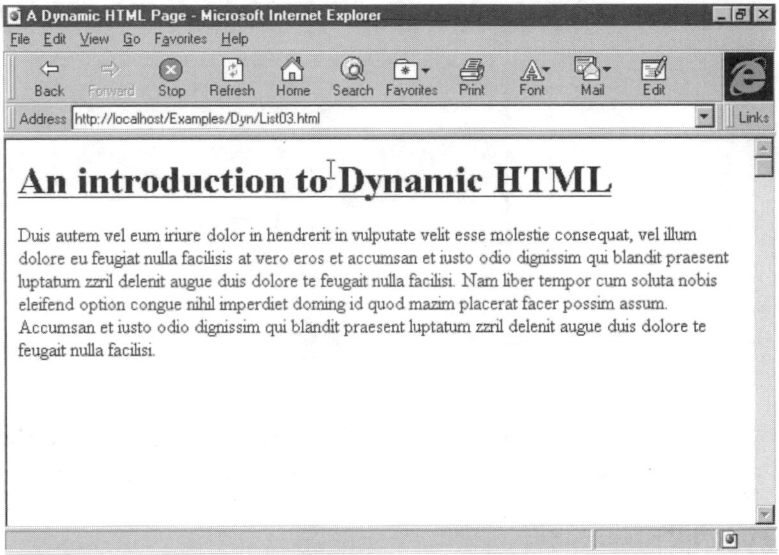
A Dynamic HTML Page - Microsoft Internet Explorer
File Edit View Go Favorites Help
Back Forward Stop Refresh Home Search Favorites Print Font Mail Edit
Address http://localhost/Examples/Dyn/List03.html
Links
An introduction to Dynamic HTML
Duis autem vel eum iriure dolor in hendrerit in vulputate velit esse molestie consequat, vel illum dolore eu feugiat nulla facilisis at vero eros et accumsan et iusto odio dignissim qui blandit praesent luptatum zzril delenit augue duis dolore te feugait nulla facilisi. Nam liber tempor cum soluta nobis eleifend option congue nihil imperdiet doming id quod mazim placerat facer possim assum. Accumsan et iusto odio dignissim qui blandit praesent luptatum zzril delenit augue duis dolore te feugait nulla facilisi.

Figure 1.10.
When the user places the pointer over the heading, it changes appearance from italics to normal underlined.

You'll dive into some more complex examples as you work your way through the next seven days, but here are some ideas to get you thinking:

- Just because the user places the pointer over the heading doesn't mean the heading is the only thing that can change. You could just as easily specify a change to any other element or elements on the page.
- With a set of mouse-click events, you can turn any element into a hyperlink, or as an impetus to trigger other activities on the page.
- Combined with layers, you can include an index at the top of a page that controls which portions of the page are displayed.

You'll learn how to do all of this and more, but your next step is to figure out who is providing all of these nifty features.

Day 1

Chapter 2

In Search of a Standard

Standards, standards everywhere, and nary a compatibility among them. Well, that's not quite true, but it's still not an easy world when you are trying to figure out whose Dynamic HTML (DHTML) proposal to follow.

Here's the problem. Microsoft and Netscape both have their ideas about what DHTML should look like, even beginning with the name. Microsoft calls its implementation Dynamic HTML (with a capital "D"), and Netscape refers to its implementation as dynamic HTML (lowercase "d"). And, the two companies' histories of happily working hand-in-hand to the common good of all Web users is what you could call...spotted.

In the case of DHTML, both Microsoft and Netscape are using a lot of the same terminology and are referring to the same set of published or proposed standards in their work toward interactive and dynamic Web pages. Both companies talk about the capability for pages to change without extra trips to the server and more extensive control of styles. But, here's the rub—the actual implementations aren't very compatible.

Netscape has added a new tag and Microsoft has added new attributes for existing tags. Netscape added load-on-the-fly typefaces, and Microsoft added ActiveX controls for database access. Between the two, the waters are getting muddier.

Speaking of standards, now is a good time to mention the World Wide Web Consortium (W3C). The W3C is developing its own recommendation for DHTML. However, true to the spirit of working by committee, the W3C standard currently exists only as a list of capabilities that a DHTML document should have. The actual appearance and prescribed behavior are still under discussion.

NEW TERM The *World Wide Web Consortium* (W3C) is the recognized organization that is responsible for developing common standards for the World Wide Web. This includes updating HTML and HTTP standards and related issues, including new markup languages, accessibility, and recommended browser implementations. It also provides a repository of information about the Web for developers, users, and anyone else interested in long specification documents. The W3C is located at www.w3.org.

NOTE

How does the W3C do its work? The first step is identification of an issue or technology that affects the World Wide Web. The W3C governing body, called the Advisory Committee, appoints a working group. This group of people consists of experts gathered to work together toward resolving a particular well-defined technical issue, such as HTML standards.

The working group develops a series of *working drafts* until they've reached a stable consensus and agreement. Then, if the W3C director approves, the draft is promoted to a *Proposed Recommendation*, also called a *Draft Recommendation*, which is sent to all W3C members for comment. Depending on the number and nature the comments, the W3C director can issue the result as a *Recommendation* as-is or with minor changes, return it to the Working Group, or scrap it altogether.

So where does that leave you? In the same place you've probably been in before—trying to develop pages that are accessible to as many people as possible while working with implementations that, while not mutually exclusive, tend to be incompatible at inopportune times.

Sounds like fun, doesn't it? To help you understand where this whole technology is headed and how we got here in the first place, here's a description of the players and the rules we'll look at in this chapter:

☐ W3C has developed a wish-list of some capabilities for DHTML, which they refer to as the *Document Object Model* (DOM). Although it sounds large and foreboding, the DOM is really just a way for the browser to identify every markup tag and page element, and make it accessible for inspection or change. More information on the W3C's DOM plan, and DOM's preliminary implementations in Microsoft and Netscape are covered in Chapter 3, "The Dynamic HTML Object Model."

☐ Netscape created its own document object model a couple of years ago with Navigator 2.0. More recently, Netscape has tried other methods of creating dynamic behavior, primarily through the use of a non-standard <LAYER> tag. However, Netscape now seems to be playing down the new tag and appears to be working toward an implementation that expands on their original document object model. This approach brings Netscape closer in this aspect of DHTML with W3C and Microsoft.

☐ As part of the Internet Explorer 4.0 release, Microsoft has released its version of what it thinks the W3C Document Object Model will look like. Microsoft's version appears to follow the wish list provided by W3C, but it's still a guess because a standard doesn't exist yet.

NOTE

> This is typical for both major browsers as they attempt to anticipate how the standards will develop. For example, both Microsoft and Netscape released their respective version 3 browsers in 1996, which implemented an HTML standard that wasn't formally accepted until 1997.

Before you get into the nuts and bolts of DHTML in Chapter 3, take some time today to explore some different visions of what DHTML could look like when its first official standard is approved by W3C.

World Wide Web Consortium

Even though it's not in anything resembling a final or usable form, the final word on the functionality of DHTML rests with the World Wide Web Consortium and its Document Object Model (DOM) Working Group. There is a bit of irony in this situation, because one of the first acts of the group's chair was to issue a statement that labeled the term Dynamic HTML as "just marketing."

NOTE

> If it's any consolation, W3C doesn't work with a blind eye to the industry it affects. The W3C is hosted by Massachusetts Institute of Technology, but the members of its various committees are representative of World Wide Web companies, including organizations such as Microsoft, Netscape, Sun Microsystems, IBM, and others. Although it costs a significant sum of money for an organization to join W3C, no single organization or company has more influence in the W3C's final recommendation than any other.

The DOM Working Group issued a statement of purpose which states that its goal is not to extend HTML or develop a standard specific to any scripting language. According to the home page for DOM on the W3C Web site, the group is working on a "platform- and language-neutral interface which allows programs and scripts to dynamically access and update the content, structure, and style of documents."

This is a mouthful, but what does it mean?

HTML 4.0 and Dynamic HTML

W3C is including several recommendations for more dynamic activity in its HTML 4.0 release, code-named Cougar. This includes the Document Object Model and scripting, mentioned earlier in this chapter.

Scripting bears further inspection. Scripting has been a part of Navigator since version 2 and Microsoft since version 3 of their respective browsers. However, scripting still is not an accepted element with HTML standards. HTML 4.0 should change this.

The W3C proposal basically reflects the current practice on the Web for including scripts, and doesn't make any suggestions for how the scripting language is interpreted or how the script interacts with the document. Scripts are provided by embedding directly in the document or through linking to a separate file.

W3C also takes no stance on which language should be used as a default, although it provides for a new META value to set the default for a specific page. For example, the following snippet sets the default for a Web page to JavaScript:

```
<META HTTP-EQUIV="Content-Script-Type" CONTENT="text/javascript">
```

If the META element is not included, then the browser has the option of determining the default language. As a generally accepted implementation, script-compatible browsers use JavaScript as the default scripting language.

HTML 4.0 also includes several other items which, while not directly part of the DHTML discussed in this book, will help the page developer create less-static documents.

First on the list are two new attributes—TITLE and TABINDEX. The first, TITLE, is added to existing elements and tags as a method for the user to request extra information or help. It includes a string of text which provides a note such as "Submit form to server." How the string is displayed is up to the browser, but on Windows you can expect an implementation using tooltips, and Macintosh versions will probably use help balloons. Another option for other platforms is the status bar.

The syntax to implement the title attribute is similar to the following:

```
<A href="http://www.w3.org/" title="World Wide Web Consortium Home Page">
```

The TABINDEX attribute sets a specific tabbing order for traversing among interactive elements (hyperlinks, form fields, and so on) on the Web page using the Tab key. This is a way of explicitly deciding which element receives the next input from the keyboard. In the past, this was accomplished by giving focus to an element with the mouse or other pointing device and then clicking on the object. The following example sets the second hyperlink to receive focus before the first by setting the second to 1 and the first to 2:

```
<a href="http://www.w3.org/" tabindex=2>
<a href="http://www.yahoo.com/" tabindex=1>
```

W3C has received several submissions from member companies, primarily Microsoft and Netscape, on how the various elements of HTML documents should be exposed to scripts. It's important to note that none of the submissions propose new HTML tags or changes to existing style sheet technology. One of the most important and hardest goals of W3C is to make sure any solution doesn't favor one company's technology to the exclusion of all others.

As mentioned earlier in this chapter, the W3C standard revolves around the Document Object Model, which is discussed in greater detail in Chapter 3. In a nutshell, the W3C model has two basic requirements:

☐ The document model can be used to take apart and build the document, even after it's loaded by the browser. Individual elements and their attributes can be added, removed, or changed within the document. This also includes a way to determine and change the content of a page, whether it's text, images, applets, or plug-ins. This is the dynamic part everyone is talking about.

☐ The DOM won't require a graphical user interface for implementation. This is part of the W3C's goal of providing standards that provide access to Web content for all types of browsers, including those based on Braille and audio technologies. Remember, DOM is way of opening the structure and contents of a Web page to the page developer so the page can interact with the user—it is not a standard for graphics or animation, although it can be utilized that way.

NOTE

> The W3C is working very hard to develop standards that don't exclude any platform or browser. This is part of an ongoing goal to provide World Wide Web standards that support specialized browsers for disabled persons, such as the blind and deaf. For this reason, each new tag or way to manipulate a tag is being developed with an eye toward providing a textual substitute that can be interpreted by browsers for special needs.
>
> To support this effort, W3C launched the Web Accessibility Initiative (WAI) to promote and achieve Web functionality for people with disabilities. The initiative involves the establishment of an International Program Office (IPO) which, according to a W3C press release, is responsible for "developing software protocols and technologies, creating guidelines for the use of technologies, educating the industry, and conducting research and development." Because the IPO office is contained within W3C, it will also ensure that all new W3C standards and technologies meet or exceed accessibility goals.

All other requirements of DOM follow from these two, including each of the major areas required by the DOM Working Group:

☐ Structure navigation—This is the capability to locate elements in a document, such as the parents or children of an object. This is how Netscape started its document model in Navigator 2.0. It begins with `window`, then down to `document`, followed by the various children of `document` including `form`, `link`, `applet`, and other page elements. Using the DOM model, all tags are exposed for the browser, including unknown tags and elements.

☐ Document Manipulation—The standard will provide a way to add, remove, or change elements and tags within the document. This also includes attributes of tags.

2

☐ Content Manipulation—This is the capability to add, change, or delete the content within a document or individual tag. It also includes a requirement for determining which tag affects text from any part of the document.

☐ Event Model—The event model is comprehensive enough to generate completely interactive documents. It includes the capability to respond to any user action within the document, including moving in and out of form fields, detecting mouse movements and clicks, and determining individual keystrokes. Although W3C is committed to accessibility for disabled persons, some of the events will apply only to a graphical interface (such as Windows), which is designed for the average user.

☐ Style Sheet Object Model—This is similar to Document Manipulation, mentioned earlier. Under DOM, cascading style sheet attributes are also exposed for modification. With an eye toward the future, W3C includes a provision to extend the style sheet model to other formats. This might be the loophole Netscape needs to include JavaScript Assisted Style Sheets while maintaining compliance with W3C standards.

☐ General Document and Browser Information—The W3C has left no stone unturned. Part of the DOM includes the capability to examine embedded objects such as cookies and the date a document was created. Other information available include the user agent (browser) brand and version, and the types of MIME types it supports.

The complete set of requirements for DOM runs about three pages and includes all the preceding items, plus document type definitions and error reporting. Essentially, all the requirements boil down to this: *Everything* within a document should be accessible for manipulation.

The first step toward creating the standard is to figure out what the current object model is. This step utilizes the models implemented by Internet Explorer 3.0 and Navigator 3.0, and will result in the Level 0 standard. After that task is completed, the Working Group will begin working toward its long-term goal of building a consensus of what should and shouldn't be part of the Document Object Model standard, which will become version 1.0.

How long will all of this head scratching and note passing take? Working Group Chair Lauren Wood said a final version of DOM 1.0 could be released as early as late as 1997 or as late as 1999.

This leads us back to the original question: What's a developer to do? The answer from W3C is to stay tuned for the level 0 specification, and write your DHTML pages to the lowest common denominator of compatibility until the consensus begins to form. This is hard for developers to swallow, especially when you want to write with the "latest and greatest" tools on the Web.

Our recommendation is similar to W3C's—if you're writing to a general audience, be wary of anything proprietary. This includes tags or attributes that are the sole domain of one browser or another. You learn more about this later, but what you'll probably start with is some combination of style sheets and JavaScript. To make sure your implementation is solid, test it with a wide variety of browsers—new and old versions of Navigator and Internet Explorer, no-frills versions such as Mosaic, and text-only applications such as Lynx. This is a reasonable precaution to take to ensure that your dynamic pages won't crater someone else's undynamic browser.

If you want to write to the evolving standard using the most advanced tools available, put it someplace separate on your Web site and mark it as "for demonstration only," along with a notation of which browser it was written for.

In short, it's still a long road to an implementation that is going to work well across all browsers, especially the major offerings from Netscape and Microsoft. If you write to the capabilities of a majority of your users and include safety nets for the rest, you won't go wrong.

Netscape

Netscape got the whole DHTML object rolling back in the old days (about 1995) with its Navigator 2.0 release. That release included a feature called JavaScript, which included a basic document object model that included access to elements such as forms, hyperlinks, colors, and various browser attributes.

That first object model was created with an instance hierarchy, which reflected the construction of the HTML page. At the top of the hierarchy was `window`—the parent of all other objects. This object included four children—`location`, `history`, `frames`, and `document`. The `document` object also included children representing selected information about the document: `alinkColor`, `bgColor`, `fgColor`, `linkColor`, `vlinkColor`, `cookie`, `lastModified`, `location`, `anchors`, `referreru`, `forms`, `links`, and `title`.

NEW TERM   An *instance hierarchy* is built from actual instances of objects rather than general classes of objects. For example, suppose the only elements allowed on a page were headings, and a particular page included three `H1`s and an `H4`. A class hierarchy would include an object for each possible header—`H1` through `H6`—including the unused `H2`, `H3`, `H5`, and `H6`. In an instance hierarchy, the same page would include only an object for the headings that actually appeared on the document—`H1` and `H4`.

As you can see, this was a mishmash of page attributes (color settings), `META` information (last modified date and referring page), and physical elements on the page (anchors, forms, and links). In the next version of Navigator (3.0), the object model was extended to include applets and other embedded objects.

Netscape had the right idea, but it was still pretty limited in scope and usage. Only a few of the items, such as form elements and some of the colors, could be changed without reloading the document. It was also possible to modify the rest of a page's contents, but only by reloading it using the *javascript* protocol.

NEW TERM The *javascript* protocol is used in the same way as other Internet protocols such as http or ftp. It enables the browser to reload a page by invoking a JavaScript method, which results in redefining the page's contents. The user still sees the page go blank and then reload. However, it's much faster than retrieving a new version from the server because the page is created by a process within the browser.

JavaScript was the other half of Netscape's big breakthrough in Navigator 2.0. JavaScript enables developers to write small applications that run on the user's browser, instead of processing through the server. The syntax was related to Java, and with Netscape 3.0, the two languages could talk back and forth across the Web page. This was also a big breakthrough, because it gave Java direct access to data on a Web page and provided a way to control Java from outside an applet.

In the early days of JavaScript, developers primarily used it and the Netscape document object model to verify form contents or make fun little 1040EZ calculators. A few hardy folks used it to create some neat effects, such as expanding and contracting outlines and Web sites with custom controls, but most of the uses were limited in scope and utility.

Netscape's Communicator release doesn't extend the document object model in any new and dramatic directions like its ancestors, but that doesn't mean Netscape doesn't have its eye on the DHTML bandwagon. Here are the three components of Netscape's vision of DHTML:

- ☐ The use of layers to move, hide, and show blocks of HTML on the Web page. The layers can be manipulated in reaction to user events, making it the only portion of Netscape's solution that meets the definition of dynamic that was adopted in Chapter 1.

NEW TERM A Netscape *layer* is a set of HTML that is displayed, hidden, moved, and altered in various ways. Essentially, it converts your HTML document into a set of slides that you can shuffle and display in any order, singly or in combination.

- ☐ Precise control over formatting, fonts, layout, and other aspects of page behavior through style sheets. Netscape includes support for the W3C CSS1 specification, which Microsoft uses, and JavaScript Assisted Style Sheets (JSSS). JSSS doesn't allow changes to the document after it's loaded, but it does allow the style sheet to ask the browser about its environment. The style sheet can then make changes to its implementation to match its specific situation.

NOTE

> Although JSSS isn't explicitly supported by W3C, part of W3C's position on the Document Object Model is to extend the CSS1 style sheet model to other style sheet formats.

☐ Dynamic fonts, which are attached to a Web page instead of dependent on the options available on a user's computer. In the past, developers have had to guess what typefaces are available on a user's machine, and then provide a list of the preferred choices for a page in the style sheet font attribute or use the <FONT> tag. Dynamic fonts uses a new method to check for the existence of the desired typeface, and if it's not found, download it from the server.

NEW TERM *Dynamic fonts* is a standard under development by W3C that will let Web browsers quickly download a copy of the fonts used within a Web page. This would eliminate some of the problems with font availability that have become more noticeable with style sheets.

A little more needs to be said about layers. With the initial betas of Navigator 4.0, Netscape decided to use a new tag to implement precise positioning of elements—<LAYER>. This caused a bit of a problem, because Microsoft wasn't going to include it on their browser, and the W3C decided not to develop the <LAYER> tag to work on other approaches to DHTML. Given a less-than-warm reception, Netscape is including more emphasis on layers implemented through the Document Object Model with the <DIV> tag. Netscape is also downplaying the <LAYER> tag, although it is still part of the Netscape Communicator release (see Figure 2.1).

Figure 2.1.

Using Netscape layers, a fish swims from left to right, in "front" of the first and last bars and "behind" the middle bar.

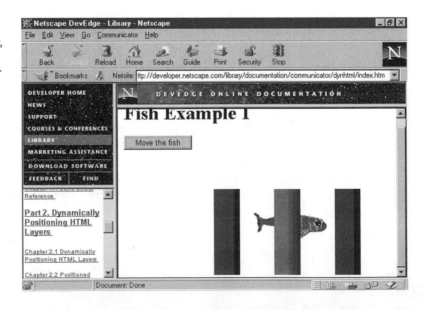

The ultimate fate of Netscape's <LAYER> tag is unclear at this point. It doesn't appear as if W3C is including any support for it in its proposed HTML 4.0 specification, although the tag appears to fulfill many of the features of the W3C draft on positioning HTML elements by using style sheets (www.w3.org/pub/WWW/TR/WD-positioning), which Netscape helped to develop in conjunction with Microsoft.

In DHTML, Netscape appears to be moving closer to working with the W3C rather than trying to set its own standards and have W3C follow its lead. Netscape Communicator is fully compatible with existing W3C recommendations or standards for HTML 3.2, plus some from the proposed HTML 4.0, Cascading Style Sheets 1, and JavaScript. It is also trying to maintain compatibility with working drafts on positioning, object models, and dynamic fonts.

Other than the implementation of the <LAYER> tag and JavaScript Accessible Style Sheets, covered in Chapter 5, "JavaScript Style Sheets," Netscape appears to be working on a version of DHTML that doesn't depend exclusively on proprietary or platform-specific controls.

Does this mean that a DHTML page that works on Netscape will also work with Microsoft if both browsers are claiming to meet the upcoming standards? Not necessarily. There are several issues at work here. First, W3C is not tying DHTML to any specific scripting language. For example, suppose Microsoft makes VBScript and Netscape makes JavaScript completely with the DHTML standard. If a Netscape browser loads a page made dynamic with VBScript, it's not going to work because Navigator still doesn't support that specific language.

Second, both companies view the standard in different ways and are claiming the exclusive privilege of being the only "real solution." This is why there's an expanded document object model on one side and layers on the other. These solutions are not compatible across the browsers, even if they both meet the letter or intent of the W3C's work. At this point, neither browser is being written to support anyone else's views on the topic, even though everyone is claiming to be "standard-compliant."

Microsoft

As has become the standard operating practice in the ongoing browser battles, Microsoft is boldly going where no standard has gone before with its definition and implementation of DHTML in Internet Explorer 4.0. You can read all about Microsoft's vision of DHTML at www.microsoft.com/workshop/author/dhtml/.

Internet Explorer 4.0 (IE4) isn't just a collection of support for a few new tags and a new user interface. Microsoft completely overhauled the HTML parsing engine.

NEW TERM The *parsing engine* in a Web browser looks at HTML documents to see what's inside them. It looks at the tagged text and the content, and then formats the content based on what it finds in the tags. In simpler terms, a parser simply breaks large units of information (such as a Web page) into smaller pieces (such as markup tags), which are easier to interpret and process, the same way you read a book.

The extended IE4 takes the individual tags and document elements and integrates them with a Scripting Object Model, which is supported by any scripting language available. As a matter of practicality, the two choices are JavaScript and VBScript, which are provided as components of IE4. The examples in this book for both Netscape and Microsoft are implemented with JavaScript.

Microsoft's vision of DHTML includes four components, which are similar to Netscape's:

☐ The Document Object Model enables any element on a page to be shown, hidden, changed, or rearranged without reloading the page from a server. One of the surprises in Microsoft's implementation of the DOM is that it isn't specific to Windows or ActiveX. It appears as if the Microsoft model were completely built into the HTML parser as part of the browser. By implementing the DOM with Jscript (Microsoft's version of JavaScript) and VBScript, developers can use the scripting languages to control page elements.

☐ A way to control elements on a page through scripts, including JavaScript and VBScript. The scripting languages include objects that relate to the various elements on the page as defined by the Document Object Model. Using the comparison and assignment features of the language, page developers can examine and change the attribute or content of any element on the page referenced by the DOM, including headings, links, text, and other items. This also includes control and manipulation of embedded Java applets, ActiveX controls, and plug-ins.

☐ Multimedia controls for animation and other effects, such as filters and transitions, without relying on downloading large files or pages. This has been implemented through Cascading Style Sheets with the use of filters for fade-in, fade-out, and other types of effects.

☐ A way to bind data to an HTML page, including automatic generation of tables, sorting tabular data, and querying local tables. This uses a special set of HTML attributes to display "live" database records in the same way you would display an applet or plug-in. In the old HTML school, displaying database records required working with CGI scripts and advanced Perl, C, or Java programming. Because DHTML supports immediate changes to page content, the database can update automatically in reaction to user typing, or the table can display live updates from third-party changes to the database.

Like Netscape, Microsoft is working with W3C standards and proposals, trying to anticipate the future of DHTML through the work of the Consortium.

The Microsoft DOM is very similar to the Netscape Navigator 2.0 model. It begins with the core objects representing the page and browser (such as `window` and `document`), and then branches into more detail (such as `form`, `applet`, and `link`). Microsoft has further expanded the model to include every element on the page. From headings to paragraphs to images to tables to horizontal rules—it's no-holds-barred access to everything on the page.

One of the big strengths touted by Microsoft is compatibility with other browsers that don't support the Internet Explorer 4.0 DHTML implementation. Microsoft calls its compatibility with other browsers *graceful degradation*. Developers and authors writing specifically to the Microsoft version of DHTML won't need to produce alternative versions for Netscape or anyone else, according to Microsoft (see sidebar). The scripting and tags used by Microsoft are accepted technologies in use by other browsers, and are blessed by the W3C.

The Reality of Graceful Degradation

Every silver lining has a dark cloud, and the DHTML story is no different. Microsoft DHTML doesn't gracefully degrade when placed on Navigator 4.0, especially when it depends on style sheets. Look at Figures 2.2 through 2.4. In Figure 2.2, you see the DHTML overview from Microsoft's site as viewed on Internet Explorer 4.0. Click on a heading, and the contents underneath appear.

The first test of graceful degradation is the old reliable Mosaic from NCSA. The same page loaded on it (Figure 2.3) degrades quite nicely. Mosaic doesn't understand style sheets or scripting, so it just ignores all the extra tags and attachments and displays the page in a clean, straightforward, and predictable manner.

In Figure 2.4, you see the same page on Navigator 4.0 (Preview Release 4). Microsoft uses the `display:none` attribute to hide the contents until the user clicks the heading, where it depends on a JavaScript method to remove the attribute so the contents can display. Here's the problem: Netscape doesn't support changing CSS1 style sheets with JavaScript, so there's no way to reveal the hidden elements without loading a new page from the server.

Why does the bulleted list appear, even though it's associated with the content under the headings? Because Navigator doesn't think it belongs with the rest of the hidden text and assumes that the `<UL>` display attribute is set for display. The effect is a list without an explanation, which is still not an acceptable interpretation of the page.

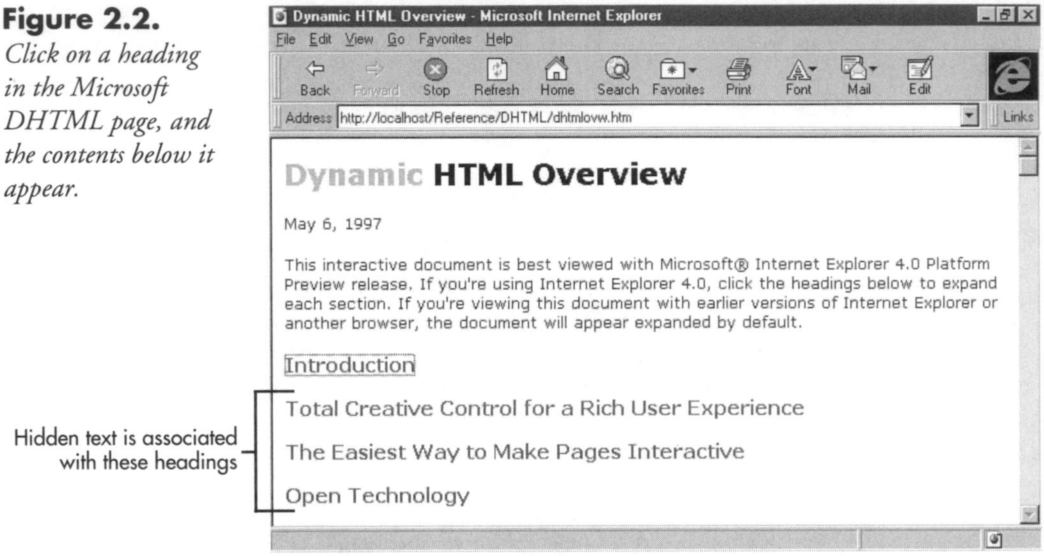

Figure 2.2.

Click on a heading in the Microsoft DHTML page, and the contents below it appear.

Hidden text is associated with these headings

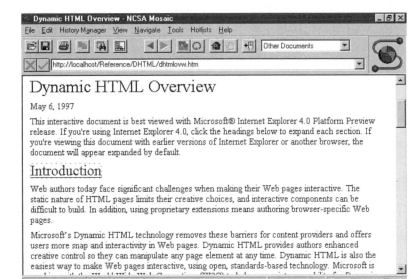

Figure 2.3.

Graceful degradation as Microsoft advertises.

Figure 2.4.

Because Netscape is compatible with CSS1 but not with JavaScript modification of CSS1, it doesn't degrade gracefully.

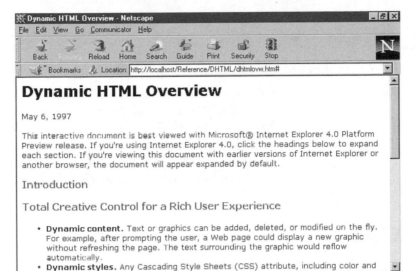

Summary

A Dynamic HTML standard is still a moving target. There are three slightly different schools of thought on what it is, but the three main players—World Wide Web Consortium, Netscape, and Microsoft—all seem to agree that an expanded Document Object Model is at the center of the solution. The expanded document model will allow access to every element, its attributes, and content, through a scripting language. With unbridled access and control over the contents, HTML pages will bear a closer semblance to putty than to tablets of stone.

From the DOM, the views start their divergence. W3C doesn't use DHTML as part of its vocabulary at all, except to acknowledge the term's use by software vendors. W3C's work is almost exclusively centered on developing the Document Object Model and its relation to style sheets, scripting languages, and other existing technologies.

Netscape includes JavaScript Assisted Style Sheets and layers in its bundle of DHTML capabilities. Layers appear to be the result of an implementation of the W3C working draft on positioning HTML elements, although the <LAYER> tag is not included as part of the proposed HTML 4.0 specification.

In addition to the Document Object Model, Microsoft is also stressing multimedia effects and data awareness with its vision of DHTML, while also relying on the object model and style sheet base similar to Netscape. However, the Microsoft solution also depends on proprietary items such as ActiveX controls to implement access to the DOM.

Unlike a year or two ago, when the two companies sought to build Web standards around their respective visions, both Netscape and Microsoft seem more eager to work with the World Wide Web Consortium in the development of standards for their browsers. Hopefully, the days are gone when each company will create their own tags and technologies in an attempt to force standards to conform to their respective software. Although competition between the two remains fierce, the user is no longer subjected to getting caught between incompatibilities.

Q&A

Q Is there a standard for DHTML?

A In a word, no. But it appears that the World Wide Web Consortium is leaning toward a Document Object Model specification where all elements on an HTML page would be accessible to the page developer through the scripting language of his or her choice.

Q Is there a standard coming soon?

A It depends on what you call soon. W3C doesn't plan on having a full recommendation on DHTML until 1999.

Q What do I do if there's no standard?

A It appears as though Netscape and Microsoft might come closer together than either would like to admit. For the time being, you might want to pick the lowest common denominator between the two—a combination of the W3C Document Object Model, cascading style sheets, and scripting—and hang with it until the W3C recommendation is finalized and the differences between browsers shake out. It's still too early in the game to depend on anything that appears to be too proprietary.

You might also need to write DHTML specifically to each browser. It's a pain, but remember, the standard is still evolving and is bound to change as the two competitors slug it out.

Q How close will the W3C recommendation be to what Microsoft and Netscape have already implemented?

A That's hard to say. I'll take a wild guess and say W3C's final recommendation will be closer to Microsoft than Netscape, and the common areas between the two won't be completely compatible. At that point, both companies will need to make sure that whatever their implementation of DHTML, it is in full compliance with the standard. However, W3C seldom moves quickly in comparison to the rest of the World Wide Web, so subsequent browser releases from Microsoft and Netscape should allow enough time for these companies to adjust to the W3C standard—whatever it looks like.

2

DAY 2

The Building Blocks of Dynamic HTML

Day 2

Chapter 3

The Dynamic HTML Object Model

So far in this book, we've tossed the Document Object Model (DOM) around like it was a sack of potatoes. It sounds pretty intimidating, conjuring visions of programmers in smoke-filled rooms gleefully rubbing their hands together over cauldrons of melted 8088 processors and chanting strange incantations. No, wait a minute, those were the witches in Macbeth.

Finally, we hope to strip away the hype and voodoo surrounding DOM and reveal it for what it is—a structured way of accessing HTML elements and content on a Web page. There's no new set of tags or attributes to learn because the goal of DOM is to work within existing HTML, style sheets, and scripting languages.

In this chapter, you'll take a look at the history of DOM with Netscape and Microsoft, what the World Wide Web Consortium (W3C) envisions for the future, and what you're going to work with in the rest of the book.

Some DOM History

DOM is not a new concept. In fact, it has been around since one of the first implementations in Netscape Navigator 2.0 in 1995. Up to this point, Netscape's version didn't generate a lot of interest except in relation to using JavaScript with forms. A new implementation of DOM in Microsoft Internet Explorer 4.0 extends the model originally created for Netscape.

Breaking New Ground: Netscape

Netscape was the first company to develop a DOM in conjunction with the creation of its JavaScript scripting language. For its first attempt, the model provided a lot of functionality for developers. Initially, the DOM was described as an *instance hierarchy* of JavaScript objects.

I'll break that mouthful apart so you can see what's happening.

- ☐ Instance—No objects are created until they appear on a Web page. For example, if no hyperlinks were on a page, the `link` object would be empty. Instance hierarchy is different from a general class hierarchy, in which an object is created for every class whether it was included as part of the Web page.

- ☐ Hierarchy—Not all objects are created equal. Each exists in a set relation to other objects (see Listing 3.1). In the case of a Web browser, the highest spot on the hierarchy food chain is the `window` object. Under the window is a `document` object, which is the current HTML page loaded in the browser. In its initial presentation, there were three objects underneath `document`: `anchor`, `link`, and `form`. Individual form elements are found under the `form` object.

 INPUT   ## Listing 3.1. The first JavaScript object hierarchy.

```
window ---> document ---> anchor
                     |
                     --> link
                     |
                     --> form ---> text
                              |
                              --> textarea
                              |
                              --> radio
                              |
                              --> checkbox
                              |
                              --> select
                              |
                              --> button
```

- ☐ JavaScript—JavaScript is a scripting language for HTML documents. Scripts are triggered after the user manipulates something on the document, such as placing the mouse over a hyperlink, clicking a button, or changing the content of a form field.

☐ Objects—An object is a construct with associated properties and methods. As an example, think of a house. The properties of a house could include items such as bedrooms, bathrooms, floors, and square feet. The first three properties could also be objects with properties of their own, such as closets, tubs, showers, flooring, and windows. Although properties describe the house, methods change it. For example, a home addition method could affect the other properties by adding rooms and square footage. Find more about objects, properties, and methods in Chapter 5, "JavaScript Style Sheets."

Now that you've seen each term, you can put the whole picture together. The first DOM was a collection of certain page elements that existed in a descending relation to each other with the JavaScript language. The topmost parent in the relationship was the browser window and continued down to individual elements on the page. Only the selected elements were accessible—you were out of luck if you wanted to work with tags such as headings or block quotes.

With that out of the way, Netscape decided to improve on a good thing with the release of Navigator 3.0. The main feature of the new JavaScript was additional objects representing plug-ins, applets, and images. Other elements on the page, such as headings and block quotes, remained inaccessible to JavaScript programmers.

With the introduction of Netscape Communicator with Navigator 4.0, Netscape hasn't extended the JavaScript DOM in any tangible fashion. You can access forms, applets, plug-ins, images, layers, frames, anchors, and hyperlinks on a page—the major page components—but nothing else.

Navigator 4.0 also includes support for JavaScript-Assisted Style Sheets, however, which uses a slightly different document object. JSSS uses JavaScript syntax to control a document's style (read more in Chapter 5). When used within <STYLE> tags, the document object picks up a whole new set of objects that aren't available when used within <SCRIPT> tags. The new objects are based on a general class hierarchy in which each HTML element is represented, along with style classes and individual identifiers (see Listing 3.2).

Listing 3.2. The JavaScript document hierarchy for style sheets.

`INPUT`

```
document ---> tags ----> all
                    |
                    --> P
                    |
                    --> DIV
                    |
                    --> SPAN
                    |
                    --> H1 through H6
```

continues

Listing 3.2. continued

```
                    |
                    --> etc.
    ---> classes ----> all
                    |
                    --> tag names
    ---> ids
```

Using this object hierarchy, you can access and modify every element on a page, whether it appears on the Web page or not. It enables the page developer to create functions to evaluate the user's browser and environment and to create a style based on that knowledge.

With that in mind, it's time to walk up the West coast to Washington and see what Microsoft has accomplished with the DOM.

Extending the Idea: Microsoft

With Internet Explorer 3.0, Microsoft jumped on the JavaScript bandwagon, adding its own scripting language (Visual Basic Scripting Edition, commonly called VBScript), as another option. The DOM, which was a part of this release, matched Netscape's implementation in Navigator 2.0, which meant that Internet Explorer lacked some of the new JavaScript objects, such as those representing applets and images.

This meant continued incompatibilities between the two versions of JavaScript and, by extension, the DOM. VBScript followed a DOM implementation compatible with Microsoft's version of JavaScript.

NOTE

It's hard to tell where VBScript is headed. Although it reaches many users just because it's a Microsoft product, it still misses many more users because Microsoft is the only company currently implementing it with its browser. VBScript's fate seems to be relegated to a minor role until more browsers support it. If you're choosing between languages and want to reach a larger audience, use JavaScript.

Old JavaScript, New ECMAScript

In early 1997, Netscape handed JavaScript to the European Computer Manufacturer's Association (ECMA) for development as a standardized language. ECMA responded in summer 1997 with ECMAScript—JavaScript in a standard form.

ECMAScript was originally designed to be a Web scripting language. However, the standardized version of ECMAScript can provide core scripting capabilities for a variety of host environments. For this reason, the specification doesn't tie the language to any particular host environment.

For now, Netscape and Microsoft are both pledging to fully support the ECMAScript standard, which should provide additional common ground for the two browsers when developing scripting and DHTML applications.

With Internet Explorer 4.0, Microsoft stopped trying to play catch-up in the JavaScript game by extending the DOM to include every tag and content on the page. The new DOM that Microsoft offers is accessible to JavaScript or VBScript and is not simply relegated to the style sheet sections of the page. It includes a new object called `all`, which is really an array of all the elements on a page (see Listing 3.3).

Listing 3.3. The Microsoft DOM looks similar to Netscape's DOM but offers access to every element (instead of just a select few) through the document's `all` property.

`INPUT`

```
document ---> all
         |
         --> anchor
         |
         --> applet
         |
         --> embed
         |
         --> frame
         |
         --> image
         |
         --> link
         |
         --> plugin
         |
         --> form ---> text
                  |
                  --> textarea
                  |
                  --> radio
                  |
                  --> checkbox
                  |
                  --> select
                  |
                  --> button
```

The other thing that the Microsoft DOM does that Netscape's doesn't do is open the world of *events* to every element. Events are how a browser detects and responds to user events, such as mouse movements or keyboard actions, and are covered in more detail in Chapter 6, "Dynamic HTML Events." With Netscape's version of the DOM, events are restricted to specific objects. For example, the only events that are affected by clicks are hyperlinks and buttons. The Microsoft model opens all page elements to virtually all events, however. For example, you can detect a user clicking a heading or moving the mouse over a block quote.

But that's not all. You can also access each attribute within an element, including settings affecting size, color, font, background, and anything else that's legal for the particular page tag. Then, to take the model one step further, Microsoft's DOM also enables you to examine and change the content between each set of tags.

Microsoft's approach is definitely in line with W3C's recommendation (covered in the next section), although it is still Microsoft's solution. So far, Microsoft is the only company to include this type of DOM in its browser. It's good to work with it and to see how to access it using scripts, but don't depend on it as the final word. Any sort of standard is still a long way off. Read on.

In Search of a Standard Revisited

The final judge in developing a universal standard is in the hands of the World Wide Web Consortium. What W3C decides will probably be adopted in major portions, if not entirely, by Netscape, Microsoft, and the other browser developers.

NOTE

> In case you skipped yesterday's reading, the W3C isn't known for its lightning speed in making decisions. A preliminary Level One DOM specification (think of it as version 1.0) is scheduled for release by the time of this book's printing. DOM Level One will fulfill only some of the requirements set forth by W3C. An extended set of specifications is not expected until mid- to late 1998.

The following sections take a look at what W3C has identified as the key requirements of a universal DOM, including an emphasis on the parts that will be addressed in the preliminary Level One specification.

General Requirements

As you've learned several times, one key component of the W3C DOM is that it should be universal—users shouldn't be required to use a specific browser or computer to take advantage of the DOM. The DOM should also be language independent. Remember that

Netscape's version began life tied to JavaScript. What the W3C wants is to separate the DOM from languages so a language can access the properties of the document object, but not dictate its structure.

Another important feature is tied to the W3C's commitment to creating accessibility for all users on the Web—a graphical user interface isn't required for conforming to the DOM.

NOTE

> A *graphical browser* can work with text, images, and other content geared toward visual manipulation of a page (tables, heading styles, frames, and so on). Graphical browsers are a relatively new invention, and their development was pioneered by NCSA's Mosaic.
>
> Several non-graphical browsers are still available, most noticeably, Lynx. Other versions are designed for people who are blind or have other disabilities that prevent them from using what we tend to think of as a "typical browser," such as Navigator. Specialty browsers can interpret HTML as speech, Braille, or special typefaces.

The capability to work within both graphical and non-graphical environments can create some confusion for developers. Throughout this book, you'll continue to explore how you can use the DOM to create decidedly graphical effects. If the DOM is used for so much graphical behavior, why go to the trouble of saying it doesn't require a graphical user interface? Because not everyone can use a graphical user interface, most notably people with vision disabilities. W3C is committed to standards that promote HTML and DOM accessibility for as many people as possible.

The last general requirement is that the DOM must not open the user's browser to problems with security, validity, or privacy. This requirement has already generated some discussion among the group working on the DOM recommendation. Although one part of the DOM says all attributes on a page must be accessible and modifiable, this can lead to problems for portions of the object model, especially where it relates to the user agent and history list.

Some pages are designed to work with specific browsers. Browsers identify themselves with a user_agent attribute, which would be accessible and available for scripts to modify. Unscrupulous page designers could use this attribute to change the way a browser views a page so that it would appear incompatible. The result would be to cause incorrect interpretation of the page or cause the browser to crash.

The other problem is with the history object. Confidential information, including passwords and credit card numbers, is often embedded or encoded in the URL, which is submitted to a CGI script for processing.

NEW TERM   The *history object* contains the URLs of pages previously navigated by the user's browser.

This attribute provides yet another method for those with less-than-honorable intentions to peruse private information for ill-gotten gain. For this reason, both Microsoft and Netscape have disabled or plan to otherwise change this part of the DOM.

Structure Navigation

This set of DOM capabilities refers to ways of moving within a document, such as finding the parent of an element or what children are contained within an element. What constitutes a parent and child? Go ask your mom and dad—that discussion is beyond the scope of this book.

Parents and Children in HTML

Beyond the birds and the bees, the parent-child relationship concerns nested tags. Look at the following snippet of HTML:

```
<DIV>This is Division 1.</DIV>
<DIV>This is Division 2 which leads to
<BLOCKQUOTE>block quote 1 which ends with</BLOCKQUOTE>
the end of Division 2.</DIV>
```

The first division is not a parent of the first division. It stands on its own, because the closing tag of the first precedes the opening tag of the second. The block quote is a child of the second division. It sits completely within the confines of the division's opening and closing tags.

Here's another parent-child relationship you might recognize:

```
<OL>
  <LI>Item 1</LI>
  <LI>Item 2</LI>
  <LI>Item 3</LI>
</OL>
```

Each of the list items is a child of the ordered list tag, which makes the list items siblings. If you nested another list by adding a new list container with its own set of list items, the new list would be a child of the outer list and a sibling to the other list items.

```
<OL id=outerlist>
  <LI>Item 1</LI>
  <LI>Item 2</LI>
  <LI>Item 3</LI>
  <UL id=innerlist>
    <LI>Sub item 1</LI>
    <LI>Sub item 2</LI>
```

```
    <LI>Sub item 3</LI>
  </UL>
</OL>
```

Using JavaScript notation, here's one way you could express the structure of the preceding snippet as a series of objects:

```
document.outerlist
document.outerlist[0] //Item 1
document.outerlist[1] //Item 2
document.outerlist[2] //Item 3
document.outerlist.innerlist
document.outerlist.innerlist[0] //Sub item 1
document.outerlist.innerlist[1] //Sub item 2
document.outerlist.innerlist[2] //Sub item 3
```

The structure of the notation reflects the structure of the document, requiring a reference to the outer list to reach the inner list nested inside. Each sibling then exists in a parallel relationship with its neighbor.

Parent-child relationship concerns in HTML do several things for you. First, they enable you to reference tags by their relationship to each other, as outlined in the sidebar. By defining a specific way to identify elements in their relationship to the document and to each other, you are given a method to express the unique structure of each document.

After each element is identified and expressed as part of the document structure, some additional structure navigation requirements fall into place, including exposing attributes and unknown tags.

You handle unknown tags the same as you would other elements. If it has an id, you could use that value to reference it within the DOM. If it doesn't, you could identify it by its relative position to other elements.

Document and Content Manipulation

Document and content manipulation follow the structure navigation standards. Document and content manipulation are used in conjunction with the event model to provide the "Dynamic" part of Dynamic HTML.

First, document manipulation enables you to change tags. For example, you could change an H1 heading into an H3 heading or into a new paragraph with P. Second, it enables you to add or remove tags from the document. The hard part of all this is that adding or removing page tags should still result in a valid document. Therefore, the DOM should provide for a way to prevent you from turning a set of LI tags into orphans by removing the parent UL or OL tag, or remove the LI tags at the same time. W3C has given no indication on what the preferred method will be on this issue.

Content manipulation will enable the page designer to script for changes to the content of any part of a document. This DOM requirement has two parts. First, like the structure navigation, you should be able to determine which element is surrounding any particular piece of text or determine the text within any given element.

After you're able to reference the content, you'll be able to add, change, or delete content at will. Microsoft added this feature to its Internet Explorer 4.0 browser with the `innerText` property. For example, with an `H1` heading named `mainHeading`, you can determine its content this way:

```
var textContent;
textContent = document.mainHeading.innerText;
```

This code creates a new string called `textContent`, which now contains all the text between the tags identified as `mainHeading`. To change this content, use the same property:

```
textContent = "This is a new heading";
document.mainHeading.innerText = textContent;
```

In addition to the content, you can use the property to add new tags or elements. You could also change the preceding line to

```
textContent = "<H2>This is a new heading</H2>";
document.mainHeading.innerText = textContent;
```

Because you're affecting only the content, the elements that surround the content do not change. Add the new content within the existing tags, resulting in HTML that now looks like this:

```
<H1 id=mainHeading><H2>This is a new heading</H2></H1>
```

If you wanted to replace the `<H1>` tags with `<H2>` tags, you can use the `outerText` property, which returns the string inside the `mainHeading` element including the elements themselves. The code would look like this:

```
TextContent = document.mainHeading.outerText;
textContent = "<H2 id='mainHeading'>This is a new heading</H2>";
document.mainHeading.outerText = textContent;
```

And the resulting HTML would look like this:

```
<H2 id=mainHeading>This is a new heading</H2>
```

Because the DOM provides a variety of ways to examine and change your document, it also needs a way to find out what the user is doing so it can react appropriately. This is the subject of the next section.

Event Model

To enable completely interactive documents, the event model must include a wide variety of possible activities for the user, including mouse movements, mouse clicks, combinations of mouse movement and clicking (drag-and-drop), key presses, and actions revolving around forms. More information about events and event handlers is provided in Chapter 6.

In Netscape's versions of object models, specific events were tied to specific objects. You could detect the user moving the mouse pointer over a hyperlink but not a heading. You could detect a click on a button but not a block quote. A key part of the W3C requirement for the DOM is that every element will accept every applicable event. Any piece of text will be able to respond to mouse activities, including clicks, double-clicks, and pointers moving over and out of their area.

This requirement also provides for a certain amount of difficulty, however, when it's merged with the user accessibility issues also stressed by W3C. What if the user interface doesn't support a mouse? That removes many potential events from the range of possibilities for a page when it's viewed on an unconventional browser. This issue hasn't been addressed yet within the requirements, but you can expect browser developers to provide for other events, such as pressing specific keys to substitute for mouse activities.

One new idea provided for HTML in the event model is a concept known as *event bubbling*. This concept allows for the fact that an event which affects an element can also affect its parent. Through scripting constructs, the event handler can let the system know whether the event was handled completely. If it wasn't, the event is passed up to the next level of the document.

For example, the user clicks an ordered list item and the event handler for the list item does its work. If the event handler is finished and the event has been completely fulfilled, the event handler returns true and the event is complete. If the event handler returns false, however, the event is passed to the parent element. The ordered list container now has the chance to perform additional actions to complete the event. If it returns true, the event is finished. If it returns false, the event is sent to the document for any default handling dictated by the user's browser.

Summary

On its simplest level, the Document Object Model is simply a way of defining how browsers can express their structure and content, regardless of the platform or scripting language. It has its roots in Netscape's JavaScript Object Model introduced in Navigator 2.0. The early Netscape model included a limited number of objects and events that provided access to some of the key components on a page, such as forms and hyperlinks, but ignored virtually all other formatting tags. Netscape's original idea is now expanded in scope and capabilities in Microsoft's Internet Explorer 4.0, which includes an object model that is closer in intent to requirements outlined by the W3C.

This isn't to say that Microsoft's solution is the final word on the Document Object Model. W3C's requirements aren't standards—they're only a list of the capabilities they expect from a DOM. The problem with conforming to this sort of list is that it doesn't create a standard—it only expresses a wish list.

A preliminary version of the DOM with the key components in place (structure navigation, document and content manipulation, and event model) is expected in 1997. Any formal W3C ruling on a complete implementation of the full DOM requirements isn't expected for another year or more. After a standard is developed, it will probably take the software developers up to another year to modify their respective browsers to make sure they work with the brave new world envisioned by W3C.

In the meantime, keep an eye on both Netscape and Microsoft. Their future browser revisions are a good indicator of which way W3C's flag is blowing, because both companies are a part of the W3C committee working on the issue. Even if they don't meet the final W3C DOM exactly, you'll be close enough to make an easy translation when both browsers come closer to compatibility with each other.

Q&A

Q I don't get it. This chapter talks about models, but I'm working with real Web pages. Why do they call this a model when it talks about real pages?

A Because the standards are driven by technical people who use neat words like "object-oriented," "paradigm," and "implementation engineering." The reality of the situation is this: The Document Object Model is nothing more than a way to describe a Web page and how developers can make the page interact with users.

Instead of getting hung up on the word "model," think more along the terms of "blueprint." The blueprint provides the standards and constraints for the building, but you can't live in it. The Web page becomes the building. Then, you can identify any section of the building using the blueprint, including additions or changes.

Q Is there any hope of compatibility between Netscape and Microsoft?

A As usual, that depends on the companies themselves. Although their past history of cooperation is less than stellar, they both have met existing HTML standards. For example, a Web page authored completely with HTML 3.2 tags might not appear exactly the same on both browsers, but they will still appear in a predictable manner and not cause any errors. Although the list of differences over the DOM is currently much longer than the list of compatibilities, our guess is that you can expect both companies will be close enough to provide basic compatibility in the next version of their respective browsers, with just enough differences to keep it from being easy. This expectation follows their respective implementations of a standardized JavaScript (called ECMAScript) plus W3C's development of the DOM standard.

3

Chapter 4

Cascading Style Sheets

In Chapter 3, "The Dynamic HTML Object Model," you had a chance to explore the Document Object Model and how it's used to represent any given Web page. Under the coming new Web order, style sheet information is also part of the DOM. After defining a style sheet or adding an inline style, you can view and alter any of the myriad of attributes that control its appearance.

NOTE

> Unlike Dynamic HTML and the Document Object Model, cascading style sheets exist as a real and accepted standard on the World Wide Web. Style sheets are in their first version accepted by the World Wide Web Consortium, and the standard is referred to as Cascading Style Sheets 1 (CSS1).

You use style sheets to control how HTML tags are formatted. The ranks of Web authors are increasingly filled with people from graphic design or desktop publishing backgrounds, and controlling the nuances of style is a part of the natural approach to design. However, a common tool to control style was missing from HTML in its first incarnations. Historically, the scripting process of HTML specifically avoided advanced style options and instead offered only very rudimentary methods for creating style elements, such as color, headers, and margins. Using special effects, such as text shadowing, has required the use of graphics, which slow the download of pages as the data shuttles between server and browser.

What exactly are Cascading Style Sheets? The word "cascading" means that multiple styles can be used in an individual HTML page, and the browser will follow an order—called a cascade—to interpret the information. Out of the three types of style sheets, a designer can use all three simultaneously, and the browser will deliver the goods in an orderly and predictable fashion.

Because style sheets are a very important method of controlling how text is displayed and moved around on the page, you'll spend the rest of the day learning how to put one together and how it's represented in the Document Object Model.

Style Control with Style Sheets

Style control with HTML is clumsy at best and non-existent at worst. With cascading style sheets, a Web designer has dramatically improved ways of working with important style issues such as fonts, including specific features such as font face, size, font weight, font style, and leading (pronounced "led-ing"). And, the controls extend beyond basic typographic functions to margins, indents, color, graphics, and a myriad of other options. Basically, if you can display it with HTML, you can control it with a style sheet.

The World Wide Web Consortium has released a definitive standard for style sheets, which is now reflected in Microsoft Internet Explorer 3.0 and later, and Netscape Navigator 4.0 and later. With both major browsers now on board with implementations, you can expect style sheets to become an integral part of many Web pages.

 NOTE

From the are-we-moving-forward-or-sideways file, when a page using style sheets exclusively is viewed by older versions of Netscape (3.0 or earlier) or Internet Explorer (2.0 or earlier), the Web page reverts back to the prison-gray backgrounds. This demotes fonts and other styles to their bare-bones defaults (see Figures 4.1 and 4.2).

Figure 4.1.

A page using cascading style sheets as it appears in Internet Explorer 4.0 is presented in all its glamour.

Figure 4.2.

The same page reverts to a bare-bone default in a non-CSS1 compliant browser such as Mosaic.

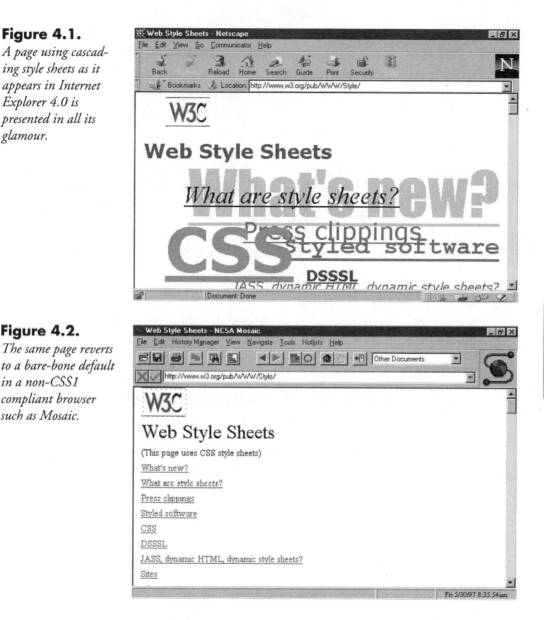

With all of their promise, there are still some challenges for style sheets. This includes problems with the difference in the selection of fonts each user holds on his or her machine— my selection of fonts is different than yours, your selection is different than your coworker's, and your coworker's selection is different from his or her neighbor's. A style sheet can call a specific typeface, but if the font and font weight aren't on the visitor's machine, the browser cannot interpret the style you've set up.

And, as mentioned in the note, a page that deals exclusively in style sheets will not achieve the desired results in a non-compatible browser. Without some allowance for the many other types of browsers on the Web, a page can look like it was created to be as ugly and unreadable as possible.

Fortunately, there are workarounds for the various problems. Wise designers will stack information into the style argument strings and back up the style with attributes in the HTML tags. This enables the browser to seek out the information it can interpret. This is good, but the designers still lose some control as a result, because they're never assured that a page is going to remain consistent regardless of where it's viewed. Old rules remain true—use prudence and caution, and, wherever possible, test the results of your work by viewing it on a variety of browsers on a variety of platforms.

Essential Style Sheets

There are three primary ways to use style sheets: the inline method, the individual page or embedded method, and linking to a master or external style sheet.

- ☐ Inline Style Sheets. This approach exploits existing HTML tags within a standard HTML document and adds a specific style to the information controlled by those tags. An example would be controlling the indentation of a single paragraph using the `style="someStyle"` attribute within the `<P>` tag. Another method of achieving this is by combining the `<SPAN>` tag and the `style="someStyle"` attribute.

- ☐ Embedded Style Sheets. This method enables the designer to control individual pages by using the `<STYLE>` tag, along with its companion tag, `</STYLE>`. This information is placed between the `<HTML>` tag and the `<BODY>` tag; the style attributes are inserted within the full `<STYLE>` container.

- ☐ External (linked) Style Sheets. This is a master style sheet stored in an external file. It uses the same syntax you would with an embedded style. This file uses the `.css` extension. Then, simply be sure that all of the HTML documents that will require those controls are linked to that document.

All three style sheets will work with Dynamic HTML, although inline and embedded style sheets are usually much more common because having all the styles and their attributes within the same file for easy review and modification is very convenient.

NOTE

The attribute syntax for embedded and linked style sheets is somewhat different than standard HTML syntax. Attributes are placed within curly brackets, whereas HTML would place an equal (=) sign; a colon (:) is used; and individual, stacked arguments are separated by semicolons rather than commas. Also, several attributes are hyphenated, such as `font-style` and `margin-left`. A style sheet string would look like this:

```
{font-style: arial, helvetica; margin-left}
```

Still, as with HTML, style sheet syntax is very logical. As you work with the examples in this chapter, you should become quite comfortable with the way style sheets work.

When you refer to the style attributes as properties of an object, the hyphen disappears and the first letter of the second word is capitalized. So, `font-style` becomes `fontStyle`, and `text-decoration` becomes `textDecoration`.

The following sections should serve as an introduction for newcomers and a review for old hands on the basics of each type of style sheet. Although you'll be using some style sheet syntax to create the examples, detailed syntax is covered later in the chapter and in Appendix D, "CSS1 Quick Reference."

Using Inline Style

An inline style is included with the tag it affects. It doesn't affect any other HTML tags on the page, whether they're the same type or not. For example, if you place an italic style with an `<H1>` tag, the style will not apply to any other `<H1>` tags on the page. You can create an inline style by following these steps:

1. Begin with a blank page in your HTML editor.

NOTE

I'm not going to make any assumptions about which HTML editor you're using. There are a billion of them to choose from (give or take), and you should use whatever you're comfortable with. There are a couple of requirements, however.

First, it should allow non-standard tags, such as `<STYLE>`. Some browsers automatically validate HTML and some don't, and those that do differ in how they handle non-standard items. If your editor doesn't directly support HTML 3.2, HTML 4.0, or CSS1, make sure your editor will still let you insert items that aren't standard to earlier versions of HTML.

> The second requirement follows from the first. If you're going to add
> non-standard elements, you'll need a way to modify the source code of
> the document. In addition to adding new tags, you'll also need a way to
> add attributes to existing tags.
>
> If your editor doesn't support this kind of activity and you can't find an
> editor you like, then you can always fall back on the old faithful text
> editor. It might not be pretty, but it works.

2. Include the following lines of HTML. Pay attention to the extra `style` attributes in
   the `<p>` and `<span>` tags.

```
<html>
<head>
<title>An Inline Style</title>
</head>
<body bgcolor="#FFFFFF">

<p style="font-size: 14pt" id="p14">
This came from a P tag with a style.
Duis autem vel eum iriure dolor in hendrerit in vulputate velit esse
molestie consequat, vel illum dolore eu feugiat nulla facilisis
at vero.</p>

<p>
This came from a P tag without a style.
Duis autem vel eum iriure dolor in hendrerit in vulputate velit esse
molestie consequat, vel illum dolore eu feugiat nulla facilisis
at vero.</p>

<span style="font-size: 18pt" id="span18">
This came from a SPAN tag with a style.
Duis autem vel eum iriure dolor in hendrerit in vulputate velit esse
molestie consequat, vel illum dolore eu feugiat nulla facilisis
at vero.</p>
</span>

<span>
This came from a SPAN tag without a style.
Duis autem vel eum iriure dolor in hendrerit in vulputate velit esse
molestie consequat, vel illum dolore eu feugiat nulla facilisis
at vero.</p>
</span>

</body>
</html>
```

3. Save the file as `inline.html`.

Figure 4.3 illustrates the finished page as it appears in Internet Explorer 4.0.

Figure 4.3.

The results of inline style sheet commands.

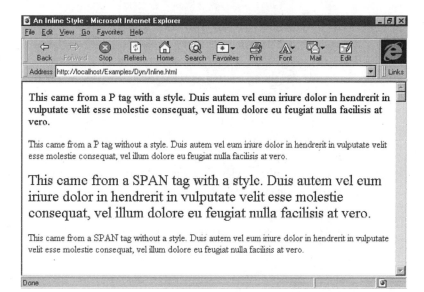

As you can see from the example, the inline style for a tag has no effect on any other tag around it. Its effect is very localized.

When you want to change these styles with Dynamic HTML, they're represented in the object model with `Object.style.fontSize`, where `Object` is the name of the `id` attribute for the tag. In this case, it's `p14.style.fontSize` and `span18.style.fontSize`.

TIP

The `<div>` (division) tag can be used like the `<span>` tag for inline control. The `<div>` tag is especially helpful for longer blocks of text, whereas `<span>` is most effective for adding style to smaller stretches of information, such as sentences, several words, or even individual letters within a word.

In one sense, an inline style defeats the ultimate purpose of cascading style sheets. The main point of the technology is to control the style for an entire page or sets of pages. For this reason, the inline method typically is used only where touches of style are required. Besides, adding style to each tag requires a lot of typing and has the potential to generate a lot of errors.

An Embedded Style for a Page

The next style you'll work with is an *embedded* style. An embedded style sheet is a set of style definitions placed within <STYLE> tags and located between the head and body of the document. It sets the style attributes for the entire page where it's located, and is created by following these steps:

1. Begin with a blank page in your HTML editor.

2. Type the following text. Be sure you place the <STYLE> tags in the proper place—immediately after </HTML> and before <BODY>. The style is similar to what you just saw in the inline styles. The exact syntax is covered in more detail as you work through the chapter.

```
<html>
<head>
<title>An Embedded Style Sheet</title>
</head>

<style>
BODY {background:#0000FF; color: #FFFF00; margin-left:0.5in;
➥margin-right:0.5in}
H2 {font-size:18pt; color:#FF0000; background:#FFFFFF}
P {font-size:12pt; text-indent:0.5in}
</style>

<body>

<h2 id="h2_1">This heading in red on a white background.</h2>

All text is yellow on a blue background.<BR>

This text is not indented, except for the margins. Duis
autem vel eum iriure dolor in hendrerit in vulputate
velit esse molestie consequat, vel illum dolore eu
feugiat nulla facilisis.

<p id="p_1">
This text is indented. Duis autem vel eum iriure dolor in
hendrerit in vulputate velit esse molestie consequat, vel
illum dolore eu feugiat nulla facilisis at vero eros et accumsan
et iusto odio dignissim qui blandit praesent luptatum.</p>

</body>
</html>
```

3. Save the file as embedded.html.

Figure 4.4 illustrates the finished page as it appears in Internet Explorer 4.0.

4

Figure 4.4.

The results of individual, or embedded, style sheet commands.

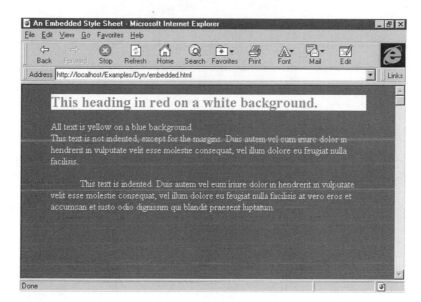

NOTE

You might have noticed by now that I'm using paragraph tags as containers, with a beginning <P> and an ending </P>. This is part of the HTML 3.2 specification, although it's not a required use. However, if you're going to work with cascading style sheets, you must get into the habit of using closing tags with elements such as paragraphs, table cells, and similar items. A style sheet won't recognize a new paragraph until you specifically mark it with a <P> and </P>. This is true even if it's a new paragraph by default, such as the first line following a heading.

When you want to change these styles with Dynamic HTML, the styles are expressed in the object model with the same syntax as inline styles—`Object.style.fontSize`. For the example in this section, it's `h2_1.style.fontSize`, `h2_1.style.color`, `h2_1.style.background`, and so on.

When you begin using style sheets, the embedded variety is probably the one you'll find yourself using most often. Its page-by-page control enables you to modify the look and feel of each page within a site. However, if strong uniformity is required for a set of pages or the entire site, a link to a master style sheet is called for.

A Linked Cascading Style Sheet

Creating a style sheet that can be linked to and used by any number of other pages is really a simple task. It's called a *linked* style sheet because all of the style definitions sit in one file, and the actual HTML page creates a link to it when the page is loaded. Creating a linked style is similar to an embedded style, as seen by following these steps:

1. Begin with a blank page in your HTML editor.

2. Start by inserting a `<STYLE>` tag and its corresponding `</STYLE>` container tag:

   ```
   <style>

   </style>
   ```

NOTE

> Many editors automatically include the basic HTML structure tags when you create a new document, including the `<HTML>`, `<HEAD>`, and `<BODY>` tags. Because a linked style sheet requires only an opening and closing `<STYLE>` tag, you will probably find the task easier to accomplish with a text editor.

3. Place the style definitions between the tags the same way you did for the embedded style sheet.

   ```
   <style>

   BODY {background:#0000FF; color: #FFFF00;
   ➥margin-left:0.5in; margin-right:0.5in}
   H2 {font-size:18pt; color:#FF0000; background:#FFFFFF}
   P {font-size:12pt; text-indent:0.5in}

   </style>
   ```

4. Now, instead of saving your work as an HTML file, save it with the extension `.css`. For this example, the entire name is `master_style.css`.

The next set of steps integrate the master style file with an HTML page. Repeat this process for any pages that use the same style definitions.

1. Select an existing HTML to which you want to apply the master style. For now, use a stripped-down version of the page from the embedded style sheet example.

   ```
   <html>
   <head>
   <title>A Linked Style Sheet</title>
   </head>

   <body>

   <h2>This is a heading.</h2>

   Duis autem vel eum iriure dolor in hendrerit in vulputate
   velit esse molestie consequat, vel illum dolore eu feugiat
   nulla facilisis.
   ```

4

```
<p>
Duis autem vel eum iriure dolor in hendrerit in vulputate
velit esse molestie consequat, vel illum dolore eu feugiat
nulla facilisis at vero eros et accumsan et iusto odio
dignissim qui blandit praesent luptatum.</p>

</body>
</html>
```

2. Open the file in your HTML editor.

3. Place the following line within the <head> tag, below the <title>:

```
<link rel=stylesheet href="master_style.css" type="text/css">
```

The <link> tag identifies another file that is related in some way to the current page, and is also used to create navigation buttons on browsers such as Mosaic. In this case, it identifies a cascading style sheet located in the same directory as the Web page. If this were a JavaScript Accessible Style Sheet (JSSS), the type would be text/jass. Creating style with JSSS is covered tomorrow.

The complete header now looks like this:

```
<head>
<title>A Linked Style Sheet</title>
<link rel=stylesheet href="master_style.css" type="text/css">
</head>
```

4. Save the file as linked.html.

All of the affected tags within the Web page will be interpreted according to the styles you've set forth in the .css file. The results of the sample page using an externally linked style sheet is shown in Figure 4.5.

Figure 4.5.

This page includes a link to an external style sheet. It doesn't contain any other style sheet information, other than the location of the .css file.

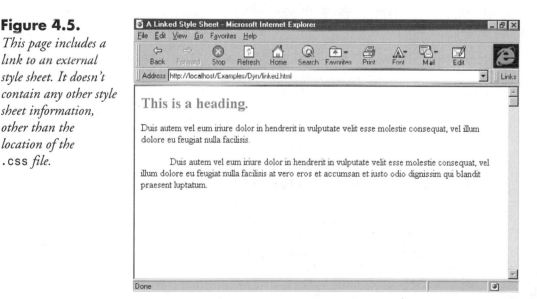

Some Web servers require registration of a MIME (Internet Media) type for style sheets before the server can deliver the linked style sheet to the browser. The Web administrator must know that the suffix is .css and the MIME type is text/css.

With the style information residing in its own file, you can use it on any number of pages by simply adding the <LINK> tag in the document header. Like the inline and embedded style sheets, all styles are accessible to scripting languages through the *object*.*style*.*styleAttribute* syntax in the Document Object Model.

Combining Style Sheet Techniques

There are times when one style sheet solution isn't enough. Designers with complex requirements are going to benefit from mixing style sheet techniques. Mixing takes full advantage of the cascading feature of style sheets. Multiple techniques are resolved by the browser in the following manner:

- ☐ First, linked style sheets are applied globally.
- ☐ If an embedded style sheet is encountered on the same page with a linked style sheet, the embedded style overrides the linked style if there's a conflict.
- ☐ Inline styles override both embedded and linked styles.

This orderly and predictable implementation enables you to define a single style sheet for an entire site, modify individual pages to support specific tasks with an embedded style, and use inline styles to tweak the details of specific lines.

TIP If your site includes a multitude of pages, linked styles, and embedded styles, it's easy to lose track of what uses what and where any one is overridden. To make your life easier, keep the linked styles as few and generic as possible, and then apply other style sheet techniques only when they're required for distinct assignments.

Text-Specific Style Attributes

Some graphic designers spend entire careers dedicated to the study of typography. It is undeniably an art, comprised of not only being familiar with countless font faces, but also related attributes such as weight, size variations, styles, families, and how to artistically use all of these aspects in attractive combinations.

NEW TERM *Typography* is the study of typefaces. A typographer is someone who is an expert at typefaces—their identification, classification, and use. These are the people who can use words like *descender, x-height, serif,* and *swash* as part of their everyday vocabulary.

The face of the Web cannot change for the better if designers don't understand some text-based fundamentals before putting style sheets to use. You'll see many tips and notes as you progress through this chapter, but be sure to refer to Day 4, "Dynamically Changing Text and Styles," where you learn in greater detail about style as it relates to text styles.

NOTE Everything you want to know about type and more is covered in *TypeStyle* by Daniel Will-Harris (Peachpit Press). It covers the issues that affect anyone who works with words—how to combine different typefaces to make pages easier to read, and more importantly, how to avoid ugly and embarrassing mistakes.

The following text and text-related attributes are available for use in all methods of style sheets:

4

- □ `font-family`: This attribute controls the face of the font by setting arguments for either of the following:

  The name of the typeface you want to use. Here is a sample style specification for Times:

  `{font-family: times}`

  Because an individual computer might not have the installed font of your preference, you might want to add a similar alternative:

  `{font-family: times, garamond}`

  As a last resort, you can add a generic family name which tells the browser to pick a typeface that at least shares the same basic attributes as your other choices:

  `{font-family: serif}`

The following type families are recognized with style sheets:

- □ *Serif.* Serif fonts are a good choice for long sections of text. Popular serifs include Times New Roman and Garamond.
- □ *Sans Serif.* This font family includes popular choices such as Arial, Helvetica, and Avante Garde. This is often used for headings to complement serif body text.
- □ *Cursive.* These are script fonts—fonts that appear as though they have been handwritten. This includes faces such as Zapf Chancery and Park Avenue.

☐ *Fantasy.* Fantasy fonts are decorative in nature and very useful for stylish headings and titles. They are typically not practical for body text or long headings. Examples include Blippo, Hobo, and Broadway.

☐ *Monospace.* This is a throwback to the days of typewriters and teletype machines. *Monospace* refers to the fact that every letter takes an equal amount of space—an i takes as much space as an m. Most fonts are proportional, which means each letter takes up a space that is proportional to the individual letter's size and style, instead of forcing it to fit in an exact amount of space—an i takes about a fourth of the space as an m. Examples of monospace include Courier or American Typewriter, and are used to represent lines of code or things the user should type.

NOTE

The traditional guideline for selecting serif versus sans serif fonts is to use serif fonts for body text and sans serif fonts for headings or small blocks of text.

There's a good reason for this. Research and experience indicate that serif fonts are easier to read. However, sans serif fonts are becoming increasingly popular as body text fonts within Web browsers. Part of the reason is that serifs don't always translate well across a variety of screens and screen resolutions. Sans serif faces don't have the extra ornamentation to worry about.

It all comes down to good judgment. You need to base the use of serif or sans serif fonts on whether the pages are attractive and easy to read.

TIP

Use a typeface family as the last item in a font-family list, because it covers your font choices as completely as possible. Even if a specific typeface is unavailable on a given computer, a similar one in the same category is likely to be available. A savvy designer includes a list of choices, from top choice through last choice, and ends with the category. For example, if you prefer three specific serif typefaces, then the final attribute would appear as

```
{font-family: garamond, goudy, times, serif}
```

☐ font size. Sizing in style sheets offers the designer five measurement options:

Points. To set a font in point size, use the abbreviation pt immediately next to the numeric size: {font-size: 12pt}. This is the standard the vast majority of designers use.

Pixels. Pixels are specified with the px abbreviation: {font-size: 24px}. A pixel is one dot on a screen; the number of pixels varies by the size of the screen. Many users use a screen 800×600 pixels in size, although there are still a lot of 640×480 screens. Incidentally, 640×480 was used for the screen images captured for this book.

> **TIP**
>
> Most Web designers are more comfortable with the point and pixel values for setting font sizes. However, if you prefer another method and find it easy for you to use, that's fine, too. The best advice I can give is to choose a method and stick with it. Consistency is a smart approach to creating style, and makes it easier to adjust the style to fit changing demands.

Inches. If you'd rather set your fonts in inches, simply place in and the numeral size, in inches, of the font size you require: {font-size: 1in}.

Centimeters. Some people might prefer centimeters, represented by cm and used in the same way as points and inches: {font-size: 5cm}.

Percentage. As a last resort, you might want to choose to set a percentage of the default point size: {font-size: 150%}.

☐ font-style. This attribute typically dictates the style of text, such as placing it in italics. The following is the appropriate syntax to do this:

{font-style: italic}

You might think that another value for font-style would be bold, but that's covered by font-weight. The other legal values for this attribute are normal and oblique. normal reverts the text to its default status, and oblique is similar to italic, except that it is slanted manually instead of relying on the true italic version of the typeface.

☐ font-weight. The thickness of a typeface is referred to as its *weight*. As with font faces, font weights rely on the existence of the corresponding font and weight on an individual's machine. A range of attributes is available in style sheets, including the following: extra-light, demi-light, light, medium, extra-bold, demi-bold, and bold.

Before you assign font weights, be certain that the font face you are applying the weight to has that weight available. Always check your work on a variety of platforms and machines, where possible, to see whether you have been able to achieve strong design despite the fact that some machines might not support the font or the font weight in question. As a general rule, bold is always available.

☐ text-decoration. This attribute decorates text, including none, underline, italic, and line-through.

NOTE

The text-decoration attribute will be a favorite of people who dislike underlined links. You can use the A {text-decoration: none} style definition to globally shut off underlined hyperlinks. For an inline style, place the value within the link you want to control:

```
<a style="text-decoration: none" href="nowhere.html">Link to
nowhere</a>.
```

☐ line-height. Another important text-related aspect is *leading*. This refers to the amount of line spacing between lines of text. This space should be consistent, or the result is uneven, unattractive spacing. The line-height attribute enables you to set the distance between the baseline, or bottom, of a line of text.

To set the leading of a paragraph, use the line-height attribute in points, inches, centimeters, pixels, or percentages in the same way you describe font-size attributes:

```
P {line-height: 14pt}
```

You've just learned a lot about syntax and attributes, so it's time to take a bit of a break. In the next section, you'll play around with some variations on the font so you can see how they display on a browser.

Using Text Attributes

This example uses an embedded style sheet with various text attributes.

1. Begin with a blank page in your HTML editor.

2. Type the structure tags and a title for the page. The attribute with the <body> attribute sets a new background color:

```
<html>

<head>
<title>Text Styles</title>
</head>

<style>
<!--
-->
</style>

<body bgcolor="#ffffff">
</body>

</html>
```

> **TIP**
>
> What are the comment tags doing between the `<STYLE>` tags? If a page with an embedded style sheet is displayed on an incompatible browser, it displays the contents of the style sheet as if it were any other text on the page. Placing a set of comment tags within the `<STYLE>` tags hides the styles from the incompatible browser.
>
> A style-compatible browser will ignore the comment tags, so you don't have to worry about mucking up your style definitions.

3. Add the following lines between the `<STYLE>` tags, which includes changes to font family, size, weight, and style for several elements, including turning off underlining in hyperlinks. You'll notice how fonts are listed under `font-family` for broad coverage:

```
H1 {font-family: verdana, helvetica, arial, san-serif ;
➥font-size: 18pt; font-style: normal}
H2 {font-family: verdana, helvetica, arial, san-serif ;
➥font-size: 14pt; font-style: normal}
P {font-family: garamond, goudy, times, serif;
➥font-size: 12pt; font-style: normal; line-height: 14pt}
A {text-decoration: none; font-weight: bold}
```

4. Finally, add the following HTML tags and text to the body:

```
<H1>Lorem ipsum dolor sit amet</H1>

<P>Consectetur <A href="tempor.html">adipisci tempor</A> incidunt
ut labore et dolore magna aliqu atib saepe eveniet ut er reupdiand
sint. Nos arsapiente delectus au aut prefer endis dol tene
sententiam, quid est cur verear ne ad eam nc quos tu paulo ante
memorite tum etia ergat.</P>

<H2>Tomporibud autem quinus</H2>

<P>Atib saepe eveniet ut er <A href="sint.html">repudiand sint</A>
et molestia tenetury sapiente delctus au aut prefer endis dol.
Endiumagist and et dodecendesse videantur, iustitiam, aequitated
fidem. Neque hominy infant efficerd possit duo contend notiner si
effecerit. Natura proficis facile explent sine julla unura aute
enim desiderable.</P>
```

Save the finished result as `text.html`. If you view it with Internet Explorer, it should resemble Figure 4.6. The headers, paragraphs, and hyperlinks give up their default presentation and follow the rules of the style sheet. The results on a browser that doesn't support style sheets, such as Mosaic, are shown in Figure 4.7.

4

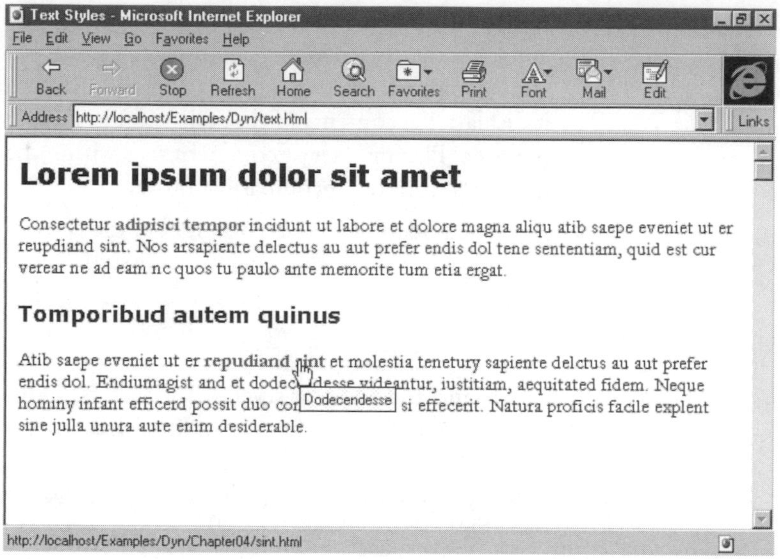

Figure 4.6.

Using an embedded style sheet; the text on this page has a variety of text controls applied to it.

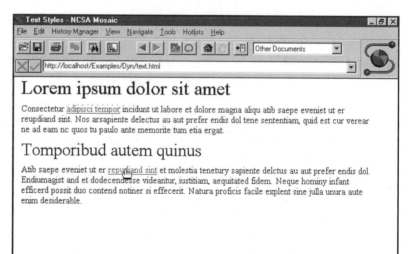

Now you have a page that has successfully employed embedded style sheets. In the next lesson, you'll work on margins, indents, and other text alignment attributes. These will help add some texture and white space to your pages.

Figure 4.7.

If the same page is interpreted by a browser that doesn't support style sheets, each element is treated in its typical default fashion.

Margins, Indents, and Text Alignment Attributes

Despite what the standard version of HTML would have you believe, pages do not exist just to have you place text from border to border with a minimum of white space. Creating a good design includes setting margins and indents so the reader's eye is guided from one element to the next, and enough white space to give the reader a break in between thoughts. The next set of attributes serves this noble purpose.

- ☐ margin-left. To set a left margin, use a distance in points, inches, centimeters, or pixels. The following sets a left margin to three-fourths of an inch:

  `{margin-left: .75in}`

- ☐ margin-right. For a right margin, select from the same measurement options as provided for the margin-left attribute:

  `{margin-right: 50px}`

- ☐ margin-top. You set top margins using the same measurement values as for other margin attributes:

  `{margin-top: 20pt)`

- ☐ text-indent. Again, points, inches, centimeters, or pixel values can be assigned to this attribute, which indents any type of text:

  `{text-indent: 0.5in)`

  Internet Explorer also allows for negative margin and text indent values. This enables you to create interesting and unusual effects, including overlapping text and hanging indents (an "outdent") for a contemporary design.

- ☐ text-align. This long-awaited feature enables you to justify text. Values include left, center, and right:

  `{text-align: right}`

Text alignment is a powerful layout tool, and as a designer, you will enjoy being able to place text in a variety of alignments without having to rely on tables, divisions, or other, less graceful HTML workarounds that existed in the past. Remember, text justification requires a fine eye. Left justification is the only reasonable choice for long selections of text, because its readability is much more accessible to the eye. Right justification comes in handy for short bursts of text, such as pull-quotes. Use centered text sparingly. Even though it seems natural to want to center text, it is actually more difficult to read and looks cliché and ungainly.

With these attributes in hand, it's time to work on another example to see how they work within an HTML page.

4

Margins and Justification Controls

This task shows how to control margins within a style sheet.

1. Open the file from the previous example, `text.html`, into your HTML editor.

2. Add the following margin syntax alongside the BODY attribute within the `<style>` tag section:

```
BODY {margin-left: 0.75in; margin-right: 0.75in; margin-top: 0.25in}
```

   You use the BODY style as the base for other elements. For example, setting the typeface to Garamond for the body makes Garamond the base typeface for paragraphs, hyperlinks, and other items.

3. Save the file as `margin.html` and view it in a browser. The results on Internet Explorer are illustrated in Figure 4.8.

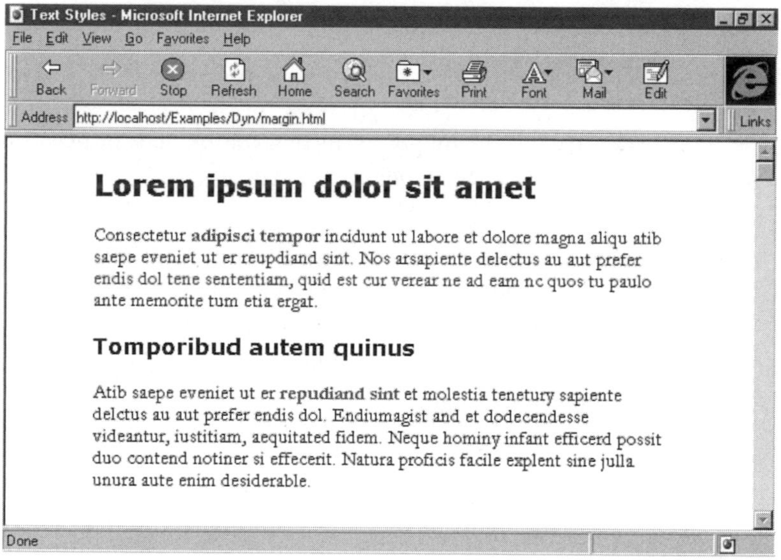

Figure 4.8.

Margins create attractive white space around the page, giving it "breathing room" from the edges of the browser window.

In this example, margin values for the entire page were changed using the BODY attribute. You can also add margins to any other HTML tag. For example, if you want to set different margins for the headers, place the margin values in the string next to the header of your choice. Similarly, you can adjust margins on individual paragraphs by adding the margin values you seek to the paragraph string.

If you're including margins for the BODY style definition as well as in the P style definition, be sure your paragraph margins are larger than those you've selected for the body of the text. Otherwise, you won't be able to see the difference. The browser ignores the lesser margin and uses the greatest value that's available between the two.

Next, add justification in order to create more visual texture on the page. Alignment, or *justification*, plays an important part in design. This example illustrates how to change the justification to affect the text.

1. Beginning with `margin.html`, add the `text-align` attribute to the two heading tags:

```
BODY {margin-left: 0.75in; margin-right: 0.75in; margin-top: 0.10in}
H1 {font-family: verdana, helvetica, arial, san-serif;
➥font-size:18pt; font-style:normal; text-align:left}
H2 {font-family: verdana, helvetica, arial, san-serif;
➥font-size:14pt; font-style:normal; text-align:right}
P {font-family: garamond; font-size: 12pt; font-style: normal;
➥line-height: 11pt}
A {text-decoration: none; font-weight: bold}
```

2. Because you're justifying paragraphs separately, add those attributes with inline style. The entire file should look like this:

```
<HTML>

<HEAD>
<TITLE>Text Styles</TITLE>
</HEAD>

<STYLE>
<!--
BODY {margin-left: 0.75in; margin-right: 0.75in; margin-top: 0.10in}
H1 {font-family: verdana, helvetica, arial, san-serif;
➥font-size:18pt; font-style:normal; text-align:left}
H2 {font-family: verdana, helvetica, arial, san-serif;
➥font-size:14pt; font-style:normal; text-align:right}
P {font-family: garamond; font-size: 12pt; font-style: normal;
➥line-height: 11pt}
A {text-decoration: none; font-weight: bold}
-->
</STYLE>

<BODY bgcolor="#ffffff">
<H1>Lorem ipsum dolor sit amet</H1>

<P style="text-align:left">Consectetur
<A href="tempor.html" title="Eveniet"> adipisci tempor</A> incidunt
ut labore et dolore magna aliqu atib saepe eveniet ut er reupdiand
sint. Nos arsapiente delectus au aut prefer endis dol tene
sententiam, quid est cur verear ne ad eam nc quos tu paulo ante
memorite tum etia ergat.</P>

<H2>Temporibud autem quinus</H2>

<P style="text-align:right">Atib saepe eveniet ut er
<A href="sint.html" title="Dodecendesse">repudiand sint</A> et
molestia tenetury sapiente delctus au aut prefer endis dol.
Endiumagist and et dodecendesse videantur, iustitiam, aequitated
fidem. Neque hominy infant efficerd possit duo contend notiner si
effecerit. Natura proficis facile explent sine julla unura aute
enim desiderable.</P>
</BODY>

</HTML>
```

4

3. Save this page as `justify.html` and view it in your browser. The look and feel of the page is becoming more and more interesting, as shown in Figure 4.9.

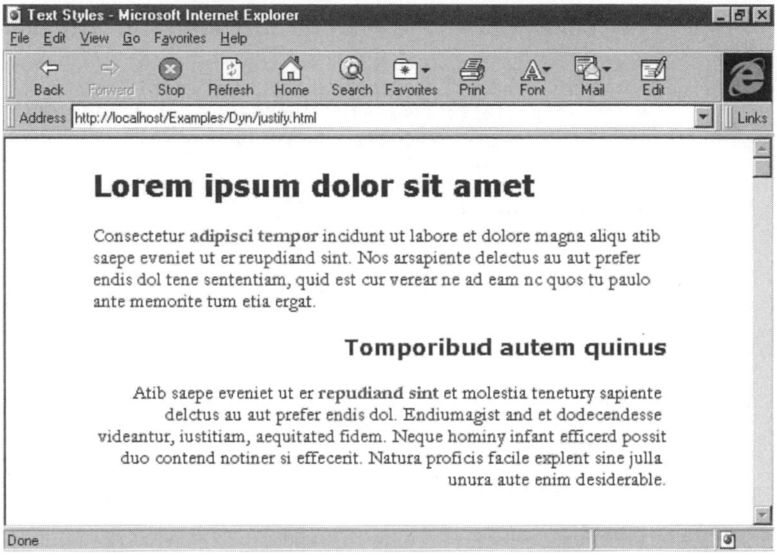

Figure 4.9.

Justification helps create a texture with words, and makes a Web page more interesting, even without pictures.

Text Styles - Microsoft Internet Explorer

File   Edit   View   Go   Favorites   Help

Back   Forward   Stop   Refresh   Home   Search   Favorites   Print   Font   Mail   Edit

Address http://localhost/Examples/Dyn/justify.html   Links

Lorem ipsum dolor sit amet

Consectetur **adipisci tempor** incidunt ut labore et dolore magna aliqu atib saepe eveniet ut er reupdiand sint. Nos arsapiente delectus au aut prefer endis dol tene sententiam, quid est cur verear ne ad eam nc quos tu paulo ante memorite tum etia ergat.

Tomporibud autem quinus

Atib saepe eveniet ut er repudiand sint et molestia tenetury sapiente delctus au aut prefer endis dol. Endiumagist and et dodecendesse videantur, iustitiam, aequitated fidem. Neque hominy infant efficerd possit duo contend notiner si effecerit. Natura proficis facile explent sine julla unura aute enim desiderable.

Done

So far, you've learned how to change the typeface and its various related attributes, changed its style, and then added some spacing and justification around the page. Now it's time to get out a paintbrush and see what can happen with the color.

Color and Background

Take a look at the `<BODY>` tag syntax and you'll notice a `bgcolor` attribute used to set the background color of the entire page. This is one way to set the background color. The other is to use the `background` attribute with the `BODY` style definition. However, there have been some problems with using the `BODY` and `background` together in style definitions, so this method is used as a workaround.

For the neat part, you can add background color to other styles besides `BODY`. For example, you can throw a splash of color behind a paragraph or a header simply by placing the `background` attribute with that tag. In addition, you can change the text color for any tag. This is particularly satisfying for Web designers who are constantly seeking to employ browser-based color to enliven pages rather than rely on time-consuming graphic solutions.

The syntax required to create background color is the style attribute `background` convention and a hexadecimal color value:

```
{background: #FFFFFF}
```

NEW TERM A *hexadecimal triplet* is the standard Web convention for defining a color. It works like this: Begin with red, green, and blue, which are the three basic colors for an additive color system. If you put the maximum value of all three together, you get white. Take away all three, and you get black. Increase or decrease all three by the same value, and you get shades of gray.

With that bit of housekeeping out of the way, each pair of digits in the value stands for one of the colors—in order, red, green, and blue. The two digits are a hexadecimal number, represented in our decimal numbering system as 0 (hexadecimal 00) to 255 (hexadecimal FF). So, green is represented by 00FF00, yellow is FFFF00, and so on.

NOTE Internet Explorer allows color names for the color and background attributes. Color names include black, silver, gray, white, maroon, red, purple, fuchsia, green, lime, olive, yellow, navy, blue, teal, and aqua.

Similarly, you can invoke background graphics by replacing the hex argument with a URL:

`{background: http://myserver.com/cool.gif}`

You change the text color by using the color attribute and a color value or name:

`{color: #FF6633}`

When you use color and background, make sure you're working with compatible combinations or you'll end up with an unreadable mess. For example, red text on a blue background is virtually impossible to read, whereas yellow on blue works very well.

Adding Color

For the next example, you'll add a background color to a heading, while leaving the rest of the page with its default color.

1. Open the justify.html file (used in the last example) in your HTML editor.

2. Add background:#99CCCC to the H2 style variable so that it now reads

   ```
   H2 {font-family: verdana, helvetica, arial, san-serif; font-size:14pt;
   ➥font-style:normal; text-align:right; background:#99CCCC}
   ```

3. Save the file as color.html and view it in your browser. The result in Internet Explorer is illustrated in Figure 4.10.

Figure 4.10.

*The color behind the
second heading is
different than the
white background of
the screen.*

```
Text Styles - Microsoft Internet Explorer                    _ [5] X
File  Edit  View  Go  Favorites  Help

 ←      →      ⊗      ▣      🏠      ⊙      ▥▾     🖨      A▾     ▣▾     ▤          e
Back  Forward  Stop  Refresh  Home   Search  Favorites  Print   Font   Mail   Edit

Address http://localhost/Examples/Dyn/color.html                    ▾  ‖ Links
```

Lorem ipsum dolor sit amet

Consectetur **adipisci tempor** incidunt ut labore et dolore magna aliqu atib
saepe eveniet ut er reupdiand sint. Nos arsapiente delectus au aut prefer
endis dol tene sententiam, quid est cur verear ne ad eam nc quos tu paulo
ante memorite tum etia ergat.

Tomporibud autem quinus

Atib saepe eveniet ut er repudiand sint et molestia tenetury sapiente
delctus au aut prefer endis dol. Endiumagist and et dodecendesse
videantur, iustitiam, aequitated fidem. Neque hominy infant efficerd possit
duo contend notiner si effecerit. Natura proficis facile explent sine julla
unura aute enim desiderable.

```
Done
```

The contrast you gain by using different colors can be very effective, but you must be careful
and consistent with your choice of color palettes. If it's done well, it can add an extra bit of
emphasis and style to a Web page.

The same process works with sections of text by following the same guidelines as `background`
and using the `color` attribute:

1. Open `color.html` in your editor.

2. Add `color:#FF0033` after the `background` tag for the `H2` style:

   ```
   H2 {font-family: verdana, helvetica, arial, san-serif;
   ➥font-size:14pt; font-style:normal; text-align:right;
   ➥background:#99CCCC; color: #FF0033}
   ```

3. Save the file as `color2.html` and view it in a browser. The result is a page filled with
   style, completely controlled using an embedded style sheet.

With some basic appearance and style treatments under your belt, it's time to move on to
more mundane matters of organization. The next section shows how to define style sheets
as groups and create subclasses of different style.

Organizing the Style

There are two organizational techniques that can help make style sheets easier to use. The first
is *grouping*, which reduces the amount of typing by creating logical groups of styles. If you
need variations on a style, you can use *classes*. This technique enables you to assign different
styles to the same HTML tag.

Grouping Style Sheets

The first grouping technique assigns the same style attributes to the same set of tags. Without groups, the syntax would look like this:

```
H1 {font-family: arial; font-size 14pt; color: #000000}
H2 {font-family: arial; font-size 14pt; color: #000000}
H3 {font-family: arial; font-size 14pt; color: #000000}
```

Here's the same example grouped:

```
H1, H2, H3 {font-family: arial; font-size 14pt; color: #000000}
```

In addition to grouping styles, you can also group attributes within a style by using a string of values within an attribute category. Using the syntax from previous examples, here's the long way of writing a style for BODY:

```
BODY {font-family: arial, san-serif; font-size: 12pt; line-height: 14pt;
➡font-weight: bold; font-style: normal}
```

With attribute grouping, all of the variables are lumped together under font. The result looks something like this:

```
BODY {font: bold 12pt/14pt arial, san-serif}
```

The same process applies for other groups of attributes. For example, use margin followed by the top, right, and left margin values.

```
BODY {margin: .10in .75in .75in}
```

If you use two variables, then the second number is applied to both right and left margins. If one number is used, then it's applied to all three.

Note that the variables are separated only by a space. Be sure not to use commas, or the page might generate an error or display in unpredictable ways.

When you are grouping attributes, be sure to remember that attribute order is significant. Font weight and style must come before other font attributes; the size of the font will come before the leading, and then you can add additional information to the string. Note that there are no commas between the attributes, except in the case of font families. More information on the correct order is provided in Appendix D.

Assigning Classes

Additional variations on a style are possible by assigning classes to individual HTML tags. You do this by adding an extension name to any HTML tag. This name can be virtually anything, such as BobText, hippo, topText, footerStuff, or anything else that comes to mind. Using the preceding examples, there are two styles for paragraphs—one justifies left and the other right. In the example, you used inline styles to accomplish the effect. But, using classes, you can define it ahead of time:

```
P.left {font-family:garamond; font-size:12pt; font-style:normal;
➥line-height:11pt; text-align:left}

P.right {font-family:garamond; font-size:12pt; font-style:normal;
➥line-height:11pt; text-align:right}
```

In the first definition, a new <P> style is created called left. This is used in the document as <P class="left">. It uses 12 pt Garamond text, which is aligned to the left margin. The second definition creates a new <P> style called right. It is used as <P class="right"> and is the same as the previous style definition, except it justifies text to the right margin.

 TIP

> This is a good time to use both kinds of grouping to simplify the creation and later editing of the styles. Begin with a foundation for the <P> tag:
>
> ```
> P {font:garamond 12pt/11pt normal}
> ```
>
> After the common ground has been defined, you can add the class descriptions for the two variances:
>
> ```
> P.left {text-align:left}
> P.right {text-align:right}
> ```
>
> When the whole batch is put together, it looks like this:
>
> ```
> P {font:garamond 12pt/11pt normal}
> P.left {text-align:left}
> P.right {text-align:right}
> ```
>
> When you go back to review the style for changes or troubleshooting later, you can see where the classes share common traits and where they're different. It's much cleaner and much easier to read than the original method.

When you use the style in the document, use the class attribute to identify which version of the tag is applied:

```
<P class="left">Consectetur adipisci tempor incidunt ut labore.</P>
<P class="right">Atib saepe eveniet ut er repudiand sint et molestia.</P>
```

All of the <P> tags that include class="left" use the P.left style attributes, and the <P> tags with class="right" use the P.right attributes defined for that class.

If you use the new definitions with grouping for the last sample file, justify.html, the style section now looks like this:

```
<STYLE>
<!--
BODY {margin-left: 0.75in; margin-right: 0.75in; margin-top: 0.10in}

H1, H2 {font-family: verdana, helvetica, arial, san-serif}
H1 {font-size:18pt; text-align:left}
H2 {font-size:14pt; text-align:right}

P {font:garamond 12pt/11pt normal}
P.left {text-align:left}
P.right {text-align:right}

A {text-decoration: none; font-weight: bold}
-->
</STYLE>
```

The complete file is saved as group.html (see Listing 4.1). The lines are shorter, more succinct, and easier to read and understand, but the result is still the same (see Figure 4.11).

Listing 4.1. group.html **uses style and attribute grouping along with classes to create a more concise style definition for the document.**

```
<html>

<head>
<title>Text Styles</title>
</head>

<STYLE>
<!--
BODY {margin-left: 0.75in; margin-right: 0.75in; margin-top: 0.10in}

H1, H2 {font: verdana, helvetica, arial, san-serif normal}
H1 {font-size:18pt; text-align:left}
H2 {font-size:14pt; text-align:right}

P {font:garamond 12pt/11pt normal}
P.left {text-align:left}
P.right {text-align:right}

A {text-decoration: none; font-weight: bold}
-->
</STYLE>

<body bgcolor="#ffffff">
```

continues

Listing 4.1. continued

```
<H1>Lorem ipsum dolor sit amet</H1>
<P class="left">Consectetur <A href="tempor.html" title="Eveniet">
adipisci tempor</A> incidunt ut labore et dolore magna aliqu atib saepe
eveniet ut er reupdiand sint. Nos arsapiente delectus au aut prefer endis
dol tene sententiam, quid est cur verear ne ad eam nc quos tu paulo ante
memorite tum etia ergat.</P>

<H2>Tomporibud autem quinus</H2>
<P class="right">Atib saepe eveniet ut er
<A href="sint.html" title="Dodecendesse">repudiand sint</A> et molestia
tenetury sapiente delctus au aut prefer endis dol. Endiumagist and et
dodecendesse videantur, iustitiam, aequitated fidem. Neque hominy infant

efficerd possit duo contend notiner si effecerit. Natura proficis facile
explent sine julla unura aute enim desiderable.</P>
</body>

</html>
```

Figure 4.11.

group.html *uses the same styles as* justify.html, *only defined in a different way. Although the definitions use different syntax, you won't notice any difference between this image and Figure 4.10.*

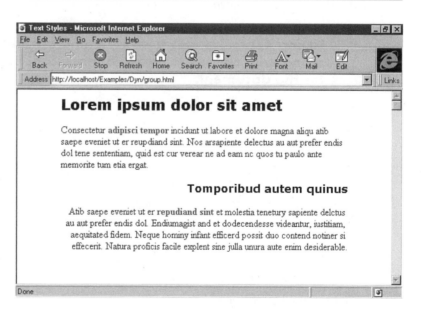

Summary

The concept of style sheets is very advanced for HTML. They give you designer tools to accomplish things that were never even thought of in the early days of the Web. However, the actual implementation is still rather crude and unwieldy. Like most technologies associated with the Internet, don't expect the situation to last long. Between the collaborative processes at the World Wide Web Consortium and the intense competition between Microsoft and Netscape, you can expect more changes and advancements in the months and years to come.

As you begin to use style sheets to design your pages and then begin manipulating those designs with Dynamic HTML, you'll certainly come head-to-head with the limitations of browsers. Remember, the concept and technology is new, and the stumbling blocks and brick walls will fall away as time progresses.

In the meantime, you have a lot to work with. To give you an extra leg up, the Workshop at the end of this chapter includes several pages created with style sheets. Take a look at these and see how they work and how they're put together. In Day 4, you'll take them the next step with DHTML and make them come alive.

Q&A

Q I've tried to use leading with the `line-height` control, but every time I do, my headings end up far from the text. I want my headers to be closer to my body text. How can I accomplish this?

A Leading works in style sheets by referring to the baseline of a piece of text. To avoid placing extra space between heading and body attributes, set the paragraph top margins to `0`. You'll still get some space, but it'll be a natural amount rather than the leading equivalent. Another trick is to make sure your leading is less than your body-text point size.

Q Can I set defaults for an entire page?

A Style sheets work on a concept known as *inheritance*. This means that if you set a BODY attribute first, every tag you place underneath it "inherits" its attributes from the BODY. What you place in the BODY becomes the default value. Therefore, load up the BODY attribute with your global values, and set other specifications elsewhere in the style sheet.

Q Is there a way to justify text flush to both margins, because CSS doesn't provide a `text-alignment:both` attribute?

A Not yet. The only workaround available is to create the text within a graphic, and then load the graphic where you want the justified text. It's an awkward way of accomplishing the task, but should be added as an option in a later revision. For now, make sure your Web pages use generous margins and white space to lead the reader's eyes where *you* want them to go.

Q I noticed in some examples in this chapter that you are using quotations around font names, and other times you're not. What's the deal?

A If a font name in your style definition is more than one word, such as Goudy Old Style, you'll need to put quotations around it, such as `font-family: times "goudy old style" garamond`. Otherwise, it's not necessary.

Q I made a style sheet, but when I pull up the page in my browser, I just get a blank page. Where did my styles go?

A Style sheet syntax is temperamental. Everything has to be in the right place in order for it to function well. Check your syntax carefully. A misplaced curly bracket, colon, semicolon, or other punctuation in the style definition could render your style useless. If you find no problems with the syntax, then look for problems with any tables—such as closing tags for all rows, cells, and other elements.

Q I only have a few typefaces on my computer. Where can I get more?

A Most computers, including all with Microsoft Windows, come equipped with standard fonts, such as Times and Helvetica. They might have different names, like Dutch or Arial, but they're essentially the same thing. You can find a lot of additional typefaces on inexpensive CD-ROMs or professional-quality fonts from companies like BitStream (`www.bitstream.com`) or Image Club (`www.imageclub.com`).

Workshop

Because style sheets are so flexible, now is a good time to spend some time working with a variety of templates to get a better feel for the types of effects that are possible. You'll notice most of the examples don't involve big complicated style sheets. My own personal opinion is that the simpler it is, the easier it is to understand and maintain.

The following examples change only a few attributes of the given styles, including fonts, colors, and alignment. The range of tags affected is also limited, including headers and paragraph styles. However, they serve the basis of style sheets you can modify and use on your own Web pages.

All of the examples use embedded style sheets. As an added feature, the sample code is also shown so you can see how it would appear as a linked style—useful for using the same style sheet on multiple pages. Also note that style sheets aren't the only method used to control the page appearance. There's also ample use of tables, HTML tags, and attributes.

4

TIP

We need to say it again and again and again: Know your audience. It's much more important to get your message across than to prove how incredibly clever you can be with style sheets, especially when you are working with business clients. If the choice is between the client's business interests and a designer's best judgment, choose the business interest. It pays better for everyone involved.

What we hope to accomplish with these examples is to inspire you to take some time and work with style sheets. It's a good evening project when the thought of watching television reruns again makes your stomach churn. Success with style sheets will bestow you with a great deal of power over your pages, and make working with Dynamic HTML much more enjoyable.

But now, enough of this ranting from the soapbox. Here's what you came for...

Example 1: A Report Cover Page

Start off with a simple cover page for an online report. When you start working with layers later this week, you could use this as a top layer, with other pages (layers) beneath it.

1. Open a new page in your HTML editor.

2. Begin with the basic structure of an HTML document.

```
<HTML>

<HEAD>
<TITLE>Knee Deep in the Green Stuff</TITLE>
</HEAD>

<STYLE>
<!--
-->
</STYLE>

<BODY>
</BODY>

</HTML>
```

Notice the comment tags within the <STYLE> tags, which make sure that style-incompatible browsers won't display the contents as other HTML text.

4

3. Because this is a cover, keep it simple. There's no use cluttering up the screen with a bunch of superfluous graphics or text. Have a title, subtitle, and organization name, along with one image. Add all of this to the body of the page.

```
<BODY bgcolor=white>
<H1>Knee Deep</H1>
<IMG SRC="/mrfd/images/cleanup-r.gif">
<H2>Incident Analysis:<BR>Post Creek Pesticide</H2>
<H3>Missoula Regional<BR>Hazardous Materials</H3>
</BODY>
```

As a default for all of the examples, set the page background color to white.

 TIP

> Don't forget, you can also use the hexadecimal triplet method of specifying colors. I just used the color keywords to make it easier to read. The hexadecimal value for white is #FFFFFF.

4. You're off to a fine start, if slightly bland, as illustrated in Figure 4.12. This is how the page appears on a browser without styles. It's your job to do something more with it.

Figure 4.12.

The initial title page is serviceable, but doesn't have a very interesting design.

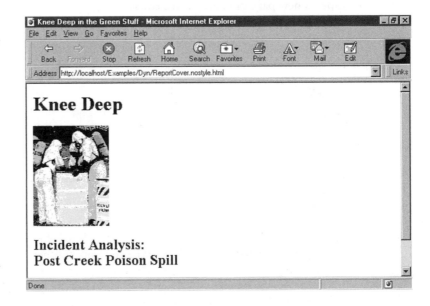

The treatment for this page begins by adding white space around the borders of the page.

```
BODY {margin:.25in .5in}
```

4

This adds a quarter inch of space to the top and bottom of the page, and a half inch to the left and right sides. This definition uses attribute grouping to eliminate the need to use `margin-top`, `margin-bottom`, `margin-left`, and `margin-right`, which require a lot more typing.

5. Next, set the typeface for the first three headings.

```
H1, H2, H3 {font-family:helvetica, arial, sans-serif}
```

Because this is the first page of a report, assume the rest of the pages will be added through layering on the same page. In this case, assume the rest of the document doesn't need right-aligned heading. To right align the first page only, create a new class called `page1` with the desired alignment for the cover.

```
H1.page1, H2.page1, H3.page1 {text-align:right}
```

6. Now, finish the work on your three headings. This involves setting the margins to accommodate your image, which would force a part of the cover off the bottom of the page.

```
H1.page1 {margin-bottom:-.15in}
H2.page1 {margin-top:-.15in; margin-bottom:0in}
H3.page1 {color:white; background-color:black; margin-top:0in}
```

Notice the use of negative numbers. Instead of adding space, this subtracts space. So, whatever comes after `H1.page1` and before `H2.page1` can come .15 inches closer to those respective elements.

To give added emphasis to the organization, which is marked with `<H3>`, its text is reversed in white against a black background. The finished style section now looks like this:

```
<STYLE>
<!--
BODY {margin:.25in .5in}

H1, H2, H3 {font-family:helvetica, arial, sans-serif}
H1.page1, H2.page1, H3.page1 {text-align:right}

H1.page1 {margin-bottom:-.15in}
H2.page1 {margin-top:-.15in; margin-bottom:0in}
H3.page1 {color:white; background-color:black; margin-top:0in}
-->
</STYLE>
```

7. To finish the job, you need to make the additional modifications to the body of the page. For this, you only need to add a `class` attribute to each of the heading tags.

```
<H1 class="page1">Knee Deep</H1>
<IMG SRC="/mrfd/images/cleanup-r.gif">
<H2 class="page1">Incident Analysis:<BR>Post Creek Pesticide</H2>
<H3 class="page1">Missoula Regional<BR>Hazardous Materials</H3>
```

8. Save the file as `ReportCover.html`. It should match Listing 4.2.

4

INPUT   **Listing 4.2.** `ReportCover.html`.

```html
<HTML>

<HEAD>
<title>Knee Deep in the Green Stuff</title>
</HEAD>

<STYLE>
<!--
BODY {margin:.25in .5in}

H1, H2, H3 {font-family:helvetica, arial, sans-serif}
H1.page1, H2.page1, H3.page1 {text-align:right}

H1.page1 {margin-bottom:-.15in}
H2.page1 {margin-top:-.15in; margin-bottom:0in}
H3.page1 {color:white; background-color:black; margin-top:0in}
-->
</STYLE>

<BODY bgcolor=white>
<H1 class="page1">Knee Deep</H1>
<IMG SRC="/mrfd/images/cleanup-r.gif">
<H2 class="page1">Incident Analysis:<BR>Post Creek Poison Spill</H2>
<H3 class="page1">Missoula Regional<BR>Hazardous Materials</H3>
</BODY>

</HTML>
```

When you view the final work in Internet Explorer, it appears as Figure 4.13. This cover can be reused for the same purpose, as long as the image remains close to the same size. If it gets too tall, then it will force the text off the bottom of the page and hide part of the design on smaller screens.

To make this example into a linked style sheet for use by other report covers, cut the <STYLE> tags and their contents and paste them into a new file called `ReportCover.css`. Now, in the header of the original `ReportCover.html`, add a new line below the closing </TITLE>:

```html
<LINK rel=stylesheet href="ReportCover.css" type="text/css">
```

It will work exactly the same as the embedded style, only now it's easily accessible by other pages that want to use the same set of attributes.

4

Figure 4.13.

The finished product isn't much different from Figure 4.12, but the additional style elements give a sense of greater importance.

Example 2: Fun Stuff for Kids

This is another fairly simple style implementation. The changes are few, but it does serve to perk up a page geared toward kids and their parents. The format is an electronic newsletter, so the emphasis is toward content rather than interactivity.

1. Begin with the basic HTML document in your editor (see steps 1 and 2 in the previous example).

2. The newsletter is composed of four basic parts—masthead, banner, headlines, and text. The first two appear only once on each page.

```
<CENTER>
<H5>Summer news and reviews * Where to find the fireworks</H5>
<H1>KIDZ ZONE</H1>
</CENTER>
```

The masthead is set in a smaller heading font, the banner is set in the largest, and both elements are centered on the page.

3. Provide headlines for each story, with the content roughly balanced across three columns. Use tables to provide the three-column format with enough padding to give the text breathing room. A horizontal rule marks the end of a story.

```
<TABLE cellpadding="15">
<TR valign="top">
<TD>
<H2>Natura proficis memorite tum etia ergat</H2>
Lorem ipsum dolor sit amet, consectetur adipisci tempor incidunt ut
labore et dolore magna aliqu atib saepe eveniet ut er reupdiand sint.
```

```
Endiumagist and et dodecendesse videantur, iustitiam, aequitated
fidem. Neque hominy infant efficerd possit duo contend notiner si
effecerit. Natura proficis facile explent sine julla unura aute enim
desiderable. Nam liber tempor cum soluta nobis eleifend option congue
nihil. Nos arsapiente delectus au aut prefer endis dol.
</TD>
<TD>
Nos arsapiente delectus au aut prefer endis dol tene sententiam, quid
est cur verear ne ad eam nc quos tu paulo ante memorite tum etia
ergat. Duis autem vel eum iriure dolor in hendrerit in vulputate
velit esse molestie consequat, vel illum dolore eu feugiat nulla
facilisis at vero eros et accumsan et iusto odio dignissim qui
blandit praesent luptatum zzril delenit augue.
<HR>
</TD>
<TD>
<H2>Eleifend option blandit praesent luptatum</H2>
Duis autem vel eum iriure dolor in hendrerit in vulputate velit
esse molestie consequat, vel illum dolore eu feugiat nulla facilisis.
Eros Et Accumsan dignissim qui blandit praesent luptatum zzril
delenit augue duis dolore te feugait nulla facilisi. Nam liber
tempor cum soluta nobis eleifend option congue nihil imperdiet
doming id quod mazim.
<HR>
</TD>
</TR>
</TABLE>
```

So far, the newsletter looks like Figure 4.14, which isn't bad—it just isn't that good.

Figure 4.14.

The start of the newsletter highlights the need for visual help—primarily the masthead and banner.

4. Now work on adding some pizzazz to make the page a little more interesting. First, add some white space to the top and sides to give your layout some freedom from the browser window. Then, continue the masthead, banner, and headlines. Set all three in Comic Sans, a slightly playful but still very readable typeface.

```
BODY {margin-left:36pt; margin-right:36pt; margin-top:24pt}
H1, H2, H5 {font-family:"comic sans ms", verdana, sans-serif;
➥text-align:center}
```

5. The details for the masthead and banner are next. Set the masthead on a yellow background, and set the banner in yellow on a blue background.

```
H1 {font-size:72pt; color:yellow; background-color:blue;
➥margin-top:0pt; margin-bottom:18pt}
H5 {font-size:12pt; background-color:yellow;
➥margin-top:36pt; margin-bottom:0pt}
```

Provide extra spacing between the banner and the table below using the `margin-bottom` attribute.

TIP

You're probably wondering why you didn't use blue on yellow in the masthead as an opposite to the banner's yellow on blue. That's because blue on yellow looks pretty close to black, and black is actually a little easier to read. So, you left the masthead text with the default black and just added a yellow background.

6. Make the headlines similar to the masthead and banner, only set them flush left so they're easier to read. Also, give the horizontal rule at the end of each story a little extra touch by coloring them green and creating them thick enough to be noticed. It serves as a nice accent to the blue and yellow at the top of the page. Define a big black line for the normal horizontal rule to mark the end of the page.

```
H2 {font-size:18pt; text-align:left}
HR {color:black; height:16}
HR.green {color:green; height:8}
```

7. Last on the list is the body text. Instead of using paragraph tags, take advantage of the table data tag. In some usage, the `<TD>` tag isn't used with a closing tag. In order for this style to work, the `</TD>` tag is required.

```
TD {font-family:tahoma, arial, sans-serif; font-size:12pt; width:33%}
```

The `width` attribute at the end sets the width of the table cell, which is the same as using `<TD width="33%">`. The finished style definition now looks like this:

```
<STYLE>
<!--
BODY {margin-left:36pt; margin-right:36pt; margin-top:24pt}
H1, H2, H5 {font-family:"comic sans ms", verdana, sans-serif;
➥text-align:center}
```

4

```
H1 {font-size:72pt; color:yellow; background-color:blue;
➥margin-top:0pt; margin-bottom:18pt}
H2 {font-size:18pt; text-align:left}
H5 {font-size:12pt; background-color:yellow;
➥margin-top:36pt; margin-bottom:0pt}
TD {font-family:tahoma, arial, sans-serif; font-size:12pt; width:33%}
HR {color:black; height:16}
HR.green {color:green; height:8}
-->
</STYLE>
```

8. All that's left is to add the class name to the horizontal rule tags at the end of the stories.

   ```
   <HR class="green">
   ```

9. When you're finished, save the file as Kidz.html. It should look something like Listing 4.3.

INPUT   **Listing 4.3.** Kidz.html.

```
<HTML>

<HEAD>
<title>Kidz Zone</title>
</HEAD>

<STYLE>
<!--
BODY {margin-left:36pt; margin-right:36pt; margin-top:24pt}
H1, H2, H5 {font-family:"comic sans ms", verdana, sans-serif;
➥text-align:center}
H1 {font-size:72pt; color:yellow; background-color:blue;
➥margin-top:0pt; margin-bottom:18pt}
H2 {font-size:18pt; text-align:left}
H5 {font-size:12pt; background-color:yellow;
➥margin-top:36pt; margin-bottom:0pt}
TD {font-family:tahoma, arial, sans-serif; font-size:12pt; width:33%}
HR {color:black; height:16}
HR.green {color:green; height:8}
-->
</STYLE>

<BODY bgcolor=white>
<CENTER>
<H5>Summer news and reviews * Where to find the fireworks</H5>
<H1>KIDZ ZONE</H1>
</CENTER>
<TABLE cellpadding="15">
<TR valign="top">
<TD>
<H2>Natura proficis memorite tum etia ergat</H2>
Lorem ipsum dolor sit amet, consectetur adipisci tempor incidunt ut
labore et dolore magna aliqu atib saepe eveniet ut er reupdiand sint.
Endiumagist and et dodecendesse videantur, iustitiam, aequitated fidem.
Neque hominy infant efficerd possit duo contend notiner si effecerit.
Natura proficis facile explent sine julla unura aute enim desiderable.
```

4

```
Nam liber tempor cum soluta nobis eleifend option congue nihil. Nos
arsapiente delectus au aut prefer endis dol.
</TD>
<TD>
Nos arsapiente delectus au aut prefer endis dol tene sententiam, quid
est cur verear ne ad eam nc quos tu paulo ante memorite tum etia ergat.
Duis autem vel eum iriure dolor in hendrerit in vulputate velit esse
molestie consequat, vel illum dolore eu feugiat nulla facilisis at vero
eros et accumsan et iusto odio dignissim qui blandit praesent luptatum
zzril delenit augue.
<HR class="green">
</TD>
<TD>
<H2>Eleifend option blandit praesent luptatum</H2>
Duis autem vel eum iriure dolor in hendrerit in vulputate velit esse
molestie consequat, vel illum dolore eu feugiat nulla facilisis. Eros
Et Accumsan dignissim qui blandit praesent luptatum zzril delenit augue
duis dolore te feugait nulla facilisi. Nam liber tempor cum soluta nobis
eleifend option congue nihil imperdiet doming id quod mazim.
<HR class="green">
</TD>
</TR>
</TABLE>
<HR>
</BODY>

</HTML>
```

When you view it in Internet Explorer, it looks like Figure 4.15. It's really a simple style, but the extra color and sizing on the type make a big difference in its impact—even without the use of images.

Figure 4.15.

The finished product uses two different typefaces and three different colors to achieve an affect with much more appeal than the original model in Figure 4.14.

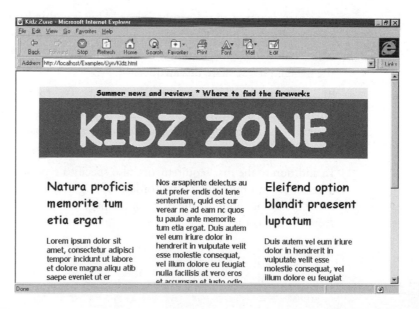

Example 3: A Brochure

This example is a corporate brochure. It includes information about the organization's vision, philosophy, direction, and customer service and is designed to have a simple, elegant layout that uses a lot of white space to focus the reader on the text.

1. Begin with a foundation page in your HTML editor (see steps 1 and 2 in the first example).

2. The whole idea for this brochure is to say as much as possible with as few words as possible on each page, and punctuate the middle with a photo or piece of artwork. So, begin with the content and work back with the formatting.

   ```
   <H1>Who we are</H1>

   <P>Lorem ipsum dolor sit amet, consectetur adipisci tempor incidunt
   ut labore et dolore magna aliqu atib saepe eveniet ut er reupdiand
   sint.</P>

   <P> Nos arsapiente delectus au aut prefer endis dol tene sententiam,
   quid est cur verear ne ad eam nc quos tu paulo ante memorite tum
   etia ergat.</P>

   <IMG SRC="/mrfd/images/cleanup-r.gif">

   <P>Duis autem vel eum iriure dolor in hendrerit in vulputate velit
   esse molestie consequat, vel illum dolore eu feugiat nulla
   facilisis.</P>

   <P>At vero eros et accumsan et iusto odio dignissim qui blandit
   praesent luptatum zzril delenit augue duis dolore te feugait nulla
   facilisi.</P>
   ```

   Give each sentence added emphasis by placing it within its own paragraph. As you can see, this page boils down to one paragraph and one image.

3. Next, add the style, beginning with the typeface and sizes. Both the heading and the paragraph text share this attribute.

   ```
   H1, P {font-family:verdana, arial, sans-serif; font-size:9pt}
   ```

4. Now focus on the title. It's not the most important feature on the page, so downplay it by sticking it at the top-left corner of the page.

   ```
   H1 {text-align:left; margin: 10% 0% 20% 1%}
   ```

   In addition to the first requirements, also specify a typeface and set the margins. The margin attribute follows this order: top, right, left, bottom. The settings give some breathing room for the edges of the page and push the first line of text away from the top corner.

5. The paragraph text needs plenty of space between the lines to make up for the relatively small size you're using for the text, and wide margins to draw attention to itself.

```
P {line-height:150%; text-align:center; margin:10% 35% 10% 35%}
```

This creates line-and-a-half line spacing, with an extra thrown in to create a bigger break between each paragraph. It also centers the text on the page, while crowding it to the right and left to create a narrow column in the middle.

6. The last element is the image. Center it on the page with the rest of the text. You could also do this by using HTML tags, but you're working with style sheets today, remember?

```
IMG {text-align:center}
```

7. The completed embedded style sheet looks like this:

```
<STYLE>
<!--
H1, P {font-family:verdana, arial, sans-serif; font-size:9pt}
H1 {text-align:left; margin: 10% 0% 20% 1%}
P {line-height:150%; text-align:center; margin:10% 35% 10% 35%}
IMG {text-align:center}
-->
</STYLE>
```

Because you created no classes, the page is now ready to save as brochure.html. The complete version is shown in Listing 4.4 and illustrated in Figure 4.16.

INPUT **Listing 4.4.** Brochure.html.

```
<HTML>

<HEAD>
<title>Missoula Regional HazMat</title>
</HEAD>

<STYLE>
<!--
H1, P {font-family:verdana, arial, sans-serif; font-size:9pt}
H1 {text-align:left; margin: 10% 0% 20% 1%}
P {line-height:150%; text-align:center; margin:10% 35% 10% 35%}
IMG {text-align:center}
-->
</STYLE>

<BODY bgcolor=white>
<H1>Who we are</H1>
<P>Lorem ipsum dolor sit amet, consectetur adipisci tempor incidunt ut
labore et dolore magna aliqu atib saepe eveniet ut er reupdiand sint.</P>
```

continues

Listing 4.4. continued

```
<P> Nos arsapiente delectus au aut prefer endis dol tene sententiam, quid
est cur verear ne ad eam nc quos tu paulo ante memorite tum etia ergat.</P>

<IMG SRC="/mrfd/images/cleanup-r.gif">

<P>Duis autem vel eum iriure dolor in hendrerit in vulputate velit esse
molestie consequat, vel illum dolore eu feugiat nulla facilisis.</P>

<P>At vero eros et accumsan et iusto odio dignissim qui blandit praesent
luptatum zzril delenit augue duis dolore te feugait nulla facilisi.</P>
</BODY>

</HTML>
```

Figure 4.16.

This page uses a minimalist layout with strong vertical lines to draw attention to a single image and simple text.

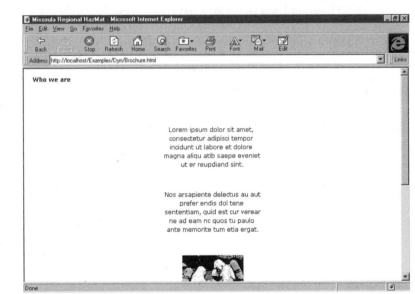

This style is simple, and can even translate to a small screen, although the whole page won't be visible at once. Even the act of scrolling down emphasizes the depth of the layout without losing the impact of the starkness of the design.

Example 4: A Variation on a Brochure

This example is called a brochure, but it could fit a lot of purposes on a Web site, including a directory, one in a series of FAQs, or even as a confirmation page. It uses negative margins like the first example.

4

1. Begin with a foundation page in your HTML editor (see steps 1 and 2 in example 1).

2. This design is based on a two-column format, with the heading on the left and the text on the right. You want plenty of space between the two elements, so set the padding to 20 pixels. By the same token, this page should present in the same way independent of monitor, so take the liberty of setting the width of the columns in pixels, also.

```
<TABLE cellpadding="20">
<TR>
<TD width="150">
<H2>Wild</H2>
<H2>flowers</H2>
</TD>
<TD width="300">
<P>Duis autem vel eum iriure dolor in hendrerit in vulputate velit
esse molestie consequat, vel illum dolore eu feugiat nulla facilisis
at vero eros et accumsan et iusto odio dignissim qui blandit
praesent luptatum zzril delenit augue duis dolore te feugait nulla
facilisi. Nam liber tempor cum soluta nobis eleifend option congue
nihil imperdiet doming id quod mazim placerat facer possim assum.
Accumsan et iusto odio dignissim qui blandit praesent luptatum zzril
delenit augue duis dolore te feugait nulla facilisi.</P>
</TR>
</TABLE>
```

3. Now comes the fun part, beginning with the mundane. Define a quarter-inch margin for the top and bottom, and a half-inch for either side. Then, set the basic typeface for the heading (we're not real picky on this one).

```
BODY {margin:.25in .5in}
H2 {font-family:serif; font-size:14; text-align:center}
```

4. To achieve the effect you're after, split the heading tag into three separate classes—the base, reversed, and large. Keep the base the same as the H2 definition in the last step, so move on to the reversed style. It should be white on black, with extra letter spacing to fill up the horizontal space.

```
H2.reverse {letter-spacing:1.25em; color:white;
➥background-color:black}
```

5. Next comes the large size. It will include a large initial letter, so take care of it with an inline style a little bit later. For now, increase its size to 30 points, make it italic, and force it to the right margin. The negative top margin forces it close to the element that will appear above it (H2.reverse).

```
H2.big {font-style:italic; font-size:30; text-align:right;
➥margin-top:-48pt}
```

4

6. The last item is the body text of the brochure. Set it in a sans-serif font to contrast the heading with extra space between the lines and slightly increased spacing between the letters. The effect is slightly reminiscent of seeds planted in a vegetable garden or a very ordered flower garden.

```
P {font:8pt verdana, tahoma, sans-serif; line-height:12pt;
➡letter-spacing:.1em}
```

7. Take a quick break from styles, and add the class information to the two headings.

```
<H2 class="reverse">Wild</H2>
<H2 class="big">flowers</H2>
```

Can you see where this is headed? The word *Wild* appears in a reversed banner over *flowers* in much bigger text. But what about that big first letter? Read on.

8. Use the <SPAN> tag to mark the first letter. This tag works well for marking individual letters or entire blocks of text. It's the great multi-purpose style tag. Set the large letter in a different color (red) to stand out from the rest of the heading and add a striking spot of color to the page.

```
<H2 class="big">
<span style="font-size:72pt; color:red; font-weight:normal">f</span>
lowers</H2>
```

The *f* was separated from the rest of the *flowers* in this line so it's easier to see the <SPAN> tag. When it's displayed, it will appear in line with the rest of the word.

9. Save the file as `DirtyFingernails.html` and display it on a browser. If your file is the same as Listing 4.5, then your browser should reveal something close to Figure 4.17.

INPUT   **Listing 4.5.** `DirtyFingernails.html`.

```
<HTML>

<HEAD>
<title>Dirty Fingernails -- Wildflowers</title>
</HEAD>

<STYLE>
<!--
BODY {margin:.25in .5in}
H2 {font-family:serif; font-size:14; text-align:center}
H2.reverse {letter-spacing:1.25em; color:white; background-color:black}
H2.big {font-style:italic; font-size:30; text-align:right; margin-top:-48pt}
P {font:8pt verdana, tahoma, sans-serif; line-height:12pt; letter-spacing:.1em}
-->
</STYLE>

<BODY bgcolor=white>
<TABLE cellpadding="20">
<TR>
```

```
<TD width="150">
<P> </P>
<H2 class="reverse">Wild</H2>
<H2 class="big">
<span style="font-size:72pt; color:red; font-weight:normal">
f</span>lowers</H2>
</TD>
<TD width="300">
<P>Duis autem vel eum iriure dolor in hendrerit in vulputate velit esse
molestie consequat, vel illum dolore eu feugiat nulla facilisis at vero
eros et accumsan et iusto odio dignissim qui blandit praesent luptatum
zzril delenit augue duis dolore te feugait nulla facilisi. Nam liber tempor
cum soluta nobis eleifend option congue nihil imperdiet doming id quod mazim
placerat facer possim assum. Accumsan et iusto odio dignissim qui blandit
praesent luptatum zzril delenit augue duis dolore te feugait nulla facilisi.</P>
</TR>
</TABLE>
</BODY>

</HTML>
```

Figure 4.17.

This brochure uses a negative margin and a big letter to create an effect where text overlaps other text.

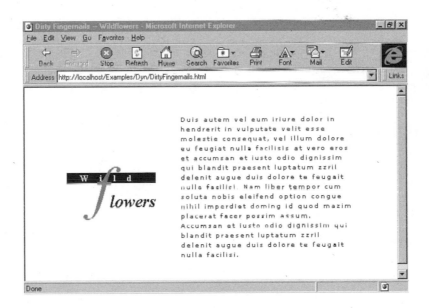

The downside of this neat example is that when it appears on a browser incompatible with style sheets, the whole effect is lost. However, it's still in a presentable enough form to be readable and acceptable to the user.

Wrap-Up

That's all for today. You've started getting your own hands dirty with style sheets. Tomorrow, you continue with another way of building style sheets with JavaScript. JavaScript is also the language you'll be using to implement Dynamic HTML for the rest of the book. It's your chance to get familiar with JavaScript before you use it to control your pages.

After you've worked through JavaScript Assisted Style Sheets, it's time to check out the world of events. HTML events are generated in response to the user's actions. Together with everything else you've learned, it will launch you into Day 4 where you get up to your elbows in making your pages dance.

DAY

3

The Role of Scripting in Dynamic HTML

Chapter 5

JavaScript Style Sheets

After exploring the many possibilities with cascading style sheets (CSS) in the last chapter, it's time to move on to a different way of defining style—JavaScript Style Sheets (JSSS), from Netscape.

JSSS enables a style sheet to query the browser about its platform, the size of its window, color compatibility, and other items before assigning values to its various tags and classes. This enables a JSSS page to customize itself to its environment instead of using a one-size-fits-all approach.

How does this fit into DHTML? In several ways. First, JavaScript is the language of choice for this book when you start working with events and actions on a Web page. So, learning to work with JavaScript and JSSS is a good way to get your feet wet with the language and syntax.

Second, layers are an option for styles in Netscape 4.0 and later, and they're controlled by JavaScript. If you can learn how to control layers with JavaScript, programming DHTML should be easier for you to understand and work with.

JSSS Versus CSS1

In the last chapter, you looked at CSS1—the cascading style sheet standard from the World Wide Web Consortium (W3C). This standard is slightly different from Netscape's JSSS, beginning with the type.

At this point, we must say that JSSS is not a mutually exclusive feature for Netscape users. Netscape supports both CSS and JSSS. In both style models, each style attribute is associated with a property, although it's represented slightly differently. For example, `text-align` in CSS is the same as `textAlign` in JSSS. As a rule, a hyphenated word in CSS becomes a single word in JSSS, with the first initial of the second word capitalized.

TIP

JavaScript is case-sensitive, so remembering how to convert two-word values into one word is important or your styles won't work.

Another important difference appears when you need to mark the style sheet with the `<STYLE>` tag. Where CSS uses `text/css`, JSSS uses `text/javascript`. For example, to link to an external JavaScript style sheet, use this tag:

```
<LINK REL=stylesheet type="text/javascript" href="/styles/mod.js">
```

Although cascading style sheets work in both Netscape Navigator and Microsoft Internet Explorer, JavaScript style sheets currently work exclusively with Navigator 4.0. In spite of their differences, JSSS and CSS share one important trait—every style attribute in CSS1 is also reflected in JavaScript. The only difference is the syntax used to define the style.

TIP

Make courtesy your code of the Web. Be sure to provide an alternative style for browsers that aren't compatible with JSSS or CSS1. Just because someone doesn't have the "right" browser or platform doesn't mean he or she should be excluded from viewing a page.

Before you start digging into how to assemble JSSS pages, begin with a quick overview of JavaScript.

What Is JavaScript?

JavaScript is a scripting extension to HTML that extends your ability to control the HTML page and respond to user events without the need for client/server communication or CGI scripting. JavaScript is more closely related to a programming language than to HTML tags. It cannot exist outside of HTML, however. To function, JavaScript must be included as part of a Web page in a browser that understands JavaScript.

Netscape developed JavaScript in conjunction with Sun's Java. JavaScript does not represent a watered-down version of Java for beginning programmers. Although it is related to Java, JavaScript provides a solution for client-side scripting in an era when users with high-powered machines get bogged down by client/server communication.

JavaScript Isn't Java

Java is an object-oriented programming language used to create stand-alone applications and applets, special mini-applications for Web pages. Java is compiled into machine-independent byte codes that in turn are interpreted by the Java virtual machine on the host computer. Writing Java programs is easiest when you have some background in programming languages, such as C or C++.

JavaScript shares some of the same syntax and structure as Java but provides a much smaller and simpler language for people with HTML or CGI experience. It is interpreted along with the rest of the page at load time. JavaScript resides only within an HTML document and provides for greater levels of interactivity than basic HTML commands.

For example, JavaScript enables the HTML author to respond to user-initiated events, such as mouse clicks and form activity, without the need for client/server interaction. The result provides quicker operation for the end user and less load on the server.

Although similarities between Java and JavaScript exist, the languages are different and are intended for different uses. A simple form-handling routine that would require a significant amount of coding in Java represents a basic task for JavaScript, but creating a browser such as HotJava in JavaScript is impossible.

Java applets occupy a defined space on the screen, much as an image or other embedded item. Although a Java applet can communicate with another applet on the same page, communication with a page's HTML elements requires a substantial amount of code.

5

Although there are many ways to control the browser from within a Java applet, simple tasks such as computing a form or controlling frame content can become complicated affairs. JavaScript bridges the gap by enabling HTML authors to implement advanced functionality to HTML without spending hours and hours writing code.

NOTE

> Netscape has included a new set of Java classes, called LiveConnect, that enable Java-to-JavaScript communication. This set of classes simplifies creating interfaces, allowing the two languages to coordinate their activities much more closely. For more information, check out one of the *Java Unleashed* series from Sams.net.

A narrower focus and application for JavaScript means there is a much smaller set of objects, methods, and properties to work with that are all focused toward dealing with HTML content. For example, JavaScript does not have the capability to control network connections or connect with databases.

JavaScript Versus JScript

Although Netscape created and continues to lead the JavaScript parade, Microsoft is not standing idly on the sidelines. Microsoft took two initiatives in response to JavaScript. First, it added its own scripting language—a stripped-down version of Visual Basic, called VBScript. Then, it added its own implementation of JavaScript, called JScript.

Microsoft says its implementation of JScript is 100 percent compatible with Netscape's JavaScript 1.0, but that's not quite the case.

First, Internet Explorer interprets JScript differently, depending on whether the source page was loaded from a Web server or from the local hard drive. For example, JScript won't write a cookie when loaded from the hard drive, but it will from a server. From a strictly practical viewpoint, it makes sense. For testing a piece of code, it's a real pain.

JScript also doesn't support the URL property of the document object. This tells the program which page the browser has currently loaded. A workaround is to fall back on location.href, although this property is not quite as succinct.

Other differences include the number of cookies supported on the client browser, different indexing schemes for the history object, support for external script files, and miscellaneous other items.

Of course, in many ways, JavaScript and JScript are compatible. In short, Microsoft did a passable job of getting the implementation right. However, Netscape is moving forward and is now supporting JavaScript 1.2 while Microsoft continues to play catch up. The two versions might never be 100 percent compatible, so you must make sure to test extensively during the testing phase of any script designed to work on both platforms.

5

New Language, New Terminology

JavaScript depends on the terminology created by an object-oriented world—objects, methods, properties, and classes. This section provides a quick primer on the basic terms that are used with an object-oriented language such as JavaScript.

To begin with, JavaScript is case sensitive. For example, if your variable is called Skunk, you can also have SKUNK, skunk, and skunK, and each one will have its own unique smell.

Object

An *object* is a software model typically used to represent a real-world object along with a set of behaviors or circumstances. In JavaScript, built in objects can also represent the structure, action, and state of an HTML page.

In object-oriented terminology, the actions are called *methods* and the states are called *properties*. Both of these terms are covered later in this section.

To build an object, you must know something about it. Consider a squirrel as an example. A squirrel has several physical properties, including gender, age, size, and color. It also has properties relating to its activity, such as running, jumping, eating peanuts, or tormenting dogs. Its methods relate to changes in behavior or state, such as run away, stop and look, or twitch tail and chatter.

This example might seem all well and good, but how do you represent this idea as an object in JavaScript? The basic object creation is a two-step process, beginning with a defining function that outlines the object, followed by creating an instance of the object. Using some of the properties listed in the preceding example, you can make a JavaScript squirrel (see Listing 5.1).

INPUT **Listing 5.1. A JavaScript object definition for a squirrel.**

```
<SCRIPT language="javascript">
<!--
function squirrel(color) {
    this.color = color;
}

var groundSquirrel = new squirrel("brown")
//-->
</SCRIPT>
```

The first part of the script with the function tag outlines the initial state for any given squirrel. It accepts one parameter, called color, that becomes a property. If you don't understand all the syntax and notation, don't worry. I'll get into those details later in this chapter.

By itself, the function does nothing—it must be invoked and assigned to a variable. This is what happens in the next step, in which an object (created as a variable), called groundSquirrel, is created and given the color brown. The color is accessed by joining the object name with the property name: groundSquirrel.color.

Property

A *property* is an individual state of an object, typically represented as a variable. In the squirrel example, color represents a property of a squirrel. An object's properties can include any of the valid JavaScript variable types.

Which Type Is Which?

A variable's *type* is the kind of value it holds. Several basic variable types are offered by JavaScript, including string, Boolean, integer, and floating-point decimal.

JavaScript utilizes loose casting, which means a variable can assume different types at will. For example:

```
squirrel.color = "pink"
...statements...
squirrel.color = 30
```

Both color values are valid. In Java, this would cause an error because it incorporates tight casting. After you assign a type to a variable in Java, you can't change it.

Loose casting can make your life easier when you are working with JavaScript. When you are building strings, for example, you can add a string to an integer, and the result will be a string. For example:

```
value = 3;
theResult = value + "is the number." //Results in "3 is the number."
```

The downside is that sometimes you can easily forget what a variable thinks it is. It's a good idea to try to keep variables to their original type unless changing them is absolutely necessary.

To access object properties, use the object's name, followed by a period and the name of the property:

```
squirrel.color
```

Assigning a new value to the property will change it:

```
squirrel.color = "pink"
```

Not all properties of all objects can change. For example, the Math object includes several properties representing constants, such as pi. Attempts to change these properties are always unsuccessful.

Function and Methods

A JavaScript *function* is a collection of statements that are invoked by using the name of the function and a list of arguments, if such a list is used. As a general rule, if you use a set of statements more than once as part of a page, it will probably be easier to include them as a function. Also, any activity used as part of an event handler should be defined as a function for ease of use.

Functions usually appear in the HEAD portion of an HTML document to ensure that they are loaded and interpreted before the user has a chance to interact with them.

The following is the syntax to define a function:

```
function functionName ([arg1] [,arg2] [,...]) {
...statements...
}
```

An example of a function that automatically generates a link to an anchor called top at the top of the current page could look like this:

```
function makeTopLink (topLinkText) {
    var topURL = "#top";
    document.writeln(topLinkText.link(topURL));
}
```

This function accepts a text string as its one argument and generates a hypertext link, similar to using the HTML <A HREF> tags.

```
makeTopLink("Return to the top.");
makeTopLink("top");
```

Method

If properties represent the current conditions of the object, methods serve as the knobs and levers that make it perform. Consider the squirrel example again. Add a property to reflect the squirrel's current state of chattering:

```
function squirrel(color) {
    this.color = color;
    this.chattering = false;
}
```

Then, add a method to change the status of his chattering:

```
function Chatter ( onOff ) {
    if (onOff == "on")
        {this.chattering = true;}
    else
        {this.chattering = false;}
}
```

Now that you have defined an extra method, you must make it a part of the object. Doing so means including the method name as part of the object definition.

5

```
function squirrel(color) {
    this.color = color;
    this.chattering = false;
    this.Chatter = Chatter;
}
```

Finally, the last step is to include the entire package as part of an HTML document, such as in Listing 5.2, and run it on a browser (see Figure 5.1).

Listing 5.2. Using the JavaScript definition of a squirrel and its behavior requires an HTML document similar to this one.

 INPUT

```
<HTML>
<HEAD>
<TITLE>A Squirrel Page</TITLE>
<SCRIPT language="javascript">
<!--
function Chatter ( onOff ) {
    if (onOff == "on")
        {this.chattering = true;
         document.writeln("Chatter, chatter.");}
    else
        {this.chattering = false;
         document.writeln("Sound of silence.");}
}

function squirrel (color) {
    this.color = color;
    this.chattering = false;
    this.Chatter = Chatter;
    document.writeln("A squirrel is born.");
}
// -->
</SCRIPT>
</HEAD>
<BODY>
<SCRIPT LANGUAGE="javascript">
var brownSquirrel = new squirrel("brown");
brownSquirrel.Chatter("on");
brownSquirrel.Chatter("off");
</SCRIPT>
</BODY>
</HTML>
```

When the browser interprets the script, it loads and interprets the functions in order. Although it would be more logical to place the squirrel's methods after the squirrel definition, the browser would generate an error because the chatter function hasn't been defined yet.

Now that you have a feel for the syntax and usage of JavaScript, let's move on to more productive endeavors, such as creating some style for your pages.

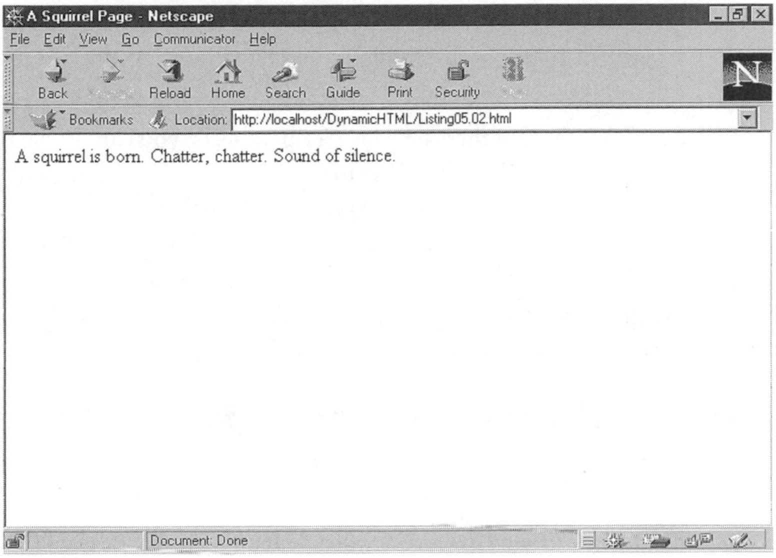

Figure 5.1.

The squirrel page instantiates its object, and then manipulates its properties through the use of its method.

Creating Style Sheets with JSSS

Following the introduction to JavaScript, it's only logical to begin with the objects that represent the style on your Web page. Netscape 4.0 introduces three new objects to provide access to changing style.

New JSSS Objects

The three new objects used with JSSS represent the three basic parts of style—tags, classes, and ids. You'll remember these from Chapter 4, "Cascading Style Sheets."

☐ *Tags* are the actual mark-up elements used in HTML. They are children of the document object, so the syntax to access them is document.tags.*tagname*, in which *tagname* is one of the valid HTML tags, such as H1, STRONG, or A.

☐ *Classes* are a further division of tags. For example, remember the left and right version of a <P> tag. It's important not to confuse the style classes with Java classes, which are the building blocks of Java code.

Classes are also children of document, so their syntax is document.classes.*classname[.tagname]*, in which *classname* is the identifier for your class and *tagname* is an optional identifier for a specific tag to which it applies. A special value for *tagname* is all, which indicates that the class can be used with any tag on the page.

☐ *IDs* are the unique identifiers for each individual tag. Think of it as the name for each tag—the first <H1> could be "Ed" (<H1 id="Ed">), the second <H1> could be "Bob" (<H1 id="Bob">), and so on.

The ID is also a child of `document` and uses the syntax `document.ids.`*`idname`*, in which *`idname`* is the name of the `id` attribute. In the first preceding example, it is `document.ids.Ed`.

By using all three of these new JavaScript objects, you can set the value of any style attribute within the document. The caveat to all of this is that you can modify JSSS only when the page loads. After the browser is finished parsing the page, the styles are set—you can't go back with Netscape Navigator 4.0 and change attributes as you can with the Microsoft Internet Explorer 4.0 model.

In addition to the three new objects, there are also a new method and property used with JSSS that you'll want to use sometimes.

New JSSS Method and Property

In addition to the three new objects, the world of JSSS offers a new method to help set contextual styles and a new property useful for assigning conditional styles.

NEW TERM   *Conditional styles* are applied depending on the status of other variables, whether it's other styles or the value on a form. For example, you could check for the existence of color combinations that are hard to read (such as red on blue) and change the colors to more palatable choices.

☐   The `contextual` method enables you to specify styles based on their relation to the position of other tags. Its purpose is the same as the contextual syntax for CSS. You can set all `<P>` tags under an `<H1>` tag to a 14-point typeface and all `<P>` tags under an `<H2>` tag to a 12-point typeface. This use is applied based on the paragraph's context to the heading tags, not on classes.

The preceding example is represented like this:

```
<style type="text/javascript">
contextual(tags.h1, tags.p).fontSize = "14pt";
contextual(tags.h2, tags.p).fontSize = "12pt";
</style>
```

TIP   You'll notice that after talking about the new objects as children of `document`, I didn't use `document` in the style definitions. Why not?

Because `document` is one of the top-level documents for a Web page, it is understood. You can use it for clarity, but it's not required.

☐   The `apply` property is used as shorthand to set the style of a tag or group of styles using a function. For example, consider the following function, which sets a background color for an unspecified tag based on the value of its color:

5

```
function setBackground(thisTag) {
    with (thisTag) {
        if (color == "yellow") {
            backgroundColor = "blue"; }
        else
            if (color == "white") {
                backgroundColor = "black"; }
    }
}
```

Nothing changes. All this processing happens when the apply property is referenced during style processing.

```
with (tags) {
    H1.color = "white";
    H2.color = "yellow";
    H3.color = "purple";
}

tags.H1.apply = setBackground(tags.H1);
tags.H2.apply = setBackground(tags.H2);
tags.H3.apply = setBackground(tags.H3);
```

This code snippet first sets the color of three heading tags. Then, it takes each of
the tags and applies the rules set forth in the function. Listing 5.3 shows the
complete page.

**Listing 5.3. In this JSSS definition, the text color is set first,
then the background is changed using the setBackground
method with the apply property.**

INPUT

```
<HTML>

<HEAD>
<TITLE>Apply and JSSS</TITLE>
</HEAD>

<STYLE type="text/javascript">
<!--
function setBackground(thisTag) {
    with (thisTag) {
        if (color == "yellow") {
            backgroundColor = "blue"; }
        else
            if (color == "white") {
                backgroundColor = "black"; }
    }
}

with (tags) {
    H1.color = "white";
    H2.color = "yellow";
    H3.color = "purple";
```

5

continues

Listing 5.3. continued

```
    }

    tags.H1.apply = setBackground(tags.H1);
    tags.H2.apply = setBackground(tags.H2);
    tags.H3.apply = setBackground(tags.H3);

    //-->
    </STYLE>

    <BODY bgcolor="white">
    <H1>This is white on black (H1)</H1>
    <H2>This is yellow on blue (H2)</H2>
    <H3>This is purple on the default background color (H3)</H3>
    </BODY>

    </HTML>
```

When the page is displayed (see Figure 5.2), each heading receives the appropriate background color, even though it wasn't set explicitly during the style definition.

Figure 5.2.

Using the apply *property is a quick way to create conditional styles.*

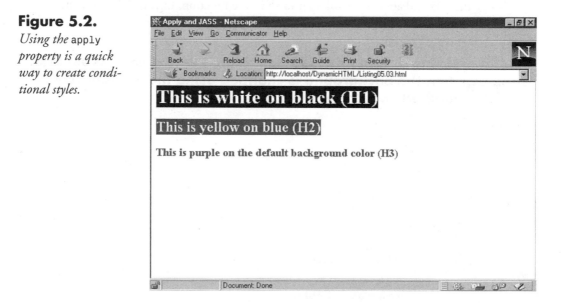

Applying JSSS to a Web Page

Now that you've had a peek at the different objects used to represent style in JavaScript, it's time to actually put JSSS to work on a real Web page. As you've seen with the objects, creating a page with JSSS is similar to creating a page with CSS, except for the syntax.

To begin, you'll work with one of the sample pages from Chapter 4 (see Listing 5.4 and Figure 5.3), and then re-create the style line-by-line with JSSS to re-create the CSS style now in place.

Listing 5.4. The complete example from Chapter 4 using CSS, which we'll replace with JSSS.

`INPUT`

```
<HTML>

<HEAD>
<TITLE>A new style</TITLE>
</HEAD>

<STYLE type="text/CSS">
<!--
BODY {margin-left: 0.75in; margin-right: 0.75in; margin-top: 0.10in}
H1, H2 {font: verdana, helvetica, arial, san-serif normal}
H1 {font-size:18pt; text-align:left}
H2 {font-size:14pt; text-align:right}
P {font:garamond 12pt/11pt normal}
P.left {text-align:left}
P.right {text-align:right}
A {text-decoration: none; font-weight: bold}
-->
</STYLE>

<BODY bgcolor="#ffffff">
<H1>Lorem ipsum dolor sit amet</H1>
<P>Consectetur <A href="tempor.html" title="Eveniet">
adipisci tempor</A> incidunt ut labore et dolore magna aliqu atib saepe
eveniet ut er reupdiand sint. Nos arsapiente delectus au aut prefer endis
dol Lene contentiam, quid est cur verear ne ad eam nc quos tu paulo ante
memorite tum etia ergat.</P>
<H2>Temporibud autem quinus</H2>
<P>Atib saepe eveniet ut er
<A href="sint.html" title="Dodecendesse">repudiand sint</A> et molestia
tenetury sapiente delctus au aut prefer endis dol. Endiumagist and et
dodecendesse videantur, iustitiam, aequitated fidem. Neque hominy infant
efficerd possit duo contend notiner si effecerit. Natura proficis facile
explent sine julla unura aute enim desiderable.</P>
</BODY>

</HTML>
```

Begin with the style tags. The basic container for JSSS is the same as for CSS, except for the type and the closing comment tag to hide the styles from incompatible browsers.

```
<STYLE type="text/javascript">
<!-- Begin hiding from incompatible browsers

// Finish hiding from incompatible browsers -->
</STYLE>
```

Figure 5.3.

The starting point for the JSSS page as it was implemented with CSS style.

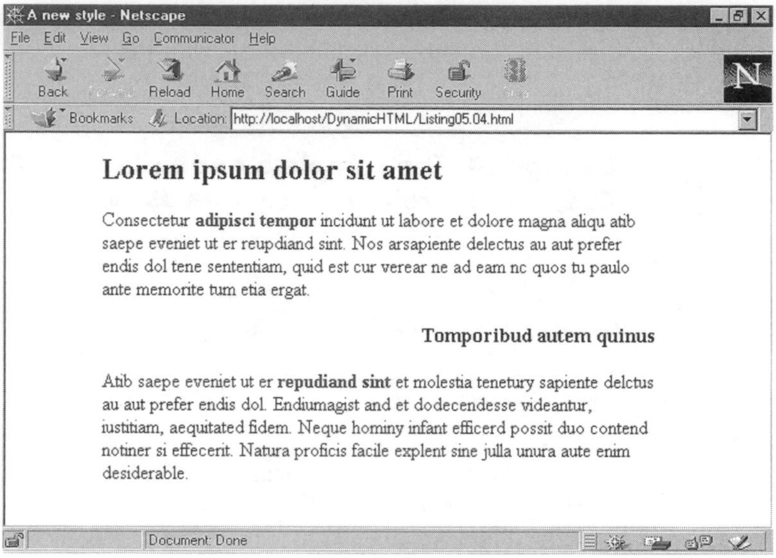

Note the two slashes before the closing comment tag. In JavaScript, two slashes mark the beginning of a comment. Use the two slashes to keep JavaScript from looking at the closing HTML comment tag (-->), which it would try to interpret as a JavaScript statement.

Next comes the body style. The original CSS version called for a left and right margin of 0.75 inches and a top margin of 0.10 inches. You'll do the same with JSSS using the tags.BODY object.

```
with (tags.BODY) {
   marginLeft = ".75";
   marginRight = ".75";
   marginTop = ".10";
}
```

The three values are set, but what about the with (tags.BODY) line at the top? This special feature of JavaScript enables you to specify an object for a set of statements. Anything that falls within the curly brackets after the with statement is interpreted as though it began with tags.BODY.

NOTE

Before style sheets, the with statement was used primarily with JavaScript's Math object. The Math object contains several constants, such as Pi and e, and a range of scientific methods such as sin and log. Instead of continually typing Math.PI, Math.e, Math.sin, or Math.log, developers can preface a mathematical section with the following followed by a set of statements enclosed in curly brackets:

```
with (Math)
```

Then, the Math object is understood, and a lot of typing and potential typos are eliminated.

Next, you'll work on the two heading tags. These two tags used CSS grouping as a shorthand to make defining the tags easier. Unfortunately, grouping is not something that JSSS handles particularly well. You will use the apply property to set the common attributes for both styles, but the end result is still a lot of additional typing.

```
function eval_Heading(thisTag) {
   thisTag.fontFamily = "verdana, helvetica, arial, sans-serif";
   if (thisTag == tags.H1) {
      thisTag.fontSize="18pt"; }
   else thisTag.fontSize="14pt";
}

tags.H1.apply = eval_Heading(tags.H1);
tags.H2.apply = eval_Heading(tags.H2);
```

Compared with the same code required to implement these styles with CSS, it's a bit of additional work. Such is the joy of working with two completely different forms of syntax. One version's drawback is another's strong point, and vice versa.

You'll also notice that you haven't implemented the left and right text alignment yet. I'll cover that next with the paragraph style. The first part of the <P> is straightforward—a font style with a typeface and size.

```
tags.P.font = "garamond, serif 12pt"
```

This is all you need for the paragraph. You'll implement the text justification with classes that you can use with the heading and paragraph tags. Like CSS, you can use JSSS and the classes object to define a class independent of a tag.

```
classes.left.textAlign = "left";
classes.right.textAlign = "right";
```

You can use these two classes with any of the tags to force right or left justification, which is what you'll do later when the HTML is created for the page.

The last style to create is for the anchor. This is a straightforward affair in which you remove the default underline attribute and add bold formatting.

```
with (tags.A) {
   textDecoration = "none";
   fontWeight = "bold";
}
```

5

The completed JSSS style section is presented in Listing 5.5.

Listing 5.5. The completed JSSS style sheet looks quite different than its counterpart in CSS.

```
<STYLE type="text/javascript">
<!-- Begin hiding from incompatible browsers

with (tags.BODY) {
   marginLeft = ".75";
   marginRight = ".75";
   marginTop = ".10";
}

function eval_Heading(thisTag) {
   thisTag.fontFamily = "verdana, helvetica, arial, sans-serif";
   if (thisTag == tags.H1) {
      thisTag.fontSize="18pt"; }
   else thisTag.fontSize="14pt";
}

tags.H1.apply = eval_Heading(tags.H1);
tags.H2.apply = eval_Heading(tags.H2);

with (tags.P) {
   fontFamily = "garamond, serif";
   fontSize = "12pt";
}

classes.justleft.all.textAlign = "left";
classes.justright.all.textAlign = "right";

with (tags.A) {
   textDecoration = "none";
   fontWeight = "bold";
}
// Finish hiding from incompatible browsers -->
</STYLE>
```

When the body of the document is created (see Listing 5.6), it changes very little from the CSS version. The notable difference is in the two classes, left and right, which are added to the two heading tags to set their alignment. Compare your starting point in Figure 5.3 with the JSSS version of the same page in Figure 5.4.

Listing 5.6. The body of this document includes the addition of classes to the heading tags.

INPUT

```html
<HTML>

<HEAD>
<TITLE>A new style</TITLE>
</HEAD>

<STYLE type="text/javascript">
<!-- Begin hiding from incompatible browsers

with (tags.BODY) {
   marginLeft = ".75";
   marginRight = ".75";
   marginTop = ".10";
}

function eval_Heading(thisTag) {
   thisTag.fontFamily = "verdana, helvetica, arial, sans-serif";
   if (thisTag == tags.H1) {
      thisTag.fontSize="18pt"; }
   else thisTag.fontSize="14pt";
}

tags.H1.apply = eval_Heading(tags.H1);
tags.H2.apply = eval_Heading(tags.H2);

with (tags.P) {
   fontFamily = "garamond, serif";
   fontSize = "12pt";
}

classes.justleft.all.textAlign = "left";
classes.justright.all.textAlign = "right";

with (tags.A) {
   textDecoration = "none";
   fontWeight = "bold";
}
// Finish hiding from incompatible browsers -->
</STYLE>

<BODY bgcolor="white">

<H1 class="justleft">Lorem ipsum dolor sit amet</H1>
<P class="justleft">Consectetur <A href="tempor.html" title="Eveniet">
adipisci tempor</A> incidunt ut labore et dolore magna aliqu atib saepe
eveniet ut er reupdiand sint. Nos arsapiente delectus au aut prefer endis
dol tene sententiam, quid est cur verear ne ad eam nc quos tu paulo ante
memorite tum etia ergat.</P>
```

continues

5

Listing 5.6. continued

```
<H2 class="justright">Temporibud autem quinus</H2>
<P class="justright">Atib saepe eveniet ut er
<A href="sint.html" title="Dodecendesse">repudiand sint</A> et molestia
tenetury sapiente delctus au aut prefer endis dol. Endiumagist and et
dodecendesse videantur, iustitiam, aequitated fidem. Neque hominy infant
efficerd possit duo contend notiner si effecerit. Natura proficis facile
explent sine julla unura aute enim desiderable.</P>
</BODY>

</HTML>
```

Figure 5.4.

The finished JSSS page with style appears to be identical to the CSS version after which it was modeled.

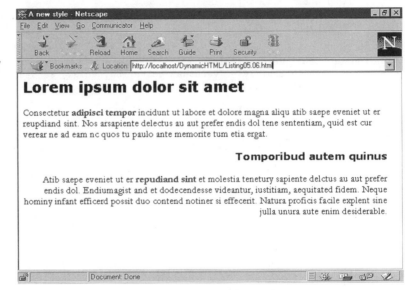

So what have you proven by re-creating a CSS page with JSSS? One important fact—the syntax might be different, but the outcome is the same. CSS and JSSS are different roads to the same result.

TIP

Now that you've created your first style sheet with JSSS, you can use it in an external style sheet, similar to CSS linked style sheets. First, save the style section of the document as its own document with a .js file extension. Then, include the <LINK> tag in the header of the document to implement the style.

```
<LINK rel="stylesheet" type="text/javascript" src="JSSS_style.js">
```
That's all there is to it. When the page is loaded, the browser will retrieve the style and apply the tags to it.

Working with Layers

Although layers are not technically a part of JSSS, I'm going to take this opportunity to show you how they work. But first, what is a layer?

A *layer* is a section of an HTML page that is handled as an independent unit. In layer-compatible browsers, each section can be displayed, hidden, moved, or otherwise manipulated independently of other sections. In Netscape, they are delineated on the Web page with the <LAYER>, <DIV>, or <SPAN> tags, while Microsoft supports the <DIV> and <SPAN> implementations. For your examples, you'll be working with <DIV> and <SPAN>.

What does all of this mean? Layers give you a whole new set of tools with which to control the position and visibility of entire segments of a Web page. You can overlap up to 10 layers and then reveal each one in turn to create an animation. Or, you can slide layers around for other transition effects.

TIP

You can define styles for layers using JSSS or CSS in the same manner as any other HTML tag.

NOTE

Layers are Netscape's way of positioning HTML elements with style sheets, which is part of a proposed W3C standard (www.w3.org/pub/WWW/TR/WD-positioning). Microsoft has a slightly different (and noncompatible way) of implementing this proposed standard, which you'll explore at the end of this section.

With this little bit of knowledge in hand, begin with a simple example (see Listing 5.7 and Figure 5.5). It is a basic HTML document that includes a paragraph for the body text and a layer that contains an image.

INPUT **Listing 5.7. This page includes a simple layer with no controls.**

```
<HTML>
<HEAD>
<TITLE>Working with layers</TITLE>
</HEAD>
<BODY>
<P>Here's some main text which is part of a paragraph.</P>
<LAYER>
<H1><FONT color="red">HERE'S SOME REALLY BIG TEXT</FONT></H1>
</LAYER>
</BODY>
</HTML>
```

Figure 5.5.

A simple layer example. With no other formatting, it displays as any other HTML document would.

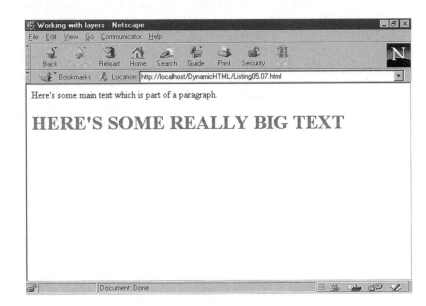

 TIP

The <LAYER> tag is proprietary to Netscape and is not compatible with any other browser.

From a design standpoint, this layer is not very interesting. Now move on to put the layer somewhere other than in line with the rest of the document.

Positioning the Layer

To position a layer, you need a coordinate system that can describe any position within the browser window, no matter the size or shape. For this reason, all coordinates are based from the top left of the browser window.

To ensure compatibility with all possible measurements used in style sheets, a layer supports figures in pixels, inches, centimeters, and percentages. If no measurement system is designated, a layer defaults to pixels.

You can see the result of positioning based on a common starting point in Listing 5.8 and Figure 5.6.

Listing 5.8. The new page includes both text items starting from the top-left corner.

`INPUT`

```
<HTML>
<HEAD>
<TITLE>Working with layers</TITLE>
</HEAD>
<BODY>
<P>Here's some main text which is part of a paragraph.</P>
<P>Here's some main text which is part of a paragraph.</P>
<P>Here's some main text which is part of a paragraph.</P>
<P>Here's some main text which is part of a paragraph.</P>
<P>Here's some main text which is part of a paragraph.</P>
<LAYER top=0 left=0>
<H1><FONT color="red">HERE'S SOME REALLY BIG TEXT</FONT></H1>
</LAYER>
</BODY>
</HTML>
```

5

Here's what happens. First, there's a bunch of body text to display, just to make sure there's plenty in the background when you get around to the layer. The layer specifies an absolute position at the top-left corner of the browser window, outlined in the top and left attributes. This is the same starting point used by all pages, but by using the two placement attributes, you've forced the heading text to the same starting point as the beginning of the page.

In addition to placement, you also can control the width of a layer. We'll use an example similar to Listing 5.8, only with two text elements instead of text and graphics (see Listing 5.9). Note the difference in the width of the text between the two paragraphs on the page (see Figure 5.7).

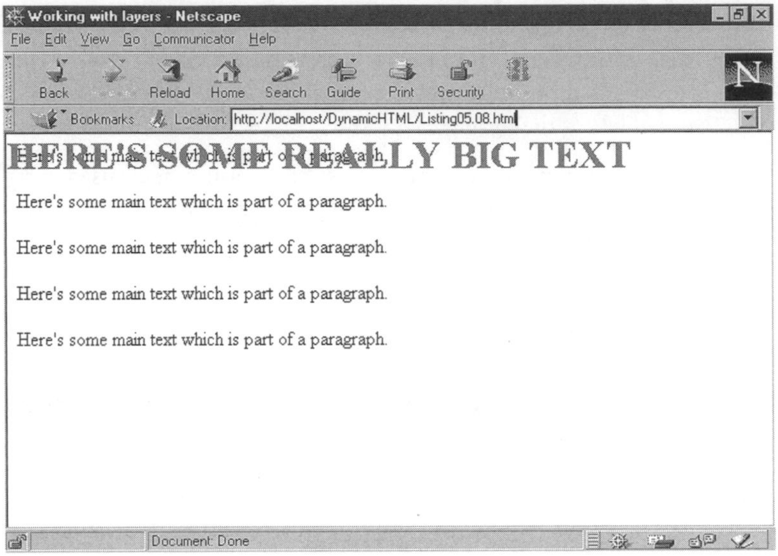

Figure 5.6.

This page uses absolute positioning to place the layer with the image at the same starting point as the rest of the page.

Listing 5.9. A new layer is added to the Web page to control the width of the body text.

INPUT

```
<HTML>
<HEAD>
<TITLE>Working with layers</TITLE>
</HEAD>
<BODY>
<P>Here's some text which is not a part of any layer anywhere, and includes
a rather long sentence which stretches clear across the page.</P>

<LAYER top=150 left=150 width=100>
<P>Here's some main text which is part of another paragraph.
Here's some main text which is part of another paragraph.
Here's some main text which is part of another paragraph.
Here's some main text which is part of another paragraph.
Here's some main text which is part of another paragraph.</P>
</LAYER>

</BODY>
</HTML>
```

The first paragraph extends all the way across the browser window and is broken according to the rules of the browser—when the line's too long, it continues to the next line. The second paragraph is contained by a layer. Its position begins further down the page, indented from the left. Then, its width is constrained to 100 pixels, forcing a long narrow column down the middle of the page.

5

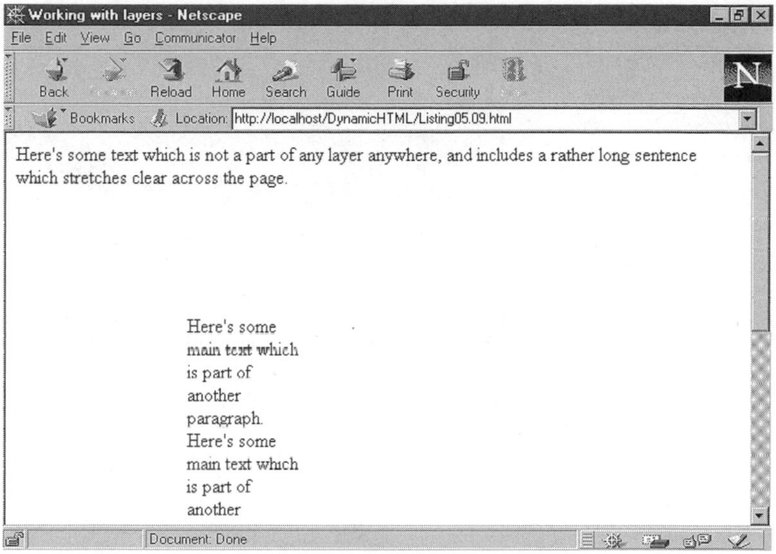

Figure 5.7.

This page uses layer width control to set margins for the text within the layer.

Working with Other Layer Attributes

Like every other element in HTML, layers have some default behavior that you should consider. First, as I mentioned earlier, layers are presented within the normal flow of a document unless additional attributes control their placement.

The second has to do with backgrounds and transparency. If no background color or graphic are specified for a layer, the layer is transparent by default. This was exhibited in Figure 5.6 when the body text appeared behind the heading text that was placed over it. Any other setting for the background renders it opaque (see Listing 5.10 and Figure 5.8).

INPUT

Listing 5.10. A background color attribute is added to the layer to make the background opaque.

```
<HTML>
<HEAD>
<TITLE>Working with layers</TITLE>
</HEAD>
<BODY bgcolor="white">
<P>Here's some main text which is part of a paragraph.</P>
<P>Here's some main text which is part of a paragraph.</P>
<P>Here's some main text which is part of a paragraph.</P>
<P>Here's some main text which is part of a paragraph.</P>
<P>Here's some main text which is part of a paragraph.</P>
<LAYER top=0 left=0 bgcolor="gray">
<H1><FONT color="white">HERE'S SOME REALLY BIG TEXT</FONT></H1>
</LAYER>
</BODY>
</HTML>
```

5

Figure 5.8.
The black-on-white body text is obscured by the white-on-gray heading text in the layer.

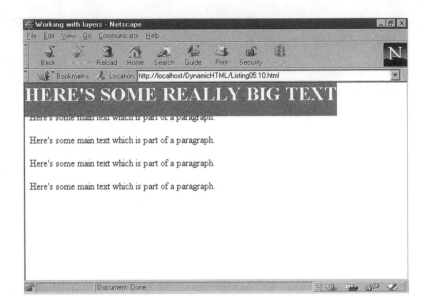

In this page, the background color of the page is set to white, and then the five lines of body text are displayed. This is followed by our faithful layer, now set in a white-on-gray color scheme. By setting a background attribute, the layer is forced to become opaque and obscures all of the text underneath it. The same effect is also achieved by using the background attribute and specifying a URL for a graphic image.

Using More than One Layer

The preceding examples have been sticking to one layer so you can see some of the basic behavior of a layer. It's possible to add more than one layer, however, by adding additional layer tags. In Listing 5.11 and Figure 5.9, four layers with absolute positioning have been added so you can see how they stack up on a page.

Listing 5.11. This page includes four layers positioned in four separate positions on the page.

INPUT

```
<HTML>
<HEAD>
<TITLE>Multiple Layers</TITLE>
</HEAD>
<BODY>
<LAYER top=0 left=0 width=150>
<P>This is layer number 1 located in the top left corner of the window.
This is layer number 1 located in the top left corner of the window.
```

5

```
This is layer number 1 located in the top left corner of the window.</P>
</LAYER>
<LAYER top=0 left=200 width=150>
<P>This is layer number 2 located in the top right corner of the window.
This is layer number 2 located in the top right corner of the window.
This is layer number 2 located in the top right corner of the window.</P>
</LAYER>
<LAYER top=200 left=0 width=150>
<P>This is layer number 3 located in the bottom left corner of the window.
This is layer number 3 located in the bottom left corner of the window.
This is layer number 3 located in the bottom left corner of the window.</P>
</LAYER>
<LAYER top=200 left=200 width=150>
<P>This is layer number 4 in the bottom right left corner of the window.
This is layer number 4 in the bottom right corner of the window.
This is layer number 4 in the bottom right corner of the window.</P>
</LAYER>
</BODY>
</HTML>
```

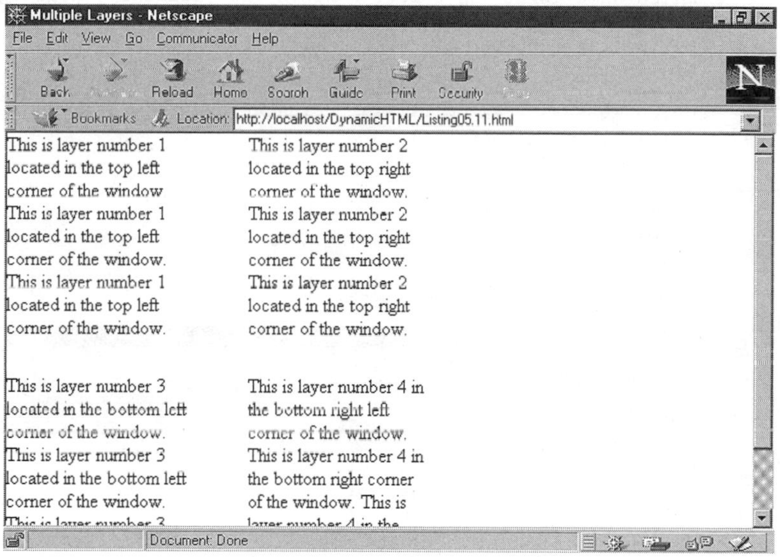

Figure 5.9.

More than one layer is placed on a page, and each is placed in its own respective position on the page.

By now, your imagination must be running wild. Next, you'll take the next big step for layers—overlapping and changing the display order at will, which involves adding one more attribute, called visibility (see Listing 5.12 and Figure 5.10). To gain additional control over each section, you also must give each layer a name.

Listing 5.12. Each layer now has the same position information but includes a name and visibility attribute to control its display status in the stack.

```
<HTML>
<HEAD>
<TITLE>Multiple Layers</TITLE>
</HEAD>
<BODY>
<LAYER name=one top=0 left=0 width=150 bgcolor=white>
<P>This is layer number 1.
This is layer number 1.
This is layer number 1.</P>
</LAYER>
<LAYER name=two top=0 left=0 width=150 visibility=hide below=1 bgcolor=white>
<P>This is layer number 2.
This is layer number 2.
This is layer number 2.</P>
</LAYER>
<LAYER name=three top=0 left=0 width=150 visibility=hide bgcolor=white>
<P>This is layer number 3.
This is layer number 3.
This is layer number 3.</P>
</LAYER>
<LAYER name=four top=0 left=0 width=150 visibility=hide bgcolor=white>
<P>This is layer number 4.
This is layer number 4.
This is layer number 4.</P>
</LAYER>
</BODY>
</HTML>
```

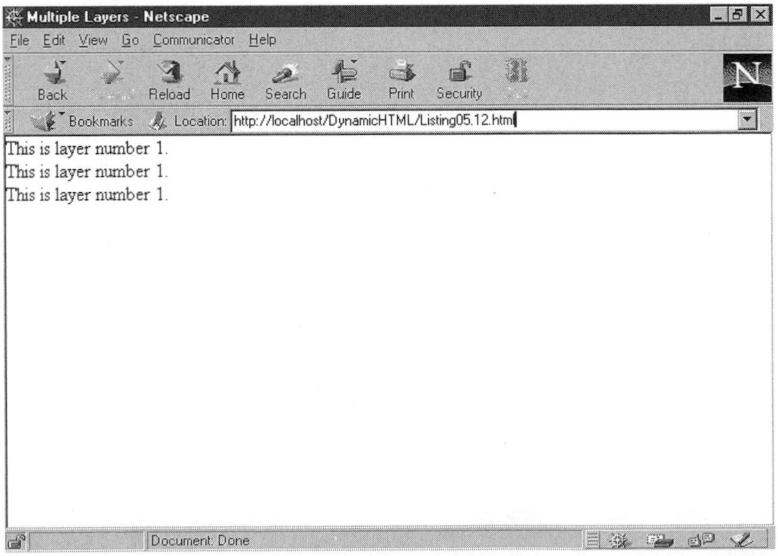

Figure 5.10.

Each layer is stacked on top of the other. Because all the layers except layer 1 are hidden from view, layer 1 is the only visible layer.

Using the same position and background information for each layer overlaps each layer but blocks the view of any layer underneath. By setting the second through fourth layers as hidden, they are blocked from view and only the first layer is seen.

Now that you have set the layers so that only the first layer is visible, you can attach a script to the document to control which layer is displayed at any given time. You'll control the layer with a form and four buttons. The script calls one function that hides the current layer and displays the selected layer (see Listing 5.13 and Figure 5.11).

Listing 5.13. The page now includes a script to display the desired layer and to hide the current layer.

`INPUT`

```
<HTML>
<HEAD>
<TITLE>Multiple Layers</TITLE>
</HEAD>

<STYLE type="text/javascript">
<!--
with (document.classes.cardStack) {
   all.top = 0;
   all.left = 0;
   all.width = 150;
}
//-->
</STYLE>

<SCRIPT language="javascript">
<!--
var topLayer = 0 //the initial layer on top
function showLayer( newTop ) {
  document.layers[newTop].visibility = "show";
  document.layers[topLayer].visibility = "hide";
  topLayer = newTop;
}
function initializeLayers () {
   for (i = 1; i<document.layers.length; i++) {
      document.layers[i].visibility = "hide";
   }
   document.layers[0].visibility = "show";
   document.layers["form"].visibility = "show";
}
//-->
</SCRIPT>

<BODY onLoad="initializeLayers()">
<LAYER name="one" class="cardStack">
<P>This is layer number 1.
This is layer number 1.
This is layer number 1.</P>
```

continues

Listing 5.13. continued

```
</LAYER>
<LAYER name="two" class="cardStack">
<P>This is layer number 2.
This is layer number 2.
This is layer number 2.</P>
</LAYER>
<LAYER name="three" class="cardStack">
<P>This is layer number 3.
This is layer number 3.
This is layer number 3.</P>
</LAYER>
<LAYER name="four" class="cardStack">
<P>This is layer number 4.
This is layer number 4.
This is layer number 4.</P>
</LAYER>
<LAYER name="form" top=150>
<FORM>
<INPUT type="button" value="Show Layer 1" onClick="showLayer('one')">
<INPUT type="button" value="Show Layer 2" onClick="showLayer('two')">
<INPUT type="button" value="Show Layer 3" onClick="showLayer('three')">
<INPUT type="button" value="Show Layer 4" onClick="showLayer('four')">
</FORM>
</LAYER>
</BODY>
</HTML>
```

Figure 5.11.

Clicking one of the buttons shows the respective layer. In Figure 5.10, layer 1 was visible. Here, layer 1 is hidden and layer 3 is visible.

As you can see, you've added a bit to this page to make it more modular. Here's what has happened. First, you've made a generic style for each of the layers in the stack. If you wanted to change the position, text color, or other style attribute, it is now much easier to change the style than to change each tag individually.

When the page loads, a script is called to initialize the visibility of all the layers. This script uses the layers object to work through each layer and set its attribute to hide, then returns to set the other layers to show.

After all this happens, the user is presented with the initial screen. The form is a straightforward affair consisting of four buttons. When a button is clicked, the function showLayer is called with one argument—the name of the layer that the user wants to see. The first two lines of the function change the desired layer's visibility attribute to show and the previous visible layer to hide. Then, the user's choice is marked as the current visible layer.

Moving a Layer Around on the Page

The last trick I'll show for layers is the ability to move a layer around on a Web page. This gives you the opportunity for some interesting, albeit superfluous, effects, such as curtains opening or graphics sliding into place (see Listing 5.14 and Figure 5.12).

Listing 5.14. By moving a layer across the screen in increments, you achieve the same effect as a curtain revealing a stage.

`INPUT`

```
<HTML>
<HEAD>
<TITLE>Multiple Layers</TITLE>
</HEAD>
<SCRIPT language="javascript">
<!--
function leftMove() {
  document.layers["curtain"].moveAbove(document.layers["thetext"]);
  curtainWidth = 800;
  var moveBy = -1;
  while ( curtainWidth> -1) {
    document.layers["curtain"].offset(moveBy,0);
    curtainWidth += moveBy;
  }
document.layers["curtain"].visibility = "hide";
}
//-->
</SCRIPT>
<BODY>
<LAYER name=curtain bgcolor="red" top=0 left=0>
<H1> Nos arsapiente delectus au aut prefer endis dol tene sententiam.</H1>
```

continues

Listing 5.14. continued

```
</LAYER>
<LAYER name=thetext top=5 left=5>
<P>Consectetur <A href="tempor.html" title="Eveniet">adipisci tempor</A>
incidunt ut labore et dolore magna aliqu atib saepe eveniet ut er reupdiand
sint. Nos arsapiente delectus au aut prefer endis dol tene sententiam, quid
est cur verear ne ad eam nc quos tu paulo ante memorite tum etia ergat.</P>
</LAYER>
<script language="javascript">
<!--
leftMove();
//-->
</SCRIPT>
</BODY>
</HTML>
```

Figure 5.12.

The curtain with the heading text is moved across the screen from left to right to reveal the body text under-neath.

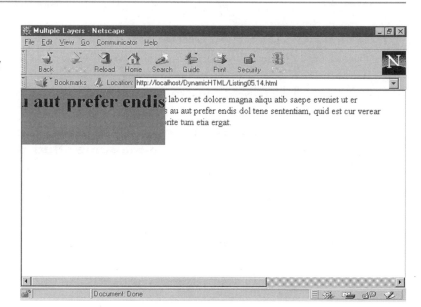

This page begins with a heading in a layer. Because it's the first element on the page, it automatically occupies the top-left position and fills the window from left to right. The red background makes the curtain opaque. The next layer is the body text. It is positioned at the top-left corner of the window below the heading text.

TIP

This page is also an example of planning for nonlayer browsers. If this page were displayed on any non-Netscape browser, the user would just see the heading over the body text in the normal HTML presentation of the elements.

5

Next, take a look at the script. To begin, get the windowWidth property from the current window, which enables you to know in how wide a space the curtain will be working. Then, begin with an offset value, which is decremented to move the curtain in a left-to-right motion using the moveTo method of the layer. After the layer is moved over, the offset is decremented by 10 pixels and the loop continues until it has traversed the screen.

As an added safety to make sure the curtain moves out of the way, you also set the visibility property of the layer to hide to ensure that it's completely hidden from view on the page.

Another Way to Work with Layers

The position properties, which have provided the foundation for Netscape layers, are also the key elements in positioning other HTML elements on a page. These properties enable you to use the position property with other tags, including <DIV>, <SPAN>, and other block elements such as headings and paragraphs.

The <LAYER> tag is not supported or endorsed by any W3C standard, although the W3C includes a specification with which Netscape is compatible. The long name is *Positioning HTML Elements with Cascading Style Sheets*, and it is available for review at

www.w3.org/pub/WWW/TR/WD-positioning

The W3C document covers new tags and attributes supported through CSS that enable the same functionality as layers. Take a look at how it works. Begin with Listing 5.11 with each of the <LAYER> tags changed to <SPAN> (see Listing 5.15 and Figure 5.13).

INPUT

Listing 5.15. This page has four layers positioned using W3C's CSS tags and attributes.

```
<HTML>
<HEAD>
<TITLE>Multiple Layers with CSS</TITLE>
</HEAD>
<BODY>
<SPAN style="position:absolute; top:0; left:0; width:150">
<P>This is layer number 1 located in the top left corner of the window.
This is layer number 1 located in the top left corner of the window.
This is layer number 1 located in the top left corner of the window.</P>
</SPAN>
<SPAN style="position:absolute; top:0; left:200; width:150">
<P>This is layer number 2 located in the top right corner of the window.
This is layer number 2 located in the top right corner of the window.
This is layer number 2 located in the top right corner of the window.</P>
</SPAN>
<SPAN style="position:absolute; top:200; left:0; width:150">
<P>This is layer number 3 located in the bottom left corner of the window.
This is layer number 3 located in the bottom left corner of the window.
```

5

continues

Listing 5.15. continued

```
This is layer number 3 located in the bottom left corner of the window.</P>
</SPAN>
<SPAN style="position:absolute; top:200; left:200; width:150">
<P>This is layer number 4 in the bottom right left corner of the window.
This is layer number 4 in the bottom right corner of the window.
This is layer number 4 in the bottom right corner of the window.</P>
</SPAN>
</BODY>
</HTML>
```

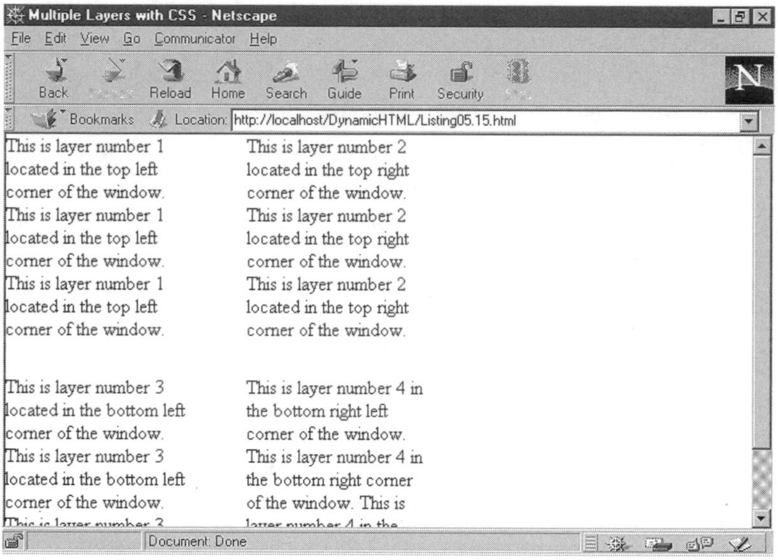

Figure 5.13.

This page creates the same result with inline CSS styles as its JSSS cousin, which uses layers.

Notice that the series of positioning attributes have been replaced by an inline `style` attribute. This attribute includes the CSS syntax for specifying absolute positioning along with the coordinates and width of the columns. The end result for the user is the same.

Using the same concepts as layers, you can also display and hide CSS elements on a page (see Listing 5.16 and Figure 5.14). Using the <DIV> tag with a style sheet, I've stacked each division and enabled its appearance or disappearance.

INPUT
Listing 5.16. The page now includes a script to display the desired layer and hide the current layer.

```
<HTML>
<HEAD>
<TITLE>Multiple Layers</TITLE>
```

```
</HEAD>

<STYLE type="text/CSS">
<!--
.cardHide, .cardShow {position:absolute; top:0px; left:0px; width=150}
.cardHide {visibility="hidden"}
.cardShow {visibility="visible"}
.formTop {position:absolute; top:100px}
-->
</STYLE>

<SCRIPT language="javascript">
<!--
var topLayer = "one" //the initial layer on top
function showLayer( newTop ) {
  document.all(topLayer).className = "CardHide";
  document.all(newTop).className = "cardShow";
  topLayer = newTop;
}
//-->
</SCRIPT>

<BODY>
<DIV id="one" class="cardShow">
<P>This is layer number 1.
This is layer number 1.
This is layer number 1.</P>
</DIV>
<DIV id="two" class="cardHide">
<P>This is layer number 2.
This is layer number 2.
This is layer number 2.</P>
</DIV>
<DIV id="three" class="cardHide">
<P>This is layer number 3.
This is layer number 3.
This is layer number 3.</P>
</DIV>
<DIV id="four" class="cardHide">
<P>This is layer number 4.
This is layer number 4.
This is layer number 4.</P>
</DIV>
<DIV class="formTop">
<FORM>
<INPUT type="button" value="Show Layer 1" onClick="showLayer('one')">
<INPUT type="button" value="Show Layer 2" onClick="showLayer('two')">
<INPUT type="button" value="Show Layer 3" onClick="showLayer('three')">
<INPUT type="button" value="Show Layer 4" onClick="showLayer('four')">
</FORM>
</DIV>
</BODY>
</HTML>
```

5

Figure 5.14.
Using CSS and <DIV> *tags, you've accomplished the same page-flipping effect as Netscape layers.*

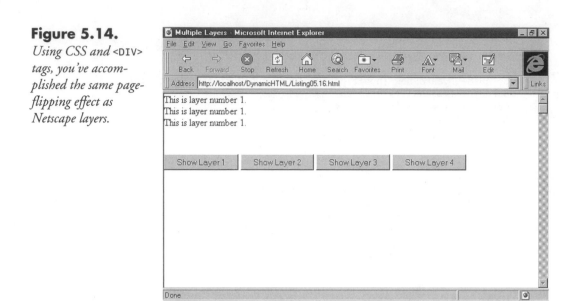

There's a little less code on this page because you're using CSS and JSSS. You start with two style class definitions that define a hidden and visible section of text located at the top-left corner of the screen. Then, add one more definition to make sure your form appears in the correct location.

When the button is pushed, your JavaScript function is invoked in the same manner as before, with slightly different syntax to account for Microsoft's document object model. Instead of directly changing the visibility attribute, you assign the page section to the appropriate class name.

As you can see with the <LAYER> and <DIV> tags, you're starting to get a taste for the fun and frustration of Dynamic HTML. The fun is making interactive pages for your users. The frustration is dealing with two technologies that can perform identical tasks but require slightly different and incompatible syntax to get the job done. Listing 5.16 won't work on Navigator, and Listing 5.13 won't work on Internet Explorer. Hang on, though, because it's only going to get more and more entertaining as you continue.

Combining Styles

For most of this chapter, I've talked about CSS and JSSS as though they were mutually exclusive implementations of styles. Now that you're approaching the end of the chapter, it's time to tell the truth: You can use both CSS and JSSS on the same page.

How does it work? It works like just about everything else in HTML—whoever has the last word wins. It's the same way style sheets cascade if you include all three types (linked, embedded, inline) on the same page. First, the browser loads the linked style sheet because it's the first style the browser encounters when parsing the page.

Then, the browser comes to the embedded style sheet. Any settings that conflict with the linked style take precedence because it's the last value the browser has encountered.

Last comes the inline style, which trumps both of the others. Neither of the other two styles ever has a chance to get the browser's attention again before the text is displayed, so the inline style is applied.

The same process works with the two methods of creating style. Instead of including one set of <STYLE> tags, you include two. If there is any difference in the styles, the last style in line gets the last say on what the style will be. To see how this works, look at Listing 5.17. After the header, the first style sheet uses CSS to set a heading and paragraph text to reverse color (white on black). Then, the next style uses JSSS to set the paragraph style back to black on white.

INPUT

Listing 5.17. This page uses the two different style sheet models to set text and background color.

```
<HTML>

<HEAD>
<TITLE>CSS and JSSS</TITLE>
</HEAD>

<STYLE type="text/css">
<!--
H1 {color:white; background:black}
P {color:white; background:black}
  >
</STYLE>

<STYLE type="text/javascript">
<!--
with (tags.p) {
   color = "black";
   backgroundColor = "white";
}
// -->
</STYLE>

<BODY bgcolor="white">
<H1>Browsers with style show white on black</H1>
<P>Internet Explorer shows this style in white on black.<BR>
Navigator shows it in white on black.</P>
</BODY>

</HTML>
```

When a user views the page on Netscape Navigator (see Figure 5.15), the result is a white-on-black heading and black-on-white paragraph. The initial black-on-white value for the paragraph was overridden by the style assignments in the JSSS section.

Figure 5.15.

Between two style sheets on the same page, the last style sheet wins, regardless of the type of style sheet syntax used.

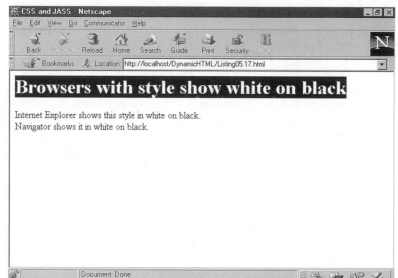

When the user views the same page in Internet Explorer (see Figure 5.16), both the heading and paragraph are displayed with white-on-black text. This occurs because Microsoft's browser doesn't know how to interpret the JSSS section, so it ignores those style values and stays with the CSS version of the style sheet.

As a general rule, this type of mixing isn't recommended for most pages when you are applying general style. Mixing the style sheets is useful if you need to generate a style or an effect for a specific browser, however. Put the default style first in the document, followed by the tags needed to create the effect.

Figure 5.16.

The same page viewed in Internet Explorer shows both heading and paragraph the same because the JSSS section is ignored.

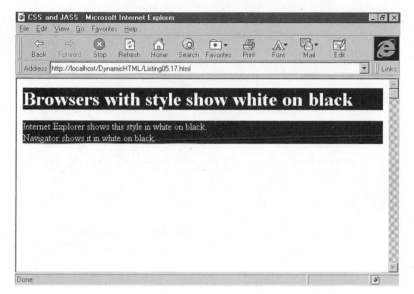

Summary

You've covered a lot of ground in this chapter, so now is a good time to step back and see where you've been. To begin, there's JavaScript. JavaScript is a special programming language used on Web pages to add interactive behavior and processing without using the Web server. JavaScript is an object-oriented language that is related to the Java programming language, although the two are quite different in implementation and usage. You'll use JavaScript for the rest of this book to implement the DHTML examples.

Next, you learned about JavaScript Style Sheets. JSSS is another way of defining the look and feel of a page and is essentially identical in use to Cascading Style Sheets. The syntax for JSSS is very different, however—not to mention incompatible—with Internet Explorer. So far, the only browser that supports JSSS is Navigator, although there is a proposal for JSSS pending with W3C.

Layers are a new part of Navigator and are also accessible for manipulation through JSSS. A layer is simply a section of a Web page—whether it's most of the body or a few lines of text—that you can position, move, or display independently of other elements on the page.

5

Layers are also a part of CSS, although the syntax is just different enough to make them incompatible with Netscape layers. CSS layers rely on the <DIV> and <SPAN> tags and do not support Netscape's <LAYER> tag. After you create a layer, you can create interactive effects using a scripting language such as JavaScript.

Although you may choose to use CSS in lieu of JSSS on your Web pages for compatibility with the most browsers, you'll probably find that you'll use JavaScript as your scripting language for the same reason. The rest of this book will rely primarily on CSS and JavaScript to implement DHTML, although we still use JSSS and VBScript to illustrate differences where we think it will help you understand what's going on.

Q&A

Q You've spent a lot of time in the last two chapters showing two different ways of creating styles. If they're both the same, which should I use?

A For now, we recommend using Cascading Style Sheets because both Internet Explorer and Navigator recognize it. Use JavaScript-Assisted Style Sheets when you want to create a specific effect just for your Netscape users.

Q JavaScript looks a lot like Java and other programming languages. Can I create programs such as word processors with it?

A JavaScript can work only within compatible browsers. Right now, it's limited to the offerings from Netscape and Microsoft. Some developers have created small Web page-based applications, such as income tax computation and shopping carts, but if you want to create a real application, you must use a real programming language. JavaScript is too limited in its capability to tackle a project like that.

Q When dividing my Web page into sections, should I use layers or divisions?

A Only Netscape understands layers right now. There's no indication that W3C will accept the <LAYER> tag as part of HTML, but there's also no clear indication that they've completely ruled it out. To maintain compatibility with as many browsers as possible, stick to the <DIV> and <SPAN> tags until W3C rules on layers.

Workshop

In this workshop, you're going to work with JSSS and layers in combination. This will give you some additional hands-on experience with JavaScript and another taste of DHTML before you take a step back to look at events in the next chapter. The first example uses positioning to display a verbose description of a hyperlink, and the second example uses layers to combine two pages into one.

5

Pop-Up Help

This example uses a familiar feature (pop-up help) applied with some Dynamic HTML features (JSSS and layers). Here's the situation. There are two hyperlinks on a page and two paragraphs of body text. You want to create a series of small pop-up windows to do two things: to give a more complete identification of where the hyperlink leads, and then to give a brief synopsis of the paragraph.

Both features will use the mouseOver and mouseOut events to detect the mouse moving over the hyperlinks and layers. You'll learn more detail about what events are and how they're handled in Chapter 6, "Dynamic HTML Events." Meanwhile, don't worry too much about that part of the code.

You'll begin with a style sheet for this example, with an added style for the text in the help box. Your HELP style creates a text style that is yellow text on a black background.

INPUT   **Listing 5.18. This JSSS document includes the addition of classes to the heading tags.**

```
<HTML>
<HEAD>
<TITLE>Pop-up Help</TITLE>
</HEAD>
<STYLE type="text/javascript">
<!-- Begin hiding from incompatible browsers
function eval_Heading(thisTag) {
    thisTag.fontFamily = "verdana, helvetica, arial, sans-serif";
    if (thisTag == tags.H1) {
        thisTag.fontSize="18pt"; }
    else {
        thisTag.fontSize="14pt"; }
}
with (tags.BODY) {
    marginLeft = ".75";
    marginRight = ".75";
    marginTop = ".10";
}
with (tags.P) {
    fontFamily = "garamond, serif";
    fontSize = "12pt";
}
with (tags.A) {
    textDecoration = "none";
    fontWeight = "bold";
}
with (classes.HELP.all) {
    color = "yellow";
    backgroundColor = "black";
}
```

continues

5

Listing 5.18. continued

```
tags.H1.apply = eval_Heading(tags.H1);
tags.H2.apply = eval_Heading(tags.H2);
classes.justleft.all.textAlign = "left";
classes.justright.all.textAlign = "right";
// Finish hiding from incompatible browsers -->
</STYLE>

<BODY bgcolor="white">
<H1 class="justleft">Lorem ipsum dolor sit amet</H1>
<P class="justleft">Consectetur <A href="tempor.html" title="Eveniet">
adipisci tempor</A> incidunt ut labore et dolore magna aliqu atib saepe
eveniet ut er reupdiand sint. Nos arsapiente delectus au aut prefer endis
dol tene sententiam, quid est cur verear ne ad eam nc quos tu paulo ante
memorite tum etia ergat.</P>
<H2 class="justright">Tomporibud autem quinus</H2>
<P class="justright">Atib saepe eveniet ut er
<A href="sint.html" title="Dodecendesse">repudiand sint</A>
et molestia tenetury sapiente
delctus au aut prefer endis dol. Endiumagist and et dodecendesse
videantur, iustitiam, aequitated fidem. Neque hominy infant efficerd
possit duo contend notiner si effecerit. Natura proficis facile explent
sine julla unura aute enim desiderable.</P>
</BODY>
</HTML>
```

With the basic page in place, begin with the layers that contain the messages in the pop-up windows.

NOTE | The windows you're creating in this example aren't really windows in the true sense of the word; they are just little boxes of HTML text that are displayed only when you want them to display.

Place each of these layers after its respective item. For example, for the first hyperlink, modify the page this way:

```
<!-- First the hyperlink... -->
Consectetur <A href="tempor.html" title="Eveniet">adipisci tempor</A>
<!-- ...then the layer providing the help... -->
<LAYER name=link_0 visibility=hide>
<TABLE border=3 cellpadding=3 bgcolor=black>
   <TD class="HELP">
      Endiumagist and et dodecendesse videantur.
   </TD>
</TABLE>
</LAYER>
<!-- ...followed by the rest of the text. -->
incidunt ut labore et dolore magna aliqu atib saepe eveniet ut
er reupdiand sint.
```

5

As you can see, this makes a bit of a mess in the middle of your otherwise clean HTML. You might want to provide more indents or comments and spaces around the layer to help isolate it from the text so editing the page later is an easier task. Add another layer after the second link in the same manner, like this:

```
<LAYER name=link_1 visibility=hide>
<TABLE border=3 cellpadding=3 bgcolor=black>
   <TD class="HELP">
     Eros Et Accumsan dignissim qui blandit.
   </TD>
</TABLE>
</LAYER>
```

Now that the layers are in place after their respective hyperlinks, it's time to work on the scripts that will control their appearance and disappearance. The first serves to display the help.

```
function displayHelp ( thisBox ) {
  document.layers[ thisBox ].visibility = "show";
}
```

There's nothing terribly complicated about this function. It takes the name of the layer and uses its value to access the layers array. The visibility attribute is changed to display the box. To clear the box, use a similar function.

```
function clearHelp ( thisBox ) {
  document.layers[ thisBox ].visibility = "hide";
}
```

This function is just like the first, except the visibility attribute is changed to hide the layer instead of show it. With your two functions in hand, you're ready to make the final changes to your page. Use the mouseOver and mouseOut events with the link tags to trigger each function (see Listing 5.19 and Figure 5.17).

Listing 5.19. The completed page includes JSS styles and two scripts to control the visibility of the layers that accompany each hyperlink.

INPUT

```
<HTML>
<HEAD>
<TITLE>Pop-up Help</TITLE>
</HEAD>

<SCRIPT language="javascript">
function displayHelp ( thisBox ) {
  document.layers[ thisBox ].visibility = "show";
}
function clearHelp ( thisBox ) {
  document.layers[ thisBox ].visibility = "hide";
```

continues

Listing 5.19. continued

```
}
</SCRIPT>

<STYLE type="text/javascript">
<!-- Begin hiding from incompatible browsers
function eval_Heading(thisTag) {
   thisTag.fontFamily = "verdana, helvetica, arial, sans-serif";
   if (thisTag == tags.H1) {
      thisTag.fontSize="18pt"; }
   else {
      thisTag.fontSize="14pt"; }
}
with (tags.BODY) {
   marginLeft = ".75";
   marginRight = ".75";
   marginTop = ".10";
}
with (tags.P) {
   fontFamily = "garamond, serif";
   fontSize = "12pt";
}
with (tags.A) {
   textDecoration = "none";
   fontWeight = "bold";
}
with (classes.HELP.all) {
   color = "yellow";
   backgroundColor = "black";
}
tags.H1.apply = eval_Heading(tags.H1);
tags.H2.apply = eval_Heading(tags.H2);
classes.justleft.all.textAlign = "left";
classes.justright.all.textAlign = "right";
// Finish hiding from incompatible browsers -->
</STYLE>

<BODY bgcolor="white">
<H1 class="justleft">Lorem ipsum dolor sit amet</H1>
<P class="justleft">Consectetur
<A href="tempor.html" title="Eveniet" onMouseOver="displayHelp('link_0')"
➥onMouseOut="clearHelp('link_0')">adipisci tempor</A>
   <LAYER name=link_0 visibility=hide>
   <TABLE border=3 bgcolor=black>
      <TD class="HELP">
        Endiumagist and et dodecendesse videantur.
      </TD>
   </TABLE>
   </LAYER>
incidunt ut labore et dolore magna aliqu atib saepe eveniet ut er reupdiand
sint. Nos arsapiente delectus au aut prefer endis dol tene sententiam, quid
est cur verear ne ad eam nc quos tu paulo ante memorite tum etia ergat.</P>
<H2 class="justright">Tomporibud autem quinus</H2>
<P class="justright">Atib saepe eveniet ut er
```

```
<A href="sint.html" title="Dodecendesse" onMouseOver="displayHelp('link_1')"
onMouseOut="clearHelp('link_1')">repudiand sint</A>
    <LAYER name=link_1 visibility=hide>
    <TABLE border=3 bgcolor=black>
        <TD class="HELP">
          Eros Et Accumsan dignissim qui blandit.
        </TD>
    </TABLE>
    </LAYER>
et molestia tenetury sapiente delctus au aut prefer endis dol. Endiumagist
and et dodecendesse videantur, iustitiam, aequitated fidem. Neque hominy
infant efficerd possit duo contend notiner si effecerit. Natura proficis
facile explent sine julla unura aute enim desiderable.</P>
</BODY>
</HTML>
```

Figure 5.17.

The finished page displays a pop-up box that provides more information about the hyperlink.

You can accomplish this task in one other way. Instead of making the help remain on the screen as long as the mouse is over the link, you can set a time limit for its display. To do this, use JavaScript's setTimeout method. Change the two script functions as follows:

```
function displayHelp ( thisBox ) {
  document.layers[ thisBox ].visibility = "show";
  window.setTimeout( "clearHelp()", 4000);
}
function clearHelp () {
  for (i=0; i<document.layers.length; i++) {
    document.layers[ i ].visibility = "hide";
  }
}
```

The first function displays the chosen box, then sets the timer for four seconds (4,000 milliseconds). When the timer runs out, it calls the `clearHelp` function, which clears all the layers. Why clear all the layers and not just those you want? Because passing arguments from within the quote marks of the `setTimeout` method is not possible.

The other modification to the page that you must make is to remove the `onMouseOut` event handlers from the hyperlink tags, because the clearing process is handled automatically through the `displayHelp` function.

Two Pages in One (Fire Department)

The last example uses JSSS to build two HTML pages that are combined into one using layers. Then, you'll add a form so that the user can pick one page he or she wants to view. The combined pages will take a bit longer to load than either page as they originally existed individually. But, the load time for the combined pages is less than the total time for loading two pages separately from the server.

Both pages were initially constructed from a template using standard HTML. We combined the content from both pages by inserting them in their own layers, adding some extra text formatting with JSSS, and then adding the layers to encompass each one.

The first page is an overview of wildland fire hazards. Begin with the body of the document (see Listing 5.20).

INPUT

Listing 5.20. The basis of the two-in-one page includes a header, footer, and a table in the middle for content.

```
<BODY BGCOLOR="white">
<!-- Heading for the whole document -->
<TABLE BORDER="0" CELLSPACING="0" WIDTH="100%"
       BGCOLOR="#000000" CELLPADDING="10">
 <TR>
  <TD ALIGN="RIGHT" VALIGN="BOTTOM">
   <H1><FONT COLOR="White">...Summer Safety...</FONT></H1>
  </TD>
  <TD ALIGN="LEFT" VALIGN="BOTTOM" WIDTH="110">
   <P><BR>
    <IMG SRC="/mrfd/Images/pointsource-posterized_92x139.jpg"
         HEIGHT="139" WIDTH="92"></P>
  </TD>
  <TD WIDTH="25"> </TD>
 </TR>
</TABLE>
<!-- Beginning of the actual content -->
<TABLE BORDER="0" CELLSPACING="15" WIDTH="100%">
 <TR>
  <TD WIDTH="25%" VALIGN="TOP">
   <H2>Living in the wildland/urban interface
    <IMG SRC="/mrfd/Images/Wildrnss.jpg" WIDTH="162" HEIGHT="122"></H2>
```

```
 </TD>
 <TD VALIGN="TOP">
  <P>Wildfire is a natural element in all ecosystems and environments, and
  Montana is no different. Our climate conditions lead to flammable ground
  cover such as grass, brush and trees. Everyone who has lived in Missoula
  County for any length of time can attest to smoky summer days, or may
  even have seen some of the larger wildfires visible from the valley. Fire
  is a part of our history and a naturally occurring element where we live.</P>
  <P>A new dimension is added to wildfires by the presence of homes. Wildfire
  quickly threatens homes and homeowners, and create a new set of issues for
  firefighters.</P>
  <P><FONT COLOR="Maroon">Missoula Rural Fire District</FONT> has firefighters
  trained for containing fires in the wildland/urban interface. But compared
  to a wildfire, they are very limited in manpower and equipment, and in the
  distances and terrain they protect. The first homes to burn in the recent
  Pattee Canyon fire were lost while firefighters were en route to the
  scene.</P>
  <P>If you're in an area which has a potential for wildfire, you can call
  for a representative from <FONT COLOR="Maroon">Missoula Rural Fire
  District</FONT> to come to your home and make
  <A HREF="/mrfd/Seasonal/Summer/Wildfire_Tips.htm">suggestions for creating
  defensible space</A> around your structures. <CITE>Defensible space</CITE>
  is an <DFN>area of reduced fuel</DFN> which gives your home greater odds of
  surviving a fire. This is a service provided free of charge to district
  homeowners. For more information, call 549-6172 or
  <A HREF="mailto:mrfd@montana.com">send us a note</A>.</P>
 </TD>
 </TR>
</TABLE>
<!-- This is the footer for the document -->
<HR>
<P ALIGN="RIGHT">
 <A HREF="/mrfd/index.htm"><STRONG>MRFD Home</STRONG>
 <IMG SRC="/mrfd/Images/cross.gif" WIDTH="113" HEIGHT="97" ALIGN="MIDDLE">
</A></P>
</BODY>
```

The first task is to create some styles for the document to spice it up a bit. Create three styles—one for the fire department name and one each for the citation (<CITE>) and definition (<DFN>) tags.

```
<STYLE type="text/javascript">
<!--
with (classes.MRFD.all) {
  color = "red";
  fontFamily = "Helvetica, sans-serif";
  fontStyle = "bold";
}
with (tags.CITE) {
  color = "green";
  fontWeight = "bold";
  fontStyle = "normal";
}
```

```
with (tags.DFN) {
  color = "green";
  fontWeight = "normal";
  fontStyle = "italic";
}
//-->
</STYLE>
```

The class for the fire department name is added to the <FONT> tag. This ensures that the text is still highlighted, even if JSSS isn't supported.

```
<FONT COLOR="Maroon" CLASS="MRFD">Missoula Rural Fire District</FONT>
```

The other tags will display according to their default representations in noncompatible browsers and with green bold or italic text in JSSS browsers.

Your next step is to add a layer to encompass the content of the document. First, add the following <LAYER> tag to the top of the content, and complete it with a closing </LAYER>:

```
<LAYER name="content_0" bgcolor="gray">
```

Doing so gives the layer a name you can use to reference it in a script and makes the background opaque so it will block anything else underneath it. Now, pull the content from the second document and add it immediately after the first, along with another set of layer tags. The content portion of your page appears in Listing 5.21.

Listing 5.21. This is the lion's share of the page. It includes the content from two pages put on one page and contained in individual layers.

```
<LAYER name="content_0" bgcolor="gray">
<TABLE BORDER="0" CELLSPACING="15" WIDTH="100%">
 <TR>
  <TD WIDTH="25%" VALIGN="TOP">
   <H2>Living in the wildland/urban interface
    <IMG SRC="/mrfd/Images/Wildrnss.jpg" WIDTH="162" HEIGHT="122"></H2>
  </TD>
  <TD VALIGN="TOP">
   <P>Wildfire is a natural element in all ecosystems and environments, and
   Montana is no different. Our climate conditions lead to flammable ground
   cover such as grass, brush and trees. Everyone who has lived in Missoula
   County for any length of time can attest to smoky summer days, or may
   even have seen some of the larger wildfires visible from the valley. Fire
   is a part of our history and a naturally occurring element where we live.</P>
   <P>A new dimension is added to wildfires by the presence of homes. Wildfire
   quickly threatens homes and homeowners, and create a new set of issues for
   firefighters.</P>
   <P><FONT COLOR="Maroon" CLASS="MRFD">Missoula Rural Fire District</FONT>
   has firefighters trained for containing fires in the wildland/urban
   interface. But compared to a wildfire, they are very limited in manpower
   and equipment, and in the distances and terrain they protect. The first
   homes to burn in the recent Pattee Canyon fire were lost while firefighters
   were en route to the scene.</P>
```

```
    <P>If you're in an area which has a potential for wildfire, you can call
    for a representative from <FONT COLOR="Maroon" CLASS="MRFD">Missoula Rural
    Fire District</FONT> to come to your home and make
    <A HREF="/mrfd/Seasonal/Summer/Wildfire_Tips.htm">suggestions for creating
    defensible space</A> around your structures. <CITE>Defensible space</CITE>
    is an <DFN>area of reduced fuel</DFN> which gives your home greater odds of
    surviving a fire. This is a service provided free of charge to district
    homeowners. For more information, call 549-6172 or
    <A HREF="mailto:mrfd@montana.com">send us a note</A>.</P>
   </TD>
  </TR>
 </TABLE>
</LAYER>

<LAYER name="content_1" bgcolor="gray" visibility="hide">
<TABLE BORDER="0" CELLSPACING="15" WIDTH="100%">
 <TR>
  <TD WIDTH="25%" VALIGN="TOP">
   <H2>Wildfire...Are you prepared?
   <IMG SRC="/mrfd/Images/flashover_small_100x118.jpg" WIDTH="160" VSPACE="10">
   </H2>
  </TD>
  <TD VALIGN="TOP">
   <P>More and more people are making their homes in woodland settings -- in
   or near forests, rural areas or remote mountain sites. There, homeowners
   enjoy the beauty of the environment but face the very real danger of
   wildfire.</P>
   <P>Wildfires often begin unnoticed. They spread quickly, igniting brush,
   trees and homes. Reduce your risk by preparing now -- before wildfire
   strikes. Meet with your family to decide what to do and where to go if
   wildfires threaten your area. Follow the steps listed here to protect your
   family, home and property.</P>
  </TD>
 </TR>
 <TR>
  <TD WIDTH="25%" VALIGN="TOP">
   <HR>
   <H2>Creating defensible space...</H2>
  </TD>
  <TD VALIGN="TOP">
   <HR>
   <UL>
    <LI>Design and landscape your home with wildfire safety in mind. </LI>
    <LI>Select materials and plants that can help contain fire rather than
    fuel it. </LI>
    <LI>Use fire resistant or non-combustible materials on the roof and
    exterior structure of the dwelling. </LI>
    <LI>Treat wood or combustible material used in roofs, siding, decking
    or trim with UL-approved fire-retardant chemicals. </LI>
    <LI>Plant fire-resistant shrubs and trees. For example, hardwood trees
    are less flammable than pine or spruce. </LI>
   </UL>
  </TD>
 </TR>
 <TR>
```

5

continues

Listing 5.21. continued

```
<TD WIDTH="25%" VALIGN="TOP">
 <HR>
 <H2>Practice wildfire safety...</H2>
 </TD>
<TD VALIGN="TOP">
 <HR>
 <P>Find out how you can promote and practice wildfire safety around your
 home and property.</P>
 <UL>
  <LI>Contact your local fire department, health department or forestry
  office for information on fire laws. </LI>
  <LI>Make sure that fire vehicles can get to your home. </LI>
  <LI>Clearly mark all driveway entrances and display your name and
  address. </LI>
  <LI>Report hazardous conditions that could cause a wildfire. </LI>
  <LI>Teach children about fire safety. Keep matches out of reach. </LI>
  <LI>Post fire emergency telephone numbers. </LI>
  <LI>Plan several escape routes away from your home -- by car and by
  foot.</LI>
  <LI>Talk to your neighbors about wildfire safety.  Plan how the
  neighborhood could work together after a wildfire. </LI>
  <LI>Make a list of your neighbors' skills such as medical or
  technical. </LI>
  <LI>Consider how you could help neighbors who have special needs such
  as elderly or disabled persons. </LI>
  <LI>Make plans to take care of children who may be on their own if
  parents can't get home. </LI>
 </UL>
 </TD>
 </TR>
</TABLE>
</LAYER>
```

Now you need a way to select a page to view. Use a drop-down list in a form near the top of the page that calls a function to display the appropriate page.

```
<FORM name="topic">
Choose a topic:
<SELECT name="choice" onChange="showPage(this.selectedIndex)">
  <OPTION>The Wildland/Urban Interface</OPTION>
  <OPTION>Preparing for Wildfire</OPTION>
</SELECT>
</FORM>
```

There are two important items in the argument for the call to showPage. The first is this, which refers to the current element in the current form. The second is selectedIndex, which returns a number corresponding to the item chosen. Because you're working with computers, the first option is 0, the second is 1, the third 2, and so on.

The last step is to create the script to hide and display each of the layers. You should recognize the function from other examples in this chapter.

5

```
<SCRIPT language="javascript">
<!--
visibleLayer = "content_0";
function showPage ( layerIndex ) {
  chosenLayer = "content_" + layerIndex;
  document.layers[ visibleLayer ].visibility = "hide";
  document.layers[ chosenLayer ].visibility = "show";
  visibleLayer = chosenLayer;
//-->
</SCRIPT>
```

Start this script by initializing the pointer to the current visible layer. Then, the function will accept the index from the selection list and use it to build the name of the desired layer. The current layer is hidden, the selected layer is displayed, and the pointer to the current layer is updated.

When you combine the style, script, and content, the result is a drop-down list with which users can select either page at their whim (see Figure 5.18). You can also easily extend it by adding additional layers and options to the form. If users view this page on an incompatible browser, each of the layer tags is ignored, and the combination is viewed as one big page.

Figure 5.18.

When the user picks a page from the list, it is automatically displayed in the window without any work from the browser.

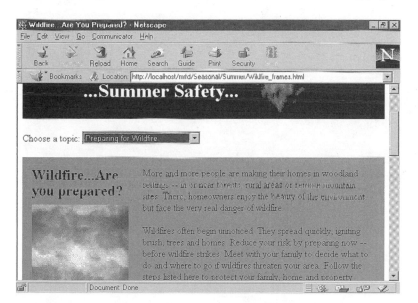

There is one last item. Did you see the hyperlink in the first layer? It used to point to the page that contained the second layer. You can make this compatible with any browser, however. First, add an anchor immediately following the second layer tag:

```
<A name="fire_tips"></A>
```

Then, modify the hyperlink to work with your script on compatible browsers and to jump to the anchor on incompatible browsers:

```
<A HREF="#fire_tips" onClick="showPage(0)">suggestions for creating
defensible space</A>
```

When a user clicks this link on a compatible browser, the `click` event handler catches the user action before an attempt is made to jump to the anchor. On an incompatible browser, the `onClick` part of the tag is ignored, and the browser jumps to the anchor.

This chapter and the few examples just scratch the surface of what's possible when you combine JavaScript with style sheets. As you've seen, you're depending a lot on event handlers to find out what the user wants to do. So you'll finish today's work with a look at the different options for determining user actions.

Chapter **6**

Dynamic HTML Events

As you'll see over the next few days, events are what drive Dynamic HTML. Dynamic HTML is not just a static process that happens regardless of what the user does—it must be able to react to the user's actions appropriately.

NEW TERM An *event* is anything that happens in the life of an HTML page while it resides on the browser. This includes loading the page from the server, unloading the page to get a new page, and everything in between, such as mouse clicks, mouse movements, and form input.

What we require for DHTML is a mechanism for responding to the events. This mechanism is called *event handling*. You saw this in Chapter 5, "JavaScript Style Sheets," in which layers were hidden and displayed in response to pressing buttons. When JavaScript detected the button push using the onClick event handler, a function was invoked that responded to that specific event.

NEW TERM *Event handling* is the process of detecting an event and performing some action as a result.

NOTE

Events are nothing new. Every programming language has them—C, Java, BASIC, Fortran, COBOL. They are a requisite item for interaction with the program's environment, which includes the user.

Why should you care about events on an HTML page? Events are the first step in transforming Web pages from electronic versions of printed books into interactive programs. With HTML events, the Web page is now enabled to also respond to its environment. This is very similar to real programs, only with much less programming involved.

Event handlers look just like any other HTML attribute. Each event begins with on and ends with the event name. The value of the attribute is the name of a scripting function.

Events happen on three basic levels: documents, forms, and individual elements. The rest of this chapter explores the different events that happen at each of these levels. In some cases, an event is unique to Netscape or Microsoft products. When this is the case, I've added a tip to let you know.

The Event Object

The Event object, a new addition to the world of event handling, enables you to receive more information about events and the conditions on the document and browser at the time the event occurred. The object is passed as an argument to an event handler when the event occurs.

For example, when the user clicks a mouse button, the Event object contains the type of event (mouseclick), the x and y positions of the cursor when the click occurred, a number indicating which button was used, and information about any modifier keys (Control, Alt, Meta, or Shift) that were pressed at the time of the event. The properties of the Event object vary from one event to another.

One of the more useful features of the Event object includes provisions for capturing events before any other function has a chance to process the event. For example, if you wanted to capture any mouse click on the page, you would include a line in your script such as this:

```
document.captureEvents(Event.CLICK);
```

This code directs the browser to intercept all events that are equal to the CLICK property of the Event property. Of course, this isn't quite enough to be effective. After you've captured the event, you must know what to do with it. The event handler for events captured in this fashion accepts one argument representing the captured Event object.

```
<SCRIPT language="JavaScript1.1">
function HandleEvent (e) {
  message = "Event = " + e.type + ". "; //identify the event type
  message += "x,y position = " + e.layerX + ", " + e.layerY; //where click was
  alert(message); //alert
  return true;
}
</SCRIPT>
```

NOTE

The last line of the function is a new addition for event handlers. It indicates to the system whether the event was handled to your satisfaction. If nothing else needs to happen, the function should return true. If you want the event to bubble up for additional handling, return false. This function enables you to build a series of event handlers to make sure each event is handled completely while using reusable code.

For example, suppose a user clicks a citation on a page (<CITE>). The citation tag does not want to deal with the event (return false). The citation tag happens to be inside a hyperlink tag (<A>) with its own event handler. The event handler evaluates what the user has done and decides it doesn't want to do anything with the mouse click either (return false). This response passes the event to the next parent object, which, in this example, is the document. If you've created a document event handler, as you're doing here, it takes over event processing. This is where you want processing to end (return true).

It's important to note that using blanket event capturing such as window.captureEvents(Event.CLICK) overrides the event bubbling behavior. If you want to return an event to normal processing after it has been captured in this manner, include window.routeEvent(e); or document.routeEvent(e) before your return statement.

With the function in place, the last step is to direct the browser to run the event handler when the click event is encountered:

```
document.onclick = HandleEvent;
```

The complete script (see Listing 6.1) tells the browser to look for all click events, creates a function to handle those clicks, and then denotes the function as the default handler for clicks. For best results, this script should be placed before the <BODY> tag so that the browser can process it and make it available before the rest of the page is loaded. If the script is placed later in the document, an event could happen before the browser knows about the event handler.

6

INPUT

Listing 6.1. A script to intercept and handle all clicks within a document.

```
<SCRIPT language="javascript">
document.captureEvents(Event.CLICK);
function HandleEvent (e) {
  message = "Event = " + e.type + ". "; //identify the event type
  message += "x,y position = " + e.layerX + ", " + e.layerY; //where click was
  alert(message); //alert
  return true;
}
document.onclick = HandleEvent;
</SCRIPT>
```

TIP

With Netscape, only three places can detect clicks with this script. The first two are hyperlinks and buttons. The last is the "dead space"—a few pixels that surround the Web page that the browser automatically adds when the page loads.

The real beauty of the Event object and event handlers is that it enables you to define generic event handlers for a group of events, because it maintains the control to override the generic handlers for specific instances.

Document Events

For the sake of events, only the part of an HTML page between the <BODY> tags is considered as the document. The <HEAD> and <STYLE> tags contain parts that relate to and control the document, but they have a behind-the-scenes role and aren't a visible part of what the user interacts with.

The `load` and `unload` Events

The load event is generated after the browser has retrieved, but not yet displayed, all the contents between the <BODY> tags. If any initialization is needed before the page is presented to the user, this is the place to put it. You can also use the load event to display copyright information, author bylines, special announcements, or other information that is displayed to users right away before they have a chance to read any other part of the page. The following section of script and HTML displays an alert box after the page is loaded (see Figure 6.1):

```
<SCRIPT language="javascript">
<!--
function showCopyright() {
  alert("All material on this Web site Copyright 1997, MRFD.");
```

 6

```
}
//-->
</SCRIPT>
<BODY onLoad="showCopyright()">
This is the page we're proud of.
</BODY>
```

Figure 6.1.

This alert box displays copyright information before any other part of the page loads. The user must click the button to continue loading the page.

As you might guess, an unload event is the opposite of the load event, although it does not depend on the page loading completely or successfully. An unload occurs any time the browser requests a new page in the same browser window. It has no relationship to whether the current page was completely loaded—it only relates to the call for a new document.

The unload event is used similarly to a load event—it's a good place to take care of housekeeping functions before the new page arrives and wipes out the current page. The primary use of the unload event is to make sure the user has completed a certain action, such as submitting a form. If the user hasn't completed the action, the function triggered by unload can inform the user or perform another action, such as submitting the form anyway. The following script and HTML wait until the browser attempts to unload the page, which will occur only if the user doesn't submit the form. If the unload event occurs, it prompts the user to confirm abandoning the form (see Figure 6.2).

```
<SCRIPT language="javascript">
<!--
function submitAlert() {
   if (confirm("Do you want to submit your form?")) {
      forms[0].submit();
   }
}
//-->
```

6

```
</SCRIPT>
<BODY onUnload="submitAlert()">
<FORM action="doSomething.pl">
Your name here: <INPUT type="text">
<INPUT type="submit" value="Submit">
</FORM>
</BODY>
```

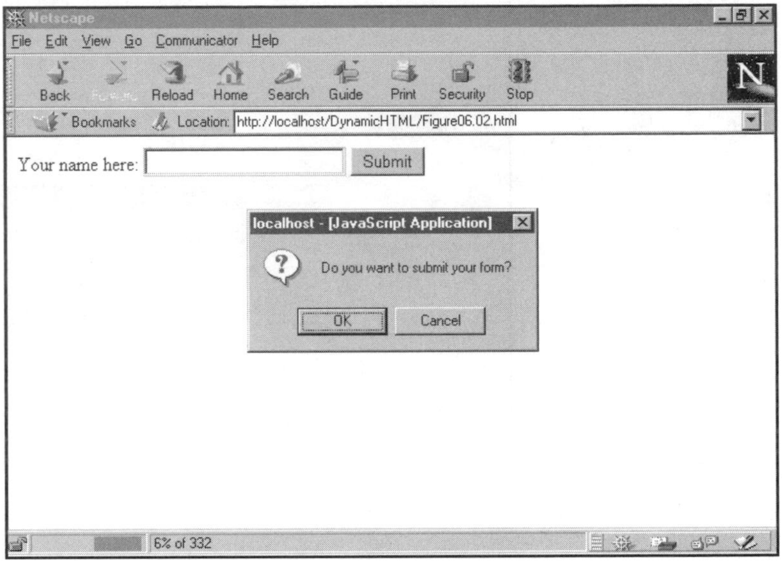

Figure 6.2.

The user entered a new URL for the browser, causing an unload *event to occur. The script confirms the user's intention about the form.*

If a user opens a new browser window, unload is not invoked because the contents of the original window stay the same.

WARNING

You can't use the unload event to create a captive audience for your Web pages. While your scripts can respond to the event, the browser will still finish unloading the current page and move on to the next page.

The mouseOver and mouseOut Events

I've combined these two events because they're typically always used together. The mouseOver event happens when the user places the mouse pointer over a hyperlink or other block element. It is accompanied by a mouseOut event, which happens when the pointer moves out of the block. These events can provide some interesting and useful effects, such as help messages similar to tooltips or message balloons or changes in style (see Listing 6.2 and Figures 6.3 and 6.4).

TIP

Internet Explorer supports mouseOver and mouseOut for all elements on a page, but Navigator supports the events only for hyperlinks and layers.

Listing 6.2. This example changes the color of the heading from green normal text to blue italic text in response to mouse movement.

INPUT

```
<HTML>
HEAD>
<TITLE>mouseover and mouseout</TITLE>
</HEAD>
<STYLE type="text/css">
<!--
H1 {color:green}
-->
</STYLE>
<SCRIPT  language ="javascript">
<!--
function changeColor() {
   head_0.style.color = "blue";
   head_0.style.fontStyle = "italic";
}
function changeColorBack() {
  head_0.style.color = "green";
  head_0.style.fontStyle = "normal";
}
//-->
</SCRIPT>
<BODY>
<H1 id="head_0" onMouseover="changeColor()" nMouseout="changeColorBack()">
This is green, except when the mouse points at it</H1>
<P>This is some body text.</P>
</BODY>
</HTML>
```

In this example, both mouseOver and mouseOut events are used to detect the presence of the mouse pointer resting over the top of the heading text. When the mouse is over the text, the style of the heading is changed. When it leaves, the effect is cleared.

6

Figure 6.3.

When the pointer isn't over the text, the text appears normal.

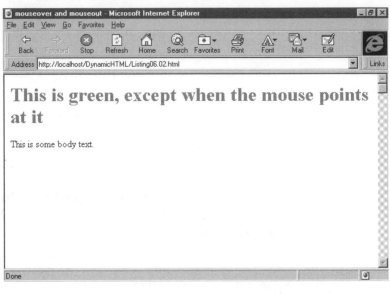

Figure 6.4.

When the pointer is moved over the heading, the color changes. I also added italic text to make the text change more pronounced.

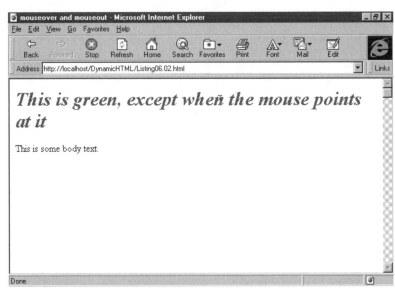

 TIP

Be careful when you use effects such as alert boxes with mouseOver events. The mouseOver event is triggered even when the user just passes the cursor over the selected text without pausing.

You'll learn a couple of other mouse events next—the mouseMove and DragDrop events.

The mouseMove Event

The mouseMove event is used exclusively with the Event object. It is used to track the location of the pointer on the screen within the current page. Implementing the mouseMove event requires a script similar to Listing 6.1 (see Listing 6.3).

INPUT

Listing 6.3. This script and accompanying HTML track the movement of the mouse on the document.

```
<HTML>
<HEAD>
<TITLE>Mouse Movements</TITLE>
</HEAD>
<SCRIPT language="javascript">
document.captureEvents(Event.MOUSEMOVE);
function HandleEvent (e) {
  message = "Event = " + e.type + ". "; //identify the event type
  message += "x,y position = " + e.layerX + ", " + e.layerY; //where click was
  document.displayForm.coordinates.value = message; //display the information
  return true;
}
document.onmousemove = HandleEvent;
</SCRIPT>
<BODY>
<H1>Here's a page</H1>
<P>Howdy</P>
<H1>Here's a page</H1>
<P>Howdy</P>
<H1>Here's a page</H1>
<P>Howdy</P>
<FORM name="displayForm">
<INPUT name="coordinates" type=text size="45">
</FORM>
</BODY>
</HTML>
```

Except for the method of displaying the results to the page, this script is virtually identical to Listing 6.1. It tells the browser to look for any mouse movements and, once found, to pass the movements to the HandleEvent function. The HandleEvent function passes the information to a form field on the screen (see Figure 6.5).

The one problem with invoking this event handler is that it tends to cloud any other events. Virtually any activity with the mouse involves a mouseMove event, so any event handling for mouseMove will always happen with clicks and mouseOver events, adding a bit of extra processing time to the page.

6

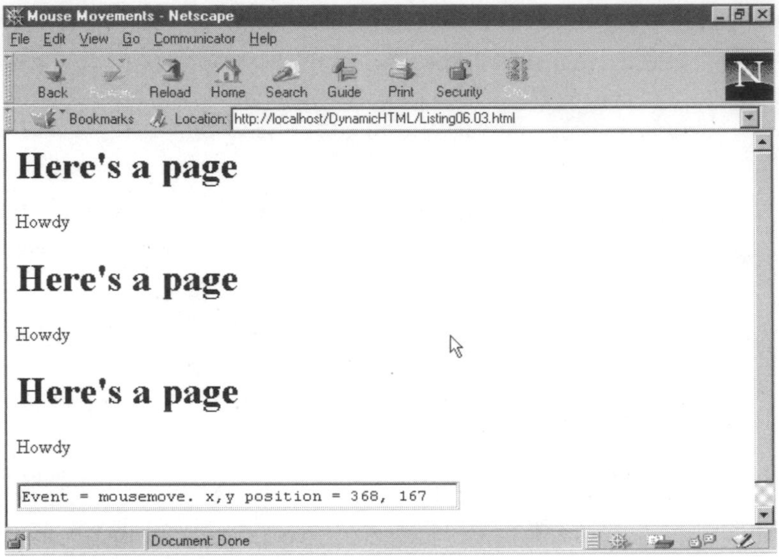

Figure 6.5.

As the pointer traverses the screen, it generates a mouseMove *event that the* HandleEvent *function handles.*

The keyPress, keyDown, and keyUp Events

These three events all relate to keyboard actions from the user. Previously, it wasn't possible to tell what the user was doing at the keyboard, other than to examine what he or she had entered into a text field using the form events discussed later in this chapter. Using these three events enables you to determine when the user presses a key and what the key is. It works very similarly to the click, mouseDown, and mouseUp events described in this chapter.

As you might guess, a keyPress is created by the combination of a keyDown and a keyUp event. The keyPress event always begins with a key pressed down, which enables you to initiate an event handler when the user holds a key down or just presses it momentarily.

All three events include two important properties. The first, the which property, identifies the specific key that the user pressed, using its ASCII code. The second, the modifiers property, returns a number indicating the status of any other special keys held down while the key was pressed (see Table 6.1).

Table 6.1. The possible values of the modifiers property for combinations of special keys.

modifiers Value	Additional Key(s) Pressed
0	None
1	Alt
2	Ctrl
3	Alt+Ctrl

modifiers Value	Additional Key(s) Pressed
4	Shift
5	Alt+Shift
6	Ctrl+Shift
7	Alt+Ctrl+Shift

TIP

> The values in Table 6.1 also apply for the various mouse click events.

The click, mouseDown, and mouseUp Events

The click event detects the user pressing a button on a form. You can also use it to detect users clicking hyperlinks or other elements on the page, depending on the document object model that the browser is using. The click event is typically used in the following form:

```
<INPUT type="button" value="Calculate Total" onClick="calculateTotal()">
```

When the user clicks the button, the event is handed off to the function, where the values from the form are totaled. The onClick event handler is used in a slightly different form with hyperlinks:

```
<A href="anotherPage.html" onClick="return newServer()">Somewhere Else</A>
```

Instead of simply performing processing, this invocation of the click event handler expects a value—either true or false.

TIP

> Actually, using return with onClick will accept virtually any value. If the value is anything but false, however, the browser will still load the destination page.

Using onClick with a hyperlink with a return value could invoke a confirmation box that checks whether the user really wants to jump from the pages on one Web server to another server.

```
<SCRIPT language="javascript">
<!--
function newServer() {
   return confirm("You are leaving our Web server. Are you sure?");
}
//-->
</SCRIPT>
```

A confirmation box has two buttons—Yes and No—that return `true` and `false`, respectively. The value of the button is returned to the browser via the hyperlink tag. If the browser sees `false`, the new page won't load.

If you remember the discussion about key press events, you'll recall that `keyPress` is a combination of `keyDown` and `keyUp`. The same is true for `click` and its two companions, `mouseDown` and `mouseUp`. The three mouse click events also use the `modifiers` property, which identifies any of the special-purpose keys that the user holds down during the click or release operation.

The `dragDrop` Event

The `dragDrop` event occurs whenever a *system* item, such as a file or Internet shortcut, is dropped onto the window using the host system's drag-and-drop mechanism. The typical response for the browser is an attempt to load the item into the browser window. If the `dragDrop` event handler returns `true`, the browser will load the item as appropriate. If the drag-and-drop operation is canceled, however, the event handler returns `false`.

The `dragDrop` event includes a property called `data`. This property is a string that contains the URL of the object that was dropped. You can use the `data` property in conjunction with a parsing script to examine the URL for attempts to load incompatible pages or undesired sites.

The `error` Event

As you'll discover when you are creating scripts to work with both Internet Explorer and Navigator, errors will occur when the browser attempts to load and interpret the page. An `error` event is provided to help you intercept and handle these errors before they generate a message for the user.

Two other items also provoke an error: an image that does not load due to a problem (not caused by a user's action) and a page that does not load completely. This can happen from several causes, such as a break in the Internet connection or a Web server closing its connections.

You have several options for handling errors when they're generated. First, you can suppress all errors and allow the execution of the script to continue by adding a line at the head of the scripting section of the document:

```
<SCRIPT>
<!--
window.onError = null;
//-->
</SCRIPT>
```

This code prevents any error from appearing to the user, although it has several drawbacks. First, it's completely useless for debugging. If you don't see any errors during testing, how are you supposed to know whether everything in your script is working as intended? Second, it prevents the user from knowing whether the script is trying to do something improper or illegal on his or her system, such as modifying a local file.

Your second option is to handle an error all on your own. This option is applied on a tag-by-tag basis with custom functions:

```
<IMG src="picture.gif" onError="imageError(text,URL,lineNum)">
```

Note the three arguments in the function call. The event handler captures the three basic pieces of information generated during an error—the text of the error message, the URL of the affected item, and the line number in the document.

The error-handling function can catch the error and handle it in any way you see fit. If you don't want the script error handler to do anything else with the error event, the function should return true. This lets the script error handler know that the error was handled successfully and that it doesn't need to do anything else.

Your third option is similar to the second. The error is captured in the same way with the same syntax in the tag, but the error-handling function returns false instead of true. This response enables you to perform any custom error handling but still passes the error on to the script error handler to complete the process and display the standard error messages.

Form Events

A lot of script functionality is implemented through forms and buttons. With buttons, users can submit and reset forms, tally totals, and perform other operations on a page. A button is a familiar and friendly tool to perform these actions, and its use is more easily understood than other items, such as text or image hyperlinks. Forms provide an intuitive way for users to enter information, and scripts can also use them as an output tool for responding to user input.

Several events are based on forms and form elements. You'll look at what's available in this section.

The submit and reset Events

The submit and reset handlers are cousins to the click event except that they only work in reaction to the two dedicated-use form buttons.

```
<INPUT type="submit">
<INPUT type="reset">
```

The event handlers for these two buttons are placed within the <FORM> tag rather than within the individual button tags because the event handlers are looking for the action generated by the button, not the button click itself.

```
<FORM name="form1" onSubmit="thankYou()" onReset="beSure()">
```

The script that could go with this form is presented in Listing 6.4.

INPUT

Listing 6.4. Two functions to handle submit **and** reset **events from a form.**

```
<SCRIPT language=javascript>
function thankYou () {
  alert("Thanks for sharing your information with us.");
  return true;
}
function beSure() {
  if ( confirm("Are you sure you want to clear the contents of this form?") )
    return true;
  else
    return false;
}
</SCRIPT>
```

The return values don't affect the event bubbling process. In this case, returning a true enables the form process to complete—submitting or resetting the form's contents, respectively. If either function returns false, their respective processes are not completed—the form is not submitted or the contents remain.

The focus **and** blur **Events**

The focus and blur events occur when a form element, window, or frame gains or loses focus. Either event can be triggered by a method of the same names, or more commonly, by the user clicking another object or using the Tab key on the keyboard to move to another element.

The most common use for the blur event is to perform element-by-element form validation. In the following snippet, you want to make sure a user makes an entry in a particular field. So, use the blur event to check the user's input as soon as the user leaves the element.

```
<SCRIPT language=javascript>
function checkNoInput( inputField ) {
  if ( inputField.value.length = 0 ) {
    alert("This value is required.");
    inputField.focus(); }
</SCRIPT>
<BODY>
...HTML stuff...
<INPUT TYPE="text" VALUE="" NAME="userName" onBlur="checkNoInput(this)">
...More HTML stuff...
</BODY>
```

When a user attempts to leave the field, the onBlur event handler calls the required function to confirm that the userName field isn't empty. If the field is empty, an alert is displayed and the focus method is used to return the user to the offending field.

The focus event is used in a similar manner, but it also has a peculiarity of which you should be wary when used with documents, windows, or frames. Using an alert or confirmation box with the onFocus event handler causes an endless loop of focus events. When you press a button to dismiss the pop-up box, the underlying section receives focus again, which in turn invokes the onFocus event handler.

The change and select Events

The change event occurs after a select, text, or text area form element loses focus (a blur event) and its value is changed from when the element received focus. In the past, the onChange event handler was used to validate data after a user modified it. You can use the change event in conjunction with Dynamic HTML to respond immediately to a user's actions (see the "Two Pages in One" example at the end of Chapter 5, "JavaScript Style Sheets").

The last event associated with forms is the select event. Contrary to the name, it doesn't have anything to do with checkboxes, radio buttons, or selection lists. A select event is triggered when a user selects some of the text within a text or text area field. This event is used very rarely because there isn't a way to determine which text was selected after the event has occurred.

An image Event

There is one final event you need to learn that is associated with the image object. The image object is actually an array of objects representing all of the <IMG> tags on a page. When the user prevents one of these images from loading, the image object generates an abort event.

The abort Event

Every browser is equipped with a stop button or hotkey to prevent a page from completely loading or displaying. The abort event is typically used to avoid loading a large image or number of images. When the user stops a page before the images are complete or prevents a specific image from loading, JavaScript returns an abort event:

```
<IMG src="image.gif" onAbort="imageAborted()">
```

It's important to note that this event isn't affected by enabling or disabling automatic image loading on a browser. This event can occur only when the user stops the image from loading. If another fault prevents the image from loading, such as an invalid image URL, then an error event is generated. The error event is discussed earlier in this chapter.

6

Summary

Events are crucial to the operation of an interactive page. If you want the user to interact with your pages, you must have a way of knowing what the user is doing. Events provide the mechanism with which you can detect the user's actions, whether it's moving the mouse, clicking a button, typing a letter, or loading a new page.

Events occur at three levels: the entire Web document, an individual form, or an element within a form. With Dynamic HTML, most events are now enabled for the entire document for virtually any element.

When an event occurs, an event handler is used to perform the necessary actions in reaction, whether it's displaying a new page, moving a layer, or clearing a form. It's important to identify which specific event you're looking for, because some actions can generate a myriad of events. For example, a mouse click results in four events: mouseDown, mouseUp, click, and mouseMove.

Events are also the conclusion to Day 3 of your exploration into Dynamic HTML. Up to this point, we've concentrated on providing you with the necessary tools to begin building DHTML pages, including the Document Object Model, style sheets, and scripts. We've provided a few examples that show some basic DHTML in action. But it's only been a taste. Starting tomorrow, the real excitement begins.

Q&A

Q You talk interchangeably about events and event handlers. Can you explain the difference between the two?

A Try this analogy. An event is like the doctor taking the little hammer that looks like a tomahawk and hitting your knee with it. The nerves in the knee send a notification of the event to your spine, which is how the event is handled. The spine tells your leg to kick the doctor in the thigh, which is the function invoked by the event handler.

Q How much difference is there between Netscape events and Microsoft events?

A Right now, quite a bit. Microsoft is much closer to the spirit of Dynamic HTML by enabling events such as click and mouseOver to occur for any element on the page. Netscape currently limits events to specific tags, such as click to buttons and hyperlinks and mouseOver to hyperlinks. Some events are also unique to each browser. What is listed in this chapter are the events that are common to both browsers. You can use proprietary events if you want, but remember, you're probably leaving a third of your users out in the cold.

Q Can I force certain events to happen, such as mouse clicks?

A You can create functions that simulate user actions, but there's no way to actually duplicate the user pressing a key or mouse button. You could stand over each user's shoulder and physically force him or her to press keys, but then that's not very practical or polite.

Workshop

The last workshop of the day uses style sheets and events to change a page in response to different user actions. The result is a show-off page—it doesn't really do anything useful, but it gives you a good idea of how to work with events and event handlers.

Anything Goes for the User

This page is one on which each element on the page responds to a different user action: key presses, mouse clicks, and document changes. You'll begin with your favorite sample document from the style sheet chapters (see Listing 6.5).

INPUT

Listing 6.5. This is our starting point—a page with style and no events.

```
<HTML>
<HEAD>
<TITLE>Events galore</TITLE>
</HEAD>
<STYLE type="text/CSS">
<!--
BODY {margin-left: 0.75in; margin-right: 0.75in; margin-top: 0.10in}
H1, H2 {font-family: verdana, helvetica, arial, sans serif}
H1 {font-size:18pt; text-align:left}
H2 {font-size:14pt; text-align:right}
P {font-family:garamond font-size:12pt}
P.left {text-align:left}
P.right {text-align:right}
A {text-decoration: none; font-weight: bold}
-->
</STYLE>
<BODY bgcolor="white">
<H1 id="head_0">Lorem ipsum dolor sit amet</H1>
<P id="para_0">Consectetur <A href="tempor.html" title="Eveniet">
adipisci tempor</A> incidunt ut labore et dolore magna aliqu atib saepe
eveniet ut er reupdiand sint. Nos arsapiente delectus au aut prefer endis
dol tene sententiam, quid est cur verear ne ad eam nc quos tu paulo ante
memorite tum etia ergat.</P>
<H2 id="head_1">Tomporibud autem quinus</H2>
<P id="para_1">Atib saepe eveniet ut er
<A href="sint.html" title="Dodecendesse">
repudiand sint</A> et molestia tenetury sapiente
delctus au aut prefer endis dol. Endiumagist and et dodecendesse
```

continues

Listing 6.5. continued

```
videantur, iustitiam, aequitated fidem. Neque hominy infant efficerd
possit duo contend notiner si effecerit. Natura proficis facile explent
sine julla unura aute enim desiderable.</P>
</BODY>
</HTML>
```

The first event you'll work with is the click. Because there are two hyperlinks on the page, you'll add a script that blocks the user from using them (nobody said this was going to be a considerate page). Add the onClick event handler to each hyperlink tag:

```
<A href="sint.html" title="Dodecendesse" onClick="stopLink()">
<A href="tempor.html" title="Eveniet" onClick="stopLink()">
```

Now you'll add the function to match the event handler. This function will display an alert box and return false so that the hyperlink is not completed:

```
function stopLink () {
  alert{"You really don't want to go there");
  return false;
}
```

That was easy enough, so now let's move on to other mischief. First, you'll add two style classes to use with the two headings:

```
.reallyBig {font-size: 72pt}
.reallySmall {font-size: 4pt}
```

For the first heading, the style will change in conjunction with a mouseOver event on the heading itself:

```
<H1 id="head_0" onMouseover="changeHead('head_0')"
  onMouseOut="changeBack('head_0')">
```

The second heading will be a little more sneaky. The user is required to hold down a mouse button over the second paragraph to change the heading's appearance.

```
<P id="para_2" onMousedown="changeHead('head_1')"
  onMouseup="changeBack('head_1')">
```

The two functions that handle all the work of changing the styles to their extremes and back again are simple affairs. First, the function checks which heading was selected, and then changes the class accordingly. The second function restores the tag to its default status:

```
function changeHead(chosenHead) {
  if (chosenHead == "head_0")
    document.all(chosenHead).className  = "reallyBig";
  else if (chosenHead == "head_1")
    document.all(chosenHead).className = "reallySmall";
}
function changeBack(chosenHead) {
  document.all(chosenHead).className = "";
}
```

For the last trick of the evening, you'll make the first paragraph change into italic when the user presses the Enter key and revert back to normal when the user presses the space bar. As before, begin by adding an event handler to the tag. In this case, add it to the <BODY> tag so you can detect the key presses at any time:

```
<BODY bgcolor="white" onKeypress="shiftItalics(event.keyCode)">
```

In this event handler, you also included a copy of the keyCode property, which provides the ASCII value of the key pressed.

TIP

The keyCode property of the Event object in Internet Explorer is identical to the which property in Navigator.

The completed document, provided in Listing 6.6, includes the functions that provide the actions for the event handlers. As you've read in the narrative up to this point, be careful to note where you place the event handlers within the tags, depending on the event and what you're looking for from the user.

INPUT

Listing 6.6. The final page with its frivolous bells and whistles.

```
<HTML>
<HEAD>
<TITLE>Events galore</TITLE>
</HEAD>
<SCRIPT language="javascript">
function stopLink() {
  alert("You really don't want to go there");
  return false;
}
function changeHead(chosenHead) {
  if (chosenHead == "head_0")
    document.all(chosenHead).className  = "reallyBig";
  else if (chosenHead == "head_1")
    document.all(chosenHead).className = "reallySmall";
}
function changeBack(chosenHead) {
  document.all(chosenHead).className = "";
}
function shiftItalics(theCode) {
  if (theCode == 13) //13 is ascii for return
    document.all("para_0").style.fontStyle = "italic";
  else if (theCode == 32)
    document.all("para_0").style.fontStyle = "normal";
}
```

continues

6

Listing 6.6. continued

```
</SCRIPT>
<STYLE type="text/CSS">
BODY {margin-left: 0.75in; margin-right: 0.75in; margin-top: 0.10in}
H1, H2 {font-family: verdana, helvetica, arial, sans-serif}
H1 {font-size:24pt; text-align:left}
H2 {font-size:12pt; text-align:right}
P {font-family:garamond; font-size:12pt}
P.left {text-align:left}
P.right {text-align:right}
A {text-decoration: none; font-weight: bold}
.reallyBig {font-size:72pt}
.reallySmall {font-size:4pt}
</STYLE>
<BODY bgcolor="white" onKeypress="shiftItalics(event.keyCode)">
<H1 id="head_0" onMouseover="changeHead('head_0')"
➥onMouseOut="changeBack('head_0')">
Lorem ipsum dolor sit amet</H1>
<P id="para_0" class="left">Consectetur
<A href="sint.html" title="Dodecendesse" onClick="stopLink()">
adipisci tempor</A> incidunt ut labore et dolore magna aliqu atib saepe
eveniet ut er reupdiand sint. Nos arsapiente delectus au aut prefer endis
dol tene sententiam, quid est cur verear ne ad eam nc quos tu paulo ante
memorite tum etia ergat.</P>
<H2 id="head_1">Tomporibud autem quinus</H2>
<P id="para_2" class="right" onMousedown="changeHead('head_1')"
➥onMouseup="changeBack('head_1')">
Atib saepe eveniet ut er
<A href="tempor.html" title="Eveniet" onClick="stopLink()">
repudiand sint</A> et molestia tenetury sapiente
delctus au aut prefer endis dol. Endiumagist and et dodecendesse
videantur, iustitiam, aequitated fidem. Neque hominy infant efficerd
possit duo contend notiner si effecerit. Natura proficis facile explent
sine julla unura aute enim desiderable.</P>
</BODY>
</HTML>
```

Figures 6.6 through 6.8 show what happens when three of the events are triggered. In each case, the page reacts according to the function called by the event handler.

This example finishes laying the groundwork for the next four days. From here, you'll get a lot of dirt under your fingernails as you take a hold of Dynamic HTML and use it to push your Web pages to new levels of functionality and interactivity.

Figure 6.6.
The first heading becomes very big when the user places the mouse over it.

Figure 6.7.
The first paragraph of text is converted to italic when the user presses the Return key.

Figure 6.8.
*An alert box is
displayed after the
user clicks a hyperlink.*

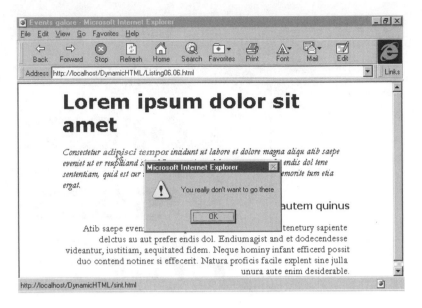

Dynamically Changing Text and Styles

Day 4

Chapter 7

Changing Text Attributes

This and the next five chapters teach you how to use the core features of Dynamic HTML so you can feel competent in using the technology. By following my examples and trying out your own, you will learn Dynamic HTML by doing—probably the best way to learn. Pay especially close attention to the "Workshop" sections at the end of each chapter. The Workshops in Chapters 7 through 12 build upon each other, so you will have created an integrated dynamic Web site by the time you finish Chapter 14.

I hope you feel comfortable with the materials covered so far in Chapters 1 through 6. The examples in Chapters 7 through 12 use both style sheets and scripting extensively. Remember that both JavaScript and CSS1 are implemented in Netscape Navigator 4.0 and Internet Explorer 4.0. You will use both JavaScript and CSS1 in Chapters 7 through 12. There are situations in which I use VBScript instead of JavaScript for Internet Explorer 4.0 Dynamic HTML examples. For the VBScript examples, my JavaScript scripts compile fine, but the features I am demonstrating are not active using JavaScript. I expect the JavaScript scripts to work in future releases of Internet Explorer 4.0.

But, for your sake, I want to provide examples that actually work with the pre-release version of Internet Explorer 4.0, which was available for download from Microsoft's Web site on July 1, 1997.

As you read the rest of the book, keep in mind the issues raised in Chapters 1 through 6 relating to Microsoft, Netscape, W3C, and Dynamic HTML. Chapter 7 begins with examples that more or less meet all three organizations' visions for Dynamic HTML. As you approach Chapter 12, the examples become more biased toward Microsoft's implementation of Dynamic HTML. Microsoft's implementation contains more sophisticated object and event models than Netscape.

In this chapter, you learn about the following:

- [ ] Why you should script in Dynamic HTML
- [ ] The <SCRIPT> tag
- [ ] Putting the script on a Web page
- [ ] Why you should change text attributes
- [ ] How to change text attributes
- [ ] Inline text attribute changes

Why Script in Dynamic HTML?

You use scripts to provide extended logic to a Web browser that places Web page processing under your control. The rest of your Web page is under complete control of the Web browser. For example, you might want to show the current stock price of your favorite company on a Web page. Web browsers are not developed with current stock price lookups as part of their functionality. You can use a script to access a stock server, obtain a stock price, and write out the latest stock price before the Web page finishes loading. On the other hand, when your Web browser encounters an <HR> tag in an HTML file, the Web browser controls how that horizontal line will be drawn on the Web page. Only through tag attributes can you choose from a limited list of variability options. The Web browser is in control.

So, why is there such an increased emphasis on scripts with Dynamic HTML? The answer lies in the event model you studied in Chapter 6, "Dynamic HTML Events." A Web browser that implements Dynamic HTML admits that it does not know how to proceed when an event triggers. Event processing is under Web author control. A Web browser can provide default event handling in obvious situations, but even those can be overridden by your scripts. Event handling scripts did not exist in the world of HTML 1.0, HTML 2.0, and HTML 3.2 because there was no significant event model associated with the mouse and keyboard—no events, no event-handling scripts.

Try to implement event handling using new tags and attributes. Extending HTML to include new tags and attributes for event handling is possible, yet the possible tags and attributes for implementing event handling are quite cumbersome. Consider a simple example of changing the color of a paragraph when a reader clicks a certain image. If you were to design new attributes for a color-changing event, you might come up with the following:

```
<IMG SRC="myimage.jpg" EVENT=onclick CHGCOLOR=PG2 EVTVALUE=Yellow>
```

Your new attributes make sense. The fictitious EVENT attribute tells the Web browser to expect a mouse click and enable the onclick event for the myimage.jpg image. The other two attributes were made up to handle the event. The CHGCOLOR attribute tells the Web browser to change the color of text identified with an ID=PG2 attribute. The EVTVALUE=Yellow attribute tells the Web browser to change PG2's text to yellow whenever the event triggers.

Whether you like my idea of new, dynamic, HTML attributes or not right now, by the end of Chapter 14, "Intelligent Dynamic Design," you will probably realize why no one has tried to create an attribute-based implementation for Dynamic HTML. The list of new attributes needed to implement Dynamic HTML would be enormous. And because you probably will want to do some conditional and looping logic within your event-handling routines anyway, you will appreciate having everything within control of scripts in the first place.

The <SCRIPT> Tag

Believe it or not, the <SCRIPT></SCRIPT> tag pair is extremely helpful in implementing a Web browser. As a Web browser reads an HTML file from left to right and top to bottom, a process called a *parser* carefully reads each <, >, /, =, and space character to determine the look and function of a Web page. The <SCRIPT></SCRIPT> tag pair parses well because it is standard HTML syntax. Imagine you are a Web browser parser. When you encounter the open <SCRIPT> tag, you say to yourself, "Here comes one of those strange scripts again. I had better carefully read the following text and pass it off to the script handler. I will wait until the end </SCRIPT> tag before resuming with my own Web page handling."

All Web browsers interpret script tags in the same way. The <SCRIPT> tag is standard HTML 3.2. Older Web browsers that have no script-handling routines simply throw away the contents of the <SCRIPT></SCRIPT> tag pair with no adverse side effects. The script will not run in older Web browsers.

Putting the Script on a Web Page

In theory, scripts do not belong within the <BODY></BODY> tag pair, but instead belong within the <HEAD></HEAD> tag pair. In practice, Web authors put <SCRIPT></SCRIPT> tag pairs anywhere between the <HTML></HTML> tags. Web browser parsers can handle scripts anywhere within the HTML file. As you surf the Web and look at HTML source code, you will notice

7

that Web authors place scripts in every possible place within the HTML file. I have seen script tags placed outside both the head and body tag pairs. In fact, I might even prefer a location between the </HEAD> and <BODY> tags if I must standardize a location. Standardization is not necessary in the script tag pair's case.

NOTE

I find it interesting to note that you make an intelligent Web browser's job easier when you place your scripts at the bottom of an HTML file. When the script-handling routine evaluates the script for syntax, the script handler can immediately verify that any referenced HTML tags already exist instead of having to wait until the parser is finished.

Every event-handling script you encounter in this book has been placed within a <SCRIPT> </SCRIPT> tag pair. Just to show you the flexibility of the script tags in my examples, I vary how many script functions I place within the script tags. In some cases, I place one function per script tag pair. In other examples, I place all the script functions within a single <SCRIPT> </SCRIPT> tag pair. Either organization works for any example.

The bottom line is that you must place your scripts inside the script tag pair in order for your scripts to be handled properly by the Web browser's parser. Continuing from the Dynamic HTML examples you learned in Chapter 5, "JavaScript Style Sheets," now learn how to use event-handling scripts to dynamically change text attributes.

Why Change Text Attributes?

Authors usually change text attributes to emphasize certain text over other text. Writers have used boldfacing and underlining for years to emphasize a phrase or word in the middle of a long paragraph. Typewriters made underlining easy by providing an underscore key. Boldfacing was a little harder to accomplish on a typewriter, but a writer could double strike characters with a slight offset to boldface them.

Today's word processor includes dozens of tricks you can use to emphasize text. To emphasize a single character in a document, you can change its color, underline it, italicize it, boldface it, superscript it, subscript it, change its font, change its size, or apply one of many different special styles such as "small caps." Many of these same features are available to a Web author using the HTML 3.2 specification. Dynamic HTML comes along only to help an author dynamically make the change. Consider the letter B. Using HTML 3.2, you can change the appearance of the letter B by using any of the tags in Table 7.1.

Table 7.1. The many ways to format the letter B.

Tag Sequence	Effect
`<B>B</B>`	Boldfaced B
`<I>B</I>`	Italicized B
`<U>B</U>`	Underlined B
`<SUB>B</SUB>`	Subscripted B
`<SUP>B</SUP>`	Superscripted B
`<FONT COLOR="#0000FF">B</FONT>`	Blue B
`<FONT FACE="Arial">B</FONT>`	Arial B
`<FONT SIZE=6>B</FONT>`	Big B

Also, remember with HTML 3.2 that you can embed one tag pair inside another to add both effects to text. For example, the following tag sequence italicizes and colors the letter B red:

```
<FONT COLOR="#FF0000"><I>B</I></FONT>
```

Dynamic HTML provides an alternative way to emphasize text through the STYLE attribute. As you learned in Chapter 4, "Cascading Style Sheets," and Chapter 5, "JavaScript Style Sheets," when you use the STYLE attribute within a <SPAN> open tag, a character enclosed by the span tag pair is styled by the STYLE attribute value. You could establish the italicized, red letter B just as easily by using the following Dynamic HTML tag sequence:

```
<SPAN STYLE="{color:red;font-style:italic;}">B</I>
```

In either case, the letter B the Web browser displays on your monitor is identical. If you did not intend for the letter B to change its attributes, you would use the HTML 3.2 tag sequence instead of the STYLE attribute. Remember that styles are new to the Dynamic HTML specification only because there is a need for Web authors to use style sheets to simplify the use of the same styles across Web pages and Web sites.

Back to my point: You change text attributes to emphasize text. Sometimes, a certain emphasis represents specific information. For example, in a list of current stock quotes, red stock values can indicate stocks that have lost value recently, and green stock values can indicate stocks that have gained value. Black quote values might not have changed in a certain time period.

Formatting conventions are great, but the convention usually must evolve over time before your readers understand its significance. Of course, you can always explicitly state your conventions on the Web page if you want to use text attributes as additional information.

7

You might already know about a feature of most Web browsers that dynamically changes text to provide additional information. Can you think of which feature that is? When you visit a link and come back to the originating page, the link text changes color to let you know that you have recently followed that link.

Changing Text Attributes

You can use Dynamic HTML to dynamically change text attributes in response to your reader's mouse or keyboard actions. Remember that JavaScript has been available in Netscape Navigator since release 2.0. Using Netscape Navigator 2.0 and JavaScript, you could change the attributes of text on a Web page each time the page was loaded in a Web browser. This is quite different from Dynamic HTML's dynamically changing text. When you use Dynamic HTML, you do not need to deliver the Web page from the Web server each time you want to change a text attribute. The Web browser simply redraws any part of the page that needs redrawing. You eliminate the download and parsing steps that are required of multiple Web page delivery.

A JavaScript snippet from a Netscape Navigator 2.0 Web page might look like the following:

```
<SCRIPT>
...
if(stockchange > 0) {
    document.writeln("<FONT COLOR="00FF00">MBO " + MBOvalue + "</FONT>");
} else {
    document.writeln("<FONT COLOR="FF0000">MBO " + MBOvalue + "</FONT>");
}
...
</SCRIPT>
```

Here, the color of a stock quote is determined by a `stockchange` value that is obtained by logic that would appear in the script before the `writeln` statements. The script is run once when the page loads and is never revisited.

On the other hand, a Dynamic HTML JavaScript snippet might look like this:

```
<SCRIPT>
...
if(stockchange > 0) {
    Q1.style.color=="green";
} else {
    Q1.style.color=="red";
}
...
</SCRIPT>
```

With Dynamic HTML, the stock coloring lines could be revisited over and over based on any available Dynamic HTML event. The script function could be run initially by the onload event and then run again each time a user clicks a certain image on the Web page. The Web server need not be disturbed to change text attributes.

NOTE

> But, of course, in the stock example the stock quote server would need to be disturbed several times if the stockchange value is to change over time.

You might still be wondering how a script refers to the text it wants to alter. In other words, what is the significance of the Q1 object identifier in the last Dynamic HTML snippet? Remember that HTML elements are instantiated as objects through the ID attribute. You can imagine that somewhere in the Web page that contains the Dynamic HTML snippet there is a <P ID=Q1> paragraph open tag that instantiates the Q1 paragraph as an object to the Dynamic HTML object model. The script then tells the Web browser to change the text in the Q1 paragraph according to the object style attribute that follows the object identifier.

The examples presented in this chapter do not use <STYLE></STYLE> tag pairs or style sheets. In Chapter 8, "Dynamically Changing Style," you learn how to use style tags. This chapter breaks dynamic changes down to the basics; nothing is more basic than changing text size and color. Two complete examples follow in the next sections.

Changing Text Size

For a dynamic changing text size example, create a simple list of 14 dynamic mouse and keyboard events on a Web page. A reader can double-click on any event name in the list to increase the font size of that word.

TECHNICAL NOTE

> The examples in this chapter comply with the latest information provided by the World Wide Web Consortium as communicated by its Web site and were tested and proven to work using the pre-release version of Microsoft's Internet Explorer 4.0. Similar effects can be created using layers and Netscape's Navigator 4.0, as seen in Chapter 5.

Often, a reader uses an online directory to look up a specific piece of information from an existing list. Perhaps a reader will visit a Web page that contains telephone numbers for a customer service department within a major airline company. You can add the capability for a user to dynamically change the appearance of a specific phone number after the online reference is created using Dynamic HTML. For a phone listing, dynamically changing text is very helpful for a reader. As she dials the phone number, she can focus on the one item in the list that looks different from all the others.

The example here uses a simple list of dynamic mouse and keyboard events to represent any online list a reader might encounter. You want to let the reader dynamically change the text for any event names in the list. Your first decision is which Dynamic HTML event to use to specify an item in the list. Probably you would agree that the onmouseover, onclick, and ondblclick events are the best events to use to select an item from a list. In this example, the ondblclick event is implemented.

Your next decision is which attribute to change to make one list item stand out from the rest of the list. If you look back to Chapter 4, you encounter many different text attributes that are specified within the CSS1 specification. You could change any of those attributes to make text stand out. In this example, the text size changes. When a reader double-clicks on a mouse or keyboard event name, her selected list item's font size changes to 32 points.

NEW TERM   A *point* is a font size unit of measurement that is equivalent to one-seventy-secondth of an inch (1/72). Points refer to vertical space (height) on a screen or paper, and font heights are independent of font widths. Fonts generally get wider as their font sizes increase, but different fonts have different height-to-width ratios.

Listing 7.1 shows the implementation of a dynamically changing text size example. Look at the example and try to anticipate how the script works, then continue reading for a detailed explanation after the listing.

INPUT   ## Listing 7.1. A changing font size example.

```
<HTML>
<HEAD>
<TITLE>Dynamic HTML Events</TITLE>
</HEAD>
<BODY BGCOLOR="#FFFFFF" TEXT="#0000FF">
<H2>Dynamic HTML Mouse and Keyboard Events</H2>
<HR>
<BR>
<P ID=PG1 ondblclick="bigPG1();">
onchange
<P ID=PG2 ondblclick="bigPG2();">
onclick
<P ID=PG3 ondblclick="bigPG3();">
ondblclick
<P ID=PG4 ondblclick="bigPG4();">
onfocus
<P ID=PG5 ondblclick="bigPG5();">
onkeydown
<P ID=PG6 ondblclick="bigPG6();">
onkeypress
```

```
<P ID=PG7 ondblclick="bigPG7();">
onkeyup
<P ID=PG8 ondblclick="bigPG8();">
onmouseover
<P ID=PG9 ondblclick="bigPG9();">
onmousedown
<P ID=PG10 ondblclick="bigPG10();">
onmousemove
<P ID=PG11 ondblclick="bigPG11();">
onmouseout
<P ID=PG12 ondblclick="bigPG12();">
onload
<P ID=PG13 ondblclick="bigPG13();">
onmouseup
<SCRIPT LANGUAGE=JavaScript>
function bigPG1() { PG1.style.fontSize = "32pt"; }
function bigPG2() { PG2.style.fontSize = "32pt"; }
function bigPG3() { PG3.style.fontSize = "32pt"; }
function bigPG4() { PG4.style.fontSize = "32pt"; }
function bigPG5() { PG5.style.fontSize = "32pt"; }
function bigPG6() { PG6.style.fontSize = "32pt"; }
function bigPG7() { PG7.style.fontSize = "32pt"; }
function bigPG8() { PG8.style.fontSize = "32pt"; }
function bigPG9() { PG9.style.fontSize = "32pt"; }
function bigPG10() { PG10.style.fontSize = "32pt"; }
function bigPG11() { PG11.style.fontSize = "32pt"; }
function bigPG12() { PG12.style.fontSize = "32pt"; }
function bigPG13() { PG13.style.fontSize = "32pt"; }
</SCRIPT>
<HR>
</BODY>
</HTML>
```

When a reader accesses the Web page in Listing 7.1, the page loads as shown in Figure 7.1. The figure shows a simple list of dynamic mouse and keyboard events and a heading. All text is the same color, and all list items are the same size.

Figure 7.2 shows the same Web page after a reader clicks three items in the event list: onclick, ondblclick, and onmouseover. Perhaps the reader is interested in creating a dynamically changing text example. She double-clicks the three dynamic events she is considering for use in her Web page.

Listing 7.1 begins with a simple <BODY> open tag that is extended to designate a white background with blue body text. Each list item is a separate paragraph identified with a <P> tag. Within each paragraph tag, the paragraph is named with an ID attribute. I also implement the Dynamic HTML event model by adding an ondblclick attribute, to which I assign the appropriate script function value. Therefore, for example, the first paragraph tag for the onchange list item looks like the following, where the paragraph name is PG1 and its respective script function is bigPG1():

```
<P ID=PG1 ondblclick="bigPG1();">
```

Figure 7.1.
A list of Dynamic HTML mouse and keyboard events.

Dynamic HTML Events - Microsoft Internet Explorer
File Edit View Go Favorites Help

Dynamic HTML Mouse and Keyboard Events

onchange

onclick

ondblclick

onfocus

onkeydown

onkeypress

onkeyup

onmouseover

onmousedown

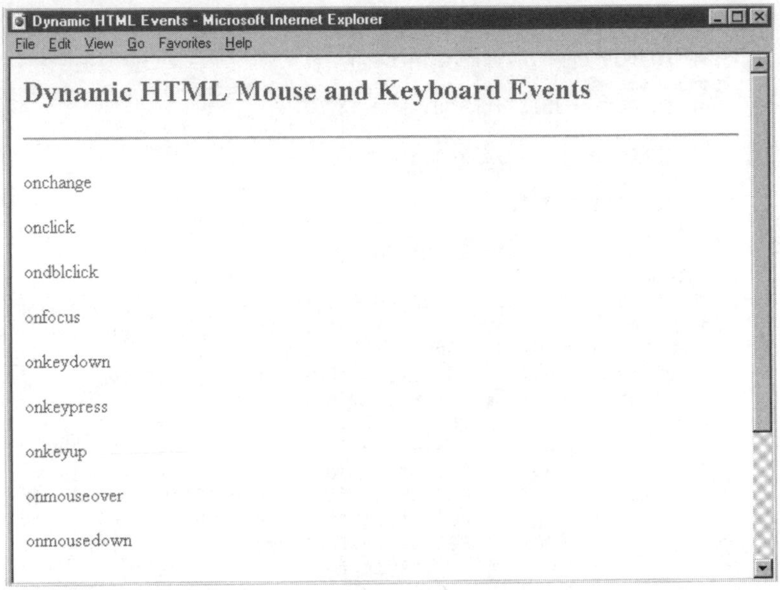

Figure 7.2.
After selecting three items in the list.

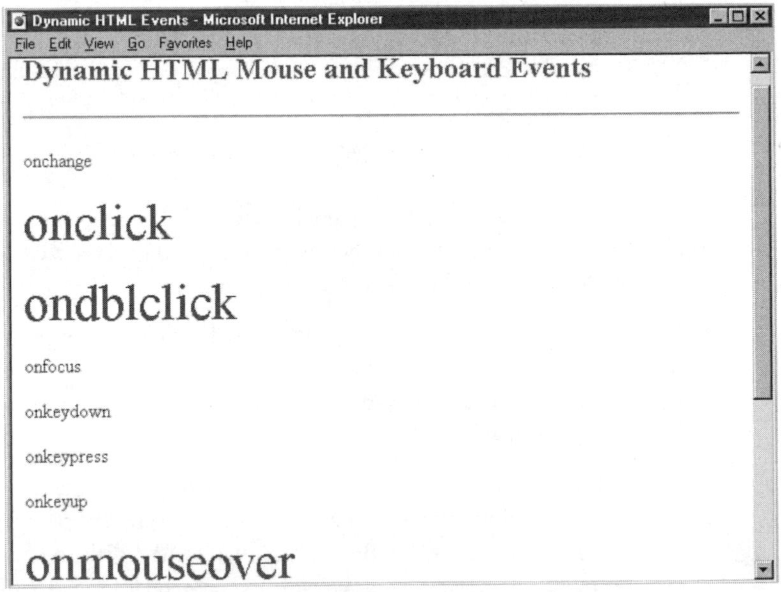

Dynamic HTML Events - Microsoft Internet Explorer
File Edit View Go Favorites Help

Dynamic HTML Mouse and Keyboard Events

onchange

onclick

ondblclick

onfocus

onkeydown

onkeypress

onkeyup

onmouseover

As you will see in upcoming chapters, you can use other tags to identify text elements in a Web page. The <P> tag is a very familiar tag. You could use <FONT>, <SPAN>, or <DIV> tags instead, for example.

After identifying your paragraphs by name and associating Dynamic HTML events with your paragraphs, write the script functions that make the dynamic changes. In Listing 7.1, 13 script functions are created to handle double-click events for the 13 paragraphs on the page. The 13 scripts are a bit redundant, as you will see later in this chapter, but I want to emphasize the basics here.

Each function is similar to the first, which follows:

```
function bigPG1() { PG1.style.fontSize = "32pt"; }
```

JavaScript was used to create the script. The JavaScript language contains the keyword function that is used to start the function bigPG1(). The function is simple. I change paragraph PG1's style by referencing the style's fontSize attribute. Through a simple assignment paragraph, PG1 becomes 32 points high on the Web page.

NOTE

JavaScript is very flexible in terms of how you physically write the script. You could just as easily write the following, because JavaScript ignores newline and carriage return characters:

```
function bigPG1() {
     PG1.style.fontSize = "32pt";
}
```

Remember for later that VBScript is not as flexible with code layout.

All 13 script functions are placed within a `<SCRIPT></SCRIPT>` tag pair. Remember that all scripts must be within a `<SCRIPT></SCRIPT>` tag pair in order to parse correctly. The opening `<SCRIPT>` tag includes the LANGUAGE=JavaScript attribute that tells the Web browser to interpret the script syntax as JavaScript syntax.

If you look at Chapter 4, you see that the CSS1 style specification identifies font size using a font-size:32pt format. For many attributes, the attribute in the CSS1 standard can be converted to its respective scripting style property by removing the hyphen and capitalizing the word after the hyphen. In my case, for the font-size CSS1 attribute I use style.fontSize within my scripts.

To recap, to create dynamically changing text you first create paragraph tags around each item you want to change independently, and add an ID attribute and event attribute to each paragraph tag. Finally, create a script function that matches the same name as the paragraph event attribute value. The script function contains a single line that assigns a new value to the appropriate style property.

7

Changing Text Color

Before I give you an example on dynamically changing text color, I want to give you a primer on color representation in Dynamic HTML. Color can be represented in two ways: by a simple string identifier or by an RGB component list. The simple string identifier is more straightforward. To represent red, you can use the string Red. To represent the color yellow, you can use the string Yellow. You can represent basic colors using their common names.

On the other hand, you can define more specific colors by using their red, green, and blue components. The physical nature of light enables you to represent most colors by levels of red, green, and blue components. Many Web technologies use a red/green/blue (RGB) color definition scheme. Televisions create every color you see on a color television screen using red, green, and blue electron beams.

The Dynamic HTML format for specifying a color using RGB values uses three short integers that vary from 0 to 255. For example, the color rgb(255,0,0) is bright red, comprised of full red, no green, and no blue. The color rgb(100,0,0) is a significantly darker red color because it uses less red. The color rgb(255,255,0) is a bright yellow. The 0 to 255 scale is linear, so a color using a 100 value is half as bright as a color using 200.

Mixing light colors is different than mixing paint pigment colors. With pigments, mixing yellow and red make orange. With light, you mix red and green to make yellow. Even for colors that can be created by mixing similar components, the relative percentages of each component needed vary between light and pigments. For example, to create the same shade of purple, you would need to combine smaller amounts of red and blue light than red and blue pigments. There are many great books that teach color theory along with all the effects of color on the human eye and the limitations of RGB. I especially find Chapter 13 of *Computer Graphics, Principles and Practice* by Foley, van Dam, Feiner, and Hughes insightful.

The following example on dynamically changing text color uses both the text string and RGB formats to specify color. In my example, I change the color of lengthy paragraphs when a reader clicks anywhere on a paragraph. I assign a new color based on the amount of time that passes between mouse clicks.

Perhaps readers could come to my Web site to test their speed reading skills. If a reader reads a paragraph in less than four seconds, the paragraph becomes red. If a reader reads a paragraph in less than eight seconds, the paragraph turns green. If a reader reads a paragraph in less than 12 seconds, the paragraph becomes blue. If a reader reads a paragraph in less than 16 seconds, the paragraph changes to cyan. If a reader reads a paragraph in over 16 seconds, the paragraph turns purple. A reader can also use the changing color as a bookmark. Any paragraph that remains black has not been read.

JavaScript contains a Date class that can be instantiated in a script. After it is instantiated, you can call one of many available methods to inquire about the system date. In my example, I instantiate a Date type object which I name t with the following line and then obtain the current system time through the getTime() method of the Date object t. The getTime() method returns a long integer that is incremented by one every millisecond.

```
t = new Date();
```

NOTE

A millisecond is one one-thousandth of a second. Although many scientists measure time in nanoseconds (one-billionths of a second), one thousandth of a second is pretty precise for Web page events.

The example in Listing 7.2 also uses the srcElement method of a window event object. The window object is the active Web browser window. The srcElement method returns the object that is the source of an event (in the example, the object on which a reader's clicks) and is assigned to a JavaScript variable as follows:

```
srcElement = window.event.srcElement;
```

A script can then use the srcElement variable to provide the same event handling logic to multiple objects on a Web page. Look at Listing 7.2 for the dynamic color changing paragraph example. Continue reading after Listing 7.2, Figure 7.3, and Figure 7.4 for a detailed explanation of my dynamic color changing paragraph Web page.

INPUT **Listing 7.2. A paragraph color changer.**

```
<HTML>
<HEAD>
<TITLE>Learning About Virtual Reality</TITLE>
</HEAD>
<BODY BGCOLOR="#FFFFFF" onload="setTime();">
<H2>Learning About Virtual Reality</H2>
<HR>
<BR>
<P ID=PG1 onclick="ColorMe();">
A <B><I>virtual reality</B></I> (VR), also called a <B><I>virtual environment
</B></I>, is a three-dimensional computer simulation that provides sensory
information (sight, sound, and/or others) to make you feel that you are in a
"place".  You can experience a virtual environment using a typical personal
computer and a few items of specialized hardware: a 3D graphics card, a  3D
sound card, a head-mounted display, and a 6D tracker. You also need software
designed to display virtual environments.
<P ID=PG2 onclick="ColorMe();">
```

continues

7

Listing 7.2. continued

In order to achieve a believable sense of reality, the computer must be
capable of calculating and displaying sensory information fast enough to fool
the senses. Not long ago such hardware and software was so expensive that
only governments, major universities, and large corporations could afford to
build virtual environments. Now, however, the price of fast computers has
come down, and the exotic peripherals have been simplified to the point that
many people will be able to explore VR.

```
<P ID=PG3 onclick="ColorMe();">
```

A key distinction to VR purists is the fact that the user is immersed in the
computer simulation. All our senses are focused on visiting this new place.
`<B><I>Desktop VR</I></B>` is a subset of VR that does not require all four
conditions of full immersion: Full field of vision display, usually produced
by the wearing of a Head Mounted Display; Tracking of the position and
attitude of the participant's body; Computer tracking of the participant's
movements and actions; Negligible delay in updating the display with feedback
from the body's movements and actions.

```
<P ID=PG4 onclick="ColorMe();">
```

Desktop VR is very popular because it can be used at little additional cost
to a typical personal computer. So, as we wait for VR accessories to come down
in price further, we can introduce VR concepts to a cross-section of society
now. Desktop VR is delivered through computer graphics and multimedia and is
not considered VR by the purists. As long as our senses are distracted by
events outside of the computer simulation, our minds are quick to remember a
virtual place is not reality.

```
<SCRIPT LANGUAGE=JavaScript>
var t,d,srcElement;
function setTime() {
  t = new Date();
  d = t.getTime();
}
function ColorMe() {
  t = new Date();
  d = t.getTime() - d;
  srcElement = window.event.srcElement;
  if (d<4000) {
    srcElement.style.color= "Red";
  } else if (d<8000){
    srcElement.style.color= "Green";
  } else if (d<12000){
    srcElement.style.color= "Blue";
  } else if (d<16000){
    srcElement.style.color= "rgb(0,200,200)";
  } else {
    srcElement.style.color= "rgb(100,0,100)";
  }
  d = t.getTime();
}
</SCRIPT>
<HR>
</BODY>
</HTML>
```

Figure 7.3 shows the HTML file produced by Listing 7.2 as rendered in a Web browser. In Figure 7.3, all paragraphs load black initially.

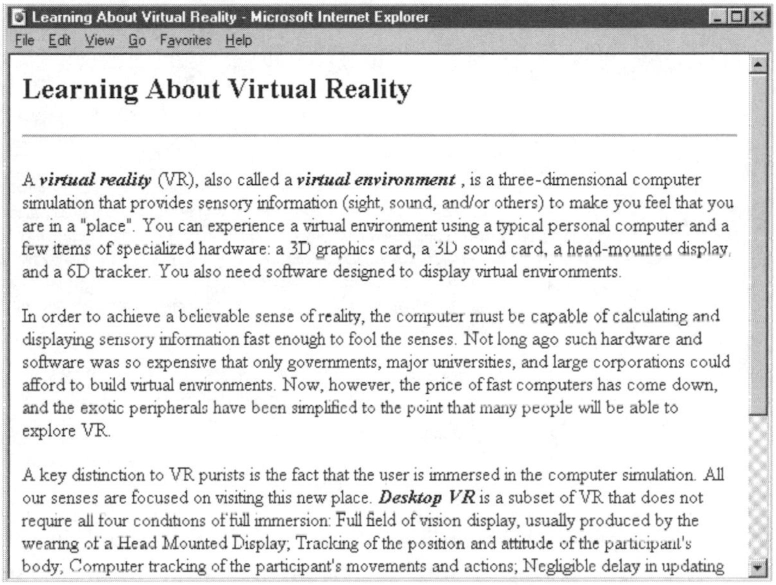

Figure 7.3.

A Web page with four paragraphs.

Figure 7.4 shows the same Web page as Figure 7.3 after you click each paragraph. In Figure 7.4, each paragraph appears in a different color as you vary the amount of time you take to read each paragraph. The paragraphs have changed color one by one as I click on a paragraph when I finish reading it.

Listing 7.2 begins similarly to Listing 7.1. In Listing 7.1, within the <BODY> opening tag, I set the body text color to black and create an onload attribute. The onload event calls my setTime() script function as the Web page loads. Each <P> tag includes two attributes. The first attribute, an ID tag, instantiates the paragraph as an object and gives the paragraph a name. The second attribute, an onclick event, associates the onclick event for each paragraph with a ColorMe() script function.

The paragraph body text in Listing 7.2 is significantly longer than Listing 7.1, but they function identically. After the four body text paragraphs, I create my two script functions within a <SCRIPT></SCRIPT> tag pair. The setText() function stores the system time when the Web page loads. The ColorMe() function colors a paragraph that a reader clicks.

The setText() function is straightforward. The first line instantiates a Date type object named t. The second stores the current system time in a variable called d.

7

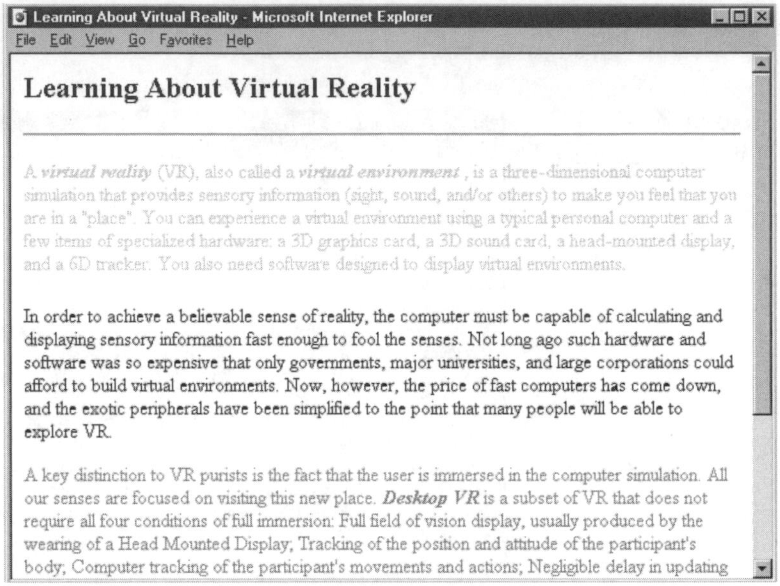

Figure 7.4.

Each paragraph changes color.

> **Learning About Virtual Reality - Microsoft Internet Explorer**
>
> File   Edit   View   Go   Favorites   Help
>
> ## Learning About Virtual Reality
>
> A *virtual reality* (VR), also called a *virtual environment* , is a three-dimensional computer simulation that provides sensory information (sight, sound, and/or others) to make you feel that you are in a "place". You can experience a virtual environment using a typical personal computer and a few items of specialized hardware: a 3D graphics card, a 3D sound card, a head-mounted display, and a 6D tracker. You also need software designed to display virtual environments.
>
> In order to achieve a believable sense of reality, the computer must be capable of calculating and displaying sensory information fast enough to fool the senses. Not long ago such hardware and software was so expensive that only governments, major universities, and large corporations could afford to build virtual environments. Now, however, the price of fast computers has come down, and the exotic peripherals have been simplified to the point that many people will be able to explore VR.
>
> A key distinction to VR purists is the fact that the user is immersed in the computer simulation. All our senses are focused on visiting this new place. *Desktop VR* is a subset of VR that does not require all four conditions of full immersion: Full field of vision display, usually produced by the wearing of a Head Mounted Display; Tracking of the position and attitude of the participant's body; Computer tracking of the participant's movements and actions; Negligible delay in updating

The ColorMe() function is more involved. In the second line of the ColorMe() function, variable d is reassigned with the amount of time that has passed since the d variable was last set. I later set a paragraph's color based on the amount of time that has passed. In the third line, I capture the initiating object in an srcElement variable. The source element will always be one of the four body text paragraphs because they are the only Web page elements that contain the onclick="ColorMe();" attribute.

The next 11 lines contain if...then...else logic. These lines compare variable d to a fixed amount of time and color a paragraph appropriately. If d currently contains less than 4000 milliseconds, the srcElement's style is set to a red color. If d is less than 8000 milliseconds, the paragraph is set to green. If d is less than 12000 milliseconds, the paragraph turns blue. If d is less than 16000 milliseconds, the paragraph is set to cyan. A strong green light added to a strong blue light produces cyan light. If d is greater than or equal to 16000 milliseconds, the paragraph is set to purple. A weak red light added to a weak blue light produces purple light.

> **NOTE**
>
> The quotes around the "rgb(0,0,0)" syntax are required. In this case, you are assigning a value to an element's style instead of calling a function. The script handler will convert the value to a color.

Finally, I set the d variable to the current system time. The system time of the current mouse click will be used in the next ColorMe() script function call to determine the amount of time a reader spends reading the paragraph on which she clicks.

Inline Text Attribute Changes

For simple dynamic text effects, you can set up your events and text attribute changes from within the HTML tags themselves. Any dynamic change to a Web page that you create solely within a single HTML tag is called an *inline* change. Inline changes are very straightforward.

As an example, consider Listing 7.3, which dynamically changes the font size of a heading. The HTML file is quite short.

INPUT   **Listing 7.3. An inline text attribute change.**

```
<HTML>
<HEAD>
<TITLE>Test</TITLE>
</HEAD>
<BODY BGCOLOR=#FFFFFF>
<H1 onmouseover="this.style.fontSize=128"
    onmouseout="this.style.fontSize=32">
Hello World
</H1>
</BODY>
</HTML>
```

In Listing 7.3, you see two event attributes on the open <H1> tag. The onmouseover attribute sets up an event to trigger when a reader places his or her mouse over the contents of the heading. When the mouse rests over the heading, the text of the heading changes to 128 points in size. The onmouseout attribute sets up an event to trigger when a reader moves the mouse off the heading. When the mouse leaves the heading area, the text of the heading changes to a much smaller 32 points.

To change text attributes dynamically within an HTML tag, you take advantage of built-in features of the Dynamic HTML object model. The this keyword refers to the HTML element identified by the tag within which the this word is contained. All text elements have a style object you can dynamically change. You then add the appropriate style property name and assign the property a new value. You could dynamically change color by assigning the this.style.color property a value such as Red.

Figure 7.5 shows the Web page in Listing 7.3 in a state in which the user has placed the mouse over the heading. Figure 7.6 shows the same Web page after the user moves the mouse off the Hello World heading.

7

NOTE   You can use the inline technique to dynamically change other Dynamic HTML object properties besides text attributes. An interesting object to consider changing is the mouse cursor. The beta 2 pre-release version of Internet Explorer 4.0 includes dynamic access to the cursor object.

Figure 7.5.

The Web page when the user places the cursor over the heading.

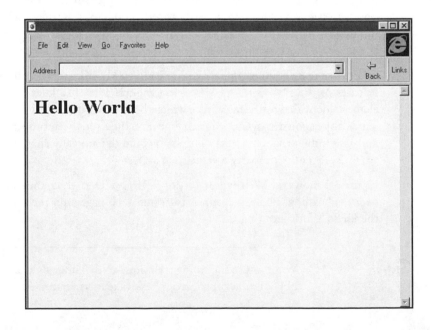

Figure 7.6.

The Web page after the user moves the cursor away from the heading.

Inlining is concise, but not especially robust. For inline dynamic changes, you do not need to create any scripts for your Web pages, yet scripts are a feature that enable you to add conditional logic to your Web pages.

Summary

In this chapter you take Dynamic HTML for a test run to make some dynamic changes to text. This chapter focuses both on dynamically changing text color and text size. All dynamic changes require that you fully understand the dynamic object model and dynamic event model as well as the JavaScript scripting language.

To create dynamically changing text, you first create paragraph tags around each text element you want to change independently. You add an ID attribute and an event attribute to each paragraph tag. For each event attribute, you create a script function that matches the same name as the paragraph event attribute value. Your script function changes the appropriate text element's style property to make the text attribute change.

The JavaScript language contains many powerful objects you can use to extend your Web page through script logic. You can use the Date object to time dynamic events through access to the system date. You can use a window event's srcElement property to reference the object on a Web page that initiates an event. Chapters 8 through 12 build on this chapter. Many of the examples you encounter in later chapters include additional scripting features you could use to extend the examples in this chapter.

Q&A

Q Why do you not use a STYLE attribute on your <P> tags, yet are still able to access the paragraph's style object dynamically?

A I could have added a STYLE attribute to set each paragraph's text attributes at load time, but the STYLE attribute is not necessary. Without a STYLE attribute, text attributes are still set by default. The capability to dynamically change text attributes is enabled through the ID attribute and the type of tag in which the ID attribute is contained. If the ID attribute exists inside an <IMG> tag, changing text attributes would have no effect on that image. After the ID attribute instantiates a text element object, you can change that text element through its style object with or without a STYLE attribute.

Q You mention the limitations of RGB in this chapter. Can you be more specific as to what limitations?

A Sure. The RGB color specification uses a positive scale for each red, green, and blue component. Some colors seen by the human eye are actually produced by a negative red value, the amount of absence of red light. Therefore, although there are more than enough colors to choose from with RGB, it is not completely whole. The French tried to popularize an altered RGB model that normalized the red component to a positive scale. But, to this day, that standard has not caught on due to the additional calculation required.

Q **I notice in Listing 7.2 that you make no distinction as to the order of the paragraphs a reader clicks on. A reader could click on the same paragraph twice to reset the clock, right?**

A Right! I like the fact that a reader can read the paragraphs in any order and still get a correct timing as long as she clicks on each paragraph she reads. If the cheating part were a concern, you could check to see whether the paragraph was still black before accepting a new timing. You use a similar technique in the second example of Chapter 9, "Dynamically Changing Content."

Quiz

Take the following quiz to see how much you've learned in this chapter.

Questions

1. How few <SCRIPT></SCRIPT> tag pairs are needed to create 20 script functions for a Web page?

2. How would you assign an Arial font face to a paragraph named PG16?

3. What scripting line(s) do you use to access the system date?

4. How would you assign a very dark brown color to the paragraph PG16?

5. How could you simplify the <SCRIPT></SCRIPT> tag pair contents in Listing 7.1?

Answers

1. Only one. You can place all your script functions within the same script tag pair.

2. Because the CSS1 standard assigns font faces through the fontFamily attribute, you can set PG16's style property with

   ```
   PG16.style.fontFamily = "Arial"
   ```

3. First, create a Date object with a line like x = new Date();. Then, call the getTime() method with a line like y = x.getTime();.

4. Brown is comprised of a low amount of red light mixed with a low amount of green light. Therefore, the following line would be appropriate:

   ```
   PG16.style.color = "rgb(20,20,0)"
   ```

5. You could combine all the scripts into a single script function such as

```
var srcElement
function bigPG() {
    srcElement = window.event.srcElement;
    srcElement.style.fontSize = "32pt";
}
```

Workshop

You will build a professional-looking, dynamic Web site incrementally in Chapters 7 through 12. I want you to demonstrate an attractive and appropriate use of Dynamic HTML complete with a quality graphics appeal. You will get started in this chapter by understanding the requirements for the Web site you have been contracted to build. Then, you will put together the static HTML tags needed to distinguish your work from the run of the mill.

In Chapters 8 through 12, I will suggest some improvements that take advantage of new Dynamic HTML features. Consistently, through all five chapters, your goal will be to build a fun and informative Web site. Use the Workshops as a place to learn and experiment with the technology. The examples embedded in the chapter text are very straightforward and not very flashy; the time to add some pizzazz is during the Workshops.

In a remote location of the South Pacific, a deep-sea marine biology team of international researchers has found a new, enormous species of squid. The squid is believed to be blind because it lives at a depth where virtually no light is present. Yet, the behavior of the South Pacific squid is complex and extremely collaborative with others of its own kind. Researchers have been able to detect a squid language spoken at very low frequencies. Two members of the research team have contacted you to build a Web site that will educate the world about the existence of these fascinating creatures. After talking with them for an extensive length of time, you determine that there should be six Web pages associated with their site. You will focus on one page per chapter, laying them out as follows:

- ☐ Chapter 7: A welcome page with anchored hyperlinks to the other five pages
- ☐ Chapter 8: A biology page with information about squid in general
- ☐ Chapter 9: An informational page about each researcher on the team
- ☐ Chapter 10: An interactive page detailing how the squid are tracked from the surface of the ocean
- ☐ Chapter 11: A biology page with information about different known squid populations in the world
- ☐ Chapter 12: A tracking page to keep up with each of the different squid groups

By the time you are finished, you will have created quite an impressive Web site that takes advantage of all the new features of Dynamic HTML. Of course, keep in mind that the content is completely fictitious and in some cases only loosely realistic in terms of the sciences involved.

This chapter gets you started with the welcome page. Open your favorite text editor, and type the text in Listing 7.4 to begin.

INPUT   **Listing 7.4. A giant squid research home page.**

```
<HTML>
<HEAD>
<TITLE>Giant Blind South Pacific Squid Welcome Page</TITLE>
</HEAD>
<BODY BACKGROUND="water.jpg" TEXT=#FFFFFF LINK=FFFF22 VLINK=FF22FF>
<H2>Welcome To The Giant Blind South Pacific Squid Research Page</H2>
<IMG SRC="giant.gif" ALIGN=RIGHT>
We hope you will visit this page often to follow the research of the world
re-knowned <FONT COLOR=#FFFF00><I>Giant Squid Marine Biology Team</I>
</FONT> and keep up with their amazing discoveries as they happen.
Go ahead and bookmark this page.  You won't regret that you have.
We all can learn a lot from blind giant squid in the South Pacific.
<P>
<TABLE BORDER=1>
<TR>
<TD WIDTH=360><CENTER><I>CHOOSE A HYPERLINK</I></CENTER></TD>
</TR><TR>
<TD WIDTH=320><CENTER><I><A HREF="dyn08wrk.htm">
What is a Squid?</A></I></CENTER></TD>
</TR><TR>
<TD WIDTH=320><CENTER><I><A HREF="dyn09wrk.htm">
Who Researches Squid?</A></I></CENTER></TD>
</TR><TR>
<TD WIDTH=320><CENTER><I><A HREF="dyn10wrk.htm">
How Do We Track Giant Squid? </A></I></CENTER></TD>
</TR><TR>
<TD WIDTH=320><CENTER><I><A HREF="dyn11wrk.htm">
How Diverse Are Squid?</A></I></CENTER></TD>
</TR><TR>
<TD WIDTH=320><CENTER><I><A HREF="dyn12wrk.htm">
Get To Know Our Blind Giant Squid Families</A></I></CENTER></TD>
</TR>
</TABLE>
</BODY>
</HTML>
```

Listing 7.4 contains a simple Web page consisting of HTML 3.2-compliant tags and body text. Figure 7.7 shows how the Web page created from Listing 7.4 appears when it is loaded in a Web browser.

Figure 7.7.

Your squid home page.

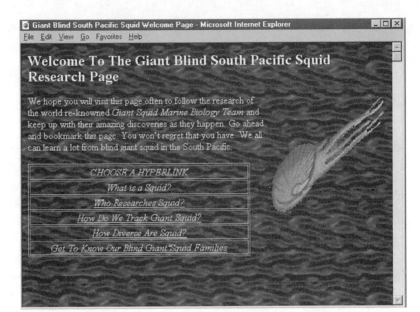

Dynamically Changing Style

In Chapter 7, "Changing Text Attributes," you reviewed examples that demonstrate the power of dynamically changing text attributes to enhance the usability and aesthetics of a Web page. You will continue along that vein in this chapter. Here, you will combine the specifics you learned in Chapter 4, "Cascading Style Sheets," about cascading style sheets with the dynamic capabilities of Dynamic HTML you have been studying in Chapters 1 through 7. The results will be impressive when compared to a static HTML page.

In this chapter, you'll learn the following:

- ☐ Why change styles?
- ☐ Adding changing styles to a Web page
- ☐ Examples of changing styles

Why Change Styles?

Basically, there are two reasons why you want to change styles within a Web page. First, you might change the style to booster a page's attention-grabbing potential and to capture the imagination of your audience. No doubt that can be very important in keeping your audience from quickly looking at your page, getting a harsh first impression of your page, and then deciding to go elsewhere. Second, you can change the style to provide feedback to your audience. Style is altered in technical books to help the reader understand the significance of the text. For example, a word in boldface and italics might be a literal string of text intended to be typed using the keyboard. Such a use of style is important in many technical Web pages.

With a dynamic page, you might want to change styles to let a reader know that he or she can interact with a part of the page in a certain way. Application programmers have acknowledged the need for user feedback and continue to provide mouse cursor feedback within the programs they write. When you use a word processor, notice how often the mouse cursor changes. All those changes are there to let you know what the computer expects to be doing on your behalf when you click the buttons or drag the mouse to a new location. As a Web page author, you can use changing styles to let a user know that a mouse click on an area within the mouse page will change the page dynamically. Perhaps that area is expandable. Or, perhaps another technology has been enabled by interacting with that part of the page.

NOTE

> Keep in mind that users do not necessarily notice visual feedback in applications or Web pages. In fact, it never hurts to train your audience. In a Web page, you can provide self training for a reader by providing a hyperlink called "This is a dynamic Web page. Click here for details."

You use Dynamic HTML to extend the concept of changing styles on a Web page. Using Dynamic HTML, your Web pages can change dramatically after their initial load into the Web browser. You can change the style of text based on the actions of your user. You can give more powerful feedback to your audience. You can better grab the attention of your audience and keep their interest longer—all without the overhead of applets, multimedia, or ActiveX.

Adding Changing Styles to a Web Page

You can create everything you need to add dynamically changing styles to a Web page in a single .htm or .html file. A recipe for creating dynamically changing styles on your Web page follows.

8

1. For each style you want to use on the Web page:

   ☐ Define two or more styles with class names and attributes within the `<STYLE></STYLE>` tag pair.

2. Within each text section that can dynamically change style:

   ☐ Define an object name with an `ID=` attribute.

   ☐ Attach a style class name to the section with a `CLASS=` attribute.

   ☐ Attach a script function name to one or more event attributes that you want to enable for the text section.

3. For each changing style routine:

   ☐ Define a script function within a `<SCRIPT></SCRIPT>` tag pair that changes styles to an available style as defined in the `<STYLE></STYLE>` tags.

You learn the steps of how to create dynamically changing styles in more detail in the following three sections.

Defining Styles

A style is defined using the style specification outlined in Chapter 4. For example, the syntax for creating a simple style that makes text red looks like the following:

```
<STYLE>
.redText   {color:Red}
</STYLE>
```

The style is defined to associate itself with the class name redText by placing a period before the redText name identifier. The period signifies that all text blocks identified with the `CLASS=redText` attribute should apply the redText style. Should you want the style to be associated with only a specific text block, you would add its identifier name in front, like `PG1.redText`. The style is defined as a red color style using the keywords color and Red, which are both part of the accepted CSS1 standard. You could also identify the red color using the rgb(255,0,0) syntax. Other examples you could place within the `<STYLE></STYLE>` tags include the following:

```
.larger {font-size:16}
H1 {font-style:italic}
.emphasis {border-color:blue}
```

In fact, you can set up any valid style following the CSS1 style sheet rules covered in Chapter 4, to be used dynamically within scripts defined in the page.

Defining Dynamic Text Blocks

A text block is defined by the HTML tags that you use. For example, you could consider a simple heading a text section by adding the necessary attributes to the opening tag of the `<H1></H1>` tag pair. Or, you could set up a more substantial paragraph as a dynamically changeable text block by including the appropriate attributes within its `<P>` tag or `<P></P>` tag pair.

TECHNICAL NOTE

You can use even a `<FONT></FONT>` tag pair to identify a text object that can have a style applied independently from the rest of the document. Although this is not technically a text block, I treat it as one for purposes of the discussion in this chapter.

A text section is a candidate for dynamically changing styles if its opening tag includes the `ID`, `CLASS`, and event name attributes. For example, a paragraph tag such as the following can change its style when the user clicks anywhere on the paragraph's text:

```
<P ID=PG1 CLASS="RedText" onclick="ChangeIt();">
```

The `ID` attribute names the paragraph so it can be identified in a script. The `CLASS` attribute defines the style to be used initially when the browser loads. The `onclick` attribute is an available Dynamic HTML event. Dynamic HTML events are reviewed in Chapter 6, "Dynamic HTML Events." As the user clicks the paragraph, the `ChangeIt()` script function is called and performed by the Web browser. The `ChangeIt()` function includes the logic to change the style.

Defining Changing Style Scripts

The Dynamic HTML event calls a script routine created with the syntax you studied in Chapter 5, "JavaScript Style Sheets." You can check and use the state of any object on the page to determine which style should be applied to that or another object. If the style is changed through a line within the script, the change is instant because a Dynamic HTML-compliant Web browser constantly waits for style changes. The script is placed within a `<SCRIPT>` `</SCRIPT>` HTML tag pair. The script language is identified as a value of a `LANGUAGE` attribute.

The following script example interrogates the `PG1` paragraph text block's current style. If paragraph `PG1` is currently blue, it dynamically changes to red; otherwise, it changes to blue.

```
<SCRIPT LANGUAGE=JavaScript>
function ChangeIt() {
   if (PG1.className=="blueText") {
      PG1.className="redText";
```

```
    } else {
       PG1.className="blueText";
    }
}
</SCRIPT>
```

A creative Web page script writer combines Web page state interrogations with actions in new and effective combinations to provide fresh and interactive content. The script is enabled from the event attribute set up with a value of the same name as the script function. In the preceding example, function `ChangeIt()` might be executed when a user moves the mouse over paragraph `PG1` through the `onmouseover` event or when a user clicks on paragraph `PG1` through the `onclick` event.

Examples of Changing Styles

Now that you know the basics of how to change styles, look at some examples of dynamically changing style so you can learn from them to improve your Web pages.

TECHNICAL NOTE
> The examples in this chapter comply with the latest information (at the time of this writing) provided by the World Wide Web Consortium (W3C) as communicated by its Web site and were tested and proven to work using the beta 2 version of Microsoft's Internet Explorer 4.0.

Changing Styles to Attract and Retain an Audience

As a first example, you will change text styles to let the audience interact with the Web page. In effect, the concept is similar to the examples of Chapter 7, but this time you will use the style technique to learn how to change and retain text styles.

The Dynamic HTML syntax in Listing 8.1 contains everything necessary to set up a style menu from within a Web page itself to give the reader the ability to change the appearance of the text. Figure 8.1 shows the result of the page as loaded in a Dynamic HTML-compliant Web browser. Figure 8.2 shows the result of the page after the reader has made a style change by interacting with the page.

In this example, you are working for an online newspaper in a small geographical region of six towns. You provide a daily Top News Stories page and want to keep your audience coming back to the page each day. You realize that your audience likes to be able to control the look of the page as it reads the stories. As a simple first addition, you decide to add a text menu that will enable the reader to change the color and text styles of the stories he or she reads. For illustration purposes, the stories used here are just headlines.

Using the <A></A> HTML tag pair, you could provide links to the full story from this page.
The example in Listing 8.1 shows the bare minimum Dynamic HTML features. Of course,
you could spruce it up with some graphics using traditional HTML tags.

INPUT   **Listing 8.1. Example of dynamic text.**

```
<HTML>
<BODY BGCOLOR=#FFFFFF>
<HEAD>
<FONT FACE="verdana,arial,helvetica" SIZE=3>
<TITLE>Today"s Top Stories</TITLE>
</HEAD>
<BODY>
<STYLE>
.redPlain     {color:rgb(255,0,0);
               font-style:normal;}
.blackPlain   {color:rgb(0,0,0);
               font-style:normal;}
.redItalic    {color:red;
               font-style:italic;}
.blackItalic {color:black;
               font-style:italic;}
</STYLE>
<H3>The Verentian Valley News</H3>
<HR>
<FONT ID=red CLASS="blackPlain" onclick="colorP();"> Red </FONT> ¦
<FONT ID=black CLASS="blackPlain" onclick="blackP();"> Black </FONT> ¦
<FONT ID=alternate CLASS="blackPlain" onclick="altP();"> Alternate </FONT> ¦
<FONT ID=italic CLASS="blackPlain" onclick="italicP();"()> Italics </FONT>
<HR>
<P ID=PG1 CLASS="blackPlain">
Argunk: The mayor here, Cora James, announces a new plan for curtailing the
current trend of juvenile delinquency: an evening curfew at 9PM.
<P ID=PG2 CLASS="blackPlain">
Henders: 500 community residents continue to keep a lid on the details of the
theme for this year's Solstice Day Festival yet smile smugly when asked
about it.
<P ID=PG3 CLASS="blackPlain">
Krikett: This year farmers suggest a winter wheat crop may be a good idea.
It has been 6 years since the last attempt.
<P ID=PG4 CLASS="blackPlain">
Lowville: Once again, the boy wonder, Jimmy Westen, has made statewide news
for his latest invention.
<P ID=PG5 CLASS="blackPlain">
Viennes: Our regional professional baseball squad wins its fifth straight
and takes solid hold of second place.
<P ID=PG6 CLASS="blackPlain">
Yinsburgh: Actress Jennifer Urgent returns home to find community support
before considering her next effort.
<SCRIPT LANGUAGE=JavaScript>
function colorP() {
   red.className="redPlain";
   black.className="redPlain";
```

8

```
        if (PG1.className=="redPlain" || PG1.className=="blackPlain") {
            PG1.className="redPlain";
            PG2.className="redPlain";
            PG3.className="redPlain";
            PG4.className="redPlain";
            PG5.className="redPlain";
            PG6.className="redPlain";
        } else {
            PG1.className="redItalic";
            PG2.className="redItalic";
            PG3.className="redItalic";
            PG4.className="redItalic";
            PG5.className="redItalic";
            PG6.className="redItalic";
        }
    }
</SCRIPT>

<SCRIPT LANGUAGE=JavaScript>
function blackP() {
    red.className="blackPlain";
    black.className="blackPlain";
    if (PG1.className=="redPlain" || PG1.className=="blackPlain") {
        PG1.className="blackPlain";
        PG2.className="blackPlain";
        PG3.className="blackPlain";
        PG4.className="blackPlain";
        PG5.className="blackPlain";
        PG6.className="blackPlain";
    } else  {
        PG1.className="blackItalic";
        PG2.className="blackItalic";
        PG3.className="blackItalic";
        PG4.className="blackItalic";
        PG5.className="blackItalic";
        PG6.className="blackItalic";
    }
},
</SCRIPT>

<SCRIPT LANGUAGE=JavaScript>
function altP() {
    red.className="redPlain";
    black.className="blackPlain";
    if (PG1.className=="redPlain" || PG1.className=="blackPlain") {
        PG1.className="blackPlain";
        PG2.className="redPlain";
        PG3.className="blackPlain";
        PG4.className="redPlain";
        PG5.className="blackPlain";
        PG6.className="redPlain";
    } else {
        PG1.className="blackItalic";
        PG2.className="redItalic";
        PG3.className="blackItalic";
```

continues

Listing 8.1. continued

```
            PG4.className="redItalic";
            PG5.className="blackItalic";
            PG6.className="redItalic";
        }
    }
</SCRIPT>

<SCRIPT LANGUAGE=JavaScript>
function italicP() {
    if (italic.className="blackPlain") {
        italic.className="blackItalic";
        if (PG1.className=="redPlain") {
            PG1.className="redItalic";
            PG3.className="redItalic";
            PG5.className="redItalic";
        } else {
            PG1.className="blackItalic";
            PG3.className="blackItalic";
            PG5.className="blackItalic";
        }
        if (PG2.className=="redPlain") {
            PG2.className="redItalic";
            PG4.className="redItalic";
            PG6.className="redItalic";
        } else {
            PG2.className="blackItalic";
            PG4.className="blackItalic";
            PG6.className="blackItalic";
        }
    } else {
        italic.className="blackPlain";
        if (PG1.className=="redItalic") {
            PG1.className="redPlain";
            PG3.className="redPlain";
            PG5.className="redPlain";
        } else {
            PG1.className="blackPlain";
            PG3.className="blackPlain";
            PG5.className="blackPlain";
        }
        if (PG2.className=="redItalic") {
            PG2.className="redPlain";
            PG4.className="redPlain";
            PG6.className="redPlain";
        } else {
            PG2.className="blackPlain";
            PG4.className="blackPlain";
            PG6.className="blackPlain";
        }
    }
}
</SCRIPT>
</FONT>
</BODY>
</HTML>
```

8

As you can see in Figure 8.1, the loaded Web page shows all news stories in black initially, yet there exists a line of text between two horizontal rules under the page heading that enables a reader to click a word and change the appearance of the page. When the user clicks the word Red, the news stories appear in red. When the user clicks the word Black, the news stories return to black. When the user clicks the word Alternate, the stories alternate red and black. Independently, the Italics option enables the user to turn italics on and off.

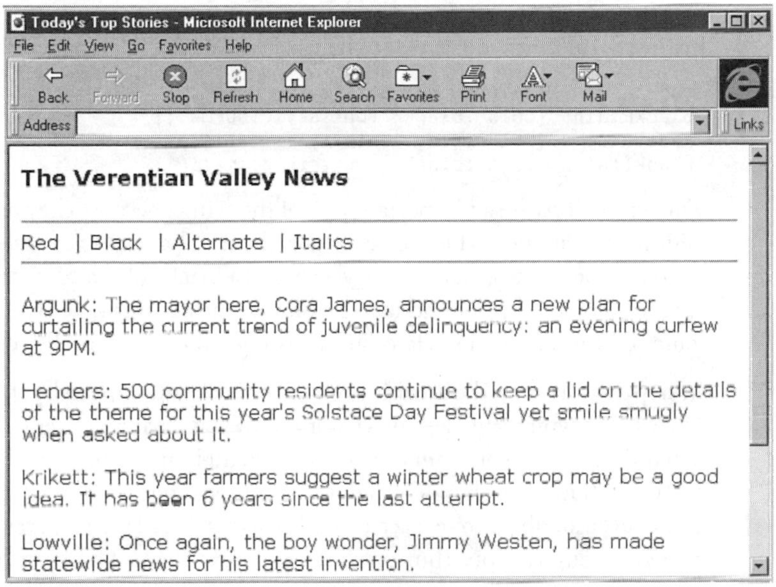

Figure 8.1.

The Top News Stories page.

> **NOTE**
>
> Use your imagination here. A user could change any feature of the text as allowed by the CSS1 style sheet standard after you define the appropriate styles. If you spent the time to understand Chapter 4, you probably are full of ideas on style features you would like to let the reader change dynamically.

You will review Listing 8.1 in detail by following the three-step process outlined in the section "Adding Changing Styles to a Web Page."

In step 1, you define the styles you want to use for the page. In Listing 8.1, four styles are defined within the <STYLE></STYLE> tags. This makes sense because the text can appear in two independent states, and each state has two options. For color, it is either red or black. For italics, it is either italicized or not.

Just like so many problems solved in Computer Science, the multiplier effect of multiple variables with multiple options quickly introduces a geometrically increasing number of states for each new variable you introduce. Use just the minimum number of text-changing variables that will make a significant difference to your audience.

Listing 8.1 defines four styles to be used within the Web page:

```
.redPlain    {color:red; font-style:normal;}
.blackPlain  {color:black; font-style:normal;}
.redItalic   {color:red; font-style:italic;}
.blackItalic {color:black; font-style:italic;}
```

The semicolons are an important part of the syntax because they define the end of each style definition statement. Do not overlook them. The redPlain style applies a red color and unstyled font. The blackPlain style applies a black color and unstyled font. The redItalic style applies a red color and italicized font. The blackItalic style applies a black color and italicized font. As you see later in the listing, all text is initially set to the blackPlain style.

In step 2, you set up the attributes on the objects you want to be able to change dynamically. In this case, you want each news story as well as each text menu item to be able to change dynamically. Yet, you want only the text menu items to be able to initiate the changes. Add an ID attribute to each open tag of the text blocks you want to change independently. Also, add a CLASS attribute to set each text block to black and unstyled text initially. I chose to enact change through a mouse button click on the text menu. Therefore, each text menu text block has an onclick attribute to initiate a script function call. Remember that the onclick event is only one of many I could have used to initiate the changes.

Because the story headlines themselves do not need to initiate changes, they do not need an event attribute within their block tags.

For example, the first text menu item is created with the HTML tag pair

```
<FONT ID=red CLASS="blackText" onclick="colorP();">Red</FONT>
```

The tag sets up the block with the name red, associates the blackText style with the block, and sets up a potential click event to initiate the colorP() script function.

The first news story is set up with the HTML tag

```
<P ID=PG2 CLASS="blackText">
```

The story's text is named PG2 and is of style blackText when the page initially loads. I did not want to initiate any dynamic changes from the text itself, so no event attribute is within the <P> tag.

In the last step, you set up the script routines to make the dynamic changes you want to happen. This is where your imagination and ability to apply logic create a potent mix. In my case, I wanted to enable a reader to click any of the four text menu items to change the style of the text in each story. The colorP() and blackP() functions are similar in that they check whether the first news story is italicized and then combine the color desired with the state of the italics already on the news stories. The altP() function alternates the color of the stories while retaining the current state of the italics.

As for the current color choice the reader makes, the menu choices Red and Black are changed to reflect the current choice. If the reader clicks Black, both the Red and Black menu choices turn black. If the reader clicks Red, both the Red and Black menu choices turn red. Finally, if the reader clicks Alternate, the Black menu choice turns black and the Red menu choice turns red.

The italicP() function is similar in syntax, yet the logic is a bit more complicated because the color decision within the news stories is not all or nothing. With italics, every story is italicized or every story is not italicized. With color, some stories can be red while others are black. So instead of interrogating just the first story for its current color, function italicP() must also interrogate the second story. If the stories are different colors, the alternate coloring must continue for the rest of the stories.

NOTE

You might notice how long each <SCRIPT></SCRIPT> tag pair is for this example. I could use some tricks within the scripting languages to shorten the number of lines that appear, or I could also interrogate the text menu instead of the first news story to find the current state of the Web page. But, the logic itself has been minimized for the features I want. By the time you have learned everything about Dynamic HTML, you will have to be sure you are not intimidated by working with long and complex functions to make the most out of what is available in the language. And, you will have to decide on the time-honored trade-off between shorter scripts that download faster and longer scripts that are better self-documenting.

Figure 8.2 shows the changes that are made dynamically to the Web page when a reader clicks the Alternate text menu option.

Figure 8.2.

*The page after the
user clicks Alternate.*

> **Today's Top Stories - Microsoft Internet Explorer**
>
> File   Edit   View   Go   Favorites   Help
>
> Back   Forward   Stop   Refresh   Home   Search   Favorites   Print   Font   Mail
>
> Address   Links
>
> ### The Verentian Valley News
>
> Red | Black | Alternate | Italics
>
> Argunk: The mayor here, Cora James, announces a new plan for
> curtailing the current trend of juvenile delinquency: an evening curfew
> at 9PM.
>
> Henders: 500 community residents continue to keep a lid on the details
> of the theme for this year's Solstace Day Festival yet smile smugly
> when asked about it.
>
> Krikett: This year farmers suggest a winter wheat crop may be a good
> idea. It has been 6 years since the last attempt.
>
> Lowville: Once again, the boy wonder, Jimmy Westen, has made
> statewide news for his latest invention.

The news story headlines now alternate between black and red and the text menu options are
black and red, respectively. If the reader then clicks the Italics text menu option, the whole
page is italicized and the colors remain as previously selected.

Changing Styles for Feedback

The example in Listing 8.1 demonstrates how you give your audience control over text styles.
A reader can color and italicize the text to make the page look more attractive to him or her,
but he or she gets little more use out of the page by doing so. In other words, the dynamically
changing styles provide no real feedback. Perhaps the alternating color choice might help him
or her distinguish the beginning and end of a certain story relative to the others, but that is
of such minimal benefit compared to other techniques you can provide with Dynamic
HTML and changing styles.

A Second Example of Dynamically Changing Text

The next example, which is laid out in Listing 8.2, improves on the usability of the Web page
by dynamically presenting the story headlines one at a time. If a reader is interested in only
one town's news, he or she will be able to move his or her mouse cursor to that town's
identifier and read just the story in which he or she is interested. If only one story is presented
at a time, you can add more information to the Web page without it appearing cluttered. As
a representation of additional information, the day's projected high temperature has been
added to the page. You probably can imagine other pieces of information a reader would
come to find at your news site.

Figure 8.3 shows an alternative presentation of the Top News Stories Web page using a more dramatic changing styles effect. The news stories are loaded initially with a font size of 2 points. At 2 points, the stories are not readable, so the emphasis is on the information to the left. A reader can see the high temperatures for each town in the valley and, if he or she is interested in the top news story for a certain town, can move the mouse over that town's name and the news story headline will appear large to the right. Figure 8.4 later in this chapter shows the effect of a reader placing the mouse cursor over the town title Krikett. The Krikett town label turns black and enlarges to a 16-point font. The news story headline for Krikett enlarges to that same font and size as well.

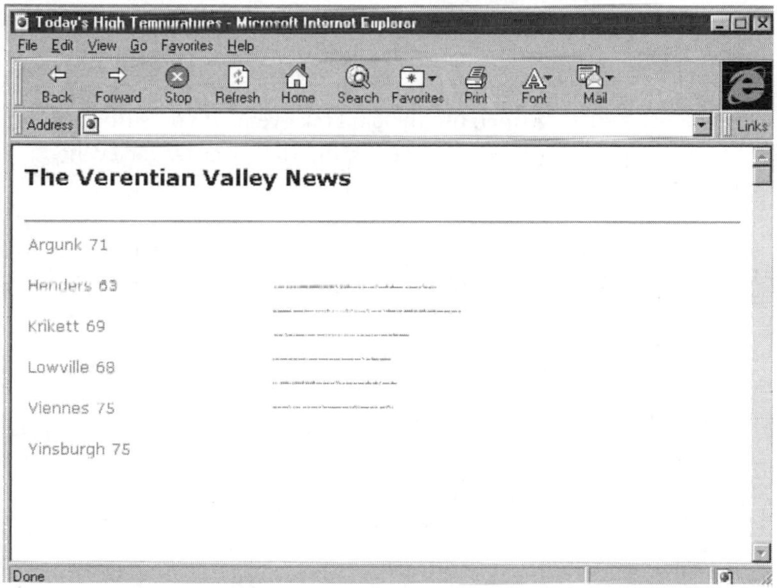

Figure 8.3.

An alternative Top Stories page.

NOTE

You might wonder why I bother showing the headline stories initially at all. At 2 points, no one will be able to read them. I like that they provide placeholders as a visual cue that something is there. In fact, I contemplated adding events that would enable a user to open the story headline by clicking the placeholder text. Instead, I decided there was enough in the example already. However, there is a question in the Q&A section at the end of the chapter to see whether you can quickly add the necessary attributes to allow for user story expansion from the story headline itself.

This enlarging feature of dynamically changing styles might be one of the most used features of Dynamic HTML. Can you already imagine how you could incorporate it into the results from today's Web search engines? A lot of scrolling will be eliminated if each link in a search result set is shown as just a single line of text and does not expand until a reader passes over it with the mouse.

 NOTE

This example focuses on the `onmouseover` event as the initiating event for changing text. The previous example from Listing 8.1 focuses on the `onclick` event as the initiator. You could just as well see them in reverse order. Your audience will be more likely to stumble on the `onmouseover` than the `onclick` event, and you can use that to your advantage. If the changes would be disruptive to an unsuspecting reader, use the `onclick` event. If you suspect that the reader would want to see the changes, use the `onmouseover` event.

In Listing 8.2, you see the Dynamic HTML syntax you can use to create the effect in Figures 8.3 and 8.4. Take a look at Listing 8.2 and then continue reading.

INPUT **Listing 8.2. Another example of dynamic text styles.**

```
<HTML>
<BODY BGCOLOR=#FFFFFF>
<HEAD>
<FONT FACE="verdana,arial,helvetica" SIZE=3>
<TITLE>Today"s High Tempuratures</TITLE>
</HEAD>
<BODY>
<STYLE>
.redPlain     {color:rgb(255,0,0);
               font-size:10pt;
               font-style:normal;}
.redSmall     {color:rgb(255,0,0);
               font-size:2pt;
               font-style:normal;}
.blackPlain   {color:rgb(0,0,0);
               font-style:normal;
               font-size:16pt;}
</STYLE>
<H3>The Verentian Valley News</H3>
<HR>
<TABLE>
<TR>
<TD WIDTH=200>
<P ID=T1 CLASS="redPlain" onmouseover="redP();">Argunk      71
<P ID=T2 CLASS="redPlain" onmouseover="redP();">Henders     63
<P ID=T3 CLASS="redPlain" onmouseover="redP();">Krikett     69
<P ID=T4 CLASS="redPlain" onmouseover="redP();">Lowville    68
<P ID=T5 CLASS="redPlain" onmouseover="redP();">Viennes     75
```

8

```
<P ID=T6 CLASS="redPlain" onmouseover="redP();">Yinsburgh    75
</TD>
<TD>
<P ID=PG1 CLASS="redSmall">
The mayor here, Cora James, announces a new plan for curtailing
the current trend of juvenile delinquency: an evening curfew at 9PM.
<P ID=PG2 CLASS="redSmall">
500 community residents continue to keep a lid on the details of the theme
for this year's Solstice Day Festival yet smile smugly when asked about it.
<P ID=PG3 CLASS="redSmall">
This year farmers suggest a winter wheat crop may be a good idea.  It has
been 6 years since the last attempt.
<P ID=PG4 CLASS="redSmall">
Once again, the boy wonder, Jimmy Westen, has made statewide news for his
latest invention.
<P ID=PG5 CLASS="redSmall">
Our regional professional baseball squad wins its fifth straight and takes
solid hold of second place.
<P ID=PG6 CLASS="redSmall">
Actress Jennifer Urgent returns home to find community support before
considering her next effort.
</TD>
</TR>
</TABLE>
<SCRIPT LANGUAGE=JavaScript>
var source
function redP() {
   source = window.event.srcElement;
   T1.className="redPlain";
   T2.className="redPlain";
   T3.className="redPlain";
   T4.className="redPlain";
   T5.className="redPlain";
   T6.className="redPlain";
   PG1.className="redSmall";
   PG2.className="redSmall";
   PG3.className="redSmall";
   PG4.className="redSmall";
   PG5.className="redSmall";
   PG6.className="redSmall";
   source.className="blackPlain";
   if (T1.className=="blackPlain")
      PG1.className="blackPlain";
   if (T2.className=="blackPlain")
      PG2.className="blackPlain";
   if (T3.className=="blackPlain")
      PG3.className="blackPlain";
   if (T4.className=="blackPlain")
      PG4.className="blackPlain";
   if (T5.className=="blackPlain")
      PG5.className="blackPlain";
   if (T6.className=="blackPlain")
      PG6.className="blackPlain";
}
</SCRIPT>
</FONT>
</BODY>
</HTML>
```

Again, in the first step, define the styles you will use within the page. The enlarging stories example used three styles. The redPlain style has been applied to all text blocks that have a CLASS=redPlain attribute in their opening tag. The redPlain style is red with a 10-point font and no styling. The redSmall style is red with a 2-point font and no styling. The blackPlain style is black with a 16-point font and no styling.

```
.redPlain    {color:rgb(255,0,0);
              font-size:10pt;
              font-style:normal}
.redSmall    {color:rgb(255,0,0);
              font-size:2pt;
              font-style:normal}
.blackPlain  {color:rgb(0,0,0);
              font-style:normal;
              font-size:16pt;}
```

In the second step, apply the appropriate attributes to the opening tags for each text block that contains the changing style feature. Each <P> tag for the town and temperature text looks like the first one:

```
<P ID=T1 CLASS="redPlain" onmouseover="redP();">
```

It contains an ID attribute to name the paragraph, a CLASS attribute to set a style for initial loading, and an EVENT attribute to initiate an action and associate the appropriate script function to that action.

Each story headline's <P> tag is similar to the story headline in the first example. The first headline tag, <P ID=PG6 CLASS="redSmall">, names the first story paragraph PG6 and initiates it to load with the redSmall style.

Notice that the two different sections, town headers and headline paragraphs, each are in a separate cell of a simple table. The WIDTH attribute of the first <TD> tag sets the width for the town headers cell.

In the third step, write the script functions that handle the events you added in the text block tags. In Listing 8.2, each town header calls only one script when the mouse passes over. The script is placed within the <SCRIPT></SCRIPT> tag pair. The redP() function resets each town header and news story back to their initial styles and then enlarges the appropriate items based on the mouse cursor position on the page. The script is simplified by the line

```
source = window.event.srcElement
```

Dynamic HTML includes the capability to read the object that initialized an event through the window.event.srcElement method. Be sure to declare the variable where you want to store the event earlier in the function. Through the source variable, the appropriate town header changes to the blackPlain style. After it is changed, the town headers are interrogated to find the black one. Then, the respective news story headline is enlarged as well.

8

Figure 8.4 shows the result of a reader placing the mouse cursor over the Krikett town header. This is a simple yet powerful presentation of the top news story. The page itself is not very attractive, but you can add traditional HTML tags and features to spruce it up significantly. As a bare-bones example, you can focus just on the Dynamic HTML enhancements.

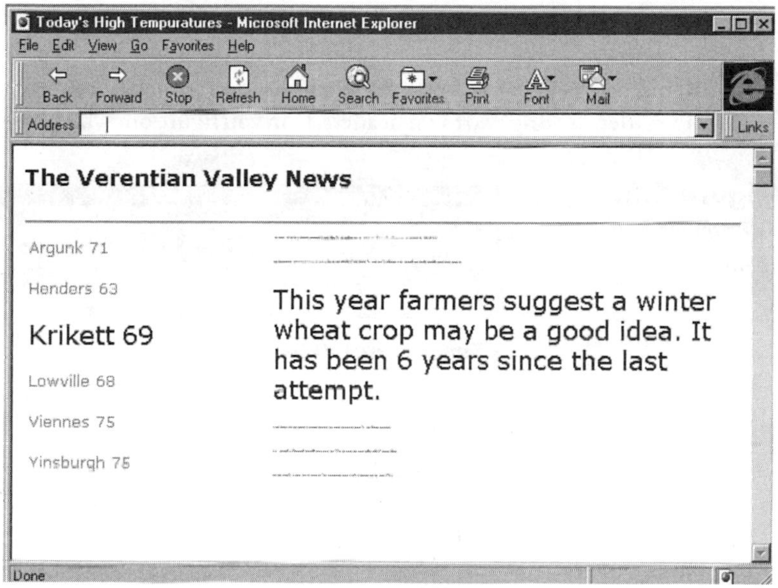

Figure 8.4.

Krikett's top story headline.

You have one more example to look at. By now, you probably have figured out the syntax for creating dynamically changing text. You just need more inspiration in terms of what the technology can do for you. If you have that already, just look at Figures 8.5 and 8.6 and skip over this example.

NOTE

And, while you follow the example, remember that lots of graphical techniques within Dynamic HTML will provide information analysis features. These features are explained on Day 5, "Dynamically Changing Content and Placement."

A Third Example of Dynamically Changing Text

The example in Listing 8.3 demonstrates two new ideas. First, changing the background color of text is another powerful way to emphasize text on a Web page. Second, you can apply changing styles to numbers to provide a simple analysis that changes over time, yet provides a consistent look and feel your audience will quickly understand.

In Figure 8.5, I create another table without borders that has six columns. The first column is the same as in Figure 8.3, except that the high temperature has been removed from the town headers. The next five columns show a range of temperatures that are reasonable for high temperatures for the towns in the valley given the time of year. Each column represents a different day of the week. A Web visitor can come to the site any time and click a town to see that town's projected high temperature for each day of the week. In fact, a visitor can click all six towns to see the range of projected highs for the valley for the upcoming week. A blue highlighting effect has been used to emphasize a temperature. Figure 8.6 shows the aftereffect of a reader clicking two town headers. Can you figure out which two towns have been clicked?

Figure 8.5.

The towns in the valley.

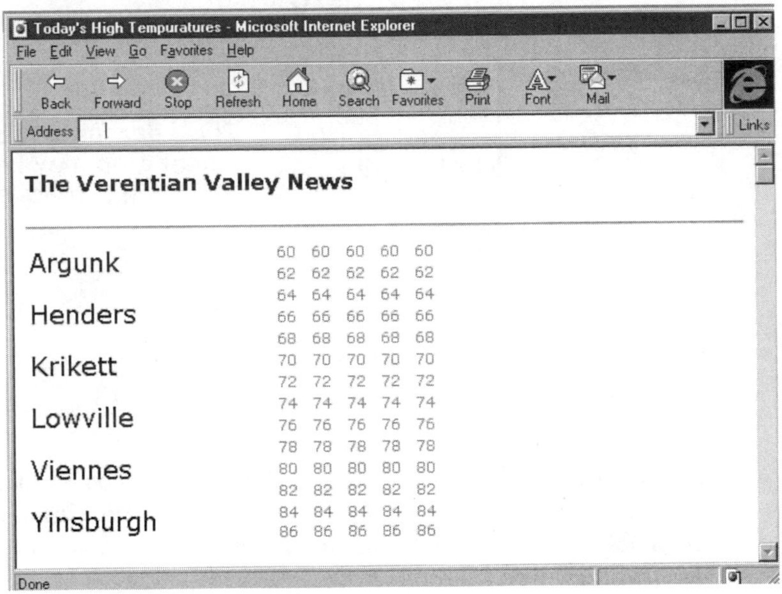

Listing 8.3 provides the syntax used to create the temperature projection Web page. Look at Listing 8.3 and continue reading for additional explanation.

Figure 8.6.
High temperatures for two towns.

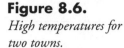

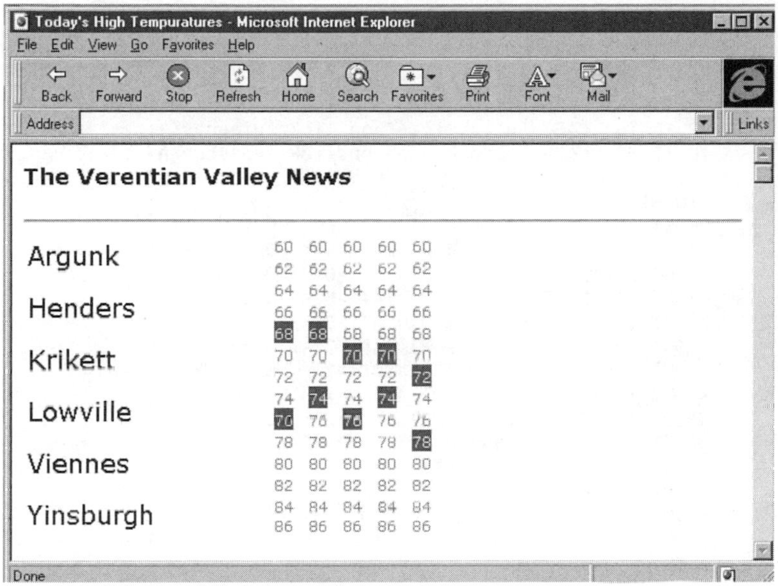

Today's High Tempuratures - Microsoft Internet Explorer
File Edit View Go Favorites Help
Back Forward Stop Refresh Home Search Favorites Print Font Mail
Address
Links
The Verentian Valley News
Argunk
Henders
Krikett
Lowville
Viennes
Yinsburgh
60 60 60 60 60
62 62 62 62 62
64 64 64 64 64
66 66 66 66 66
68 68 68 68 68
70 70 70 70 70
72 72 72 72 72
74 74 74 74 74
76 76 76 76 76
78 78 78 78 78
80 80 80 80 80
82 82 82 82 82
84 84 84 84 84
86 86 86 86 86
Done

INPUT

Listing 8.3. A third example of dynamic text.

```
<HTML>
<BODY BGCOLOR=#FFFFFF>
<HEAD>
<FONT FACE="verdana,arial,helvetica" SIZE=3>
<TITLE>Today"s High Tempuratures</TITLE>
</HEAD>
<BODY>
<STYLE TYPE="text/css">
.redPlain    {color:rgb(255,0,0);
              font-size:10pt;
              font-style:normal;
              line-height:1.1;}
.blackPlain  {color:rgb(0,0,0);
              font-style:normal;
              font-size:16pt;}
.highlight   {color:rgb(255,255,255);
              background:rgb(0,0,255);
              font-style:normal;
              font-size:10pt;}
</STYLE>
<H3>The Verentian Valley News</H3>
<HR>
<TABLE>
<TR>
<TD WIDTH=200>
<P ID=T1 CLASS="blackPlain" onclick="argunk();">Argunk
<P ID=T2 CLASS="blackPlain" onclick="henders();">Henders
```

continues

Listing 8.3. continued

```
<P ID=T3 CLASS="blackPlain" onclick="krikett();">Krikett
<P ID=T4 CLASS="blackPlain" onclick="lowville();">Lowville
<P ID=T5 CLASS="blackPlain" onclick="viennes();">Viennes
<P ID=T6 CLASS="blackPlain" onclick="yinsburgh();">Yinsburgh
</TD>
<TD WIDTH=25>
<FONT ID=TP1 CLASS="redPlain" >60</FONT>
<FONT ID=TP2 CLASS="redPlain" >62</FONT>
<FONT ID=TP3 CLASS="redPlain" >64</FONT>
<FONT ID=TP4 CLASS="redPlain" >66</FONT>
<FONT ID=TP5 CLASS="redPlain" >68</FONT>
<FONT ID=TP6 CLASS="redPlain" >70</FONT>
<FONT ID=TP7 CLASS="redPlain" >72</FONT>
<FONT ID=TP8 CLASS="redPlain" >74</FONT>
<FONT ID=TP9 CLASS="redPlain" >76</FONT>
<FONT ID=TP10 CLASS="redPlain" >78</FONT>
<FONT ID=TP11 CLASS="redPlain" >80</FONT>
<FONT ID=TP12 CLASS="redPlain" >82</FONT>
<FONT ID=TP13 CLASS="redPlain" >84</FONT>
<FONT ID=TP14 CLASS="redPlain" >86</FONT>
</TD>
<TD WIDTH=25>
<FONT ID=TTP1 CLASS="redPlain" >60</FONT>
<FONT ID=TTP2 CLASS="redPlain" >62</FONT>
<FONT ID=TTP3 CLASS="redPlain" >64</FONT>
<FONT ID=TTP4 CLASS="redPlain" >66</FONT>
<FONT ID=TTP5 CLASS="redPlain" >68</FONT>
<FONT ID=TTP6 CLASS="redPlain" >70</FONT>
<FONT ID=TTP7 CLASS="redPlain" >72</FONT>
<FONT ID=TTP8 CLASS="redPlain" >74</FONT>
<FONT ID=TTP9 CLASS="redPlain" >76</FONT>
<FONT ID=TTP10 CLASS="redPlain" >78</FONT>
<FONT ID=TTP11 CLASS="redPlain" >80</FONT>
<FONT ID=TTP12 CLASS="redPlain" >82</FONT>
<FONT ID=TTP13 CLASS="redPlain" >84</FONT>
<FONT ID=TTP14 CLASS="redPlain" >86</FONT>
</TD>
<TD WIDTH=25>
<FONT ID=WTP1 CLASS="redPlain" >60</FONT>
<FONT ID=WTP2 CLASS="redPlain" >62</FONT>
<FONT ID=WTP3 CLASS="redPlain" >64</FONT>
<FONT ID=WTP4 CLASS="redPlain" >66</FONT>
<FONT ID=WTP5 CLASS="redPlain" >68</FONT>
<FONT ID=WTP6 CLASS="redPlain" >70</FONT>
<FONT ID=WTP7 CLASS="redPlain" >72</FONT>
<FONT ID=WTP8 CLASS="redPlain" >74</FONT>
<FONT ID=WTP9 CLASS="redPlain" >76</FONT>
<FONT ID=WTP10 CLASS="redPlain" >78</FONT>
<FONT ID=WTP11 CLASS="redPlain" >80</FONT>
<FONT ID=WTP12 CLASS="redPlain" >82</FONT>
<FONT ID=WTP13 CLASS="redPlain" >84</FONT>
<FONT ID=WTP14 CLASS="redPlain" >86</FONT>
</TD>
```

```
<TD WIDTH=25>
<FONT ID=RTP1 CLASS="redPlain" >60</FONT>
<FONT ID=RTP2 CLASS="redPlain" >62</FONT>
<FONT ID=RTP3 CLASS="redPlain" >64</FONT>
<FONT ID=RTP4 CLASS="redPlain" >66</FONT>
<FONT ID=RTP5 CLASS="redPlain" >68</FONT>
<FONT ID=RTP6 CLASS="redPlain" >70</FONT>
<FONT ID=RTP7 CLASS="redPlain" >72</FONT>
<FONT ID=RTP8 CLASS="redPlain" >74</FONT>
<FONT ID=RTP9 CLASS="redPlain" >76</FONT>
<FONT ID=RTP10 CLASS="redPlain" >78</FONT>
<FONT ID=RTP11 CLASS="redPlain" >80</FONT>
<FONT ID=RTP12 CLASS="redPlain" >82</FONT>
<FONT ID=RTP13 CLASS="redPlain" >84</FONT>
<FONT ID=RTP14 CLASS="redPlain" >86</FONT>
</TD>
<TD WIDTH=25>
<FONT ID=FTP1 CLASS="redPlain" >60</FONT>
<FONT ID=FTP2 CLASS="redPlain" >62</FONT>
<FONT ID=FTP3 CLASS="redPlain" >64</FONT>
<FONT ID=FTP4 CLASS="redPlain" >66</FONT>
<FONT ID=FTP5 CLASS="redPlain" >68</FONT>
<FONT ID=FTP6 CLASS="redPlain" >70</FONT>
<FONT ID=FTP7 CLASS="redPlain" >72</FONT>
<FONT ID=FTP8 CLASS="redPlain" >74</FONT>
<FONT ID=FTP9 CLASS="redPlain" >76</FONT>
<FONT ID=FTP10 CLASS="redPlain" >78</FONT>
<FONT ID=FTP11 CLASS="redPlain" >80</FONT>
<FONT ID=FTP12 CLASS="redPlain" >82</FONT>
<FONT ID=FTP13 CLASS="redPlain" >84</FONT>
<FONT ID=FTP14 CLASS="redPlain" >86</FONT>
</TD>
</TR>
</TABLE>

<SCRIPT LANGUAGE=JavaScript>
function argunk() {
   TP5.className="highlight";
   TTP5.className="highlight";
   WTP6.className="highlight";
   RTP6.className="highlight";
   FTP7.className="highlight";
}
</SCRIPT>

<SCRIPT LANGUAGE=JavaScript>
function henders() {
   TP4.className="highlight";
   TTP6.className="highlight";
   WTP6.className="highlight";
   RTP5.className="highlight";
   FTP7.className="highlight";
}
</SCRIPT>
```

continues

Listing 8.3. continued

```
<SCRIPT LANGUAGE=JavaScript>
function krikett() {
   TP7.className="highlight";
   TTP6.className="highlight";
   WTP8.className="highlight";
   RTP8.className="highlight";
   FTP8.className="highlight";
}
</SCRIPT>

<SCRIPT LANGUAGE=JavaScript>
function lowville() {
   TP9.className="highlight";
   TTP8.className="highlight";
   WTP9.className="highlight";
   RTP8.className="highlight";
   FTP10.className="highlight";
}
</SCRIPT>

<SCRIPT LANGUAGE=JavaScript>
function viennes() {
   TP5.className="highlight";
   TTP6.className="highlight";
   WTP7.className="highlight";
   RTP8.className="highlight";
   FTP7.className="highlight";
}
</SCRIPT>

<SCRIPT LANGUAGE=JavaScript>
function yinsburgh() {
   TP7.className="highlight";
   TTP8.className="highlight";
   WTP8.className="highlight";
   RTP8.className="highlight";
   FTP7.className="highlight";
}
</SCRIPT>
</BODY>
</HTML>
```

In the first step, define your styles. Three styles for the example in Listing 8.3 were defined:

```
.redPlain      {color:rgb(255,0,0);
                font-size:10pt;
                font-style:normal;
                line-height:1.1;}
.blackPlain    {color:rgb(0,0,0);
                font-style:normal;
                font-size:16pt;}
.highlight     {color:rgb(255,255,255);
                background:rgb(0,0,255);
                font-style:normal;
                font-size:10pt;}
```

The redPlain style is for temperature numbers that are not emphasized. The blackPlain style is for the town headers that are black and significantly larger than the temperature numbers (16 points versus 10 points). The highlight style is for emphasizing temperature numbers that are projected highs for one or more selected towns. The new component of the style is the background color, which is set to blue.

In the second step, set up the attribute you need within the text block opening tags. The town headers are similar to the second example in Listing 8.2. The temperature headers look like the following, where each temperature is given a name and an initial class to use when the page is loaded:

```
<FONT ID=FTP13 CLASS="redPlain" >84</FONT>
```

In the third step, write the script functions you need to enact style changes dynamically. In Listing 8.3, there is a separate script for each town header event. Each script is in its own <SCRIPT></SCRIPT> pair. Look at the script for the argunk() function:

```
<SCRIPT LANGUAGE=JavaScript>
function argunk() {
   TP5.className="highlight";
   TTP5.className="highlight";
   WTP6.className="highlight";
   RTP6.className="highlight";
   FTP7.className="highlight";
}
</SCRIPT>
```

In this script, a different temperature is highlighted for each day of the week. The first two letters of the class name identify which day of the week is being identified (TP is Monday, TT is Tuesday, WT is Wednesday, RT is Thursday, and FT is Friday). The number represents the temperature range (a 7 is four degrees hotter than a 5, 72 degrees versus 68).

Because all the functionality is defined in a single .htm or .html file, an automated computer process can more cleanly create the page dynamically by running a process that spits out this text on a weekly basis. A reader need only download the page once a week, and he or she can use the page for hours without ever having to be assisted by the server again.

NOTE

In Listing 8.3, there is no clear function to clear out the highlighted temperatures and start again. A reader would have to reload or refresh the Web page to begin with fresh temperature readings. Based on the first example in Listing 8.1, you should feel comfortable adding a Clear text item that would set all the numbers back to the redPlain style.

You could add a lot more to this example to spruce up the information content. You could add a fourth style to highlight the projected lows and more styles to handle average temperatures or other useful comparisons. Use standard HTML tags to make the static features of the page more attractive.

Summary

You can easily add dynamically changing styles to a Dynamic HTML Web page through syntax standardized by the Cascading Style Sheets specification, known as CSS1. Chapter 4 introduces you to those specific details. After you define the styles within the Web page, you can change named objects between the styles by altering their CLASS attributes. The changes are made by script functions that are very flexible in allowing for creative effects based on the state of the page, mouse, and keyboard.

This chapter introduced you to three examples of using dynamic styles to improve your Web page's attractiveness and usability. You could use the highlighting feature in other ways, such as to highlight a form after the form had been submitted. Dynamic HTML provides an onsubmit event you can use to provide feedback on a form. In fact, it is the feedback feature of dynamic styles that is most important if Web pages are to become self-contained applications delivered over the Web. Only then will the mindset of the reader move away from thinking of Web pages as encyclopedia pages and toward interactive information applications.

Q&A

Q I noticed in Listing 8.3 that you included the attribute TYPE="text/css" in your opening <STYLE> tag. Can you tell me more about the TYPE attribute and why you did not include a TYPE attribute in Listings 8.1 and 8.2?

A Sure. The TYPE attribute identifies the style sheet convention you are using in the style declarations within the <STYLE></STYLE> tag pair. The W3C tries to be open with its specifications to enable Web browser developers to use alternative technologies that their markets demand. Other style sheet specifications are popular beside the Cascading Style Sheet specification that the W3C promotes. Yet, if no TYPE attribute is included in a <STYLE> open tag, the W3C recommends that the CSS specification be the default. Note that the W3C calls a Web browser a *user agent* to expand on usability of the HTML standard.

Q **In your previous answer, what do you mean about user agents?**

A A user agent is software running on any device that reads HTML files and formats the information on behalf of the user. You probably use a Web browser only to read HTML files on the Web. But, in the future, pagers, telephones, automobile dashboards, and special devices for the physically challenged might access the Web and present information to an audience. The W3C intends to use the same HTML specification for those devices as well.

Q **I suspect you are going to show me how I could create a Web page similar to that in Figure 8.6 using graphics instead of text with changing styles. Is there an advantage to using text over graphics?**

A By the time you finish reading Chapter 9, "Dynamically Changing Content," and Chapter 10, "Dynamically Altering the Placement of Elements," you should be able to create the same effect with a bitmap image of thermometers and moving temperature indicators. You will even know how to add some animation to a weather report Web page. However, text often is more exact to a reader than a graphical representation. If the data you present is very precise, you might want to use text instead of graphics to be very explicit with the numerical values. Also, if you expect your audience to visit your site with older technologies and slow modem connections, you might want to use text because it uses less bandwidth and loads faster in older Web browsers.

Quiz

Take the following quiz to see how much you've learned in this chapter.

Questions

1. How would you create a CSS style specification that styles all <H2></H2> heading elements in italics?

2. How would you create a CSS style specification that sets up a highlight of white on red for 12-point, italicized text for a class named reverse?

3. How would you apply your reverse class style to set a paragraph named PG16?

4. In Listing 8.2, what changes do you need to make to enable the news story font expansion for mouse clicks on the news stories themselves?

Answers

1. `H2 {font-style:italic;}`

2. ```
.reverse {color:rgb(255,255,255);
background:rgb(255,0,0);
font-style:italic;
font-size:12pt;}
```
```

3. You can apply the reverse class style in two ways. You can add the attribute `CLASS=reverse` to the `<P>` open tag or you can set the style in a script function with the line `PG16.className="reverse";`.

4. You must make two changes. First, add an `onclick="redP();"` attribute to each paragraph opening tag for paragraphs `PG1` through `PG6`, like

```
<P ID=PG1 CLASS="redSmall" onclick="redP();">
```

Then, update the `redP()` function script to include six additional `if...then` statements near the end, like the following, for each of the `PG` and `T` pairs 1 through 6:

```
if (PG1.className=="blackPlain")
T1.className="blackPlain";
```

Workshop

You created your giant squid Web site welcome page in Chapter 7, "Changing Text Attributes"; now, create the page your readers will access from the first welcome page link, called `What Is a Squid?`. The What Is a Squid? Web page contains basic information about squid that identifies squid from the rest of the animal kingdom.

NOTE

> I did not know much about squid when I started this project. Everything I learned I read on the Web. I will provide enough facts for you to piece together a basic informational page on squid, but if you want to do your own research, look at the list of URLs in Listing 8.5 at the end of this Workshop section. Access each URL in Listing 8.5 with the `http://` protocol in your favorite Web browser.

You will create an interactive Web page that enables a reader to click one aspect of squid at a time to get more information about that aspect. The information on squid used in this implementation follows.

☐ **Aspect: Cephalopoda (Group)**

The Cephalopoda are an ancient and very successful group of the Mollusca. They have been among the dominant, large predators in the ocean at various times in geological history. Two groups of cephalopods exist today: the extant Nautiloidea, containing the pearly nautiluses that are phylogenetic relics and represented by only a few species, and the Coleoida.

☐ **Aspect: Coleoida (Subgroup)**

The Coleoida group contains the squids, cuttlefishes, octopods, and vampire squids that are represented by about 700 species. Cephalopods are the most active of the mollusks, and some squids rival fishes in swimming speed. Although there are only about 700 species of living cephalopods, they occupy a variety of habitats in all of the world's oceans. Individual species are often very abundant and provide major targets for marine fisheries.

☐ **Aspect: Identifying Characteristics**

A cephalopod has identifying characteristics that categorize it separately from all other animals. A squid has a funnel derived from the molluscan foot. A squid has circumoral arms that are probably derived from the molluscan head. A squid has chitinous beaks. A squid has a shell bearing a phragmacone and siphuncle. A squid has image-forming eyes.

☐ **Aspect: Propagation**

All squid move through the ocean using a jet of water forced out of the body by a siphon. Many squid prefer to move about in very deep water where the water temperature is colder. Recent studies indicate that the blood of deep water squids does not carry oxygen very well at higher temperatures. Those squid will actually suffocate in warm water. There are warm water squid that swim closer to the surface, however. Warm water squid are migratory because water temperature changes more dramatically nearer to the surface.

☐ **Aspect: Food**

Squid are carnivorous. They eat fish, other squid, and, in the case of the largest species, whales.

☐ **Aspect: Geography**

Different species of squid are seen in the seas of the entire world. They have evolved to take advantage of many different environmental conditions. Their geography is more interesting at the species-specific level.

Consider the different aspects of squid similar to the different town news stories presented earlier in this chapter. Create a table with a listing of the aspect categories in the left column of the table. The information on each aspect should expand in the right column when a reader clicks the word identifying an aspect of squid. Make your presentation attractive to your audience. When you are finished, look at Listing 8.4 for my implementation. If you are unsure of what you should do, look at a screen shot of the implementation in Figure 8.7 before you begin.

Finally, when you are finished with your What Is a Squid? Web page, save the HTML file with the same filename you referenced in the What Is a Squid? link of your Welcome page.

Listing 8.4. A What Is a Squid? page.

```
<HTML>
<HEAD>
<TITLE>A Giant Squid Is One Type Of Squid</TITLE>
</HEAD>
<BODY BACKGROUND="water.jpg" TEXT=#FFFFFF LINK=FFFF22 VLINK=FF22FF>
<STYLE>
.yellowPlain  {color:rgb(255,255,0);
               font-size:10pt;
               font-style:italic}
.yellowSmall  {color:rgb(255,255,0);
               font-size:2pt;
               font-style:normal}
.whitePlain   {color:rgb(250,250,250);
               font-style:normal;
               font-size:12pt;}
</STYLE>
<IMG SRC="giant.gif" WIDTH=128 ALIGN=RIGHT>
<H2>So, What is a Squid?</H2>
<TABLE BORDER=1>
<TR>
<TD WIDTH=200>
<P ID=T1 CLASS="yellowPlain" onclick="yellowP();">Cephalopoda
<P ID=T2 CLASS="yellowPlain" onclick="yellowP();">Coleoidea
<P ID=T3 CLASS="yellowPlain" onclick="yellowP();">Characteristics
<P ID=T4 CLASS="yellowPlain" onclick="yellowP();">Propagation
<P ID=T5 CLASS="yellowPlain" onclick="yellowP();">Food
<P ID=T6 CLASS="yellowPlain" onclick="yellowP();">Geography
</TD>
<TD WIDTH=400>
<P ID=PG1 CLASS="yellowSmall">
The Cephalopoda is an ancient and very successful group of the Mollusca.
They have been among the dominant large predators in the ocean at various
times in geological history. Two groups of cephalopods exist today: The
extant Nautiloidea, containing the pearly nautiluses which are phylogenetic
relicts, are represented by only a few species, and the Coleoida.
<P ID=PG2 CLASS="yellowSmall">
The Coleoida group contains the squids, cuttlefishes, octopods and vampire
squids which are represented by about 700 species. Cephalopods are the most
active of the mollusks and some squids rival fishes in their swimming speed.
Although there are only about 700 species of living cephalopods, they occupy
a great variety of habitats in all of the world's oceans. Individual species
are often very abundant and provide major targets for marine fisheries.
<DIV ID=PG3 CLASS="yellowSmall">
Coleoida Characteristics
<OL>
<LI>A funnel derived from the molluscan foot.
<LI>Circumoral arms that are probably derived from the molluscan head.
<LI>Chitinous beaks.
<LI>Shell bearing a phragmacone and siphuncle
(lost in most Recent cephalopods).
<LI>Image-forming eyes.
</OL></DIV>
<P ID=PG4 CLASS="yellowSmall">All squid move through the ocean using a jet
of water forced out of the body
by a siphon. Many squid prefer to move about in very deep water where the water
```

8

```
temperature is colder. Recent studies indicate the blood of deep water squids
does not carry oxygen very well at higher temperatures. Those squid will
actually suffocate in warm water. There are as well warm water squid that swim
closer to the surface. Warm water squid are migratory because water temperature
changes more dramatically nearer to the surface.
<P ID=PG5 CLASS="yellowSmall">Squid are especially carnivorous.
They eat fish, other squid, and, in the case
of the largest species, whales.
<P ID=PG6 CLASS="yellowSmall">Different species of squid are seen in the seas
of the entire world.
They have evolved to take advantage of many different environmental
conditions. Their geography is more interesting at the species specific level.
</TD>
</TR>
</TABLE>
Click on a word in the left column to learn more about squid on the right!
<SCRIPT LANGUAGE=JavaScript>
var source
function yellowP() {
    source = window.event.srcElement;
    T1.className="yellowPlain";
    T2.className="yellowPlain";
    T3.className="yellowPlain";
    T4.className="yellowPlain";
    T5.className="yellowPlain";
    T6.className="yellowPlain";
    PG1.className="yellowSmall";
    PG2.className="yellowSmall";
    PG3.className="yellowSmall";
    PG4.className="yellowSmall";
    PG5.className="yellowSmall";
    PG6.className="yellowSmall";
    source.className="whitePlain";
    if (T1.className=="whitePlain")
        PG1.className="whitePlain";
    if (T2.className=="whitePlain")
        PG2.className="whitePlain";
    if (T3.className=="whitePlain")
        PG3.className="whitePlain";
    if (T4.className=="whitePlain")
        PG4.className="whitePlain";
    if (T5.className=="whitePlain")
        PG5.className="whitePlain";
    if (T6.className=="whitePlain")
        PG6.className="whitePlain";
}
</SCRIPT>
</BODY>
</HTML>
```

Figure 8.7 shows what happens after clicking the word Characteristics in the left column:
The informational list in the right column expands.

Figure 8.7.
The What Is a Squid?
page.

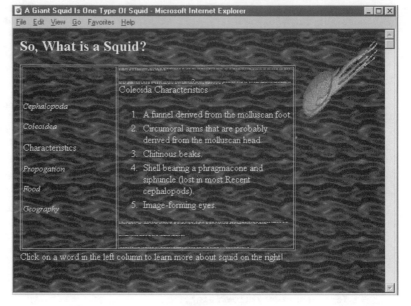

Remember to access each URL in Listing 8.5 with the `http://` protocol in your favorite Web browser. Include even the URLs that begin with the word `gopher`.

INPUT   **Listing 8.5. Squid-related URLs.**

```
www.nmnh.si.edu/departments/invert.html -- Smithsonian Zoology
www.nmnh.si.edu/cephs/ -- Smithsonian Cephalopods in Action
www.abdn.ac.uk/~nhi104/ -- The EuroSquid Page
www.abdn.ac.uk/~nhi104/workers.htm -- Cephalopod Researchers
is.dal.ca/~ceph/wood.html -- The Cephalopod Page
www.soest.hawaii.edu/tree/cephalopoda/cephalopoda.html -- Cephalopoda Tree
www.york.biosis.org/zrdocs/zoolinfo/grp_moll.htm -- Mollusca Resource Guide
www.nrcc.utmb.edu/ -- National Resource Center for Cephalopods
www.nbs.ac.uk/public/mlsd/ciac/index.html -- Cephalopod Int'l Advisories
www.oit.itd.umich.edu/bio/doc.cgi/Mollusca/Cephalopoda - Animal Diversity
www.stl.nps.navy.mil/~iirg/fieldnotes/ - California Field Notes
www.mindspring.com/~webrx/squid/squid.html -- The Squid Page
www.rsmas.miami.edu:80/sea-frontiers/fall-95/thrills.html -- Deep Thrills
www.abdn.ac.uk/~nhi104/far.htm -- North East Atlantic Squid Stocks
kingfish.ssp.nmfs.gov/olo/unit2.html -- Northeast Pelagic Fisheries
gopher.wh.whoi.edu/library/sos94/spsyn/iv/lfsquid.html -- Long-finned Squid
gopher.wh.whoi.edu/library/sos94/spsyn/iv/sfsquid.html -- Short-finned Squid
fisheries.com/SQUIDNET.HTM -- Squid Net from British Columbia
www.mbl.edu/html/life_sci/nerve.html -- The Giant Axon Research at MBL
www.clever.net/kerry/creature/creature.htm#Cephalopods -- Cephalopods from BC
www.nhm.ac.uk/museum/lifegal/13/13.html -- Marine Invertebrates
www.paragon.nf.ca/eastcost/squid.htm -- The Giant Squid by Robin McGrath
www.newstimes.com/archive/jan3196/inb.htm --Rare Giant Squid in New Zealand
www.ncf.carleton.ca/~bz050/HomePage.archi1.html -- Elusive Giant Squid
```

```
www.scholastic.com/public/Network/Antarctica/NZJournal1.html -- Giants
www.brainiac.com/aquanet/news/newslist/item2_1.htm -- Giant Squid Captured
www.vpm.com:80/cordova/squid.htm -- Teacher to Teacher Talk about Squidology
www.vpm.com:80/cordova/sqdpix_a.htm -- Squid Lesson Diagram
199.2.210.97:80/squid.html -- Squids A Student's Perspective
www.aai.org/opar/poster/squid.html -- Squid Poster
www.skio.peachnet.edu/noaa/tw/activities/actinvert.html -- Invertebrates
www.uwsports.ycg.com/magazine/1995/november_december/marinlif.htm -- Critters
www.calfish.com:80/calfish/fishop/squid.htm - Squid Fishing Tips
www.cs.cmu.edu:80/afs/cs/Web/People/mjw/recipes/seafood/squid-coll.html
www.newstimes.com/archive/apr2996/tvh.htm -- How Real is the Giant Squid
unmuseum.mus.pa.us/squid.htm -- Giant Squid Museum of Unnatural Mystery
userweb.lightspeed.net/~auntjudy/ -- The Great Squid Society of America
www.magi.com/%7Ekady/squid.html -- All Things Tentacled
www.okeanos.com/gallery/bbsqgal.html -- Squid Images
```

8

Dynamically Changing Content and Placement

Chapter 9

Dynamically Changing Content

Chapter 8, "Dynamically Changing Style," provided examples that demonstrated the power of dynamically changing styles by reviewing the Dynamic HTML syntax that adds interactivity to the Web page. This chapter introduces the concept of dynamically changing content through HTML replacement. You will be able to identify an object within your Web page and change the actual text or graphics that appear within the HTML tags that define the beginning and end of that object.

Specifically, in this chapter, you will learn

- ☐ What HTML replacement is
- ☐ Why change text contents?
- ☐ Changing text content
- ☐ An example of HTML text replacement
- ☐ Why change graphics content?
- ☐ An example of HTML graphics replacement

What Is HTML Replacement?

HTML replacement is a feature of Dynamic HTML that enables you to change the text or graphics that are associated with a specific HTML tag or tag pair. The <P></P> paragraph tag pair is an especially useful tag pair to use as the point of reference for setting up an object that enables you to change content. The <DIV></DIV> division tag pair is another useful tag pair to use when you want to replace whole sections of tags at a time. The examples in this chapter often use the <DIV></DIV> tag pair.

 NOTE One proposal for HTML's next official specification is the creation of an <IFRAME> tag to work similarly to a <FRAME> tag, except within the body of a scrollable document (thus completely scrolling off the visible window at times when traditional frames will not do). If you define a very large section with the <DIV></DIV> tag pair, you might want to investigate the <IFRAME> tag further to provide independent scrolling of the section within a defined area on your Web page.

Using HTML replacement, you can set up a paragraph that appears on a Web page as the following:

Step One—Create HTML Tags

Then it changes to the following when a reader initiates an event by interacting with the Web page:

1. Create HTML tags that can reference a block of Web page content and instantiate that block as a dynamic object using the ID attribute.

In other words, a Dynamic HTML Web page can load as shown in Figure 9.1 and then dynamically change to appear as in Figure 9.2 when the reader clicks the Step One—Create HTML Tags text. The page dynamically changes without an additional trip to the Web server.

You can enable a similar replacement for graphics so that a graphic image changes from one .gif or .jpg file to another. To enable graphics replacement, you simply place the changing <IMG> tags within the tag pair that sets up the changeable range within the page. In fact, you can vary the text and graphics so that a reader can click text and see a graphic appear or click a graphic and see text appear. Think of HTML replacement as having control of separate Web pages within one Web page that change not through links but through the new features of Dynamic HTML.

9

Figure 9.1.

The initial Web page.

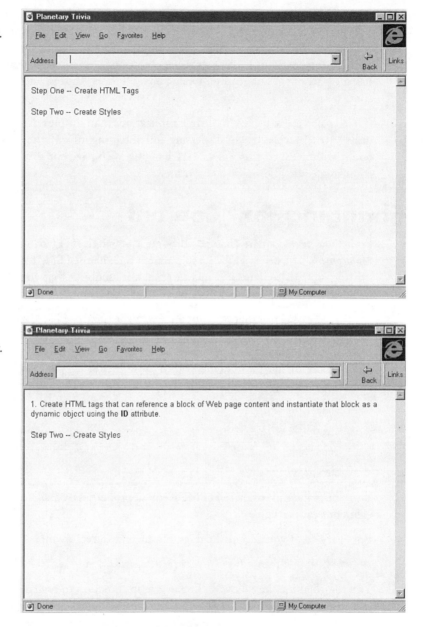

Why Change Text Contents?

Changing text content takes the concept of changing styles you studied in Chapter 8 one step further. Your motives for changing content will be similar to that for changing styles: to retain an audience and provide feedback on possible interactions or respond to interactive events triggered by a reader. Think how traditional graphical applications interact with users. When a program needs information from the user or has a message to communicate to the user, a dialog box, message box, or status bar comment appears on the screen temporarily to get or disperse information. Each interactive object appears on the screen when the user uses a specific part of the application. Dialog boxes, message boxes, and status bar comments are context sensitive.

If Web pages are to behave more like applications than simple encyclopedia pages, they, too, must have a mechanism for dispersing and obtaining information from the reader (who no doubt will be called a *user* as well). Changing Web page content is a great way to provide context-specific information to a reader.

Changing Text Content

You make text content changes through a Dynamic HTML mechanism called *HTML replacement*. The key to HTML replacement is Dynamic HTML's approach to defining the existing HTML tags and text in a text block as an object that you can change dynamically by an on-page script routine.

Every HTML tag pair that can contain text can be used for HTML content replacement. You identify the elements you want to change dynamically by instantiating them as objects through the ID= attribute. You then have four text element properties at your disposal to dynamically change the contents within the element's tag pair. An HTML element tag pair can change through the four following properties:

- [ ] `innerHTML`
- [ ] `outerHTML`
- [ ] `innerText`
- [ ] `outerText`

You can change any of these HTML element properties by assigning a new text string to the element's property.

For example, if you declare a paragraph, such as the following:

```
<P ID=PG1>I <B>love</B><I> Dynamic HTML</I></P>
```

You can then use the following line in a script function to reference the existing I `<B>love` `</B><I>Dynamic HTML</I>` HTML tags and text within the paragraph text block and change the contents:

```
PG1.innerHTML="as much as I <B>love</B> breathing";
```

After that, at any time within the flow of a script function, you can change the contents of paragraph PG1 by reassigning any of the four element range properties to a new string, a string I refer to as the assignment string.

NEW TERM It is important to understand exactly what an *element range* defines. An *element* is any HTML tag or tag pair that is parsed and treated as a unique item on a page. An element differs from an object in that an element is an object only if it is named with an ID attribute. The *range* is the span of influence an element has within the Web page. The range of a text block or section is defined by the HTML tags and text that appear between the opening and closing tags of the tag pair.

The innerHTML property defines the contents of an element object with HTML tags and maintains the existing tags that define the element. The outerHTML property also defines the contents of an element object with HTML tags, yet replaces the element itself with the outer tags identified in the assignment string.

The innerText property defines new contents of an element, but evaluates the assignment string as text only. The outerText property defines new contents of an element and eliminates the element tags in the process. The outerText property also evaluates the assignment string as text only. Any tags placed in the assignment string will appear as text on the page if you use the innerText or outerText properties.

Therefore, changing the innerHTML property of the PG1 paragraph maintains the <P></P> tag pair as part of the page. If instead you write the following statement and change the outerHTML property, you replace the <P></P> tags with new <DIV></DIV> tags:

```
PG1.outerHTML="<DIV>as much as I <B>love</B> breathing</DIV>";
```

Quite powerful, eh? These four properties can be changed for any valid HTML element tag pair. Even the <BODY></BODY> tag pair contents can be replaced with the innerHTML property. The outerHTML property is not available for the body tag pair. The HTML page would be invalid without the <BODY></BODY> tag pair.

Any Dynamic HTML event could trigger the script function that makes the dynamic content change. To make the example even cuter (is that possible?), replace the <B>love</B> HTML text with <IMG SRC="heart.gif">. The example still works with graphics included.

An Example of HTML Text Replacement

Now that you have the basics in hand, you are ready to see HTML text replacement in action. Here you will see an example that uses only text. You will see another HTML content replacement example using graphics later in this chapter, in Listing 9.2.

For this first example, you are a planetary expert from a university astronomy department who has a worldwide following. For years, you have been giving away interesting trivia about the planets in the solar system through magazine articles and an online Web site. Now with Dynamic HTML, you want your Web audience to have to work a little to get to some of the information. In fact, you are pretty sure they will enjoy playing a round of planetary trivia and will be more apt to come to the Web site more often if there are new trivia games to play each week. Yes, the advertisers are licking their chops just at the thought of it.

NOTE   If you are interested in a really great Web site on the planets and the expeditions that have been made to visit them, check out the Web site of the Jet Propulsion Laboratory at `http://pds.jpl.nasa.gov/planets/`

You decide to create your first Planets Test Web page complete with dynamically changing content. You provide a clean Web page table with four planets: Mars, Venus, Saturn, and Uranus, each as a separate row in the table. You provide four columns in your table, each with text edit boxes, one for each planet in each column. The first column is for your audience to enter the numbers 1 through 4 to rank the planets in terms of their distance from the sun (closest to furthest). The second column wants your users to order the planets by size (smallest to largest). The third column is for ranking the planets by day length (shortest to longest), and the fourth is for ranking the planets by surface temperature (coldest to warmest).

When readers want to see whether their answers are correct, they click the page heading, Planets Test, and, for each planet they have correct, they see the facts about that planet expand (through dynamic text replacement). To try again, they must click the Planets Test heading to collapse any answers they have correct so far.

On first loading the page, your audience will encounter the page as it is shown in Figure 9.3. Listing 9.1 provides the Dynamic HTML syntax that creates Figure 9.3. Look at the syntax and continue reading after the listing for a review of the details.

TECHNICAL NOTE   As in Chapter 8, the examples in this chapter comply with the latest information provided by the World Wide Web Consortium (W3C) as communicated by its Web site and were tested and proved to work using the beta 2 pre-release version of Microsoft's Internet Explorer 4.0.

Figure 9.3.
The Planets Test page.

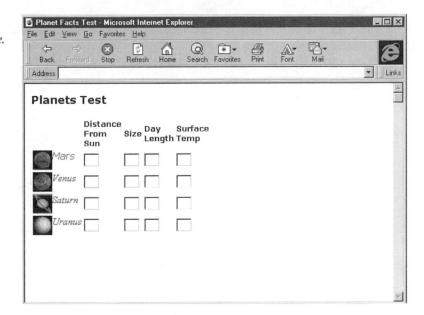

Listing 9.1. A Planets Test Web page.

```
<HTML>
<HEAD>
<FONT FACE="verdana,arial,helvetica" SIZE=3>
<TITLE>Planet Facts Test</TITLE>
</HEAD>
<BODY BGCOLOR="#FFFFFF">
<STYLE>
.redText {color:Red;
          font-style=italic;}
.blueText {color:Blue;
           font-style=italic;}
</STYLE>
<H3 onclick="expandP();">Planets Test</H3>
<TABLE><TR>
<TD> </TD>
<TD><H5>Distance<BR>From<BR>Sun</H5></TD>
<TD><H5>Size</H5></TD>
<TD><H5>Day<BR>Length</H5></TD>
<TD><H5>Surface<BR>Temp</H5></TD>
</TR>
<TR><TD>
<IMG SRC="mars.gif" ALIGN=LEFT HEIGHT=32>
<DIV id=mars CLASS="blueText">Mars</DIV>
</TD>
<TD><INPUT NAME="Q11" SIZE=2></TD>
<TD><INPUT NAME="Q21" SIZE=2></TD>
<TD><INPUT NAME="Q31" SIZE=2></TD>
<TD><INPUT NAME="Q41" SIZE=2></TD>
```

continues

Listing 9.1. continued

```
</TR><TR><TD>
<IMG SRC="venus.gif" ALIGN=LEFT HEIGHT=32>
<DIV id=venus CLASS="blueText">Venus</DIV>
</TD>
<TD><INPUT NAME="Q12" SIZE=2></TD>
<TD><INPUT NAME="Q22" SIZE=2></TD>
<TD><INPUT NAME="Q32" SIZE=2></TD>
<TD><INPUT NAME="Q42" SIZE=2></TD>
</TR><TR><TD>
<IMG SRC="saturn.gif" ALIGN=LEFT HEIGHT=32 WIDTH=32>
<DIV id=saturn CLASS="blueText">Saturn</DIV>
</TD>
<TD><INPUT NAME="Q13" SIZE=2></TD>
<TD><INPUT NAME="Q23" SIZE=2></TD>
<TD><INPUT NAME="Q33" SIZE=2></TD>
<TD><INPUT NAME="Q43" SIZE=2></TD>
</TR><TR><TD>
<IMG SRC="uranus.gif" ALIGN=LEFT HEIGHT=32>
<DIV id=uranus CLASS="blueText">Uranus</DIV>
</TD>
<TD><INPUT NAME="Q14" SIZE=2></TD>
<TD><INPUT NAME="Q24" SIZE=2></TD>
<TD><INPUT NAME="Q34" SIZE=2></TD>
<TD><INPUT NAME="Q44" SIZE=2></TD>
</TR>
</TABLE>
<SCRIPT LANGUAGE=JavaScript>
function expandP() {
   if (Q11.value=="2" && Q21.value=="1" && Q31.value=="3" && Q41.value=="3") {
      mars.innerHTML="<B><I>Mars</I></B><BR><BR>Diameter: 6,787 km<BR>" +
         "Rotation: 1.02 days<BR>Temperature: 230 K<BR> Distance From Sun: " +
         "1.52<BR>";
      mars.className="redText";
    } else {
      mars.innerHTML="Mars<BR><BR>";
      mars.className="blueText";
    }
   if (Q12.value=="1" && Q22.value=="2" && Q32.value=="4" && Q42.value=="4") {
      venus.innerHTML="<B><I>Venus</I></B><BR><BR>Diameter: 12,104 km" +
         "<BR>Rotation: 243 days<BR>Temperature: 726 K<BR>Distance From " +
         "Sun: .723<BR>";
      venus.className="redText";
    } else {
      venus.innerHTML="Venus";
      venus.className="blueText";
    }
   if (Q13.value=="3" && Q23.value=="4" && Q33.value=="1" && Q43.value=="2") {
      saturn.innerHTML="<B><I>Saturn</I></B><BR><BR>Diameter: " +
         "120,660 km<BR>Rotation: 10.2 hours<BR>Temperature: 88 K<BR>" +
         "Distance From Sun: 9.54<BR>";
      saturn.className="redText";
    } else {
      saturn.innerHTML="Saturn";
      saturn.className="blueText";
```

```
    }
    if (Q14.value=="4" && Q24.value=="3" && Q34.value=="2" && Q44.value=="1") {
        uranus.innerHTML="<B><I>Uranus</I></B><BR><BR>Diameter: " +
            "51,118 km<BR>Rotation: 17.9 hours<BR>Temperature: 59 K<BR>" +
            "Distance From Sun: 19.18<BR>";
        uranus.className="redText";
    } else {
        uranus.innerHTML="Uranus";
        uranus.className="blueText";
    }
}
</SCRIPT>
</FONT>
</BODY>
</HTML>
```

Figure 9.4 shows the state of the Web page after a reader has entered the correct numbers for ranking the planet Saturn. He or she has clicked the heading Planets Test to see how many he or she has correct, and the Web page responds that only one is correct.

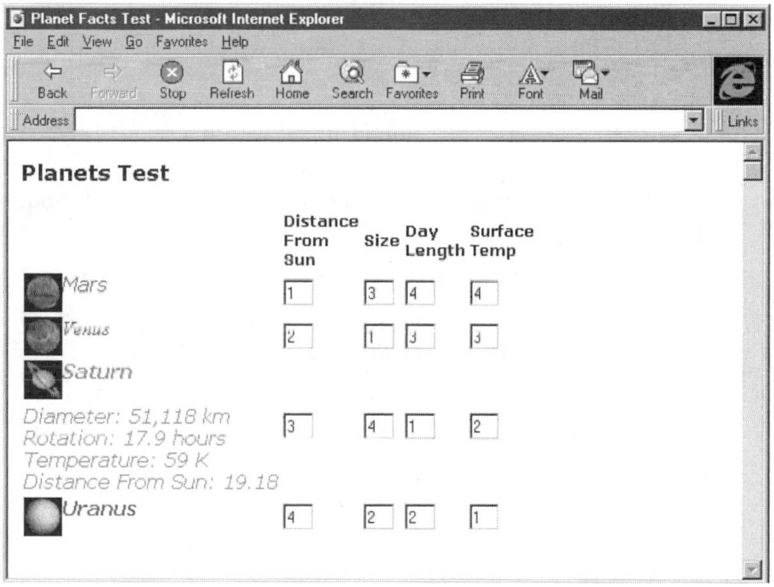

Figure 9.4.

Planets Test after text replacement.

Listing 9.1 is rather long, but fortunately, quite redundant. Review the listing from top to bottom to learn the significant parts related to Dynamic HTML.

Listing 9.1 starts out similar to the examples in Chapter 8 by defining several styles within a <STYLE></STYLE> tag pair. In fact, the redText and blueText are exactly the same as in Listing 8.1. Remember that you could define a style sheet in an external file and reference the same style sheet file in multiple pages.

The `blueText` style is used initially to set all the planet names to a simple, blue text style. The `redText` style becomes active only when the expanded planet information is displayed when a reader correctly answers all the values for a specific planet. Remember, with the method demonstrated in Chapter 8, the `CLASS` attribute is used to change the text style over time.

The Planets Test page heading contains the attribute `onclick="expandP();"`, which sets up an event for a reader's mouse to click the heading. When a reader clicks the heading, a script function named `expandP()` will be executed. Notice that `expandP()` is the only script function on the page and is called only from a single mouse click on the Planets Test text.

The components within the page are created within a standard HTML table. After the column header row, the next four rows contain a planet image, planet name, and four text boxes. Each planet name is set up similar to `<DIV ID=venus CLASS="blueText">Venus</DIV>`, the specific Venus division. The `<DIV></DIV>` division tag pair sets up each planet name as an element range. Venus is named through the `ID` attribute with value venus. The venus value will be loaded as blue text, as the `CLASS="blueText"` attribute dictates.

Each text box is set up similarly to `<INPUT NAME="Q13" SIZE=2>`. The box is set up with a `NAME` attribute to be interrogated from within a script function. The `SIZE` specifies how wide the text box will appear to a reader. In this particular text box, the `Q13` name stands for question 1, choice 3.

The `expandP()` script function is placed within a `<SCRIPT></SCRIPT>` tag pair. The script is written in JavaScript and requires no local variables. The logic contains four similar sections. Each section compares the values a reader has entered into the four text boxes for a planet with the correct answers.

The script logic for Mars follows:

```
if (Q11.value=="2" && Q21.value=="1" && Q31.value=="3" && Q41.value=="3") {
    mars.innerHTML="<B><I>Mars</I></B><BR><BR>Diameter: 6,787 km " +
        "<BR>Rotation: 1.02 days<BR>Temperature: 230 K<BR> Distance " +
        "From Sun: 1.52<BR>";
    mars.className="redText";
  } else {
    mars.innerHTML="Mars<BR><BR>";
    mars.className="blueText";
  }
}
```

The first line of the script compares the values the reader has entered for Mars with the correct answers. From left to right, the correct answers are 2, 1, 3, and 3. If all four values are in fact those that the reader entered, the HTML text replacement is made. The element range's `innerText` property for the division with the attribute `ID=mars` is assigned a new string that changes the element range's contents. The text style changes to `redText` for a more dramatic effect on a correct answer.

If, on the other hand, a planet's answers are incorrect, the text element's range is set back to a simple planet name string with a couple of line breaks. The text style remains the `blueText` style to provide additional feedback that the answer is still incorrect. Mars-similar logic is repeated three other times for Venus, Saturn, and Uranus.

Why Change Graphics Content?

A better question than "WHY change graphics content?" might be "Why NOT change graphics content?" Everywhere we go nowadays, graphics are changing all the time. It is no longer good enough that a roadside billboard proudly displays a time-honored marketing slogan. No, billboards have all kinds of moving parts nowadays. Imagine television if the picture did not change. Silly thought, eh? We have become quite the point-and-click, image-hungry society. Our brains are attracted to motion and our brains process images efficiently, so why not?

Changing graphics is a must if Web pages are to corral their share of the software application market. Video games always change the player's graphical representation to give him or her special powers or to finish him or her off. Software toolbars change tool button shapes and colors to provide feedback on the state of each tool. Animations are a series of changing images that appear to be continuous to a reader's brain. Such is the case for Web-based movie watching or virtual environment exploration.

NOTE

> A virtual environment is a three-dimensional model that you can load in your computer's memory and traverse in six directions: forward, backward, up, down, left, and right. If you are interested in the concept of virtual environments on the Web, do some research on VRML 2, the Virtual Reality Modeling Language's second specification. VRML 2 is an attempt to define interactive virtual environments within a singular file for a Web browser to load. Sound familiar to what Dynamic HTML is doing to HTML for Web pages?

I am not sure whether a movie or virtual environment will ever be self-contained in an HTML Web page without requiring an additional file of some sort. Imagine the length of the scripts that would be involved. However, there is no need for you to get that far ahead of yourself now. The example that follows shows the power of just a few timely graphical changes.

An Example of HTML Graphics Replacement

In this example of HTML graphics replacement, you will revisit the planet trivia test from the last example. This time, though, the feedback will be more immediate and colorful.

You are interested in providing a multiple choice quiz in which a reader can click on one of four planets to get a visual response as to whether they chose the right answer. You obtain images for each planet from an Internet Web site with no copyright restrictions, and create your own images for the correct and incorrect answer feedback. Then you write a Dynamic HTML Web page to put it all together, complete with dynamically changing graphics.

NOTE

> To create the images for the correct and incorrect answers, I used the Paint program, which comes as an accessory in Windows 95. It took me about three minutes. Hopefully, to my audience it will look as though I spent a little more time than that.

Figure 9.5 shows a question from the multiple choice planet trivia game example before a reader clicks one of the planets to submit an answer. Listing 9.2 provides the Dynamic HTML syntax that created the page after the reader loaded it in a Web browser. Take a look at the listing, and then continue reading for an explanation.

Figure 9.5.

The multiple choice planets test.

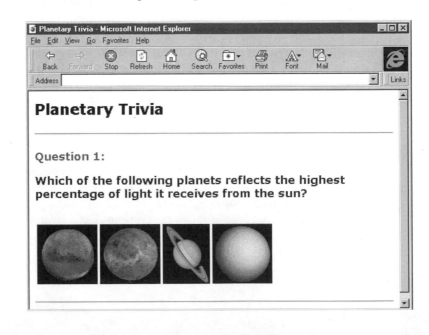

INPUT **Listing 9.2. A planets test trivia question.**

```
<HTML>
<HEAD>
<FONT FACE="verdana,arial,helvetica" SIZE=2>
<TITLE>Planetary Trivia</TITLE>
</HEAD>
<BODY BGCOLOR="#FFFFFF">
<H2>Planetary Trivia</H2>
<HR>
<BR>
<H3><P ID=Q1 STYLE="color:Blue">
<B>Question 1: </B>
<P>
Which of the following planets reflects the highest percentage
of light it receives from the sun?
</H3>
<BR>
<TABLE>
<TR><TD><IMG SRC="mars.gif" ID=A11 onclick="Answer1();"></TD>
<TD><IMG SRC="venus.gif" ID=A12 onclick="Answer1();"></TD>
<TD><IMG SRC="saturn.gif" ID=A13 onclick="Answer1();"></TD>
<TD><IMG SRC="uranus.gif" ID=A14 onclick="Answer1();"></TD></TR>
</TABLE>
<P ID=A1></P>

<SCRIPT LANGUAGE=JavaScript>
var srcElement
function Answer1() {
  srcElement = window.event.srcElement;
  if (Q1.style.color=="blue") {
     if (srcElement.id=="A12") {
        srcElement.src = "correct.gif";
        Q1.style.color= "Green";
     } else {
        srcElement.src = "wrong.gif";
        Q1.style.color= "Red";
     }
     A1.innerHTML="<B>Venus</B> has an albedo of 59% " ¦
        "which is much higher than the other answers";
  }
}
</SCRIPT>

<HR>
</FONT>
</BODY>
</HTML>
```

Figure 9.6 shows the Web page after a reader clicks a correct answer. Figure 9.7 shows the Web page after a reader clicks an incorrect answer.

Figure 9.6.
A Planets Test guess is made correctly.

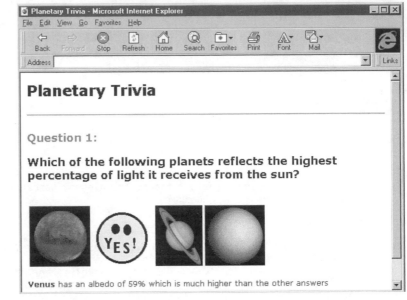

Figure 9.7.
A Planets Test guess is made incorrectly.

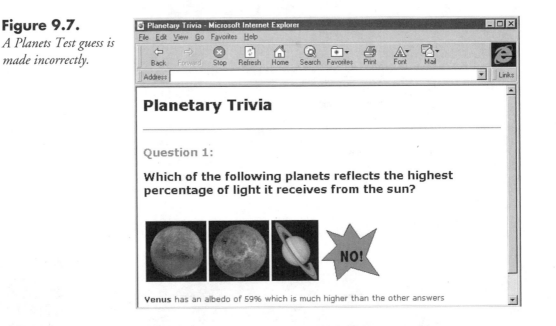

The first thing you might notice in Listing 9.2 is that there is not a single <STYLE> tag. Instead, I used a STYLE attribute, placed within the <P> tag in the location where the CLASS attribute was placed in previous examples. The STYLE attribute value of "color:Blue" defines a blue text color for the paragraph named Q1. I chose the name Q1 to signify question 1.

Listing 9.2 is unique as well in that I am actually setting up the <IMG> tags with an ID attribute and an event attribute for each planet. The two attributes share space with the traditional SRC attribute. The event I chose to use for selecting a question answer is the onclick event. What else would a reader expect? The onclick event is associated with the Answer1() script function with the onclick=Answer1() attribute.

NOTE

> You could use the document_onclick event that is available for each Web page loaded in a Dynamic HTML-compatible browser. Then, you could interrogate which image had been clicked and perform the appropriate steps for that question, all within one long script. For this example, however, a separate script function for each answer would be more self-documenting and flexible for adding new questions. Either method would be quite acceptable, though.

The <P ID=A1></P> line sets up a paragraph named A1, which is an element range that will house question 1's answer after the reader has made a guess by clicking a planet image. Notice that it is perfectly fine to create a text block with no text in it.

I have used a traditional HTML table to organize the planetary pictures.

The script function Answer1() is contained within a <SCRIPT></SCRIPT> tag pair, as usual. The function uses a single local variable: srcElement holds a reference to the element in the page that triggers an event. The source element of the event is set in the following line:

```
srcElement = window.event.srcElement;
```

As for the core logic of the script function, the current style of the Q1 text block is interrogated. If Q1 is blue, the reader is choosing an answer for the first time for question 1. If not, the color of the text is either red or green, based on the reader's first answer attempt. Red reflects an incorrect answer. Green reflects a correct answer.

If Q1 is blue, the function logic checks whether the reader has selected the correct answer. For question 1, the image named A12, Venus, is the correct answer. If A12 has been clicked, Venus's image is replaced with a new image, a smiley face that represents choosing the right answer. That replacement is made possible with the following line:

```
srcElement.src = "correct.gif";.
```

Yes, changing an image that is the source of an event is that easy.

The color of the Question 1: text changes to green with the following line, which is feedback to the reader that he or she chose the correct answer:

```
Q1.style.color= "Green";
```

If, on the other hand, the reader selects the Mars, Saturn, or Uranus image, the image is replaced with `"incorrect.gif"` and the Question 1: text becomes red.

In either case, as long as a reader is choosing an answer for a first time, the answer appears as a line of text after the row of images. The HTML text replacement is accomplished through the following lines:

```
A1.innerHTML="<B>Venus</B> has an albedo of 59% " +
     "which is much higher than the other answers";
```

The script is set up to easily define a second function named `Answer2()`. You could just copy and paste parts of the question 1 listing and change a few things to reflect the details of question 2. In fact, you will do that as part of a quiz question at the end of this chapter.

NOTE Now that you have seen an example of graphics replacement, you can look forward to Chapter 10, "Dynamically Altering the Placement of Elements," when you will add animation to a Web page similar to the one in Figure 9.6 to create an Old Shell Game Web page. Basically, the HTML tags and text will be the same. Only the script will change to add movement to the graphical objects created by the `<IMG>` tags.

NOTE If you want to mix text with graphics in the example from Listing 9.2, you would need to return to the `document.rangeFromElement()` and `pasteHTML()` methods of the text replacement example. Within the element range you are replacing, you can include or exclude one or more `<IMG>` image tags to include or exclude the graphics, respectively.

As more questions are added to the planetary trivia Web page, creating a subprocedure that can automatically correct each question a reader answers makes more and more sense.

Take a look at the answer processing logic for question 1:

```
if (srcElement.id=="A12") {
   srcElement.src = "correct.gif";
   Q1.style.color= "Green";
} else {
   srcElement.src = "wrong.gif";
   Q1.style.color= "Red";
}
```

The only parameters that are required to generalize a subroutine are the "A12" and "Q1" strings, as well as the srcElement. Such a subroutine could significantly reduce the download time for the page because the page would contain less text. You should always look for such opportunities.

Such a Web-based trivia page could be the cornerstone behind distance learning for diploma or degree consideration. Certainly the average middle school student might prefer to click a computer screen than slave at a desk with pen and paper. As you will see in the next chapter, Dynamic HTML enables a reader to move images around on the page. You will be able to place the planets randomly on the page and ask the reader to put them in the appropriate place on a map of the solar system. Cool, huh? Don't just jump there now, though. There are Q&A, Quiz, and Workshop sections to do before you move on to Chapter 10.

Summary

HTML tag replacement takes style changes a step further. Instead of changing how text appears to the reader, you can change the text itself to say something completely different. In fact, with HTML tag replacement, you can insert graphics into a text block that were not there when the page loaded. An HTML tag that is appropriate for HTML replacement is called a *range element*. Popular tags used to mark a range for replacement include the <P> and <DIV> tags.

This chapter provided an example in Listing 9.2 that replaces graphics without a range element. Instead, the graphic is changed within the <IMG> tag using its src attribute, which is available to be interrogated and changed in a script function. Continuing with the momentum from Chapter 8, style changes are also made to reflect the significance of the graphic replacements.

This chapter is a stepping stone to further dynamic changing graphics effects explored in Chapter 10. In Chapter 10, you create simple animations from the same script functions demonstrated in this chapter. You just add a loop to the script and vary the location of the graphic over time. During the animation, a graphical image can change to reflect something that happens to the image as it moves about on the page. Animated behavior is required of graphics in many applications.

However, with all the excitement about graphics, the ability to dynamically change text content is just as powerful. Using text leaves visualization to the imagination of the reader. Some readers will prefer to create their own images sometimes. Listing 9.1 provides a typical example of using dynamically changing text to keep a reader interested in your page.

Q&A

Q **Because the World Wide Web Consortium is expanding HTML to become more useful to electronic publishers and word processors, why isn't the `<DIV>` tag instead a `<SECTION>` or `<SECT>` tag? I mean, I use sections all the time when I do word processing. What is the difference between a section and a division?**

A Usually when I use a word processor, I create a section to provide a format to one page or paragraph that is different than the page or paragraph preceding that section. For example, I create a section to add an extra column on a page. The use of divisions in HTML is extremely flexible. I can create a division that includes just a single word, like `<DIV>Word</DIV>`. I suspect many people would not feel comfortable calling that a section because it is so small.

Q **HTML replacement seems extremely flexible. Is it true that I can replace current HTML element range contents with any HTML tags I want?**

A I suspect that you should be able to add any tags to an element range as long as those tags would make sense if they had been there in the first place. For example, if the range originally contained an end tag of a tag pair, you might need to provide that end tag in your replacement tags. Remember that HTML replacement opens up a tremendous number of possible states for a Web page. If a certain order of tags you devise does not work as a replacement, consider what you are asking the Web browser to do. Perhaps some special processing would need to take place to do what you are asking the browser to do through the replacement. If so, it is possible that particular processing has not been added to the Web browser yet. My approach is to try anything, but use only what works. A more aggressive approach is to get involved with the Web browser developer and send e-mail or phone messages when things do not work.

Q **In your previous answer, what do you mean by *special processing* that might be necessary by the Web browser?**

A Web browsers have been evolving their processing logic based on the needs of readers. For example, initially, images were loaded at the point they were encountered in the HTML file, and Web browsers did not continue until the image was completely loaded. Yet, readers preferred to continue reading text while the images were loading. Therefore, Web browser developers changed the processing to continue loading Web page text while the images were loading as well.

Now, all of sudden with Dynamic HTML, readers are making even more requests. The processing logic is that much more complex. If a reader clicks a dynamic

HTML element while the Web page has not yet finished loading, what response should the Web browser give to the click? I would call that decision point a special processing decision because it was not required of Web browsers before Dynamic HTML was incorporated. A new set of tags might radically change the appearance of a Web page. Perhaps it might affect the other elements on the page that are not changing directly in the tag replacement. The Web browser might not yet know how to gracefully handle that request. Be patient with tag replacement while dynamic Web browsers mature.

Quiz

Take the following quiz to see how much you've learned in this chapter.

Questions

1. Which new HTML tag pair is very flexible for defining sections on a Web page?

2. What is the difference between an object and an element?

3. Are objects a subset of elements or are elements a subset of objects?

4. Which object or objects are automatically defined on a dynamic Web page at load time?

5. To perform HTML tag replacement, you use which key line in your script function?

6. Without looking at Listing 9.2 unless absolutely necessary, can you create a second question asking which of the planets rotates on its axis in the opposite direction of all other planets in the solar system? Again, Venus is the answer because its rotation is considered retrograde.

Answers

1. The `<DIV></DIV>` tag pair is very flexible. You will compare that with Netscape's `<LAYER></LAYER>` tag pair in Chapter 10.

2. An object is an element that has been named with an `ID` attribute (or, in some cases, with a `NAME` attribute).

3. Objects are subsets of elements on a Web page. Not every element is an object, but all objects continue to be elements.

4. The document object is automatically available for you to use in a script function. The document object is automatically defined at load time.

5. The `document.rangeFromElement()` line is critical to HTML replacement because it defines the element for which you are replacing tags.

6. The following is a possible implementation of trivia question 2:

```
<HTML>
<HEAD>
<TITLE>Planetary Trivia</TITLE>
</HEAD>
<BODY BGCOLOR="#FFFFFF">
<H2>Planetary Trivia</H2>
<HR>
<BR>
<H3><P ID=Q2 STYLE="color:Blue">
<B>Question 2: </B>
<P>Which planet rotates on its axis in the opposite direction
   of all other planets in the solar system?</P>
</H3>
<BR>
<TABLE>
<TR><TD><IMG SRC="mars.gif" ID=A21 onclick="Answer2();"></TD>
<TD><IMG SRC="venus.gif" ID=A22 onclick="Answer2();"></TD>
<TD><IMG SRC="saturn.gif" ID=A23 onclick="Answer2();"></TD>
<TD><IMG SRC="uranus.gif" ID=A24 onclick="Answer2();"></TD></TR>
</TABLE>
<P ID=A2></P>

<SCRIPT LANGUAGE=JavaScript>
var srcElement
function Answer2() {
  srcElement = window.event.srcElement;
  if (Q2.style.color=="blue") {
     if (srcElement.id=="A22") {
        srcElement.src = "correct.gif";
        Q2.style.color= "Green";
     } else {
        srcElement.src = "wrong.gif";
        Q2.style.color= "Red";
     }
     A2.innerHTML="<B>Venus</B> is the only planet that rotates against " +
         "the grain, a condition called <I>retrograde</I> rotation";
  }
}
</SCRIPT>
<HR>
</BODY>
</HTML>
```

Workshop

In this workshop, you will continue building your Giant Blind South Pacific Squid Research Web site. Remember that the second link on the welcome page you created in Chapter 7, "Changing Text Attributes," is named Who Researches Squid?. In this workshop, create a Web page that introduces a reader to the key members of the research team. In your key researcher Web page, use the HTML tag replacement features of this chapter to provide dynamic interactivity for your readers. Blend this page in with the look and feel of the rest of your Web site. Do not forget to save your work in an HTML file with the right filename that the HREF attribute value in the link's anchor tag on the welcome page expects.

There are five key members of the giant squid research team. Each has a specialty that is invaluable to the team's success. Here is the data I want you to use for the page you create.

Goreng Veng is a 33-year-old cephalopod specialist from Vietnam. He knows much about the octopus and squid, and began his fascination with the sea when he was six years old. He can speak four southeast Asian languages and impressive English. Goreng is always smiling while he works and has an outgoing personality.

Chaka Binte is a 31-year-old marine biologist from Philadelphia, Pennsylvania, in the United States. She has been working in the water since her father taught her how to fish off the coast of West Africa at the age of seven. The team always admires her natural sixth sense of intuition that has saved the team countless hours of wasted effort.

Ernesto Charrez is a 36-year-old technologist from Santiago, Chile. He has an amazing grasp of today's computer capabilities, as well as a great philosophical attitude toward computer use. He always reminds the team that technology does not make human beings any more important, but, instead, gives humanity more responsibility in the future of all living things.

Carl Genf is a 42-year-old head diver from Munich, Germany. He is a fanatic when it comes to marine exploration. He often drives the team on to new accomplishments with a friendly reminder that he does not have as many years ahead of him as the rest of them. He consistently demonstrates the attitude that nothing is impossible.

Thomas White is a 33-year-old marine biologist from Adelaide, Australia. He prefers the nickname Tommy. He kids the team that they are in his part of the world and he should have first say on the issues. Another of the natural outdoorsmen of the group, he balances his talents with a quick wit and incredible athletic preparation.

For my implementation, I have chosen to create a table with each key researcher as a separate row. The first column in the table contains a picture of the researcher. A user is able to move the mouse over any picture to see the comments associated with that researcher. I provide a larger picture of that researcher to the reader based on the mouse position as well. Note that I also have chosen VBScript for the scripting language. You can also use JavaScript instead.

After you are finished creating your implementation, look at mine in Listing 9.3. If you need inspiration, look at Figure 9.8 before you get started. I am sure you can outdo my example.

Listing 9.3. My key researchers HTML file.

```
<HTML>
<HEAD>
<TITLE>The Giant Squid Research Team</TITLE>
</HEAD>
<BODY BACKGROUND="water.jpg" TEXT=#FFFFFF LINK=FFFF22 VLINK=FF22FF>
<STYLE>
.redText {color:Red;
          font-style=italic;}
.yellowText {color:Yellow;
          font-style=italic;}
</STYLE>
<IMG SRC="giant.gif" WIDTH=128 ALIGN=RIGHT>
<H2>The Research Team</H2>
<TABLE><TR>
<TD></TD>
<TD WIDTH=120><B>Name</B></TD>
<TD WIDTH=120  CLASS="yellowText">Nationality</TD>
<TD WIDTH=50   CLASS="yellowText">Age</TD>
<TD CLASS="yellowText">Duties</TD>
</TR>
<TR><TD>
<IMG ID=R1 SRC="1.jpg" onmouseover="ExpandR();" ALIGN=LEFT HEIGHT=32>
</TD>
<TD><DIV ID=veng CLASS="yellowText">Goreng Veng</DIV></TD>
<TD>Vietnamese</TD>
<TD>33</TD>
<TD>Cephalopod Specialist</TD>
</TR><TR><TD>
<IMG ID=R2 SRC="2.jpg" onmouseover="ExpandR();" ALIGN=LEFT HEIGHT=32>
</TD>
<TD><DIV ID=binte CLASS="yellowText">Chaka Binte</DIV></TD>
<TD>American</TD>
<TD>31</TD>
<TD>Marine Biologist</TD>
</TR><TR><TD>
<IMG ID=R3 SRC="3.jpg" onmouseover="ExpandR();" ALIGN=LEFT HEIGHT=32>
</TD>
<TD><DIV ID=charrez CLASS="yellowText">Ernesto Charrez</DIV></TD>
<TD>Chilean</TD>
<TD>36</TD>
<TD>Technologist</TD>
</TR><TR><TD>
<IMG ID=R4 SRC="4.jpg" onmouseover="ExpandR();" ALIGN=LEFT HEIGHT=32>
</TD>
<TD><DIV ID=genf CLASS="yellowText">Carl Genf</DIV></TD>
<TD>German</TD>
<TD>42</TD>
<TD>Head Diver</TD>
</TR><TR><TD>
<IMG ID=R5 SRC="5.jpg" onmouseover="ExpandR();" ALIGN=LEFT HEIGHT=32>
</TD>
<TD><DIV ID=white CLASS="yellowText">Thomas White</DIV></TD>
<TD>Australian</TD>
<TD>33</TD>
<TD>Marine Biologist</TD>
```

```
</TR>
</TABLE>
<IMG ID=feature src="1.jpg" HEIGHT=128 WIDTH=128 ALIGN=RIGHT>
<P ID=detail>Details:</P>
<SCRIPT LANGUAGE=JavaScript>
var srcElement
function ExpandR() {
  veng.className="yellowText";
  binte.className="yellowText";
  charrez.className="yellowText";
  genf.className="yellowText";
  white.className="yellowText";
  srcElement = window.event.srcElement;
  if (srcElement.id=="R1") {
     veng.className="redText";
     feature.src = "1.jpg";
     detail.innerHTML="<B>Goreng</B> began his fascination with the " +
        "sea at 6 years of age.  He is an integral member of the " +
        "team for both his deep understanding of the Cephalopod " +
        "species and his ability to speak 4 southeast Asian languages " +
        "and impressive English.  Goreng is always smiling while he works";
  } else if (srcElement.id=="R2") {
     binte.className="redText";
     feature.src = "2.jpg";
     detail.innerHTML="<B>Chaka</B> has been working in the water " +
        "since her father taught her how to fish off the coast of West " +
        "Africa at the age of seven.  The team always admires her " +
        "natural sixth sense of intuition that has saved the team " +
        "countless hours of wasted efforts.";
  } else if (srcElement.id=="R3") {
     charrez.className="redText";
     feature.src = "3.jpg";
     detail.innerHTML="<B>Ernesto</B> has an amazing grasp of today's " +
        "computer capabilities as well as a great philosophical attitude " +
        "towards its use.  He always reminds us that technology does not " +
        "make human beings any more important, but instead, gives us " +
        "more responsibility in the future of all living things.";
  } else if (srcElement.id=="R4") {
     genf.className="redText";
     feature.src = "4.jpg";
     detail.innerHTML="Every team has its fanatic.  Ours is no " +
        "exception.  <B>Carl</B> drives us on to new accomplishments " +
        "with a friendly reminder that he does not have as many years " +
        "ahead of him as the rest of us.  We have yet to hear him say the " +
        "word <I>impossible</I>";
  } else if (srcElement.id=="R5") {
     white.className="redText";
     feature.src = "5.jpg";
     detail.innerHTML="<B>Tommy</B> tries to tell us that we are in his " +
        "part of the world so he should have first say.  Another one of " +
        "the natural outdoorsmen of the group, he balances his talents " +
        "with a quick wit and incredible athletic preparation.";
  }
}
</SCRIPT>
</BODY>
</HTML>
```

Figure 9.8 presents my key researcher Web page after a reader has clicked Thomas White's photo in the first column.

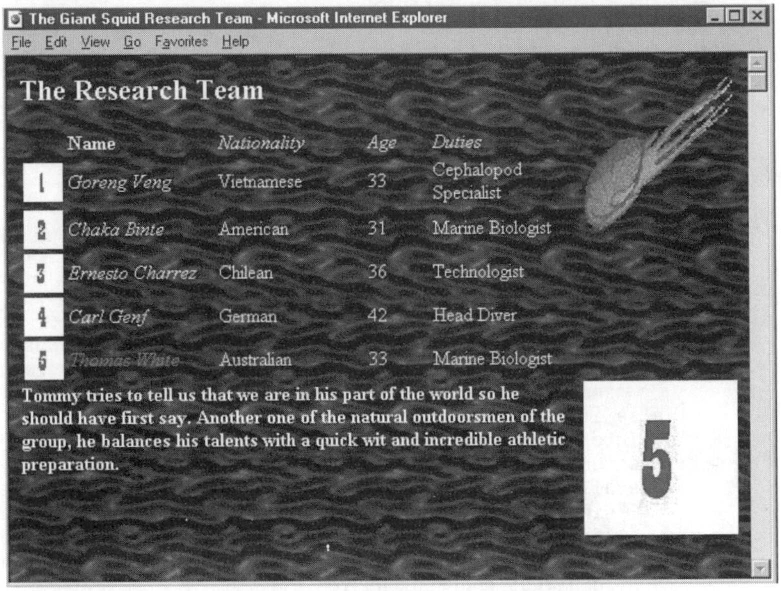

Figure 9.8.

A key researcher Web page.

The Giant Squid Research Team - Microsoft Internet Explorer

File   Edit   View   Go   Favorites   Help

The Research Team

	Name	Nationality	Age	Duties
1	Goreng Veng	Vietnamese	33	Cephalopod Specialist
2	Chaka Binte	American	31	Marine Biologist
3	Ernesto Charrez	Chilean	36	Technologist
4	Carl Genf	German	42	Head Diver
5	Thomas White	Australian	33	Marine Biologist

Tommy tries to tell us that we are in his part of the world so he should have first say. Another one of the natural outdoorsmen of the group, he balances his talents with a quick wit and incredible athletic preparation.

5

Chapter 10

Dynamically Altering the Placement of Elements

In Chapter 9, "Dynamically Changing Content," you saw examples that demonstrated the power of dynamically changing Web page content, both text and graphics, using Dynamic HTML. This chapter expands on the examples in Chapter 9 to introduce both reader control of Web page element placement and graphics animation. With the skills you learn in this chapter, you will be off and running in creating all kinds of interesting, interactive Web pages. And each page will continue to be delivered as a single .htm or .html file through a single trip to the Web server.

In this chapter, you learn the following:

☐ Positioning elements

☐ An example of reader positioning control

☐ Why animate?

☐ Animation through looping scripts

☐ Using depth in a script

☐ Examples of animations

Positioning Elements

Every Web page element occupies a position within the Web page browser window. In traditional Web browsers that are compliant with older HTML specifications, the Web browser positions elements once when the page is loaded and then fixes the element in that location. Some elements have attributes that enable a Web page author much control over how the element should be placed relative to other elements that are nearby in the .html file. For example, the <IMG> tag has an ALIGN attribute that positions an image relative to any body text that follows.

NOTE

> To be more accurate, with traditional HTML, the elements stay in their loaded position unless the reader changes the browser window size. If the reader changes the window dimensions, the Web browser repositions the elements, and they are then fixed to the new window dimensions.

Dynamic HTML still relies heavily on the initial position in which a Web author places elements within a Web page. But after the page is loaded, Dynamic HTML provides a mechanism with which a reader can change the position of elements using the events and scripts you make available in the page.

Why Position Graphics?

Your motives for positioning graphics are similar to your motives for controlling text style and content. You want to place graphics on a page in a manner that looks as pleasing to the eye as possible. Yet your readers might want to position graphics in order to play a game or provide feedback to the Web page provider. With the prerelease version of Internet Explorer 4, Microsoft provides an application in its online gallery that enables a reader to drag and drop vegetable images onto the silhouette of an alien to make alien faces. Such an application is cute and enjoyable to tinker around with because it stirs up creative thinking and imagination.

Imagine instead that there was a local police crime-reporting Web site to which a citizen who witnessed a crime could go to drag and drop realistic facial components and provide feedback about a suspected criminal he or she had seen at the scene of the crime. That could be not only entertaining but of societal value as well. Dynamic HTML provides a framework for authoring Web pages that gives your readers control over where graphics are placed. So you could easily create a crime-reporting Web page in a single .html file that accesses all the separate image files you want to provide as movable elements.

Movable objects on a Web page were one of the showcased, exciting features of the alpha Java Development Kit. On one initial Java informational Web page, a first-time user could download Java's HotJava browser and download a Java applet that enabled the reader to apply different makeup effects to the picture of a member of the Java team. The Java language has pushed Web technology and enabled the Web community to accept or reject new features. The HTML specification need not compete with full-fledged programming languages such as Java, but there is a wonderful opportunity to expand the specification for those features that are proven winners on Web pages. Element positioning is a clear winner.

NOTE

> What a perfect time for interactive element positioning to be introduced to the Web. Most computer users are finally comfortable using the mouse and consider it an extension of their hand. Most Web surfers are getting tired of just reading pages of information and are starving for interactivity.

10

The next few sections detail the specific features of Dynamic HTML that allow for text and graphics positioning in new and novel ways.

The ZINDEX Style Attribute

Because you want to give some freedom to your audience to move text and graphics around on the Web page, you also want to control how multiple images appear when they share the same position on a page. Eager readers will move images on top of other images—you can be sure of that.

The ZINDEX is a component of the style specification that enables you to define where a Web page element is located on the z axis. The z axis is the third dimension that is not often considered in typical office computer applications. Office software is flat and defines only x (left to right) and y (top to bottom) axes. The z axis is defined as back to front, actually moving toward and away from your computer monitor's screen at a perpendicular angle. When you are sitting in front of your computer and reading this paragraph on a computer screen, you are actually sitting in a positive z coordinate.

Using a ZINDEX, you can tell the Web browser how to show two images that overlap in the same area of the Web page. If one element has a STYLE attribute like the following:

```
STYLE="ZINDEX:1"
```

and a second element has a STYLE attribute like the following:

```
STYLE="ZINDEX:2"
```

the first element would always appear behind the second one if their positions overlapped on the page. Why? Because the larger the ZINDEX value, the closer the element considers itself to be to the reader. In a Report A Crime Web site, I would give the head shape image the lowest ZINDEX value so it always appears behind a nose. I would give the mustache images a higher ZINDEX than the noses so a mustache always appears in front of a nose.

NOTE

In true 3D graphics specifications, z-axis values are maintained true to scale, and objects are shown smaller to appear farther away from the reader as their z values decrease. The ZINDEX used in Dynamic HTML is not an absolute scale. A reader cannot tell which element is going to appear in front of another because no visual sizing takes place. The ZINDEX is used only as a relative value to resolve conflicts over shared space on a Web page. Each element maintains the same size, effectively ignoring the ZINDEX for sizing purposes. Perhaps some day the Dynamic HTML specification will change to allow for some great, automatic, 3D perspective to appear on a Web page.

Defining a Graphical Area

You can specify the exact area in a Web page within which you want your readers to be able to position elements. In the case of the vegetable alien, crime suspect, and applying makeup Web pages, you might want to provide a wide open area in the middle of the page for the reader to play around with positioning. However, you might not want to let a reader place images over the title of your document or some of the informational text.

The <DIV></DIV> tag pair is convenient to use for defining a rectangular area on a page. Look at the following division:

```
<DIV ID=playarea STYLE="position:relative;
                        width:100%;
                        height:600px">
</DIV>
```

In this case, you create an area on the Web page that is set up as an object called playarea. Once again, the ID attribute identifies the name for the object. The STYLE attribute defines the size of the area and where it will appear on the Web page. The position:relative component tells the Web browser to create the area in its usual manner, considering the size of the Web browser window and resolution of the monitor. You could alternatively specify exactly where on the page you want the area to appear by using the absolute keyword. However, using absolute positioning provides no freedom for the Web browser to use its best algorithms that have already been optimized for many situations that might occur.

10

NOTE

> I would like to see absolute positioning tied to the current monitor screen coordinates. With such a feature, you could enable HTML elements that could be positioned off the Web browser window. Imagine minimizing your browser window and still being able to drag Web images around on your operating system's desktop. With Dynamic HTML, absolute positioning is absolute to the Web browser window, not to the entire monitor screen.

The `width:100%` component tells the browser to register `playarea` as consisting of the complete width of the page. Finally, the `height:600px` style component tells the browser to allow 600 pixels for the height of the area. Because a VGA resolution is only 480 pixels high to begin with, 600 pixels is a lot for a VGA monitor resolution. Yet it will look great on some of the more advanced resolutions.

As you will see in the section "An Example of Reader Positioning Control," later in this chapter, the elements you will want to enable a reader to move are listed in your HTML file between the opening and closing `<DIV></DIV>` tags. However, you will set up restrictions in your script functions that keep the objects from escaping outside the area.

Events Generated By the User

As a reader holds a mouse button down and moves the mouse simultaneously on a Web page, Dynamic HTML automatically registers an `onmousemove` event for the entire document. Remember that every Web page is considered a document object to the Dynamic HTML object model. If you never create a script function that uses that event, the event is effectively rendered useless. But that does not cause any harm to anyone.

If, on the other hand, you want to capture the mouse-dragging movement, you need only create an appropriate script function to handle the logic you want to enact. Look at the following function declaration:

```
function document_onmousemove()
```

This `document_onmousemove` function is available to any Dynamic HTML Web page document to capture a user's mouse movements. By declaring the function, you can create code that is executed each time a user moves the mouse with a mouse button held down. To get the most out of the `document_onmousemove` function, you declare and initialize three key variables: `button`, `x`, and `y`. The `button` variable is either a 1, 2, or 3, depending on which mouse button the reader presses while dragging the mouse. Button 1 is the primary mouse button that is usually defined as the left mouse button for a right-hand installation. Button 2 is the right mouse button, and button 3 is a third, middle button available on the mouse.

Variables x and y correspond with the current position of the mouse when the event is generated. In the example in this chapter, you will use x and y to determine where to place a Web page element that is being legally moved according to your wishes. To use the three variables (button, x, and y) in your scripts, assign them their respective window.event object properties with the following statements near the beginning of the document_onmousemove script function:

```
button = window.event.button
x = window.event.x
y = window.event.y
```

Giving the User Control of Element Placement

You give a user control of an element's placement by providing the appropriate logic within the onmousemove script function. Consider an example in which you create a playarea object and a nose object that is a 64×64 pixel image. You can control where the nose is placed relative to the mouse cursor that drags it by using the following logic:

```
srcElement = window.event.srcElement;
if (srcElement.id=="nose") {
    nose.style.posWidth = x - document.all.playarea.docLeft - 32;
    nose.style.posHeight  = y - document.all.playarea.docTop - 32;
}
```

The 32 that is subtracted from both the nose.style.posWidth and posHeight assignments centers the team logo image at the current mouse location. The 32 represents half the width and height of the 64 pixel sides of each logo. Basically, you are setting the new top-left corner of the nose image to the mouse coordinates minus their appropriate offsets for the location of the playarea relative to the page.

The following is a recap of the steps for providing the user element positioning control:

1. Create the area of the page over which you want the user to have positioning control.

2. Create the elements you want to enable the user to move and place them within the area you defined in step 1.

3. Declare the document_onmousemove script function and provide the logic that handles the positioning of elements by the user.

With those steps in mind, look at a complete example of user element positioning control that will fill in some informational gaps and provide useful details.

An Example of Reader Positioning Control

The HTML Web page detailed in Listing 10.1 contains eight .jpg graphic files, one for each team logo in the fictitious Web Baseball League. When the reader initially loads the page in a Web browser, the team logos are presented on the page, as seen in Figure 10.1. The page is presented with the expectation that a reader will drag and drop the logos on the page to place them in the order in which he believes the teams will finish after the upcoming season. After he drags them into place, he enters into the text boxes the number of wins and losses he expects each team to have after the season is over. Or perhaps a contest could be held weekly or monthly instead.

NOTE

> In the fictitious Web Baseball League, players from all over the world create teams that play virtual baseball over the Internet. Farm leagues allow new players to gain experience and attempt to make the big leagues. Games are heavily attended by others on the Web, and each whole game is captured as a computer animation so that a Web visitor can fast forward through the game to the highlights. The real players continue to make four million dollars a year and fans attend those games for a suntan from time to time. Yet the Web Baseball League is a lot more interactive. Fans vote by computer for rules changes, expansion teams, and all-star teams.

When the reader is satisfied with his choices, he can click OK and a process on the Web server evaluates his choices and enters the choices into a relational database. Yet the Web server need not even be aware of what the reader is doing after the server delivers the Web page initially. A reader could take 10 minutes to reposition the team logos and the server would be off serving other requests for the page.

Look at Listing 10.1 and Figure 10.1 and then continue reading for explanatory details.

INPUT   **Listing 10.1. Example of reader positioning control.**

```
<HTML>
<HEAD><TITLE>WBL Standings Contest</TITLE></HEAD>
<BODY BGCOLOR="#FFFFFF">
<H2>Predict The Web Baseball League Standings</H2>
<FONT FACE="Verdana, Arial, Helvetica" SIZE="4">
```

continues

Listing 10.1. continued

```
<B>Use the mouse to position the team logos in order of finish</B>
<BR><BR></FONT>
Then predict the number of wins and losses for the 112 game schedule<BR>
Click OK to submit your selections<BR>
<DIV ID=OuterDiv STYLE="position:relative;width:100%;height:280px">

 <IMG ID="bear" STYLE="position:absolute;TOP:32pt;LEFT:0px;
 WIDTH:64px;HEIGHT:64px;ZINDEX:-1;" SRC="Bears.jpg">
 <IMG ID="frog" STYLE="position:absolute;TOP:32pt;LEFT:66px;
 WIDTH:64px;HEIGHT:64px;ZINDEX:-2;" SRC="Frogs.jpg">
 <IMG ID="lion" STYLE="position:absolute;TOP:32pt;LEFT:134px;
 WIDTH:64px;HEIGHT:64px;ZINDEX:-3;" SRC="Lions.jpg">
 <IMG ID="robin" STYLE="position:absolute;TOP:32pt;LEFT:202px;
 WIDTH:64px;HEIGHT:64px;ZINDEX:-4;" SRC="Robins.jpg">
 <IMG ID="rhino" STYLE="position:absolute;TOP:32pt;LEFT:270px;
 WIDTH:64px;HEIGHT:64px;ZINDEX:-5;" SRC="Rhinos.jpg">
 <IMG ID="shark" STYLE="position:absolute;TOP:32pt;LEFT:338px;
 WIDTH:64px;HEIGHT:64px;ZINDEX:-6;" SRC="Sharks.jpg">
 <IMG ID="spider" STYLE="position:absolute;TOP:32pt;LEFT:406px;
 WIDTH:64px;HEIGHT:64px;ZINDEX:-7;" SRC="Spiders.jpg">
 <IMG ID="tiger" STYLE="position:absolute;TOP:32pt;LEFT:474px;
 WIDTH:64px;HEIGHT:64px;ZINDEX:-8;" SRC="Tigers.jpg">

 <H1> --1--  --2--  --3--  --4--  --5--  --6--  --7--  --8--</H1>
 <PRE>



 </PRE>
 <TABLE>
 <TR>
 <TD WIDTH=64><INPUT TYPE=text NAME="wins1" SIZE=5 VALUE="" MAXLENGTH=3></TD>
 <TD WIDTH=64><INPUT TYPE=text NAME="wins2" SIZE=5 VALUE="" MAXLENGTH=3></TD>
 <TD WIDTH=64><INPUT TYPE=text NAME="wins3" SIZE=5 VALUE="" MAXLENGTH=3></TD>
 <TD WIDTH=64><INPUT TYPE=text NAME="wins4" SIZE=5 VALUE="" MAXLENGTH=3></TD>
 <TD WIDTH=64><INPUT TYPE=text NAME="wins5" SIZE=5 VALUE="" MAXLENGTH=3></TD>
 <TD WIDTH=64><INPUT TYPE=text NAME="wins6" SIZE=5 VALUE="" MAXLENGTH=3></TD>
 <TD WIDTH=64><INPUT TYPE=text NAME="wins7" SIZE=5 VALUE="" MAXLENGTH=3></TD>
 <TD WIDTH=64><INPUT TYPE=text NAME="wins8" SIZE=5 VALUE="" MAXLENGTH=3></TD>
 <TD WIDTH=64><< Wins</TD>
 </TR>
 <TR>
 <TD WIDTH=64><INPUT TYPE=text NAME="loss1" SIZE=5 VALUE="" MAXLENGTH=3></TD>
 <TD WIDTH=64><INPUT TYPE=text NAME="loss2" SIZE=5 VALUE="" MAXLENGTH=3></TD>
 <TD WIDTH=64><INPUT TYPE=text NAME="loss3" SIZE=5 VALUE="" MAXLENGTH=3></TD>
 <TD WIDTH=64><INPUT TYPE=text NAME="loss4" SIZE=5 VALUE="" MAXLENGTH=3></TD>
 <TD WIDTH=64><INPUT TYPE=text NAME="loss5" SIZE=5 VALUE="" MAXLENGTH=3></TD>
 <TD WIDTH=64><INPUT TYPE=text NAME="loss6" SIZE=5 VALUE="" MAXLENGTH=3></TD>
 <TD WIDTH=64><INPUT TYPE=text NAME="loss7" SIZE=5 VALUE="" MAXLENGTH=3></TD>
 <TD WIDTH=64><INPUT TYPE=text NAME="loss8" SIZE=5 VALUE="" MAXLENGTH=3></TD>
 <TD WIDTH=64><< Losses</TD>
 </TR>
 </TABLE>
 <INPUT TYPE=submit VALUE="OK">
 </FONT>
 <SCRIPT LANGUAGE="VBScript">
```

```
function document_onmousemove()
dim newleft, newtop, srcElement, x, y, button
button = window.event.button
x = window.event.x
y = window.event.y
  if (button = 1) then
    set srcElement = window.event.srcElement
    ' if mouse is dragging and IMG, move it.
    if srcElement.tagname="IMG" then
        ' move team logo
        newleft=x-(srcElement.style.posWidth/2) - 32
        if newleft<0 then newleft=0
        srcElement.style.posLeft=newleft
        newtop=y-(srcElement.style.posHeight/2) - 150
        if newtop<0 then newtop=0
        if newtop>120 then newtop=120
        srcElement.style.posTop=newtop
        srcElement.style.zindex=z
        z = z + 1
        window.event.returnValue = false
        window.event.cancelBubble = true
    end if
  end if
end function

function document_ondragstart()
  window.event.returnValue = false
end function

</SCRIPT>
</BODY>
</HTML>
```

Figure 10.1.

A drag-and-drop baseball team standings page.

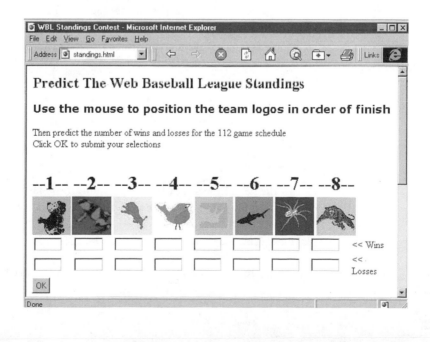

NOTE

Note that the script in Listing 10.1 uses the VBScript scripting language. The JavaScript version of Listing 10.1 did not work appropriately using the latest pre-release version of Internet Explorer 4.0 as of this book's press time (beta 2). In fact, even the VBScript version in Listing 10.1 did not produce a perfectly smooth drag-and-drop motion for the dynamic positioning of graphics on a Web page. The translation from VBScript syntax to JavaScript syntax is straightforward for the team standings example. If the JavaScript version of this example works in the final release as I suspect it should, you can replace the <SCRIPT> </SCRIPT> tag pair contents in Listing 10.1 with the following JavaScript code:

```
<SCRIPT LANGUAGE="JavaScript">

function document_onmousemove() {
var newleft, newtop, srcElement, x, y, button;
button = window.event.button;
x = window.event.x;
y = window.event.y;
  if (button==1) {
    srcElement = window.event.srcElement;
    if (srcElement.tagname=="IMG") {
    newleft=x-(srcElement.style.posWidth/2) - 32;
    if (newleft<0) { newleft=0; }
    srcElement.style.posLeft=newleft;
    newtop=y-(srcElement.style.posHeight/2) - 150;
    if (newtop<0) { newtop=0; }
    if (newtop>120) { newtop=120; }
    srcElement.style.posTop=newtop;
        srcElement.style.zindex=z;
        z = z + 1;
        window.event.returnValue = false;
        window.event.cancelBubble = true;
    }
  }
}

function document_ondragstart() {
  window.event.returnValue = false;
}

</SCRIPT>
```

In the beta 2 version of Internet Explorer, the JavaScript script loaded without error, yet did not enable the user to drag and drop the team logos.

Now review the steps to create a drag-and-drop graphics Web page for Listing 10.1.

In step 1, create the area of the page over which you want the user to have positioning control. In Listing 10.1, a division is created to define the region of allowable movement. The OuterDiv division starts with the following lines and continues with the user input field definitions that appear within a table:

```
<DIV ID=OuterDiv STYLE="position:relative;width:100%;height:280px">
                (details on team logos here)
<H1> --1--  --2--  --3--  --4--  --5--  --6--  --7--  --8--</H1>
<PRE>


</PRE>
```

You can use a table to control how input controls such as text boxes appear on a Web page.

The vertical white space between the <PRE></PRE> tags was placed intentionally. Readers will drag and drop the team logos within the white space the <PRE></PRE> tag pair creates. The <H1></H1> tag pair header line places the numbers 1 through 8 on the page to represent the place in the standings each team occupies. The opening <DIV> tag contains the attributes that set up the constrained area in the page where readers will be able to reposition the team logo images. The ID attribute names the division OuterDiv. The OuterDiv region is the full width of the Web page (100%) and is 280 pixels high at the relative point in the page at which the Web browser encounters the division when parsing the .htm file. When the OuterDiv is 280 pixels high, the team standings Web page does not provide scrollbars to the user on an 800×600 monitor when the Web browser window is maximized.

In step 2, create the elements you want to allow to be moved, and place them within the area you defined in step 1. In this example, eight team logo images are defined, each with an <IMG> tag that defines an ID attribute to name the image and a STYLE attribute to size, position, and provide a ZINDEX for the image. The team logo images are placed within the <DIV></DIV> tag pair so that they will be constrained by the division.

In step 3, declare the document_onmousemove script function and provide the logic that handles the positioning of elements by the user. In Listing 10.1, the document_onmousemove() function contains three important variables that are obtained from the window.event object: the mouse button the user is currently holding down, the x location of the mouse pointer, and the y location of the mouse pointer.

If the user is dragging an object by the left mouse button (button 1), the function associates the dragged object with an srcElement variable declared in the function body. Next, the script interrogates the srcElement variable to determine whether the object being dragged exists as the result of an <IMG> tag. If so, the source element is a graphical object and the script continues. If not, the function exits without interest in the mouse movement because only images should be repositioned.

If the function determines that the user is dragging a bitmap with the left mouse button, the bitmap location is changed dynamically on the screen to reflect the current x and y values of the mouse pointer.

Two variables declared in the function body, `newleft` and `newtop`, are used to determine where an image should be placed. The movement of the images is constrained by a region created by the Web author in the `OuterDiv` division. The script further constrains the left movement to the left edge of the division. The script also constrains vertical movement within the top of the division and 120 pixels down from the top. After repositioning the bitmap image, the script sets the `ZINDEX` for the most recently dragged bitmap to the highest value yet. The `ZINDEX` assignment assures that the most recently dragged bitmap image appears in front of any other team logos.

The line `window.event.cancelBubble = true` tells the browser window to refrain from *bubbling* up the event in case the document cannot handle the event. The concept of bubbling has to do with the automatic passing of events up to a parent class of an object when an object is not equipped to handle that event. Bubbling helps reduce the amount of function writing that is necessary in cases where some objects on a page can handle an event by themselves. Objects that can't handle the event can use the same function, and the event automatically is passed up the class hierarchy until it can be handled.

NOTE

> If you don't know anything about class hierarchies, don't sweat it. Class hierarchies are fundamental to object-oriented programming (OOP). Because Dynamic HTML scripting does not demand a hard-core object-oriented programming style, you can get by without understanding all the nuances of object-oriented programming. If you are interested in object-oriented programming, go to the technical section of your favorite bookstore and you will find more than one decent book title on OOP.

You can add substantial interactivity to your Web pages by allowing users to drag and drop component objects. Such interactivity is critical if the Web is to be able to compete with successful CD-ROM titles. Figure 10.2 shows the team standings Web page after a user has begun to move the team logos around.

Figure 10.2.

The baseball team standings page after dragging team logos.

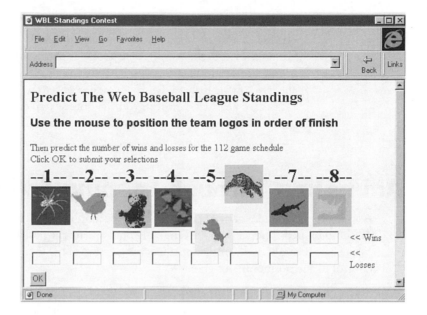

Why Animate?

Human beings enjoy animation. Young toddlers smile and point at animated images even before they can talk. Computer animation attracts attention, especially when the rest of your field of view is static.

However, animation goes beyond entertainment. Animation contains informational value not found in static pictures. An animation shows you how to get from step A to step B in an exact and specific manner. I know I have run into problems building sophisticated furniture from kits even though I have a clear picture of every major step in the process. If only the manual had shown me an animation of how to get from step 23 to step 24, I would not have had to try to rip those two pieces of wood apart before the glue dried.

There is much focus on animation as a needed feature of the Web to compete with television. I figure it is mainly for entertainment purposes that I hear people say that. But really, to me the power is in the interactiveness of the Web versus TV. I want to start an animation of the solar system and then pull Jupiter off its orbit to see what would happen to the solar system. Let me fire an enormous comet at the planet Venus. Interactive means I am in control.

There are Java-based Web pages that enable you to do exactly what you want with scientific simulations. Animation in Dynamic HTML combined with element positioning should enable you to build interesting pages that entertain and teach, often in a much more efficient manner than printed text.

In fact, if you are interested in scientific simulations and you have a Java-enabled Web browser, take a look at the list of links at The American Institute of Physics. The URL is `http://www.aip.org/aip/physres.html`. If that URL is down, just enter the query `physics and links` (or `physics+links`) in your favorite search engine. Consider how you would begin to create such Web sites using just Dynamic HTML.

Animation Through Looping Scripts

Animation works in Dynamic HTML through the looping construct of scripting languages. Within a loop, positional variables can change and update the position of graphics within the Web page. Basically, with animation, the script, instead of the user's mouse movement, takes control of the positioning of graphics.

Web-based animations usually are specified through a key frame sequence. As a Web author, you specify the locations on a Web page a graphic visits and the time in the sequence it appears at each location. Each of those pairs of time and location are called a *key frame*. For example, a key frame could look like this as part of a list of key frames:

```
35,50,80;
```

A Web browser reads this key frame and thinks to itself, "OK, I need to get that graphic to location (50,80) after 35 seconds." If the previous key frame was `25,100,25`, the browser interpolates the movement from (100,25) to (50,80) to create a smooth, straight-line movement over 10 seconds (the 35 seconds of the next key frame minus the 25 seconds of the previous key frame).

NEW TERM The word *interpolate* comes from an estimation technique used in mathematics. *Linear interpolation* is the mathematical process of estimating points along a sophisticated curve based on the assumption that each two consecutive points are connected in a straight line. If you interpolate between the two key frames from the example, you assume the line between them decreases along the x axis by 5 units every second (50 minus 100 divided by 10 seconds) and increases along the y axis by 6 units every second (80 minus 20 divided by 10 seconds).

At a time equal to 28 seconds, you would interpolate a position for your graphic at (85,38). The x coordinate would be 85 because you started at 100 and decreased 5 units per second for 3 seconds (28 seconds is 3 seconds after the 25 second mark, where you started). The y coordinate would be 38 because you started at 20 and increased 6 units per second for 3 seconds. A Web browser will do the same calculation to show the graphic at (85,38) 28 seconds after starting the animation.

Therefore, when you work with the specifics of implementing animation with Dynamic HTML, you should expect to see a way to define key frames and a way to loop through them within a script function. You learn the specifics soon, in the two examples that follow the next section.

Using Depth in a Script

Animation looks better if it takes advantage of the third dimension on a Web page. You can alter the way your graphics are presented to provide some depth to your animation. Surprisingly, as you learned earlier, you cannot provide a real depth perspective by altering the ZINDEX style parameter. The ZINDEX style does not resize graphics when its value changes dynamically.

Instead, if you want to add depth perspective to animation, you must alter the HEIGHT and WIDTH attributes from within a script. As you decrease the width and height of an image, the image appears to move farther behind the other images in animation. As you increase the width and height of an image, the image appears to move farther in front of the other images. Unfortunately, the implementation of Dynamic HTML you will see here for Internet Explorer 4.0 and Netscape Navigator 4.0 does not include interpolation for the resizing of graphics. Therefore, if you do alter the height and width of your graphics in a script, the images will resize in a step fashion. That could look a bit jumpy to your Web audience and lose the effect for which you were hoping.

Examples of Animations

With Dynamic HTML, you can create animated Web pages using one of many possible techniques. The example in Listing 10.2 uses Netscape's layering technique and an appropriate JavaScript script. The example in Listing 10.3 uses a Microsoft ActiveX control, two VBScript functions, and the object specification recommended by the W3C. As you play with them, you might notice that you can use part of one example with a part of the other and still have the examples work fine for at least one Dynamic HTML-enabled Web browser.

For the examples in Listings 10.2 and 10.3, I selected the old shell game. I was introduced to the old shell game in the 1980s when I watched a school chum get taken for $20 by a street con artist (or, perhaps, a very good magician) in New York City. The goal of the shell game is to select the correct walnut shell under which a stone is hiding. The hard part is that you see the stone only once as your opponent puts it under one shell and moves the shells around on a flat surface to confuse you.

You will see the old shell game implemented as a Dynamic HTML Web page. In both listings, the animation starts automatically when the Web page is loaded. A Netscape Navigator 4.0 implementation is provided in Listing 10.2. Look at the listing and then continue reading for a detailed explanation. Figure 10.3 contains a picture of the old shell game.

```
<HTML>
<HEAD>
</HEAD>
<BODY onload="cycle();">
<H2>The Shell Game</H2>
<LAYER name="gem" left=142 top=192 visibility="hidden">
<img src="gem.gif" id=gem border=0 width=64 height=64>
</LAYER>
<LAYER name="shell1" left=0 top=50 visibility="hidden">
<img src="walnut.gif" id=shell1 border=0 width=132 height=132>
</LAYER>
<LAYER name="shell2" left=142 top=50 visibility="hidden">
<img src="walnut.gif" id=shell2 border=0 width=132 height=132>
</LAYER>
<layer name="shell3" left=284 top=50 visibility="hidden">
<img src="walnut.gif" id=shell3 border=0 width=132 height=132>
</LAYER>
<SCRIPT>
var TimingsX
var TimingsY
var currentTick = 0
var gemshell
function cycle() {
        TimingsX = new Array(4);
        TimingsY = new Array(4);
        gemshell = Math.random();
        if(gemshell<.333) {
            gemshell=1;
            TimingsX[0] = new Array(0,126,0,284,0,142,284,142,142);
            TimingsY[0] = new Array(50,176,50,176,50,176,50,176,50);
            TimingsX[1] = new Array(142,142,142,142,284,0,0,0,284);
            TimingsY[1] = new Array(50,50,50,176,50,176,50,176,50);
            TimingsX[2] = new Array(284,284,284,0,142,284,142,284,0);
            TimingsY[2] = new Array(50,50,50,176,50,176,50,176,50);
            TimingsX[3] = new Array(142,142,16,300,16,158,300,158,158);
            TimingsY[3] = new Array(192,192,66,192,66,192,66,192,66);
        } else if(gemshell<.667) {
            gemshell=2;
            TimingsX[0] = new Array(0,0,0,284,0,142,284,142,142);
            TimingsY[0] = new Array(50,50,50,176,50,176,50,176,50);
            TimingsX[1] = new Array(142,126,142,142,284,0,0,0,284);
            TimingsY[1] = new Array(50,176,50,176,50,176,50,176,50);
            TimingsX[2] = new Array(284,284,284,0,142,284,142,284,0);
            TimingsY[2] = new Array(50,50,50,176,50,176,50,176,50);
            TimingsX[3] = new Array(142,142,158,158,300,16,16,16,300);
            TimingsY[3] = new Array(192,192,66,192,66,192,66,192,66);
        } else {
            gemshell=3;
            TimingsX[0] = new Array(0,0,0,284,0,142,284,142,142);
            TimingsY[0] = new Array(50,50,50,176,50,176,50,176,50);
```

```
                TimingsX[1] = new Array(142,142,142,142,284,0,0,0,284);
                TimingsY[1] = new Array(50,50,50,176,50,176,50,176,50);
                TimingsX[2] = new Array(284,126,284,0,142,284,142,284,0);
                TimingsY[2] = new Array(50,176,50,176,50,176,50,176,50);
                TimingsX[3] = new Array(142,142,300,16,158,300,158,300,16);
                TimingsY[3] = new Array(192,192,66,192,66,192,66,192,66);
        }

        document.layers["shell1"].visibility="show";
        document.layers["shell2"].visibility="show";
        document.layers["shell3"].visibility="show";
        document.layers["gem"].visibility="show";
        setTimeout("Moves()", 450);
}
function Moves() {
        document.layers["shell1"].moveTo
                (TimingsX[0][currentTick], TimingsY[0][currentTick]);
        document.layers["shell2"].moveTo
                (TimingsX[1][currentTick], TimingsY[1][currentTick]);
        document.layers["shell3"].moveTo
                (TimingsX[2][currentTick], TimingsY[2][currentTick]);
        document.layers["gem"].moveTo
                (TimingsX[3][currentTick], TimingsY[3][currentTick]);
        currentTick++

        if (currentTick < 9)
                setTimeout("Moves()", 450)
}
</SCRIPT>
</BODY>
</HTML>
```

Figure 10.3.

The shell game.

Listing 10.2 sets up an event attribute within the opening <BODY> tag. As a result of the onload="cycle();" attribute, the Web browser will run the script function cycle() when the page is loaded.

I create independent regions within the Web page by using the <LAYER></LAYER> tag pair. Layers can be located without consideration of other objects on the Web page. Each layer open tag contains a NAME attribute to name the layer. The name is used later in a script function. The location of a layer on a Web page is identified by the top-left corner. At Web page load time, the LEFT and TOP attributes identify the x and y values of the layer coordinate respectively. The VISIBILITY attribute is set initially to hidden. Later, in a script function, the value is changed to show when the animation begins.

The size of a layer is determined by the HTML elements that are nested within the <LAYER></LAYER> tag pair. In Listing 10.2, a single image file is placed within each layer. The <IMG> tag contains an ID attribute that sets up the image as a named object you can manipulate from within a script function. Because you are using images with a transparent background color, use a BORDER=0 attribute to turn off any borders. Set the size of the image with the WIDTH and HEIGHT attributes that, in effect, set the size of the layer as well.

NOTE	Note how easy it would be for you to include text in a layer. Just add the appropriate HTML tags, and the text becomes as movable as the team logo images used for example purposes.

I create two functions within the <SCRIPT></SCRIPT> tag pair that together create the animation. The cycle() function sets up all the variables needed for the animation and makes the layers visible. The Moves() function actually performs the required looping to move the images around on the Web page.

In function cycle(), two arrays are defined to hold the x and y coordinates of the shells: TimingsX and TimingsY. You need four lists for each coordinate because there are four images involved in the animation. Fill each array based on which shell will hold the stone. To choose a shell, use a random function available to JavaScript scripts: Math.random(). The Math.random() function returns a random number between 0 and 1. Interrogate the random number and break its possibilities into three ranges. If the random number is less than .333, animate the left shell to go down to pick up the stone. If the random number is less than .667, animate the middle shell to go down to pick up the stone. Otherwise, the right shell picks up the stone. Set the variable gemshell to the appropriate shell number to be able to test a reader's guess at the end of the animation.

The last line of the `cycle()` function starts the `Moves()` function and sets a timeout for the function at `450`:

```
setTimeout("Moves()", 450);
```

The `Moves()` function is pretty straightforward. For each loop, `currentTick` is incremented by one and then used as an index into the timing array lists. The resulting array list values are used as new coordinates for each team logo image layer. The Web browser moves the images as directed by the `Moves()` function. The `setTimeout()` function is a built-in Dynamic HTML function that automatically runs its first parameter as a function call. You will see the same function in the Internet Explorer implementation coming up next in Listing 10.3.

Listing 10.3 shows an alternative animation approach for the old shell game. Currently, such an approach is appropriate only for Internet Explorer 4.0 because it uses an ActiveX control and VBScript. The timing sequences are defined within the HTML tags instead of within a script function. The timing sequences also include specific timing points for each image coordinate. Notice that the Navigator implementation in Listing 10.2 does not specify timings, so each new coordinate in the animation is reached after an equal amount of time.

Look at Listing 10.3 and then continue reading a detailed explanation.

INPUT **Listing 10.3. Example of animations using objects.**

```
<HTML>
<HEAD>
</HEAD>
<BODY onload="cycle();">
<H2 ID=sg STYLE="color:Black;">Shell Game</H2>
<IMG SRC="gem.gif" ID=gem BORDER=0
 STYLE="container:positioned;position:absolute;
 TOP:192pt;LEFT:142px;WIDTH:32px;HEIGHT:32px;ZINDEX:0;">
<IMG SRC="walnut.gif" ID=shell1 BORDER=0 onclick="Guess();"
 STYLE="container:positioned;position:absolute;
 TOP:50pt;LEFT:0px;WIDTH:64px;HEIGHT:64px;ZINDEX:1;">
<IMG SRC="walnut.gif" ID=shell2 BORDER=0 onclick="Guess();"
 STYLE="container:positioned;position:absolute;
 TOP:50pt;LEFT:142px;WIDTH:64px;HEIGHT:64px;ZINDEX:2;">
<IMG SRC="walnut.gif" ID=shell3 BORDER=0 onclick="Guess();"
 STYLE="container:positioned;position:absolute;
 TOP:50pt;LEFT:284px;WIDTH:64px;HEIGHT:64px;ZINDEX:3;">
<OBJECT ID="pathone"
        CLASSID="CLSID:E0E3CC60-6A80-11D0-9B40-00A0C903AA7F">
<PARAM NAME=XSeries
        VALUE="0,0;10,126;20,0;30,284;40,0;50,142;60,284;70,142;80,142">
<PARAM NAME=YSeries
        VALUE="0,50;10,176;20,50;30,176;40,50;50,176;60,50;70,176;80,50">
</OBJECT>
<OBJECT ID="pathtwo"
        CLASSID="CLSID:E0E3CC60-6A80-11D0-9B40-00A0C903AA7F">
```

continues

10

Listing 10.3. continued

```
<PARAM NAME=XSeries
       VALUE="0,142;10,142;20,142;30,142;40,284;50,0;60,0;70,0;80,284">
<PARAM NAME=YSeries
       VALUE="0,50;10,50;20,50;30,176;40,50;50,176;60,50;70,176;80,50">
</OBJECT>
<OBJECT ID="paththree"
       CLASSID="CLSID:E0E3CC60-6A80-11D0-9B40-00A0C903AA7F">
<PARAM NAME=XSeries
       VALUE="0,284;10,284;20,284;30,0;40,142;50,284;60,142;70,284;80,0">
<PARAM NAME=YSeries
       VALUE="0,50;10,50;20,50;30,176;40,50;50,176;60,50;70,176;80,50">
</OBJECT>
<OBJECT ID="pathfour"
       CLASSID="CLSID:E0E3CC60-6A80-11D0-9B40-00A0C903AA7F">
<PARAM NAME=XSeries
       VALUE="0,142;10,142;20,16;30,300;40,16;50,158;60,300;70,158;80,158">
<PARAM NAME=YSeries
       VALUE="0,192;10,192;20,66;30,192;40,66;50,192;60,66;70,192;80,66">
</OBJECT>
<SCRIPT LANGUAGE=VBScript>
function cycle()
       dim itimer
       pathone.Target = shell1.Style
       pathtwo.Target = shell2.Style
       paththree.Target = shell3.Style
       pathfour.Target = gem.Style
       shell1.style.visibility="visible"
       shell2.style.visibility="visible"
       shell3.style.visibility="visible"
       gem.style.visibility="visible"
       pathone.Play
       pathtwo.Play
       paththree.Play
       pathfour.Play
       itimer = setTimeout( "Moves()", 50)
End function

Sub Moves
       dim itimer
       pathone.Tick
       pathtwo.Tick
       paththree.Tick
       pathfour.Tick
       if currentTick < 9 then
            itimer = setTimeout("Moves()", 50)
       end if
End Sub
</SCRIPT>

<SCRIPT LANGUAGE=VBScript>
function Guess()
  dim r, srcElement
  set srcElement = window.event.srcElement
  if (srcElement.id="shell1") then
     srcElement.src = "gem.gif"
  else
```

```
      srcElement.src = "wrong.gif"
  end if
end function
</SCRIPT>
</BODY>
</HTML>
```

Without the use of a layer tag, an image tag in Listing 10.3 is significantly more complicated than an image tag in Listing 10.2. The SRC, ID, and BORDER attributes are similar, but the positioning is defined within the STYLE attribute.

The <OBJECT></OBJECT> tag pairs contain two key frame sequences for each team logo image. Each key frame sequence is identified as a value to a PARAM NAME attribute. The XSeries object VALUE attribute contains a key frame sequence for the x component of each image coordinate. The YSeries object VALUE contains the y component. Each key frame contains a time value and a location value. Key frames are separated by semicolons.

The CLASSID attribute for each object specifies a very specific string that identifies the appropriate ActiveX control that can interpret the XSeries and YSeries parameters. In a script function, object parameters become active through their object name, which is defined in the ID attribute.

Although the cycle() and Moves functions look quite different syntactically, they in fact perform the same function as in Listing 10.2. In the cycle() function, each team logo image is associated with a timing object through a line such as the following:

```
pathone.Target = shell1.Style.
```

Each object with the appropriate CLASSID has a Play method that is called to start the timing sequence. The Play method is activated for each shell game image with lines like the following:

```
pathone.Play
```

The timing objects also have a Tick method that increments the index into the timings. The Tick method is called in the Moves subfunction, which provides the looping construct an animation requires.

NOTE

I find it interesting that the second parameter to the setTimeout() function, the timing component, is different in the Microsoft and Netscape implementations. To get a similar total time for the animation, for the Netscape timing parameter, you must multiply the Microsoft timing parameter by the number of timing points in the key sequence. That explains the 50 parameter for Listing 10.3 and the 450 parameter (50 times 9) for Listing 10.2.

Randomness is not included in the example in Listing 10.3; the left shell always picks up the stone initially. However, the shell selection routine that is not complete in Listing 10.2 is included in Listing 10.3. The Guess() function looks a lot like the Answer1() function from Listing 9.2 in Chapter 9. The Guess() function is enabled as an onclick attribute of each shell <IMG> tag. Figure 10.4 shows the old shell game after the animation is complete and a reader clicks the wrong shell.

Figure 10.4.

Choosing the wrong shell.

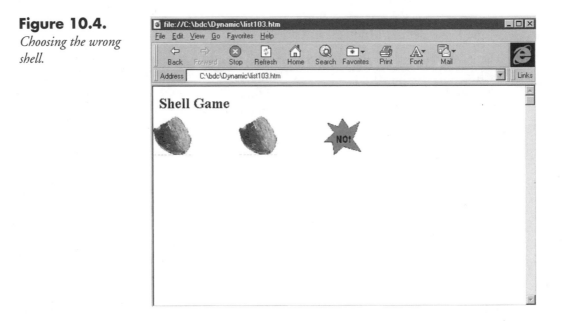

Summary

In this chapter, you learned how to control image positioning with Dynamic HTML. First, you learned how you can pass positioning control to your reader so he or she can position images anywhere within an area you define. The <DIV></DIV> tag pair is especially appropriate for defining a constrained area on a Web page. The reader repositions images by dragging and dropping them with the mouse.

Second, you learned how to position graphics in a script-controlled loop. With animations, the reader sits back and watches as you bedazzle him or her with interesting effects. Instead of specifying exactly where each image moves in an animation, you define key frames that the browser uses to create a smooth-moving animation. After an animation runs, you can continue with additional script functions that give control back to the reader. With multiple functions and mouse-enabled events, you can put together a game or interactive presentation.

The functionality reviewed in this chapter also applies to text manipulation. You can define traditional text tags within a layer tag pair and position the layer just as you position a layer containing an image. Graphics were demonstrated here only as a contrast to the time you spend covering text effects in Chapters 7, "Changing Text Attributes," 8, "Dynamically Changing Style," and 9, "Dynamically Changing Content." Many Web sites show off attractive techniques of text manipulation. The Workshop in this chapter integrates text with the sample techniques covered in the chapter.

Q&A

Q **I noticed that in your examples the animation plays once and then stops. Is there any way to keep an animation playing over and over in a script function?**

A Both the JavaScript and VBScript scripting languages include `while` keywords that you can use to run the animation multiple times. For example, with JavaScript, you could place your animation logic within the following syntax to run the animation five times:

```
function animate() {

count=0;
while(count<5) {
    -- animate here --
    count = count + 1;
}
```

To run the animation indefinitely, declare `while` as `while(true)` or `while(1)`. The animation will keep playing until the reader exits the page or loads another page on top of it.

Q **I notice that when I load the Netscape version of the old shell game in my Netscape Navigator browser, the animation is much more jumpy than the Internet Explorer version. Why?**

A I have noticed the same thing. For some reason, the Navigator browser does not interpolate the key frames as smoothly as Internet Explorer does. The interpolation routines are not rocket science, so I suspect that Netscape will smooth out its animation processing in a future release of the Netscape Navigator or Netscape Communicator Web browser. I would compensate for the jumpiness of Netscape's implementation by adding more key frames to the key frame sequence. However, I did not do so in this chapter because the listing would have been too long for an introductory example.

Q **You mentioned the fact that the HEIGHT and WIDTH attributes of images currently are not interpolated by Dynamic Web browser. Could you review interpolation by explaining how those would be interpolated to provide a depth perspective in an animation?**

10

A Sure. If I were to change the width of an image from 96 pixels at time 20 seconds to 64 pixels at time 30 seconds, an improved Web browser would interpolate values between those times to show the width changing smoothly. The width interpolation calculation would inform the browser to change width at 3.2 pixels per second ([96 pixels minus 64 pixels] divided by [30 seconds minus 20 seconds]) during the animation from time equals 20 seconds to time equals 30 seconds. The height calculation would be exactly the same for a transition from 96 to 64 pixels. When both height and width decrease over time, an improved Web browser would show an image that appeared to be smoothly moving farther away from the reader and toward the background of the Web page. I personally like the 3D effect, but not if the Web browser is not smooth in producing the effect.

Quiz

Take the following quiz to see how much you've learned in this chapter.

Questions

1. True or False: An image with a ZINDEX style parameter value of -3 will appear in front of an image with a ZINDEX of 3.
2. Can you create a keyframe sequence that animates an image in a square path over 12 seconds? Prove it.
3. Can you create the Internet Explorer 4.0 XSeries and YSeries VALUE attributes for the key frame sequence you created in question 1?
4. What line could you use in a script function to hide a graphic named G12 from the reader?
5. Which function is available in Java or JavaScript for use in obtaining a random number between 0 and 1 in a script function?

Answers

1. False. Greater ZINDEX values appear in front of lower ZINDEX values. 3 is greater than -3.
2. 0,0,0;3,100,0;6,100,100;9,0,100;12,0,0
3. XSeries: VALUE="0,0;3,100;6,100;9,0;12,0"
   YSeries: VALUE="0,0;3,0;6,100;9,100;12,0"
4. G12.style.visibility="hide"
5. The Math.random() function returns a random number between 0 and 1. You can use the Math.random() function to set variable key frame sequences in animation. To the reader, it will appear that the animation is different each time he or she visits the page. Supposedly, Web readers like a changing experience.

10

Workshop

Now that you finally have dynamic animation under your belt, you can jazz up the giant squid research Web site significantly. If you want to warm yourself up, revisit your Web pages from Chapters 7, 8, and 9 and add some cute animations to the graphical objects on those pages. In this Workshop, add an educational animation to the How Do We Track Giant Squid? Web page.

The animation I have in mind shows how, from the surface, a research boat can emit sonar sound waves down into the water and time how long the waves take to bounce back to the surface. By knowing the depth of the ocean floor at each location, researchers can track the squid when the sound waves come back to the surface faster than if they had hit the ocean floor.

Assume that the sonar approach is so sensitive that it can recognize the individual squids from the group as a whole. Perhaps this is unreasonable for the depths involved, but don't get caught up in the feasibility. (I hope you will let me slide by without presenting a complete explanation of the technology.)

The animation is a simplified one. It shows a boat at the surface under a blue sky. The boat emits sound waves down into the water. Three squid images swim by under the sound waves at just the exact time they reach their depth. The sound waves bounce off the squid and return to the surface at the point where the boat is waiting. I do not bother animating the boat, but do not let me stop you from using your full creativity.

If my text explanation does not create a distinct picture in your mind, look at Figure 10.5 to see my implementation. Now, try to create the animation for yourself. When you are finished, look at my implementation in Listing 10.4. I downloaded the image of the squid from the Web and created the boat, bottom, and sonar wave images using Microsoft's Paint application that comes with Windows 95.

INPUT Listing 10.4. A sonar tracking animation.

```
<HTML>
<HEAD>
</HEAD>
<BODY BACKGROUND="water.jpg" TEXT=#FFFFFF LINK=FFFF22 VLINK=FF22FF>
<H2>Squid Tracking -- How Do We Do It?</H2>
<TABLE>
<TR><TD WIDTH=320>
<DIV ID=AnimDiv STYLE="position:relative;width:320px;height:320px">
<IMG SRC="sonard.gif" ID=sonard BORDER=0
 STYLE="container:positioned;position:absolute;
 TOP:0pt;LEFT:150px;WIDTH:32px;HEIGHT:32px;ZINDEX:0;">
<IMG SRC="sonaru.gif" ID=sonaru BORDER=0
 STYLE="container:positioned;position:absolute;
```

continues

Listing 10.4. continued

```
        TOP:0pt;LEFT:150px;WIDTH:32px;HEIGHT:32px;ZINDEX:0;">
<IMG SRC="squid2.gif" ID=squid1 BORDER=0 onclick="Guess();"
 STYLE="container:positioned;position:absolute;
 TOP:170pt;LEFT:20px;WIDTH:64px;HEIGHT:64px;ZINDEX:1;">
<IMG SRC="squid2.gif" ID=squid2 BORDER=0 onclick="Guess();"
 STYLE="container:positioned;position:absolute;
 TOP:190pt;LEFT:20px;WIDTH:64px;HEIGHT:64px;ZINDEX:2;">
<IMG SRC="squid2.gif" ID=squid3 BORDER=0 onclick="Guess();"
 STYLE="container:positioned;position:absolute;
 TOP:180pt;LEFT:0px;WIDTH:64px;HEIGHT:64px;ZINDEX:3;">
<IMG SRC="boat.jpg" BORDER=0 STYLE="container:positioned;position:absolute;
 TOP:0pt;LEFT:0px;WIDTH:320px;HEIGHT:50px;ZINDEX:5;" onclick="cycle();">
<IMG SRC="bottom.gif" BORDER=0 STYLE="container:positioned;position:absolute;
 TOP:240pt;LEFT:0px;WIDTH:320px;HEIGHT:50px;ZINDEX:5;">
</DIV></TD><TD>
<FONT COLOR=#FFFF00><I>To track squid we use a sophisticated sonar device
 that emits sound waves down into the ocean
from the surface.  The sound waves will either bounce off the ocean floor
or bounce off the squid if they get between the emitting boat and the
ocean floor. We get very precise images of each squid that gets in the way of
the sound waves.  In fact, we can identify each squid as an individual unique
from all squid we have catalogued.</I></FONT><BR>
<B>Go ahead and click on the boat to start an animation.</B>
</TD></TR></TABLE>
<OBJECT ID="pathone"
        CLASSID="CLSID:E0E3CC60-6A80-11D0-9B40-00A0C903AA7F">
<PARAM NAME=XSeries
        VALUE="0,20;10,50;20,80;30,115;40,150;50,185;60,220;70,255;80,300">
<PARAM NAME=YSeries
        VALUE="0,170;10,170;20,170;30,170;40,170;50,170;60,170;70,170;80,170">
</OBJECT>
<OBJECT ID="pathtwo"
        CLASSID="CLSID:E0E3CC60-6A80-11D0-9B40-00A0C903AA7F">
<PARAM NAME=XSeries
        VALUE="0,20;10,55;20,80;30,110;40,135;50,170;60,200;70,230;80,270">
<PARAM NAME=YSeries
        VALUE="0,190;10,190;20,193;30,195;40,197;50,194;60,192;70,190;80,190">
</OBJECT>
<OBJECT ID="paththree"
        CLASSID="CLSID:E0E3CC60-6A80-11D0-9B40-00A0C903AA7F">
<PARAM NAME=XSeries
        VALUE="0,0;10,20;20,50;30,80;40,100;50,128;60,148;70,178;80,210">
<PARAM NAME=YSeries
        VALUE="0,180;10,182;20,185;30,190;40,185;50,181;60,179;70,176;80,179">
</OBJECT>
<OBJECT ID="pathfour"
        CLASSID="CLSID:E0E3CC60-6A80-11D0-9B40-00A0C903AA7F">
<PARAM NAME=XSeries
        VALUE="0,150;10,150;20,150;30,150;40,150;50,150;60,150;70,150;80,150">
<PARAM NAME=YSeries
        VALUE="0,20;10,50;20,90;30,135;40,180;41,0">
</OBJECT>
<OBJECT ID="pathfive"
        CLASSID="CLSID:E0E3CC60-6A80-11D0-9B40-00A0C903AA7F">
```

```
<PARAM NAME=XSeries
       VALUE="0,150;10,150;20,150;30,150;40,150;50,150;60,150;70,150;80,150">
<PARAM NAME=YSeries
       VALUE="40,0;41,180;50,135;60,90;70,50;80,20">
</OBJECT>
<SCRIPT LANGUAGE=VBScript>
function cycle()
       dim itimer
       pathone.Target = squid1.Style
       pathtwo.Target = squid2.Style
       paththree.Target = squid3.Style
       pathfour.Target = sonard.Style
       pathfive.Target = sonaru.Style
       squid1.style.visibility="visible"
       squid2.style.visibility="visible"
       squid3.style.visibility="visible"
       sonard.style.visibility="visible"
       sonaru.style.visibility="visible"
       pathone.Play
       pathtwo.Play
       paththree.Play
       pathfour.Play
       pathfive.Play
       itimer = setTimeout( "Moves()", 50)
End function

Sub Moves
       dim itimer
       pathone.Tick
       pathtwo.Tick
       paththree.Tick
       pathfour.Tick
       pathfive.Tick
       if currentTick < 9 then
           itimer = setTimeout("Moves()", 50)
       end if
End Sub
</SCRIPT>

<SCRIPT LANGUAGE=VBScript>
function Guess()
  dim r, srcElement
  set srcElement = window.event.srcElement
  if (srcElement.id="squid1") then
     srcElement.src = "gem.gif"
  else
     srcElement.src = "wrong.gif"
  end if
end function
</SCRIPT>
</BODY>
</HTML>
```

I captured Figure 10.5 halfway into the sonar tracking animation key frame sequence. The sound waves are just about to reflect off the squid and head back up toward the surface.

Figure 10.5.

The Squid Tracking Web page.

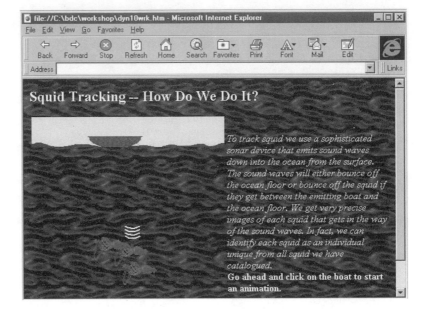

DAY

6

Creating Data-Aware Documents

Day 6

Chapter 11

Data-Bound Form Fields

You have learned all about how to change Web content dynamically within a Web page, so Chapters 11 and 12 focus on dynamic Web data delivery. We live in the information age. People, organizations, and automated processes create enormous amounts of data, and there is no doubt that the Web is a satisfactory vehicle for delivering data around the world. The more you and I decide to be data consumers, the more Web data must be retrieved and delivered efficiently to be able to meet everyone's requests.

Microsoft has incorporated data-awareness into its Internet Explorer 4.0 Web browser. If a Web page is data-aware, the page can refer to the same downloaded data set from the Web and present the data in several different ways, without having to return to a server on the Web. The World Wide Web Consortium (W3C) has not yet addressed the standardization of HTML data-awareness. Netscape does not consider data-awareness part of Dynamic HTML's realm of influence. Yet, to me, data-awareness is a powerful and needed Web browser feature; enough so to warrant a full day's consideration in this book.

This chapter starts slowly in explaining the significance of data-awareness. You learn how data is stored and accessed outside of the Web. Then, you will see examples of how to add data-awareness to your Web pages. You can make up your own mind about data-awareness, and you can decide whether it should be standardized within the Dynamic HTML specification.

Specifically, in this chapter, you will learn the following:

- [ ] What data-awareness is
- [ ] Why you should use data-awareness
- [ ] Data delivery today
- [ ] The Web browser's role
- [ ] The data form
- [ ] Adding data-awareness using Dynamic HTML
- [ ] Examples of data-aware Web forms

What Is Data-Awareness?

Something is *data-aware* if it associates itself with a data source. Data-awareness is a feature of a computer application that enables it to access data and keep a reference to that data source. The application, in effect, continues to be aware of the data.

A video game is data-aware if it has access to high scores and earlier game states that you saved while playing. Such data-awareness is a great feature for an adventure game. As you play and realize that you have gone down an unfortunate path, you can reload an earlier position in the game and resume from that place. Because the video game is a data-aware video game, the game can access the data immediately and restore the game to that particular state.

Now, imagine that you are playing a video game on the Web, and you would like to have the game downloaded once so that it runs local on your machine. As you begin to save game states, you should not have to request the Web server to save the game state for you. There is no need to create unnecessary Web traffic. You have the mind set of a good Internet citizen.

In the case of a Web browser, data-awareness is a feature of a browser that requests all the possible data for a Web page once, disconnects from the Web server, and then interacts with the data locally for as long as the user wants to interact.

Why Use Data-Awareness?

To understand why you should use data-awareness, look at a real-world example. Suppose you are shopping for Christmas gifts for your family and friends, and you flip through your favorite mail order catalog and are amazed at how easy you find 10 items that should make your loved ones happy. Your sister's birthday is coming up on December 18, and you are celebrating the holidays early with your in-laws on the 21st.

You have a decision to make. To you, there is no difference between requesting three different shipments to arrive for the three different dates you need presents (the 18th, 21st, and 25th) or having them all shipped at the same time. However, having a delivery truck stop by on three different occasions is using up additional natural resources, not to mention creating additional paperwork (or computer record entries) for the mail order company. You might make others wait longer for their deliveries as the delivery truck stops at your home before going on to theirs. Your simple actions related to a mail-order purchase have an effect on many other things and people.

Data delivery on the Web is similar to goods delivery by mail. Today, you jump from one page to another, and the server delivers the next page's data each time you click a link. Any of the examples from Chapters 7–10 could deliver Web pages in this manner. News stories can be delivered one page at a time for each town in a region. Trivia questions can be delivered one page at a time. Baseball statistics can be delivered one team at a time. Delivery of one page at a time is similar to delivery of one package at a time. Other Web visitors wait for their Web page delivery (albeit microseconds) while the server distributes other people's pages.

With a data-aware Web browser, all the data can be delivered with a single Web server visit, and the browser stays aware of the data. With Dynamic HTML, the Web page can dynamically change to present the data based on interactive mouse clicks from the reader. In fact, a reader could add new data to the data source if needed. Hopefully, by now, you can see the benefit of adding data-awareness to the Web browser and Dynamic HTML specification.

NOTE

The biggest drawback to data-awareness is the fact that often more data is delivered than will actually be used by the recipient. Extra data uses up network bandwidth that could be used for data that will actually be consumed. However, as data compression methods for compressing data sources keep getting better, it appears that the trade-off is usually worth it for the Web server's sake.

Data Delivery Today

Today, much data is delivered to corporate data consumers through *Local Area Networks* (LANs). Most corporate data is stored in relational databases. *Relational* database theory has been institutionalized into computing environments for its capability to deliver data efficiently and non-redundantly. Usually, data is delivered to a PC in a manner that can be efficiently presented by a relational database front-end tool such as Access, Paradox, or FoxPro (to name just a few).

NOTE

If the words used in this section seem Greek to you, at least you are getting a sense of the technospeak of database professionals. Database theory is really quite amazing to me. *Relational* theory is a specific theory of storing and accessing data to make it self-validating and efficient in speed and size. The theory has been working remarkably well in practice. *Local Area Networks* are networks of computing devices that are contained within a small area and are secure against outside connections. A *front-end tool* is a computer application that knows how to request specific data from a database server and then knows how to present the data to you in an easy-to-understand and easy-to-manipulate manner. Read a good book on databases to learn more of the technospeak.

Corporate consumers can request data from data servers by creating a query through a query language. A *query* is just a fancy word for a request for information in a specific format from the database in which the information is stored. The *Structured Query Language* (SQL) is the standard language of relational data requests and manipulation. Almost all data servers understand SQL. A data server accepts a query, runs the query, and sends back the query result set over the corporate network. Only recently has the business world considered using the Internet as part of its network.

NOTE

As you think about the benefit of a standard, structured way of requesting database information, you begin to see all the benefits that the HTML standard has had for Web presentation. With HTML, you can use one of many browser software applications to request a Web page from any one of many server applications. With SQL, you can use one of many data analysis tools to request data from any one of many data server applications. The standard (HTML or SQL) is the go between for independent technology improvements at either end.

Not every data consumer in the business world knows how to properly request data to be most efficient with shared computing and networking resources. Public Web consumers cannot be expected to understand the trade-offs either. Every time I request relational data over a corporate network, I make a decision. Should I request more data than I need currently in order to have it on my PC when the time comes to use it? Or, should I request only the summary information I need at this time?

Data access decisions have been around for a long time. For the business world, technologists have worked on both ends of the spectrum to deliver the best of both worlds. Data analysis tools are ready to accept all the data at once and provide the tools to analyze it in pieces locally on a PC. Web servers are optimized to simultaneously analyze, calculate, and deliver data requests from tens to hundreds of simultaneous requests. Because the technologists have been working on these same fundamental opportunities for decades, many believe it seems proper to provide the same benefits to the rest of the world on the Web.

The more that technologists look to apply the time-honored benefits of relational data theory to the Web, the more readers are confronted with wanting to have the best of both worlds within the Web page. Again, you arrive at a place where you should consider data-aware Web pages and Web browsers.

The Web Browser's Role

In order for a data-aware Web page delivery strategy to work, a Web browser must be capable of understanding the data format the Web server delivers. The browser must put the data in a place in memory from which it can easily retrieve it. The Web browser also must remember where it put the data when the Web page wants to display more of the data.

The Internet Explorer 4.0 Web browser has the capability to do the receiving, placing, calculating, and presenting needs of data-aware Web pages. For Microsoft, I would assume, adding the necessary data-aware functionality was not very difficult because it has been creating the Access data analysis tool for several years. Yet, without Dynamic HTML, adding data-awareness would be awkward because there would be no simple way to communicate a reader's desire for more data with the data source that had been delivered.

The event model of Dynamic HTML provides more than enough interactivity on a Web page to provide clean and intuitive data presentation and alteration strategies. You can click a button to see the next row of data in the data source. You can enter a date in a text box to see the information for a particular day. You can pass your mouse over a particular image file to request that particular image's data.

The Data Form

You create a *data form* to present data in a Web page. A data form is a presentation object that contains labels that define the significance of each piece of data and fields in which to display the data for a particular piece of the data source. Usually, a piece of a data source that refers to a specific data object is called a *record*. In the case of the geographical region from Chapter 8, "Dynamically Changing Style," each town's specific information would be stored in a data source as a separate record. You use a data form to present each record one at a time. You use Dynamic HTML to give a reader the chance to indicate she would like to see a different record.

Data forms can look very glamorous as you add graphics and color using the appropriate HTML tags. I want my readers to be unsuspecting of the fact that they are not getting each record from the Web one at a time. Of course, a trained eye will know the difference, but I want the untrained eye to not have to worry about the details.

Adding Data-Awareness Using Dynamic HTML

So far, this chapter has been mainly definitions and vision. The data analysis community is constantly thinking up new terms and providing visions for the future. It likes doing both. This section covers the technical details of how to add a data source to a Dynamic HTML Web page intended for viewing with the Internet Explorer 4.0 Web browser. I hope you will agree that the process is straightforward. If not, keep going to the examples that follow this section.

To add data-awareness to a Web page, supply an <OBJECT></OBJECT> tag pair with all the appropriate attributes. Look at an example:

```
<OBJECT ID="townnews"
    CLASSID="clsid:333C7BC4-460F-11D0-BC04-0080C7055A83"
    BORDER="0" WIDTH="0" HEIGHT="0">
    <PARAM NAME="DataURL"   VALUE="towndata.txt">
    <PARAM NAME="UseHeader" VALUE="True">
</OBJECT>
```

The opening <OBJECT> tag contains an ID attribute that gives the data source a name. In this case, the data source contains town news for several towns. The CLASSID attribute references the ActiveX control that provides data-awareness to an Internet Explorer 4.0 Web page. The data-awareness ActiveX control comes with the standard Internet Explorer 4.0 application.

Note that the data source object takes up no space on the Web page; instead, components of the data source will be accessed and presented in other tags on the Web page. The nested <PARAM> tags and their attributes are required because the Web browser uses the parameters to set up the data source properly. The NAME=DataURL parameter provides a VALUE that identifies the filename of the data source. The UseHeader parameter identifies whether to use the first row in the data source as a header for the rest of the records in the data source. a VALUE of True tells the Web browser to refer to each column in the data source by the name at the top of the column.

To create the data form within your Web page, associate a label and data field to each column in your data source. The following example creates a label, where a <LABEL></LABEL> tag pair is used to define the label:

```
<LABEL FOR=hightemp>Today's High Temperature: </LABEL>
```

The opening <LABEL> tag contains a FOR attribute that identifies the field for which the label is intended. You put the text for the label between the <LABEL></LABEL> tag pair.

You create a field similar to the following, where an <INPUT> tag contains the appropriate attributes that create the form field:

```
<INPUT ID=hightemp TYPE=text DATASRC=#townnews DATAFLD="High">
```

The ID attribute names the field. The TYPE attribute defines the type of data the field holds. The DATASRC attribute associates the field with the correct data source object, and the DATAFLD attribute associates the field with the correct column of data in the data source.

You create the process of label and field creation for each field in the data source. You can align the labels and fields nicely by using HTML table tags, or you can leave them to scatter within the page to create the appearance of a form letter or mailing label. The definition of labels and fields are as flexible as any other HTML element.

Examples of Data-Aware Web Forms

This chapter presents two examples of data-aware Web forms that you can embed into a Web page. Listing 11.1 presents a sports page that is organized along the locker room concept. A reader can point and click on the Web page to visit each team's locker room and see statistics specific to that team. Listing 11.3 presents an interactive, geographical Web page.

A First Example

In the example from Listing 11.1, the locker rooms are pages for the teams of the Web Baseball League introduced in Chapter 10, "Dynamically Altering the Placement of Elements." In fact, the same team logos are used to identify each team. Each locker room page shows the number of team wins and losses, the team batting average, and the team ERA through the last game played. Initially when the page loads, the Tigers team locker room is presented as shown in Figure 11.1. Then, a reader can use the two buttons provided to move forward or backward between the different locker rooms.

Almost all of the big sports information providers on the Web use a locker room concept so readers can quickly go directly to their favorite teams. If a reader then decides to go to another team's locker room, a second request is made to the Web server to deliver that team's information. With the example in Listing 11.1, all the data is delivered initially in a single file. As a reader browses the different teams, she is not dependent on any additional data delivery from the Web.

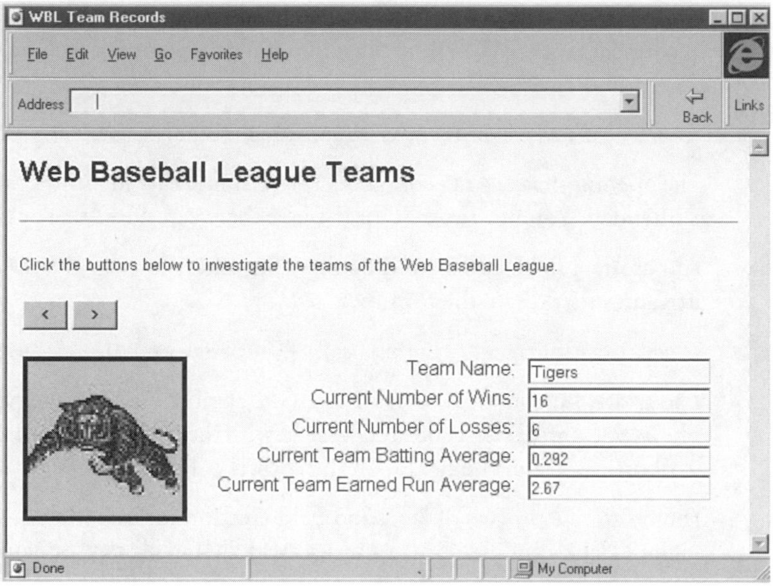

Figure 11.1.

A presentation of the Tigers team locker room.

> **WBL Team Records**
>
> File   Edit   View   Go   Favorites   Help
>
> Address |
>
> Back   Links
>
> ## Web Baseball League Teams
>
> Click the buttons below to investigate the teams of the Web Baseball League.
>
> < >
>
> Team Name: Tigers
> Current Number of Wins: 16
> Current Number of Losses: 6
> Current Team Batting Average: 0.292
> Current Team Earned Run Average: 2.67
>
> Done   My Computer

NOTE

The locker room concept could easily be taken one level deeper. Imagine that after you are in a specific team's locker room, the Web site shows you lockers for each player on the team. By selecting the locker of your favorite player, you get access to his page, presented as a data form with his specific statistics. Because this is a Web-based baseball league, you might even get an e-mail address. With the data delivery structure in Listing 11.1, you could provide the data for all the players for a team at once and then give your readers an attractive method to move from player to player.

Look at Listing 11.1, and then continue reading for a detailed explanation. Figure 11.2 shows the locker room for the Frogs team as presented in a Dynamic HTML Web browser.

INPUT   **Listing 11.1. Example of dynamic record presentation.**

```
<HTML>
<HEAD>
<FONT FACE="verdana,arial,helvetica" SIZE=2>
<TITLE>WBL Team Records</title>
</HEAD>
<BODY BGCOLOR="#FFFFFF">
<H2>Web Baseball League Teams</H2>
```

11

```
<HR>
<P>Click the buttons below to investigate the teams of the Web Baseball
League.</P>
<P>
<OBJECT ID="teamlist"
        CLASSID="clsid:333C7BC4-460F-11D0-BC04-0080C7055A83"
        BORDER="0" WIDTH="0" HEIGHT="0">
  <PARAM NAME="DataURL" VALUE="wblteam.txt">
  <PARAM NAME="UseHeader" VALUE="True">
</OBJECT>

<TABLE>
  <TR>
    <TD ALIGN=RIGHT><INPUT TYPE=BUTTON ID=backward VALUE="   <   "></TD>
    <TD ALIGN=LEFT><INPUT TYPE=BUTTON ID=forward VALUE="   >   "></TD>
  </TR>
</TABLE>
<P>
<IMG ID=Picture SRC="Tigers.jpg" BORDER=4 HEIGHT=128 WIDTH=128 ALIGN=LEFT>

<TABLE ALIGN=CENTER CELLSPACING=0 CELLPADDING=0>
<TR>
<TD ALIGN=RIGHT VALIGN=TOP><LABEL FOR=team>Team Name: </LABEL></TD>
<TD ALIGN=LEFT VALIGN=TOP WIDTH="10"></TD>
<TD ALIGN=LEFT VALIGN=TOP><INPUT ID=team TYPE=text
DATASRC=#teamlist DATAFLD="Team"></TD>
</TR>

<TR>
<TD ALIGN=RIGHT VALIGN=TOP><LABEL FOR=wins>
Current Number of Wins: </LABEL></TD>
<TD ALIGN=LEFT VALIGN=TOP WIDTH="10"></TD>
<TD ALIGN=LEFT VALIGN=TOP><INPUT ID=wins TYPE=text
DATASRC=#teamlist DATAFLD="Wins"></TD>
</TR>

<TR>
<TD ALIGN=RIGHT VALIGN=TOP><LABEL FOR=losses>
Current Number of Losses: </LABEL></TD>
<TD ALIGN=LEFT VALIGN=TOP WIDTH="10"></TD>
<TD ALIGN=LEFT VALIGN=TOP><INPUT ID=losses TYPE=text
DATASRC=#teamlist DATAFLD="Losses"></TD>
</TR>

<TR>
<TD ALIGN=RIGHT VALIGN=TOP><LABEL FOR=BA>
Current Team Batting Average: </LABEL></TD>
<TD ALIGN=LEFT VALIGN=TOP WIDTH="10"></TD>
<TD ALIGN=LEFT VALIGN=TOP><INPUT ID=BA TYPE=text
DATASRC=#teamlist DATAFLD="BA"></TD>
</TR>

<TR>
<TD ALIGN=RIGHT VALIGN=TOP><LABEL FOR=ERA>
Current Team Earned Run Average: </LABEL></TD>
```

continues

Listing 11.1. continued

```
<TD ALIGN=LEFT VALIGN=TOP WIDTH="10"></TD>
<TD ALIGN=LEFT VALIGN=TOP><INPUT ID=ERA TYPE=text
DATASRC=#teamlist DATAFLD="ERA"></TD>
</TR>
</TABLE>

<SCRIPT LANGUAGE=JavaScript>
function documentClick() {
    Picture.src = team.value + ".jpg";
}

document.onclick = documentClick;

</SCRIPT>

<SCRIPT LANGUAGE=JavaScript>
function backwardClick() {
  if (teamlist.recordset.AbsolutePosition > 1) {
     teamlist.recordset.MovePrevious();
  } else {
     alert("Already at first team");
  }
}

backward.onclick = backwardClick;

function forwardClick() {
  if (teamlist.recordset.AbsolutePosition != teamlist.recordset.RecordCount) {
     teamlist.recordset.MoveNext();
  } else {
     alert("Already at last team");
  }
}

forward.onclick = forwardClick;

</SCRIPT>
</FONT>
</BODY>
</HTML>
```

The data control object used in this example is an ActiveX control a reader can download once from the Internet to extend the capabilities of his or her Web browser. In fact, Internet Explorer 4.0 includes the data-awareness control in its standard package. The same control will be used for all the data-aware examples in Chapters 11 and 12. The data control object is included in the HTML page by way of the <OBJECT></OBJECT> tag pair. The <OBJECT> </OBJECT> pair is an attempt by the HTML specification to standardize a tag that encompasses browser-specific tags of the past, such as the <EMBED></EMBED> tag pair Netscape uses to enable the plug-in architecture in HTML Web pages. The ActiveX control identification lines from Listing 11.1 follow:

```
<OBJECT ID="teamlist"
        CLASSID="clsid:333C7BC4-460F-11D0-BC04-0080C7055A83"
        BORDER="0" WIDTH="0" HEIGHT="0">
  <PARAM NAME="DataURL" VALUE="wblteam.txt">
  <PARAM NAME="UseHeader" VALUE="True">
</OBJECT>
```

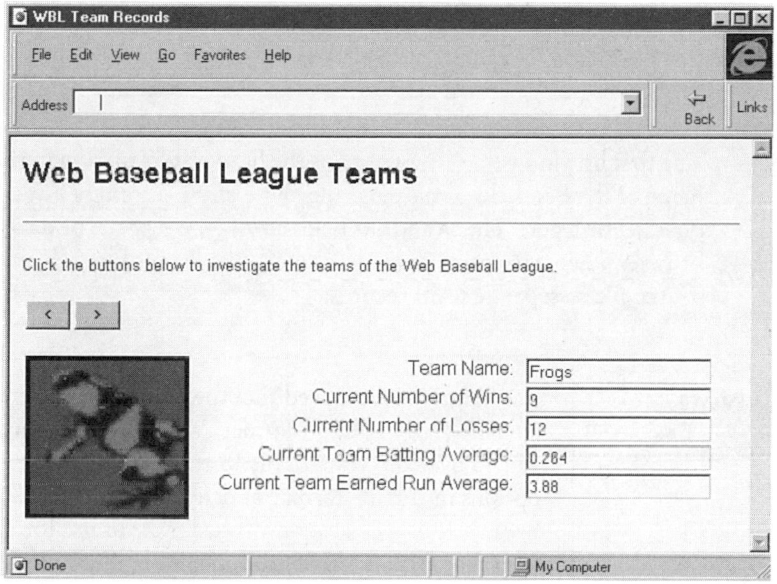

Figure 11.2.

A dynamic record presentation of the Frogs team locker room.

The ID attribute value instantiates teamlist as the data source object. The CLASS_ID attribute value of the <OBJECT> tag is a sophisticated code with embedded security used to select the appropriate ActiveX control for data-set management. The control requires two parameters identified in <PARAM> tags with NAME and VALUE attributes. The DataURL parameter supplies to the Web browser the URL of the data source. The UseHeader parameter identifies whether to use the header row of the data set as column name information.

A table with two buttons is added to the Web page to give the user controls to move from team to team. Both are instantiated as objects with the ID attribute. One button is instantiated as backward and the other as forward.

The bitmap image for the Tigers team logo is placed on the page in an <IMG> tag instantiated as an object with the ID=Picture attribute. The team logo image will change through the document_onclick() function declared later within a script. The Tigers team information is the first row of the data set wblteam.txt. Listing 11.2 shows the wblteam.txt file's contents.

INPUT   **Listing 11.2. Contents of** `wblteam.txt`.

```
Team,Wins:INT,Losses:INT,BA:FLOAT,ERA:FLOAT
Tigers,16,6,.292,2.67
Bears,14,8,.244,2.87
Robins,13,8,.267,2.67
Lions,11,10,.282,4.07
Rhinos,10,10,.255,3.55
Frogs,9,12,.264,3.88
Sharks,8,12,.251,4.15
Spiders,4,14,.212,3.86
```

The first line in Listing 11.2 contains the header information for the data source. `Team` is the name of the first field, and `Wins` is the name of the second. The `Wins` and `Losses` fields are of type `INT` (integer). The `BA` and `ERA` fields are of type `FLOAT`. The data types are used by the Web browser when presenting data to a reader. The details for each team then follow in the data source file as separate team records.

 NOTE   You might have noticed that the `wblteam.txt` file is in a simple *comma separated values* (CSV) format. With all the expertise Microsoft has gained over the years in file formats, be sure that you will have lots of options in the file format of delivered data to a Web surfer. I use CSV because it is very straightforward, easy to use for debugging, and almost all personal data software applications allow for a database table to be exported in that format.

After you add the team logo image to the page, you are ready to create the data form. The data form has five labels and five fields. Create each label with a `<LABEL></LABEL>` tag pair like the following:

```
<LABEL FOR=team>Team Name: </LABEL>
```

and each field with an `<INPUT>` tag like this:

```
<INPUT ID=team TYPE=text DATASRC=#teamlist DATAFLD="Team">.
```

The tags for each data form label and field are similar. For the `team` field, the `TYPE` attribute identifies the presentation type for the field. The `DATASRC` attribute identifies the source of the data (which has the same value as the data source object name that points to the `wblteam.txt` file). The `DATAFLD` attribute identifies the field in the data source from which the input box expects to get data. The field name is obtained from the first row of the `wblteam.txt` file.

11

NOTE

In the example in Listing 11.1, I chose to present the data form in a table for a more organized look and feel. The table tags are straight out of the HTML 3.2 specification. Listing 11.3 provides an example that shows a less organized method of presenting data.

The first `<SCRIPT></SCRIPT>` tag pair includes a script with the `documentClick()` function. Remember that the `documentClick()` function is available to any Web page loaded in a Web browser supporting Dynamic HTML. In this case, the `documentClick()` function is used to keep the locker room team logo in agreement with the current data row being shown on the Web page. The single line `Picture.src = team.value + ".jpg";` handles every mouse click on the page for every team. It changes the `SRC` attribute for the `Picture` object based on the `team` field of the current data row. The `team` field is instantiated with the `ID=team` attribute of its `<INPUT>` tag.

NOTE

The code in this chapter was heavily tested to comply with the beta 2 pre-release version of Microsoft's Internet Explorer 4.0, which was the latest available version at press time.

Within the other `<SCRIPT></SCRIPT>` tag pair, two functions are created to handle the user button mouse clicks. The `backwardClick()` function moves the user back up the data set one row at a time until the first row is encountered. The `forwardClick()` function moves the user down the data set rows one row at a time until the last row is encountered. The fact that the functions start with the same string as existing, instantiated objects is critical. Without using the exact same strings of `backward` and `forward`, the function would not work as intended.

A Second Example

The second example presents a geography Web site where data is presented more as a flow of each page instead of in a neat and orderly table. Instead of moving through the data sequentially one record at a time, a reader can click an image to see information about that particular item. The data form presents the specific, absolute record related to the selected land mass.

This example uses the six states of New England in the United States. Perhaps I am a little sentimental because I grew up in that part of the world. Perhaps not, because those six states just happen to fit together so well and look great on a Web page. In either case, the area of New England was named so by the first English residents of the Massachusetts Bay Colony. Figure 11.3 shows the presentation for the state of Maine.

Figure 11.3.

A presentation on the state of Maine.

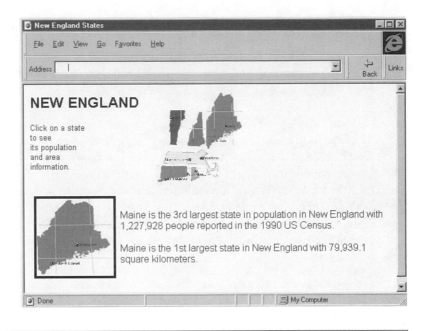

NOTE

In order to obtain population and area figures for the United States, I visited the United States Government's census Web site. There is so much information available online at http://www.census.gov/ it is overwhelming to a statistics addict like myself. If you visit the census Web site, notice how parts are organized as data forms in which you request certain information and wait for the request to be served back to you. As of June 1997, the census Web site is still using CGI scripting to communicate with a CD-ROM reader on its server. Therefore, the census Web site is a great example of the old way of interacting with a data source.

In this example, you want to share some basic information with people from around the world about the six New England states. Using Dynamic HTML, you add six attractive bitmap images to a New England States Web page, one for each state. You add the appropriate scripting to enable a reader to click a state image to see that state's record from the data source you deliver to the reader. In other words, you create the New England States Web page as a data-aware Web page.

The Dynamic HTML syntax necessary to create the example in Listing 11.3 is more similar to Listing 11.1 than different. Look at Listing 11.3 and Figure 11.4, and then continue reading for the details.

Listing 11.3. A point-and-click dynamic record presentation.

```
<HTML>
<HEAD>
<FONT FACE="verdana,arial,helvetica" SIZE=2>
<TITLE>New England States</title>
</HEAD>
<BODY BGCOLOR="#FFFFFF">
<H2>NEW ENGLAND</H2>

<P>Click on a state <BR>
to see <BR>
its population <BR>
and area <BR>
information.</P>
<P>
<OBJECT ID="statelist"
        CLASSID="clsid:333C7BC4-460F-11D0-BC04-0080C7055A83"
        BORDER="0" WIDTH="0" HEIGHT="0">
  <PARAM NAME="DataURL" VALUE="newengld.txt">
  <PARAM NAME="UseHeader" VALUE="True">
</OBJECT>
<P>
 <IMG ID="Maine" STYLE="container:positioned;position:absolute;TOP:10pt;
   LEFT:300px;WIDTH:64px;HEIGHT:96px;ZINDEX:1;" src="Maine.jpg">
 <IMG ID="Vermont" STYLE="container:positioned;position:absolute;TOP:30pt;
   LEFT:240px;WIDTH:32px;HEIGHT:64px;ZINDEX:6;" src="Vermont.jpg">
<IMG ID="New Hampshire" STYLE="container:positioned;position:absolute;TOP:30pt;
   LEFT:270px;WIDTH:32px;HEIGHT:64px;ZINDEX:3;" src="New Hampshire.jpg">
<IMG ID="Massachusetts" STYLE="container:positioned;position:absolute;TOP:80pt;
   LEFT:230px;WIDTH:96px;HEIGHT:48px;ZINDEX:2;" src="Massachusetts.jpg">
<IMG ID="Connecticut" STYLE="container:positioned;position:absolute;TOP:100pt;
   LEFT:220px;WIDTH:64px;HEIGHT:32px;ZINDEX:4;" src="Connecticut.jpg">
<IMG ID="Rhode Island" STYLE="container:positioned;position:absolute;TOP:100pt;
   LEFT:270px;WIDTH:32px;HEIGHT:32px;ZINDEX:5;" src="Rhode Island.jpg">
<TABLE><TR><TD>
<IMG ID=Picture SRC="Maine.jpg" BORDER=4 HEIGHT=128 WIDTH=128 ALIGN=RIGHT>
</TD><TD>
<SPAN ID=state DATASRC=#statelist DATAFLD="State">
</SPAN>is the
<SPAN ID=pr DATASRC=#statelist DATAFLD="Pop_Rank">
</SPAN> largest state in population in New England with
<SPAN ID=pop DATASRC=#statelist DATAFLD="Population">
</SPAN> people reported in the 1990 US Census.
<P>
<SPAN ID=state2 DATASRC=#statelist DATAFLD="State">
</SPAN> is the
<SPAN ID=ar DATASRC=#statelist DATAFLD="Area_Rank">
</SPAN> largest state in New England with
<SPAN ID=area DATASRC=#statelist DATAFLD="Area">
</SPAN> square kilometers.
</TD></TR></TABLE>
<SCRIPT language=JavaScript>
var srcElement
```

continues

Listing 11.3. continued

```
function documentClick() {
    srcElement = window.event.srcElement;
    if (srcElement.id=="Maine") {
      statelist.recordset.AbsolutePosition = 1;
    } else {
      if (srcElement.id=="Vermont") {
        statelist.recordset.AbsolutePosition = 2;
      } else {
        if (srcElement.id=="New Hampshire") {
          statelist.recordset.AbsolutePosition = 3;
        } else {
          if (srcElement.id=="Massachusetts") {
            statelist.recordset.AbsolutePosition = 4;
          } else {
            if (srcElement.id=="Rhode Island") {
              statelist.recordset.AbsolutePosition = 5;
            } else {
              if (srcElement.id=="Connecticut") {
                statelist.recordset.AbsolutePosition = 6;
              }
            }
          }
        }
      }
    }
    Picture.src = srcElement.id + ".jpg";
}

document.onclick = documentClick;

</SCRIPT>
</FONT>
</BODY>
</HTML>
```

By now, Listing 11.3 might be self-explanatory to you if you have been reading this book sequentially. Try to understand how it works without reading the following details. The <OBJECT></OBJECT> tag pair that sets up the data source is identical to the pair in Listing 11.1 except that the data source name and file are changed to statelist and newengld.txt, respectively.

The inclusion of the six states' images is right out of Chapter 10. Each <IMG> tag has an SRC attribute to identify the URL of the image file, an ID attribute to give each object image a name, and a STYLE attribute to place and size the image on the Web page.

Similar to Listing 11.1, a larger image object is added to the page to provide an image of the state the reader selects through a mouse click. Initially, the image is set to the state of Maine. As a reader clicks a different state, the larger image is replaced with that state's. This is done through the first script function in Listing 11.1.

Figure 11.4.

The New England States Web page with Connecticut chosen.

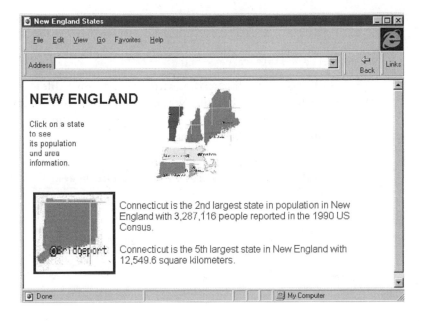

Each data record field is set up as a separate form field on the Web page. For the New England States data form, I use <SPAN></SPAN> tag pairs instead of the <INPUT></INPUT> tag pairs used in Listing 11.1. The difference for Listing 11.3 is that the data form fields are placed within free-flowing body text instead of in a neat and orderly table. Remember that the difference between division tags and span tags is that span tags do not include a line feed. Because you are creating a free-flowing presentation, you do not need to create labels.

As for the script function created to tie everything together, the srcElement feature from Chapter 8 is used. I interrogate the source element of a reader's mouse click with the following line within the function documentClick:

```
srcElement = window.event.srcElement;
```

The documentClick() function is always available as a part of Dynamic HTML.

The ID attribute of the image selected by the user is interrogated. Depending on which image a reader clicks, the data source record is set to that row with a line in the function like the following:

```
statelist.recordset.AbsolutePosition = 6.
```

Here, the row indicator is set to row 6 (its absolute position), which contains the information for the state of Connecticut. Six such lines are created in the script function because there are six states.

Finally, the larger image's source is set to the bitmap image file of the state that the reader selects. The following line is used to change the image:

```
Picture.src = state.value + ".jpg";
```

The New England-specific data comes from the data source file named `newengld.txt`. Listing 11.4 shows the contents of the file. Note that the file format is Comma Separated Values. Also note that the string data includes a space character at the end of each string to provide appropriate spacing on the Web page.

 Listing 11.4. Contents of the file `newengld.txt`.

```
State,Pop_Rank,Area_Rank,Population,Area
Maine ,3rd ,1st ,"1,227,928 ","79,939.1 "
Vermont ,6th ,2nd ,"562,758 ","23,955.8 "
New Hampshire ,4th ,3rd ,"1,109,252 ","23,230.7 "
Massachusetts ,1st ,4th ,"6,016,425 ","20,300.3 "
Rhode Island ,5th ,6th ,"1,003,464 ","2,706.5 "
Connecticut ,2nd ,5th ,"3,287,116 ","12,549.6 "
```

NOTE

All the examples in this chapter have used data forms for data presentation only. Microsoft has implemented an architecture in its Internet Explorer 4.0 Web browser that permits you to author data form Web pages that your readers can use to update data as well. Microsoft's Dynamic HTML architecture includes form field validation events you can use to check a Web-based form's contents before or after you update a database.

Summary

This chapter introduced the concept of data-awareness. Data-awareness is a feature of the Internet Explorer 4.0 Web browser that enables flexible data delivery by a Web author. A data-aware Web page stays aware of a data source that is downloaded at the same time as the page. Using Dynamic HTML, you then provide a way for the reader to interact with the Web page and filter or sort the data. The data is then presented anew.

This chapter reviews two examples of using data-awareness to present data sources one record at a time. Chapter 12, "Dynamic Table Generation and Expansion," focuses on interactive expansion and sorting.

The advantages of using data-awareness include eliminating multiple Web server requests and eliminating reader wait time. The disadvantage lies in the initial download time of the data source. The corporate world has been accessing data over a network for years, and Information Services (IS) specialists are always considering data delivery strategy trade-offs when providing new applications. Web page data-awareness brings those same trade-off decisions to the Web author. With multiple delivery strategies available, the Web author can control the best way to deliver Web page data to the user.

Q&A

Q I noticed that an incredible amount of data is available at the U.S. Census Web site. Certainly, you are not suggesting that all that data should be delivered to each reader who comes to the site?

A Exactly. If everything were to come down at once, each reader would have to wait for an entire CD-ROM's worth of information to be delivered. But, I might suggest that all the data for one state be available for a single download in order to make the Web page presentation of that state's information more fluid in a highly interactive and dynamic presentation. In a perfect world, the site would let you choose either presentation, one page at a time or one state at a time.

Q I noticed that, in the team locker room example, you use the same image you use in Chapter 9 in the dynamic team placement example. The resolution does not look very good when blown up. Shouldn't you have used a better resolution for the team locker room images?

A Yes. I used the low-resolution images solely for simplicity purposes. I would have been better off creating larger images and then shrinking them for the movable images example from Chapter 9. In fact, I thought about including the images again in this chapter after I had created the example in Chapter 9. I would not publish the locker room example from this chapter on the Web unless I knew most of my readers had very low-tech computers and modem connections.

Q If I want to access more than one data source from within a single Web page, how can I access both from the same mouse event?

A If you want to access two separate data sources from your Web page, you must create a second `<OBJECT></OBJECT>` tag pair to reference the second data source. You also must add the appropriate labels and fields to your data form for the second data source. Interesting to note is the fact that you can intermix the fields on the same data form even though they are presented from different data sources. Then, in your scripts, add both data set controls within the same logical sections. As an example, look at the following code, in which the current record position of two data sources is set within the same `if...then` construct:

```
if (srcElement.id="conn") {
    statelist.recordset.AbsolutePosition = 6;
    taxinfo.recordset.AbsolutePosition = 36;
}
```

Quiz

Take the following quiz to see how much you've learned in this chapter.

Questions

1. What is data-awareness?
2. What are the primary advantages of using a data-aware Web page data delivery strategy?
3. Which file format is used in this chapter for the data source examples?
4. Why did you use that particular data source file format?
5. In a data-aware script function, what are the three commands you can use to move to a different record in a data source?

Answers

1. Data-awareness is a feature of a computing process that enables the process to communicate with an external data source as if it were part of the process. To a Web browsing process, a Web page is data-aware if it binds to a data source and then references the data source elsewhere throughout the Web page.
2. There are two primary advantages: First, such a strategy requires only a single request to the Web server. Second, such a strategy eliminates reader download wait time between presenting different records on the Web page.
3. The comma separated values (CSV) file format.
4. I used the CSV format because it is a very common standard to which most data tools can export. By the way, tab-delimited file formats are also popular for importing and exporting between different data presentation tools.
5. `MoveNext` moves to the next record, `MovePrevious` moves to the previous record, and `AbsolutePosition` moves to a specific record number in the data source. All three are called using the *datasourceid.recordset.command* syntax such as `statelist.recordset.MovePrevious`.

Workshop

Chapter 10's workshop is as creative as they come, and you can continue to add animation to the workshops in Chapters 11 and 12. In this workshop, though, focus primarily on an interactive data form. Listing 11.5 provides you with a data source I would like you to present to a Web reader on a dynamic Web page. The data source contains a header row and five data records. Each record contains information about a different species of squid. Listing 11.5 provides you with each squid's name, geography, environment, size, and species-specific comments.

Because most Web visitors prefer graphics over text, add images to your Web page that users can click on to see the data form fill with that species' information. Feel free to have those images moving around in a simple animation because the onclick event is still available for moving images. You will be filtering the data source to present just one record at a time. In my implementation, I have fixed the location of each squid species on the page. I also include an image that moves around to highlight the squid that is currently being presented in the data form.

If you do not have a clear understanding of what to do, look at Figure 11.5 for some clarification or inspiration. After you create your How Diverse Are Squid? Web page, look at the implementation in Listing 11.6. Be sure to save your page with the filename the hyperlink on your giant squid welcome page expects for the How Diverse Are Squid? link. Put the file in the same subdirectory on your hard drive as your welcome page. Make sure the link works.

INPUT   ## Listing 11.5. My How Diverse Are Squid? data source.

```
Type,Geography,Environment,Size,Comments
Giant,Worldwide colder oceans such as Soviet Union and South Africa,
Deepwater,Up to 30 Meters, Beak-like mouth strong enough to cut
through steel cable. Five pairs of arms. Eyes that are the largest
in the animal kingdom - as big as eighteen inches across.
Long-finned,From Newfoundland Canada to the Gulf of Venezuela,Pelagic
schooling loliginid distributed in continental shelf and slope waters,
Up to 40 cm,The short lifespan of long-finned squid combined with their
 rapid growth and capacity to spawn year-round leads to a seasonally
dynamic resource for fishermen.Short-finned,from Florida USA to Labrador
Canada in the Western Atlantic,
Gulf Stream is thought to be an important transport mechanism for larvae
and juveniles. As adults they stay on the continental shelf, Up to 35 cm,
Short-finned squid are essentially an annual species with a life cycle
of roughly one year.
Stubby,Range is from Japan around to southern California, Found most
often at night below about 30 feet on a sand or mud bottom or where that
kind of bottom meets a rock wall,Up to size of a golf ball,They lay a real
```

continues

Listing 11.5. continued

```
distinctive egg that looks like a fake plastic pearl attached to a rock
usually in a small crevice. This animal does not normally inhabit the
intertidal zone so you are very unlikely to find it beachwalking or
tidepooling.
Opalescent,Range is southern Alaska to Baja but this animal is palagic,
Continental shelf dweller,up to 40 cm, A rare but wonderful site this
is the squid of Calamari fame. Their eggs called squid candles
(white tubes about 3 inches long) are a more likely find.
```

Listing 11.6 shows my implementation of the How Diverse Are Squid? Web page. Notice that I have not used any animation in my example. The image with the ID=pointer attribute is used solely as an image that highlights the squid a user clicks last. The information for the highlighted squid is shown in the data form.

INPUT **Listing 11.6. My How Diverse Are Squid? Web page.**

```
<HTML>
<HEAD>
<TITLE>5 Species of Squid</TITLE>
</HEAD>
<BODY BACKGROUND="water.jpg" TEXT=#FFFFFF LINK=FFFF22 VLINK=FF22FF>
<H2>Species of Squid</H2>
<FONT COLOR=#FFFF00>
<I>Click on a squid to learn more about that type</I></FONT>
</P>
<P>
<OBJECT ID="squidlist"
        CLASSID="clsid:333C7BC4-460F-11D0-BC04-0080C7055A83"
        BORDER="0" WIDTH="0" HEIGHT="0">
  <PARAM NAME="DataURL" VALUE="types.txt">
  <PARAM NAME="UseHeader" VALUE="True">
</OBJECT>
<P>
<IMG ID="pointer" STYLE="container:positioned;position:absolute;TOP:400pt;
LEFT:0px;WIDTH:156px;HEIGHT:156px;ZINDEX:0;" src="hilite.gif">
<IMG ID="s1" STYLE="container:positioned;position:absolute;TOP:10pt;
LEFT:480px;WIDTH:128px;HEIGHT:96px;ZINDEX:1;" src="Squid1.gif">
<IMG ID="s2" STYLE="container:positioned;position:absolute;TOP:30pt;
LEFT:340px;WIDTH:128px;HEIGHT:64px;ZINDEX:6;" src="Squid5.gif">
<IMG ID="s3" STYLE="container:positioned;position:absolute;TOP:55pt;
LEFT:40px;WIDTH:128px;HEIGHT:64px;ZINDEX:4;" src="Squid4.gif">
<IMG ID="s4" STYLE="container:positioned;position:absolute;TOP:50pt;
LEFT:270px;WIDTH:64px;HEIGHT:96px;ZINDEX:3;" src="Squid3.gif">
<IMG ID="s5" STYLE="container:positioned;position:absolute;TOP:80pt;
LEFT:400px;WIDTH:128px;HEIGHT:64px;ZINDEX:2;" src="Squid2.gif">
<TABLE><TR><TD>
<TR>
<TD ALIGN=RIGHT VALIGN=TOP><LABEL FOR=type>Squid Type: </LABEL></TD>
<TD ALIGN=LEFT VALIGN=TOP WIDTH="10"></TD>
<TD ALIGN=LEFT VALIGN=TOP><INPUT ID=type SIZE=20 TYPE=text DATASRC=#squidlist
```

11

```
DATAFLD="Type"></TD>
</TR>
<TR>
<TD ALIGN=RIGHT VALIGN=TOP><LABEL FOR=geography>Geography: </LABEL></TD>
<TD ALIGN=LEFT VALIGN=TOP WIDTH="10"></TD>
<TD ALIGN=LEFT VALIGN=TOP><INPUT ID=geography SIZE=60 TYPE=text
DATASRC=#squidlist DATAFLD="Geography"></TD>
</TR>
<TR>
<TD ALIGN=RIGHT VALIGN=TOP><LABEL FOR=environment>Environment: </LABEL></TD>
<TD ALIGN=LEFT VALIGN=TOP WIDTH="10"></TD>
<TD ALIGN=LEFT VALIGN=TOP><INPUT ID=environment SIZE=200 TYPE=text
DATASRC=#squidlist DATAFLD="Environment"></TD>
</TR>
<TR>
<TD ALIGN=RIGHT VALIGN=TOP><LABEL FOR=size>Size: </LABEL></TD>
<TD ALIGN=LEFT VALIGN=TOP WIDTH="10"></TD>
<TD ALIGN=LEFT VALIGN=TOP><INPUT ID=size SIZE=20 TYPE=text DATASRC=#squidlist
DATAFLD="Size"></TD>
</TR>
<TR>
<TD ALIGN=RIGHT VALIGN=TOP><LABEL FOR=comments>Comments: </LABEL></TD>
<TD ALIGN=LEFT VALIGN=TOP WIDTH="10"></TD>
<TD ALIGN=LEFT VALIGN=TOP><INPUT ID=comments SIZE=200 TYPE=text
DATASRC=#squidlist DATAFLD="Comments"></TD>
</TR>
</TABLE>
<SCRIPT language=JavaScript>
var srcElement
function documentClick() {
    srcElement = window.event.srcElement;
    if (srcElement.id=="s1") {
       squidlist.recordset.AbsolutePosition = 1;
       pointer.style.top="0px";
       pointer.style.left="440px";
    } else {
       if (srcElement.id=="s2") {
          squidlist.recordset.AbsolutePosition = 2;
          pointer.style.top="0px";
          pointer.style.left="320px";
       } else {
          if (srcElement.id=="s3") {
             squidlist.recordset.AbsolutePosition = 3;
             pointer.style.top="35px";
             pointer.style.left="20px";
          } else {
             if (srcElement.id=="s4") {
                squidlist.recordset.AbsolutePosition = 4;
                pointer.style.top="30px";
                pointer.style.left="200px";
             } else {
                if (srcElement.id=="s5") {
                   squidlist.recordset.AbsolutePosition = 5;
                   pointer.style.top="60px";
                   pointer.style.left="360px";
```

11

continues

Listing 11.6. continued

```
                    }
                }
            }
        }
    }
}

document.onclick = documentClick;

</SCRIPT>
</BODY>
</HTML>
```

Figure 11.5 shows my implementation of the How Diverse Are Squid? Web page after I clicked on the giant squid in the upper-right corner of the page.

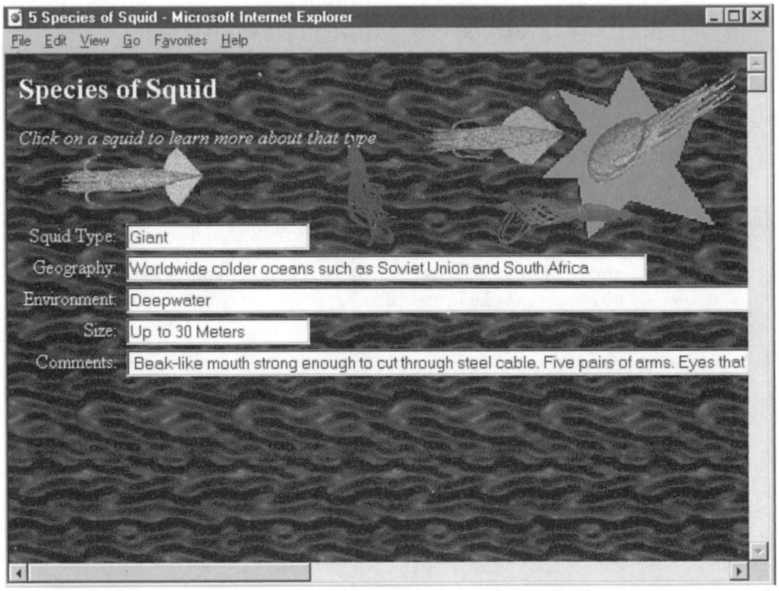

Figure 11.5.

After the giant squid is selected.

Day 6

Chapter 12

Dynamic Table Generation and Expansion

This chapter continues with the data-awareness theme. Chapter 11, "Data Bound Form Fields," introduced you to new data delivery strategies made available to a Web author by Microsoft's Internet Explorer 4.0 Web browser. You saw examples of how to deliver a data source along with a Web page. You then used Dynamic HTML to interact with the data one record at a time. Presenting just a subset of records within a data source is called data filtering. In Chapter 11, you filtered a data source to show one record at a time in a data form on the Web page.

In this chapter, you learn how to present more than one data source record at a time on a Web page. You learn how to create Web pages that automatically generate tables from a data source. Then you will add the appropriate lines to your HTML file in order to let the data be sorted dynamically by a reader. A reader will thank you as she gains control over the appearance of the data in Web page tables.

Specifically, in this chapter, you learn the following:

☐ What dynamic table expansion is

☐ Why to use dynamic table generation and expansion

☐ The Web browser's role

☐ How to add dynamic table generation with Dynamic HTML

☐ An example of dynamic table generation

☐ An example of dynamic table sorting

What Is Dynamic Table Expansion?

Dynamic table expansion is a feature of a data presentation tool that enables variable-length data sources to automatically be presented in a table of any length necessary. For a Web browser, dynamic table expansion means that you, the Web author, must identify only the first row of the table with the appropriate headers and then identify which column from the data source belongs with which header field. The Web browser does the rest, dynamically creating the necessary table tags to show the complete contents of the data source.

The dynamic table expansion feature works especially well with variable-length data sources that change over time. You do not have to change the Web page, because the Web browser does all the work in creating the appropriate tags depending on the number of records in the data source. Only the data source changes to present more recent data.

For example, imagine you provide a daily ski report Web site's New Snow Page. Every day you list in a table on a Web page all the mountains that received new snow in the last 24 hours. For each mountain, there is a mountain name column, a new centimeters of snowfall column, and a current centimeters of snow base column. To present the information each day, you could take advantage of dynamic table expansion on a data-aware Web page. The HTML file you create can stay the same day after day. Only the data source that includes a variable number of records (depending on the number of mountains that received snow in the last 24 hours) must change daily. The Web browser knows how to present the variable information in a table based on the first row you identify with the appropriate HTML tags.

Why Use Dynamic Table Generation and Expansion?

You use dynamic table generation for its simplicity and flexibility in presenting changing data. This book does not present examples of how to use multiple data sources on the same Web page. That probably would be redundant and detract from your core learning. There is no reason why you could not have multiple tables on a Web page, each with its own dynamic table.

NOTE

In fact, I encourage you to try to add several dynamic tables to see the technology in action. Use the cut-and-paste feature of your favorite text editing tool to copy one table's tags and add a new table. When you compare Listing 12.1 with Listing 12.4 later in this chapter, you will see how easy putting both tables on the same Web page would be.

Perhaps you want to present on a Web page daily baseball standings for all the Major League, AAA, and AA teams in the United States and Canada. Each night, each league could send you a data source of the team standings for that league. Daily, on the Web server, you would replace each data source's file with a file of the same name. A reader who downloads the standings page then would get the latest standings for each team.

Dynamic expansion means that each league's standings are already expanded and visible on the page when the Web browser finishes loading the Web page. After loading, a reader might want to collapse some of the league standings he was not interested in. I call that dynamic collapse. Many readers would prefer to have expansion and collapse control of the detail on a Web page. I expect Microsoft to add dynamic table collapse to Internet Explorer soon.

The Internet Explorer 4.0 Web browser also comes with the capability to dynamically sort data in a dynamically generated table. Each time you click a table header to sort the data by that column, the table collapses and then regenerates in a different order. The table automatically re-expands. There are many reasons why you might want to sort a data source. Sorting shows you the relative ordered position of a data item. For example, I like to sort baseball team standings by ERA to see where my favorite pitching staff ranks relative to the rest of the league.

12

NOTE

Actually, I should be happy the Web did not exist in 1984. During that summer, I could not stop reading baseball statistics every day because my favorite team had the lowest team earned run average as well as the highest team batting average in the whole Major Leagues. Imagine if I had been able to access a statistics Web page from my desk at work. I think I would have checked every half hour just to make sure I was not dreaming.

Dynamic sorting provides an interactive activity to a Web-based visitor. Many Web surfers want to be able to do other things on the Web besides just read and look at pictures. Even if it seems like a basic feature, dynamic sorting is quite useful in the battle of trying to keep your readers coming back to your site.

The Web Browser's Role

Just as with the Web pages you saw in Chapter 11, dynamically generated and expanding tables rely on the Web browser in order to function properly. The Web browser downloads the Web page and the data source. Then, the Web browser puts the data source in a place where the browser can reference it often to present the results from a user's interactions with the Web page.

The Web browser reads the definition of the first table row from the `<TABLE>`, `<TR>`, and `<TD>` HTML tags that define the row. Then, through the attributes associated with a second row of table tags, the Web browser associates the appropriate columns from the data source with the different cells in the table. After that, the browser reads through all the data and expands the table to make room for each row of data in the data source.

The Web browser must contain the different file translation logic that is necessary to interpret different data source file types. The Web browser must contain any sorting logic in order to dynamically sort a data source before presenting a table.

Adding Dynamic Table Generation with Dynamic HTML

To add dynamic table generation to your Web pages, you insert into your HTML file the same `<OBJECT></OBJECT>` tag pair you use to present data-aware data forms. Then, you create the first row of the table using a `<THEAD></THEAD>` tag pair. You nest the table header within a `<TABLE></TABLE>` tag pair. The opening `<TABLE>` tag needs a few attributes such as the following, where an `ID` attribute gives the table the name `mytable` and a `DATASRC` attribute associates the appropriate data source object with the table:

```
<TABLE BORDER="1" ID="mytable" DATASRC="#mydata">
```

The `BORDER` attribute defines the thickness of the border to be used between cells in the table.

You then create three lines after the opening `<TABLE>` tag to look like the following, which begins the table head with a `<THEAD>` tag, begins the first row with a `<TR>` tag, and begins the first column header cell with a `<TD>` tag:

```
<THEAD>
<TR>
<TD><FONT COLOR="#0000FF"><B><U><DIV ID=col1>Name</DIV></U></B></FONT></TD>
```

Of all the tags nested within the `<TD></TD>` table cell tag pair, the `<DIV ID=col1>Name</DIV>` sequence is the most critical. The division creates an object with the name `col1`. Remember that a division is just another word for a section, but a division is a section that can be much smaller than a typical word processing section. You can reference `col1` from any script function in order to modify the appearance or contents of the division.

12

The text Name actually appears within the table cell on the Web page. You should recognize the <FONT>, <B>, and <U> tags as older HTML tags that affect the appearance of the text. In this case, the table headings are colored blue and the table headings are boldfaced and underlined. I recommend adding some form of text formatting to the header row to make it stand out from the rest of the table.

NOTE

Remember that in Chapters 7, "Changing Text Attributes," and 8, "Dynamically Changing Style," you learned to vary text format or style as a way to provide feedback to the user. Table headers are a great example of where you should vary text attributes in order to draw attention to the fact they are available for interaction. If you add dynamic sorting to your table, be sure to make the headers stand out. A user will be more apt to click on a header if a header jumps out at him or her.

For each column in your data source, add an additional <TD></TD> tag pair similar to the preceding example. After you declare all the column headers, close off the first table row with a </TR> tag, and close off the table head with a </THEAD> tag.

After the table head, you create a table body identifier by using a <TBODY></TBODY> tag pair. In a table with four columns, the table body identifier might look like the following:

```
<TBODY>
<TR>
<TD><DIV DATAFLD="Col1"></DIV></TD>
<TD><DIV DATAFLD="Col2"></DIV></TD>
<TD><DIV DATAFLD="Col3"></DIV></TD>
<TD><DIV DATAFLD="Col4"></DIV></TD>
</TR>
</TBODY>
```

Each cell in the table body identifier contains a division with a DATAFLD attribute. The value of the DATAFLD attribute is the column name as specified in the data source you identified in the opening <TABLE> tag. In this case, you are using the mydata data source.

NOTE

As a review, don't forget that the mydata data source identifier is the object ID attribute name for the <OBJECT></OBJECT> tag pair. You add the object tag pair to the page in order to supply the appropriate ActiveX control the Web browser uses to handle the dynamic data-aware functionality of the Web page.

That is all you need to do to add dynamically expanding tables to a Web page that follows Microsoft's approach to data-awareness. The Web browser does the rest.

An Example of Dynamic Table Generation

This chapter presents two examples of how to dynamically generate tables from a data source. The first, in Listing 12.1, demonstrates the flexibility of a dynamic Web page to handle variable-length data sources. The second, in Listing 12.4, shows how to provide the dynamic sorting feature to your readers.

As I mentioned earlier, you take more advantage of dynamic table generation when you provide a variable-length data source often over a period of time. A daily New Snow Report Web page is one example. Listing 12.1 provides another variable-length data source example.

For a first example, imagine you are providing a Web site that announces new births for a busy city hospital. Any town citizen can visit your Web page on a daily basis to see information about babies that have been delivered by the hospital's staff. You want to provide the name of the mother, name of the baby if available, sex of the baby, weight of the baby, length of the baby, and the mother's comments, if any, all within a dynamic table on the Web page.

Look at Listing 12.1 and Figure 12.1, and then continue reading for a detailed explanation.

INPUT **Listing 12.1. Hospital births Web page.**

```
<HTML>
<HEAD><TITLE>Recent Hospital Births</TITLE></HEAD>
<BODY BGCOLOR= "#FFFFFF">
<H2>This Month's Births</H2>
<HR>
<P>
<OBJECT ID="babylist"
    CLASSID="clsid:333C7BC4-460F-11D0-BC04-0080C7055A83"
    ALIGN="baseline" BORDER="0" WIDTH="0" HEIGHT="0">
    <PARAM NAME="DataURL" VALUE="babies1.txt">
    <PARAM NAME="UseHeader" VALUE="True">
</OBJECT>

<TABLE BORDER="1" ID="elemtbl" DATASRC="#babylist">
<THEAD>
<TR>
<TD><B><U><DIV ID=mom>Mom</DIV></U></B></TD>
<TD><B><U><DIV ID=name>Baby</DIV></U></B></TD>
<TD><B><U><DIV ID=sex>Sex</DIV></U></B></TD>
<TD><B><U><DIV ID=weight>Weight</DIV></U></B></TD>
<TD><B><U><DIV ID=length>Length</DIV></U></B></TD>
<TD><B><U><DIV ID=comment>Comment</DIV></U></B></TD>
</TR>
</THEAD>
<TBODY>
<TR>
<TD><DIV DATAFLD="Mom"></DIV></TD>
<TD><SPAN DATAFLD="Baby"></SPAN></TD>
<TD><DIV DATAFLD="Sex"></DIV></TD>
```

```
<TD><DIV DATAFLD="Weight"></DIV></TD>
<TD><DIV DATAFLD="Length"></DIV></TD>
<TD><DIV DATAFLD="Comment"></DIV></TD>
</TR>
</TBODY></TABLE>
<HR>
</BODY>
</HTML>
```

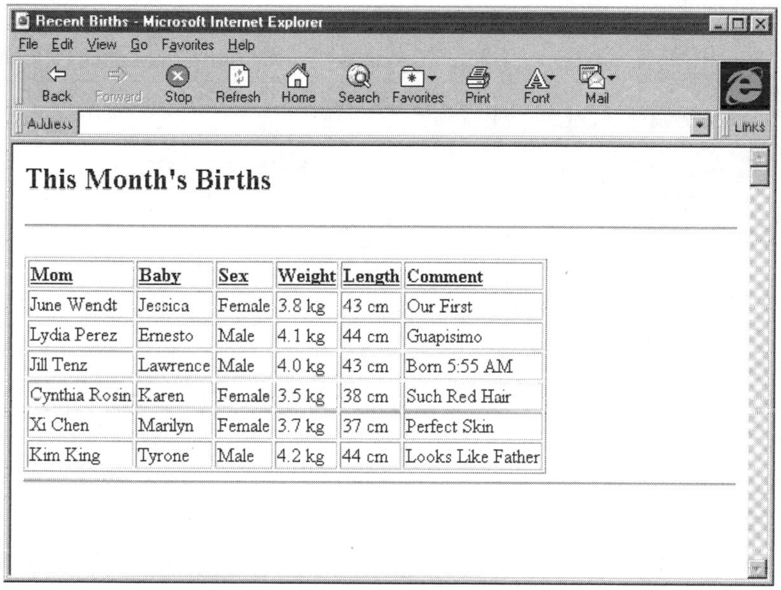

Figure 12.1.

Births for three days in May.

Before you review Listing 12.1 in detail, focus on the benefits of using dynamically generating tables. Figure 12.1 shows the This Month's Births Web page as it displays the data source in Listing 12.2. After the column header row, the table dynamically expands to include six additional rows, each with a separate baby record.

INPUT **Listing 12.2. Contents of the `babies1.txt` file.**

```
Mom,Baby,Sex,Weight,Length,Comment
June Wendt,Jessica,Female,3.8 kg,43 cm,Our First
Lydia Perez,Ernesto,Male,4.1 kg,44 cm,Guapisimo
Jill Tenz,Lawrence,Male,4.0 kg,43 cm,Born 5:55 AM
Cynthia Rosin,Karen,Female,3.5 kg,38 cm,Such Red Hair
Xi Chen,Marilyn,Female,3.7 kg,37 cm,Perfect Skin
Kim King,Tyrone,Male,4.2 kg,44 cm,Looks Like Father
```

Go ahead and edit the babies1.txt file to include two new births for May 4. You can change the file, save it, and then reload the Web page. If you are short on creativity, just copy and paste or type the two new rows from the babies2.txt file from Listing 12.3. The table will automatically generate two new rows as it expands for the new data source. Remember that any computer process could automatically generate the baby births data source by accessing a database on the hospital's network and running a query. Also, keep in mind that you do not need to re-create the Web page each time the data source changes.

INPUT   **Listing 12.3. Contents of the babies2.txt file.**

```
Mom,Baby,Sex,Weight,Length,Comment
June Wendt,Jessica,Female,3.8 kg,43 cm,Our First
Lydia Perez,Ernesto,Male,4.1 kg,44 cm,Guapisimo
Jill Tenz,Lawrence,Male,4.0 kg,43 cm,Born 5:55 AM
Cynthia Rosin,Karen,Female,3.5 kg,38 cm,Such Red Hair
Xi Chen,Marilyn,Female,3.7 kg,37 cm,Perfect Skin
Kim King,Tyrone,Male,4.2 kg,44 cm,Looks Like Father
Jen Georgeson,Lyle,Male,4.1 kg,42 cm,First on Fourth
Tin Xin,Yu,Male,3.9 kg,42 cm,Very Easy Birth
```

The result of adding two new lines to the data source is shown in Figure 12.2. The data from Listing 12.3 is presented in Microsoft's Internet Explorer 4.0 Web browser. This time, the table displays eight rows for the eight baby records in the data source plus one for the column headers.

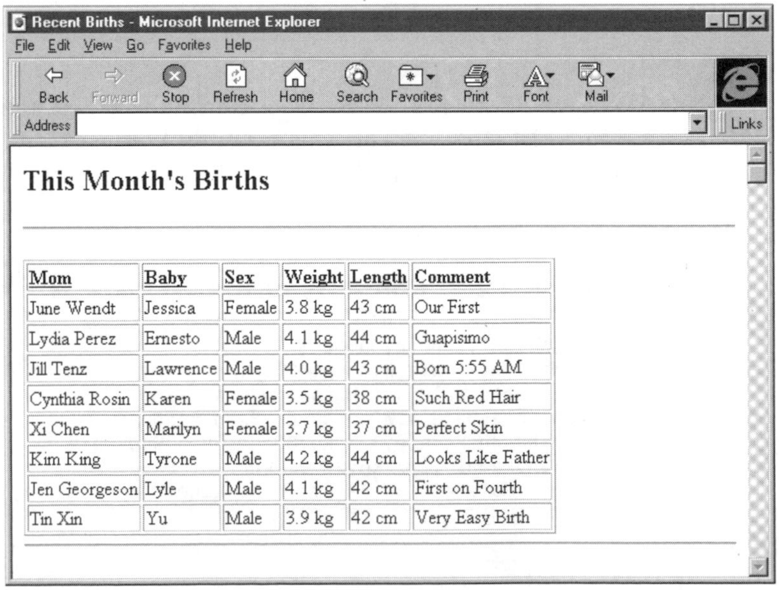

Figure 12.2.

Births for four days in May.

Mom	Baby	Sex	Weight	Length	Comment
June Wendt	Jessica	Female	3.8 kg	43 cm	Our First
Lydia Perez	Ernesto	Male	4.1 kg	44 cm	Guapisimo
Jill Tenz	Lawrence	Male	4.0 kg	43 cm	Born 5:55 AM
Cynthia Rosin	Karen	Female	3.5 kg	38 cm	Such Red Hair
Xi Chen	Marilyn	Female	3.7 kg	37 cm	Perfect Skin
Kim King	Tyrone	Male	4.2 kg	44 cm	Looks Like Father
Jen Georgeson	Lyle	Male	4.1 kg	42 cm	First on Fourth
Tin Xin	Yu	Male	3.9 kg	42 cm	Very Easy Birth

12

Return your focus to Listing 12.1. You probably have noticed that Listing 12.1 does not require a script. In fact, you did not even need to use the onLoad() event handling function to start the table generation process. The browser starts the table and generation process solely from the other HTML tags on the Web page.

First, you add the object tags to activate the ActiveX control that handles table generation and expansion. You name the object with the ID="babylist" attribute. You will refer to the babylist name whenever you want to use the data source object within the other HTML tags on the page. The CLASSID attribute defines the proper value for the control. As with Chapter 11, you need no physical space on the Web page for the data-awareness control, so you set the BORDER, WIDTH, and HEIGHT attributes to 0. You add an ALIGN attribute and set it to baseline, which aligns each row along the baseline for the table.

The two <PARAM> tags are expected by the ActiveX control. The first parameter the ActiveX control expects is a DataURL for the data source. The data is saved in a comma separated value (CSV) file named babies1.txt. You want to use the first row in the data file as a header record. So, set the UseHeader parameter to True.

When you are finished, the data source object looks like this:

```
<OBJECT ID="babylist"
    CLASSID="clsid:333C7BC4-460F-11D0-BC04-0080C7055A83"
    ALIGN="baseline" BORDER="0" WIDTH="0" HEIGHT="0">
    <PARAM NAME="DataURL" VALUE="babies1.txt">
    <PARAM NAME="UseHeader" VALUE="True">
</OBJECT>
```

After you define the data source object, refer to the data source ID attribute value within the table. The opening <TABLE> tag includes a DATASRC attribute, which has been set to be the name of the babylist data source object. The leading pound symbol (#) is required syntax when you are referring to a data source name.

Next, create the first two rows of the table. The first is nested within a <THEAD></THEAD> tag pair. The first row is a row of column headers for the table. You create the first row with simple HTML tags, and the second row is nested within a <TBODY></TBODY> tag pair. The second row is just as clean, but includes a DATAFLD attribute for each opening <DIV> tag. The DATAFLD attribute value for each division had better agree with the header row in the data source. If not, the Web page will not present the correct data in the column as the table expands.

As you will see in the "Quiz" section later in this chapter, adding dynamic sorting to the This Month's Births Web page is straightforward. If you can guess how to do it, try it now. If you can't, read the next section.

12

An Example of Dynamic Table Sorting

Earlier in the chapter, I mentioned a baseball statistics Web page as an example of a useful dynamically sorting page. You will now build a simplified baseball statistics Web page that provides dynamic sorting. You can extend this page to include more interesting statistics such as team home runs, team stolen bases, team shutouts, and team home winning percentage. In fact, to me, statistics are the most amazing aspect of baseball. So are the people who have memorized them for the last 50 years worth of games.

Take a look at Listing 12.4, and then continue reading for the details. Of most interest to you should be the script functions near the bottom of the listing.

INPUT   **Listing 12.4. A sortable baseball statistics Web page.**

```
<HTML>
<HEAD><TITLE>WBL Current Standings</TITLE></HEAD>
<BODY BGCOLOR= "#FFFFFF">
<H2>WBL Current Standings</H2>
<HR>
<P>
<OBJECT ID="teamlist"
     CLASSID="clsid:333C7BC4-460F-11D0-BC04-0080C7055A83"
     ALIGN="baseline" BORDER="0" WIDTH="0" HEIGHT="0">
     <PARAM NAME="DataURL" VALUE="wblteam.txt">
     <PARAM NAME="UseHeader" VALUE="True">
</OBJECT>

This Table is Sortable By Clicking on the Column Header<P>
<TABLE BORDER="1" ID="elemtbl" DATASRC="#teamlist">
<THEAD>
<TR>
<TD><FONT COLOR="#0000FF"><B><U><DIV
     ID=team>Team</DIV></U></B></FONT></TD>
<TD><FONT COLOR="#0000FF"><B><U><DIV
     ID=wins>Wins</DIV></U></B></FONT></TD>
<TD><FONT COLOR="#0000FF"><B><U><DIV
     ID=losses>Losses</DIV></U></B></FONT></TD>
<TD><FONT COLOR="#0000FF"><B><U><DIV ID=BA>
     Batting Avg</DIV></U></B></FONT></TD>
<TD><FONT COLOR="#0000FF"><B><U><DIV ID=ERA>
     ERA</DIV></U></B></FONT></TD>
</TR>
</THEAD>
<TBODY>
<TR>
<TD><SPAN DATAFLD="Team"></SPAN></TD>
<TD><DIV DATAFLD="Wins"></DIV></TD>
```

```
<TD><SPAN DATAFLD="Losses"></SPAN></TD>
<TD><DIV DATAFLD="BA"></DIV></TD>
<TD><DIV DATAFLD="ERA"></DIV></TD>
</TR>
</TBODY></TABLE>
<SCRIPT LANGUAGE="JavaScript">
function teamClick() {
  teamlist.Sort = "Team";
  teamlist.Reset();
}

team.onclick = teamClick;

function winsClick() {
  teamlist.Sort = "Wins";
  teamlist.Reset();
}

wins.onclick = winsClick;

function lossesClick() {
  teamlist.Sort = "Losses";
  teamlist.Reset();
}

losses.onclick = lossesClick;

function baClick() {
  teamlist.Sort = "BA";
  teamlist.Reset();
}

ba.onclick = baClick;

function eraClick() {
  teamlist.Sort = "ERA";
  teamlist.Reset();
}

era.onclick = eraClick;

</SCRIPT>
<HR>
</FONT>
</BODY>
</HTML>
```

I feel no need to insult your intelligence, so let me just say that other than the functions inside the <SCRIPT></SCRIPT> tag pair, Listing 12.4 is very similar to Listing 12.1. The data source used for this example is the same wblteam.txt file used for the team locker room example in Chapter 11. Refer to Listing 11.2 if you want to see the data source again.

12

The following are the changes you needed to make from Listing 12.1 to create Listing 12.4:

☐ Change the data source object ID attribute to teamlist, and change the DataURL parameter to wblteam.txt.

☐ Change any DATASRC attributes from #babylist to #teamlist.

☐ Change the text in the table header row (I also added the blue font color).

☐ Change any DATAFLD attributes to the appropriate values provided in the data source header line.

A script function was then added to handle a reader's mouse click on each table header cell. All the functions were placed within the same <SCRIPT></SCRIPT> tag pair. Each function adds the suffix Click() to the ID value of the column header opening <DIV> tag in order to define a function name. For example, the function for the wins column is named winsClick().

Each function contains two simple lines. The first line tells the Web browser to re-sort the table based on the column the reader clicked with the mouse:

```
teamlist.Sort = "Wins";,
```

All sorts are done in ascending order. The second line tells the Web browser to regenerate and re-expand the table, which is done with the new sort:

```
teamlist.Reset(),
```

NOTE

> That's right, the sort script function events are not referenced as attributes of the table row <DIV> tags, but instead are automatically associated through the ID attribute value. I think that is a clever way of associating an element with an event, but puts more burden on the browser to implicitly notice the connection. For documentation purposes, I like adding the event attribute to the HTML element that initiates the event. You can decide whether you agree.

Adding dynamic sorting to your Web pages is simple when the data source awareness is done properly. You might want to point out to your readers the fact that they can sort the table dynamically. In Figure 12.3, text has been added to the page to indicate that the table can be sorted. I sorted the table you see in Figure 12.3 by team earned run average by clicking the ERA column heading before I took the screen capture.

Figure 12.3.
Dynamic standings sorting.

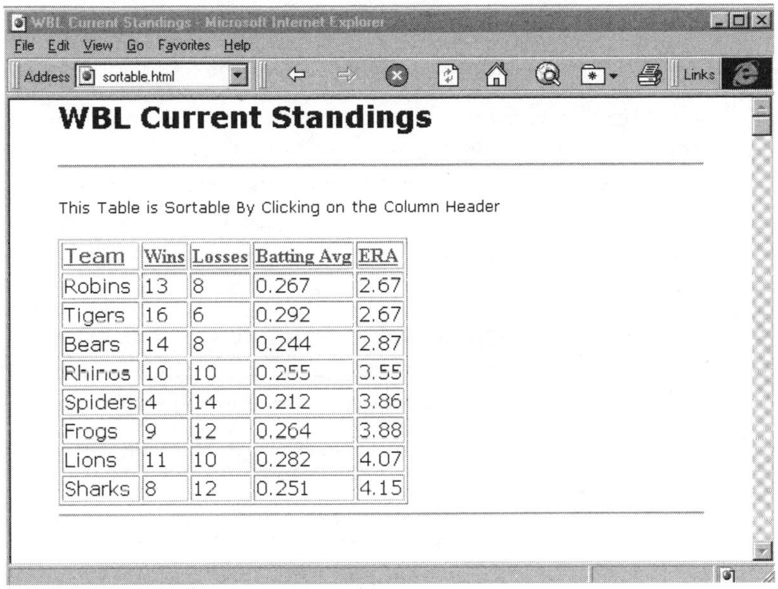

DATAFORMATAS **and** DATAPAGESIZE

You can use the DATAFORMATAS attribute in the same tag pair as a DATAFLD attribute to identify two different types of data in a database: text and html. If you store HTML tags within the text of a database field and author a Web page data field with a DATAFORMATAS=html attribute, the Internet Explorer 4.0 Web browser will format the text using the HTML tags. In fact, you can even specify an image by storing an <IMG></IMG> tag pair in your database field. If you do not identify a DATAFORMATAS attribute, the browser uses the text type as default.

As an example of using the DATAFORMATAS attribute, consider the following <DIV></DIV> tag pair, which accesses a data source dynamically:

```
<DIV DATAFLD="Element" DATAFORMATAS=html></DIV>
```

If in the database, the Element column fields looks like this:

```
<B>Na</B> is the symbol for <I>Sodium</I>
```

the field would appear on the Web page as this:

Na is the symbol for Sodium

On the other hand, if the DATAFORMATAS attribute is set to text or does not appear at all like the following:

```
<DIV DATAFLD="Element"></DIV>
```

the field would appear on the Web page as

```
<B>Na</B> is the symbol for <I>Sodium</I>
```

In the latter case, the tags actually appear as text. No doubt you would want to avoid having tags appear on your Web page as text. Still, the capability to store HTML tags in a database and let a Web browser present the formatted text and graphics is a powerful feature. More and more, Web authors will store changing data in a database because the cost of maintaining Web pages drops significantly if the dynamically changing facts are kept separate from the static text.

You can use the DATAPAGESIZE attribute to identify how many rows of data you want to present to a user at one time. For very long tables, a user might want to manage how many rows he or she sees at one time. You can create the controls that let a user manage table presentations.

As an example of using the DATAPAGESIZE attribute, consider the following dynamic table open <TABLE> tag:

```
<TABLE DATAPAGESIZE=10 id=Periodic DATASRC="#ElementTable"
```

Now, a user will see only 10 records at a time when the table generates. In your scripts, you can move forward in the table by using the .nextPage method or dynamically change the page size using the .dataPageSize property of the table name object.

When a user clicks a button you provide, your onmouseclick event can execute a script function with the following line:

```
Periodic.nextPage
```

and you can change the table size dynamically to 15 records with the following line:

```
Periodic.dataPageSize=15
```

Both DATAFORMATAS and DATAPAGESIZE are new Dynamic HTML attributes with powerful capabilities.

Summary

With Internet Explorer 4.0, you can present more than one record at a time from a data source within a Web page. Presenting only a subset of records at a time is called filtering. If you want to present the entire data source, you can set up an automatically generated and expanding table by using the appropriate Dynamic HTML tags. The table will automatically fill up with the data from the data source file you identify.

After a Web page automatically loads a data source in a file, you can indicate by which columns a reader can sort the table. A reader sorts a column by clicking on it with his or her mouse. When a sort is requested, the table dynamically regenerates and re-expands the table in the row order of the sorted column. All dynamic sorts are ascending.

A big advantage to delivering data as a separate data source is the flexibility it presents. Your Web page does not need to be edited if only the data source changes. The Web browser builds the table on the fly even if the data source record length varies over time. As more data sources are created by automated processes involving sensors and computing algorithms, expect to see more data-aware Web pages delivered in this fashion.

You might be noticing a trend here. Chapters 7 through 10 provided examples of Web pages that were enabled with a single HTML file. Chapters 11 and 12's examples required two files: an HTML file and a data source file. The examples in Chapters 13 and 14 will require multiple files as you see examples of how to integrate Dynamic HTML with other existing technologies.

Q&A

Q You reference other data presentation tools in this chapter. I use one that lets me filter out columns of a data set. Is there any way I can dynamically rearrange the order or filter out columns from a data set?

A Good point. Dynamically filtering or sorting rows from a data source in Internet Explorer's 4.0 pre-release Web browser is easy. The technology to do the same for columns is very simple to implement. I would expect more dynamic tools to be at your disposal as version 4.0 of Internet Explorer develops further. In fact, some day relatively soon I would expect to be able to dynamically manipulate a data set on a Web page as I can a table in a personal database tool. You might have a different opinion.

Q I realize that I must use an ActiveX control to enable data awareness and dynamic sorting. Because ActiveX technology is a Microsoft invention, is there any chance it will become a standard endorsed by the W3C?

A Well, there are several things to consider in response to your question. First, because Netscape and Microsoft own so much of the Web browser market, it is not imperative that the W3C endorse ActiveX controls as a standard to make the technology worthwhile. In fact, Microsoft endorsed Netscape's plug-in technology, and many third parties have successfully used the plug-in implementation. I am more interested in whether Netscape would endorse ActiveX controls. I suspect it will not because Netscape has so many other technologies in the works that fill the same need as ActiveX controls. It would be great if either the W3C endorsed ActiveX, Netscape endorsed ActiveX, or Microsoft stopped promoting ActiveX. Web users might become frustrated by the fact that so many ActiveX components are being added to their hard drives as they use Internet Explorer. What do you think?

12

Q The **Sort** method you use to choose a new dynamic sort always performs ascending sorts. Can I perform descending sorts as well?

A Yes. Not only can you perform descending sorts, you can identify multiple sorts of more than one column within a single script function. The details are available from Microsoft's sitebuilder Web pages at

```
http://www.microsoft.com/workshop/author/dhtml/
```

Quiz

Take the following quiz to see how much you've learned in this chapter.

Questions

1. How many rows of tags must you set up in order to create a dynamically expanding table?

2. What two new tag pairs are introduced to HTML tables in order to create a dynamically expanding table?

3. In order to enable dynamic sorting for a table column, what function must you create?

4. What line is necessary in the dynamic sort function in order to actually perform the sort?

5. Using Listing 12.4 as a guide, can you add dynamic sorting to the This Month's Births Web page from Listing 12.1?

Answers

1. You should create the first two rows, but you could actually ignore the first table heading row if you were not going to enable dynamic sorting.

2. The `<THEAD></THEAD>` table head tag pair and the `<TBODY></TBODY>` table body tag pair are not traditional tags associated with HTML tables, but should be used for a dynamically generated and expanding table.

3. You create a function that connects the `ID` attribute value for that column header data cell and `Click`. For example, if a table column header data cell includes a `<DIV ID=head1>` open tag, the appropriate function name would be `head1Click()`.

4. You must use the `datasourcename.Reset()` line, which regenerates and re-expands the table using the new sort. The data source name comes from the `ID` attribute value of the `<OBJECT></OBJECT>` pair you create to connect your data file with the Web page.

5. Adding dynamic sorting to Listing 12.1 is pretty straightforward. Just add the following script before the closing </BODY> HTML tag:

```
<SCRIPT LANGUAGE="JavaScript">
function momClick() {
  babylist.Sort = "Mom";
  babylist.Reset();
}

mom.onclick = momClick;
function nameClick() {
  babylist.Sort = "Baby";
  babylist.Reset();
}
name.onclick = nameClick;

function sexClick() {
  babylist.Sort = "Sex";
  babylist.Reset();
}

sex.onclick = sexClick;

function weightClick() {
  babylist.Sort = "Weight";
  babylist.Reset();
}

weight.onclick = weightClick;

function lengthClick() {
  babylist.Sort = "Length";
  babylist.Reset();
}
length.onclick = lengthClick;

function commentClick() {
  babylist.Sort = "Comment";
  babylist.Reset();
}

comment.onclick = commentClick;</SCRIPT>
```

Workshop

In this workshop, you finish the giant squid research Web site. In the workshop in Chapter 9, "Dynamically Changing Content," you personalized the research team by introducing a reader to the key team members. This chapter's workshop is a little more far-fetched because you will personalize the giant squid families themselves. I watched a great science television special on how researchers got to know each of the whales in the whale families that live around Vancouver Island in Canada. Those whales come to the surface often and are recognized by sight by the researchers.

12

On the Get to Know Our Blind Giant Squid Families Web page you will create in this workshop, you will introduce your readers to the individual squid that make up each squid family. You will present each of three squid families in separate, dynamically generated and expanding tables. The data for the tables is provided in Listing 12.5. I have invented some silly names for the squid in my data sources; feel free to change them to your liking. The data provided on each squid include the squid's name, weight, sex, age, and the name of the researcher who first discovered the squid. The three different families are named Group A, Group B, and Group C. Show the families one at a time on the Web page, and provide a method for a reader to switch between the three families.

Feel free to look at Figure 12.4 before you begin your implementation. After you finish, look at the implementation in Listing 12.6. Be sure to save your HTML file with the same filename your Get to Know Our Blind Giant Squid Families link on your welcome page expects.

INPUT   **Listing 12.5. The data sources.**

```
Group A:

Name,Weight,Sex,Age:INT,Discoverer
Sqibbles,657 kg,Female,12,Chaka Binte
Grant,633 kg,Male,13,Chaka Binte
Bubbles,433 kg,Female,3,Chaka Binte
Feebee,356 kg,Female,3,Chaka Binte
Linlin,402 kg,Female,3,Chaka Binte
Trent,457 kg,Male,3,Chaka Binte

Group B:

Name,Weight,Sex,Age:INT,Discoverer
Alta,643 kg,Male,17,Chaka Binte
Ellen,603 kg,Female,9,Thomas White
Swifty,639 kg,Male,9,Chaka Binte
Wobbles,456 kg,Female,5,Chaka Binte
Dilly,282 kg,Female,2,Chaka Binte
TinTin,357 kg,Male,3,Chaka Binte

Group C:

Name,Weight,Sex,Age:INT,Discoverer
Dinky,555 kg,Female,8,Goreng Veng
TuTu,673 kg,Male,11,Chaka Binte
TuTuToo,412 kg,Female,7,Chaka Binte
Nuctong,556 kg,Male,7,Chaka Binte
Tina,302 kg,Female,2,Thomas White
Dilbert,347 kg,Male,2,Thomas White
Dally,319 kg,Male,2,Thomas White
```

In the implementation in Listing 12.6, I created three separate range elements with the Group A, Group B, and Group C family names identified as separate elements. I use a <SPAN></SPAN>

12

tag pair for each family name element. The span tags work similar to division tags but keep placing consecutive elements on the same Web page line. When a reader clicks on a family name, the color of that family name changes to yellow and the appropriate table's division moves into view. The other two family names are colored white, and their tables move off the visible window at location (20,800). The reader can dynamically sort the first four columns of all three tables. The Discoverer column cannot be sorted.

INPUT ## Listing 12.6. My HTML file implementation.

```
<HTML>
<HEAD><TITLE>Get to Know Our Giant South Pacific Squids</TITLE></HEAD>
<BODY BACKGROUND="water.jpg" TEXT=#FFFFFF LINK=FFFF22 VLINK=FF22FF>
<H2>Our Giant Squid Families</H2>
<HR>
<SPAN ID=GA STYLE="color:Yellow" onclick="A();"><B> Group A </B></SPAN>
<SPAN ID=GB STYLE="color:White" onclick="B();"><B>  Group B </B></SPAN>
<SPAN ID=GC STYLE="color:White" onclick="C();"><B>  Group C </B></SPAN>
<P>
<IMG SRC="Squid1.gif"
 STYLE="position:absolute;top:30;left:360;width:120px;height:155px">
<IMG SRC="Squid1.gif"
 STYLE="position:absolute;top:120;left:380;width:150px;height:170px">
<IMG SRC="Squid1.gif"
 STYLE="position:absolute;top:80;left:400;width:160px;height:180px">
<IMG SRC="Squid1.gif"
 STYLE="position:absolute;top:100;left:370;width:120px;height:155px">
<IMG SRC="Squid1.gif"
 STYLE="position:absolute;top:160;left:450;width:112px;height:140px">
<OBJECT ID="groupAlist"
     CLASSID="clsid:333C7BC4-460F-11D0-BC04-0080C7055A83"
     ALIGN="baseline" BORDER="0" WIDTH="0" HEIGHT="0">
     <PARAM NAME="DataURL" VALUE="groupA.txt">
     <PARAM NAME="UseHeader" VALUE="True">
</OBJECT>

<OBJECT ID="groupBlist"
     CLASSID="clsid:333C7BC4-460F-11D0-BC04-0080C7055A83"
     ALIGN="baseline" BORDER="0" WIDTH="0" HEIGHT="0">
     <PARAM NAME="DataURL" VALUE="groupB.txt">
     <PARAM NAME="UseHeader" VALUE="True">
</OBJECT>

<OBJECT ID="groupClist"
     CLASSID="clsid:333C7BC4-460F-11D0-BC04-0080C7055A83"
     ALIGN="baseline" BORDER="0" WIDTH="0" HEIGHT="0">
     <PARAM NAME="DataURL" VALUE="groupC.txt">
     <PARAM NAME="UseHeader" VALUE="True">
</OBJECT>
```

12

continues

Listing 12.6. continued

```
<DIV ID=DivA
 STYLE="position:absolute;top:100;left:20;width:320px;height:320px">
<TABLE BORDER="1" ID="elemtbl" DATASRC="#groupAlist">
<THEAD>
<TR>
<TD><B><U><DIV ID=nameA STYLE="color:Yellow">Name</DIV></U></B></TD>
<TD><B><U><DIV ID=weightA STYLE="color:Yellow">Weight</DIV></U></B></TD>
<TD><B><U><DIV ID=sexA STYLE="color:Yellow">Sex</DIV></U></B></TD>
<TD><B><U><DIV ID=ageA STYLE="color:Yellow">Age</DIV></U></B></TD>
<TD><B><U><DIV ID=discovererA STYLE="color:Yellow">Discovered By
</DIV></U></B></TD>
</TR>
</THEAD>
<TBODY>
<TR>
<TD><I><DIV DATAFLD="Name"></DIV></I></TD>
<TD><SPAN DATAFLD="Weight"></SPAN></TD>
<TD><DIV DATAFLD="Sex"></DIV></TD>
<TD><DIV DATAFLD="Age"></DIV></TD>
<TD><DIV DATAFLD="Discoverer"></DIV></TD>
</TR>
</TBODY></TABLE>
</DIV>
<DIV ID=DivB
 STYLE="position:absolute;top:800;left:20;width:320px;height:320px">
<TABLE BORDER="1" ID="elemtblB" DATASRC="#groupBlist" STYLE="visibility:hide">
<THEAD>
<TR>
<TD><B><U><DIV ID=nameB STYLE="color:Yellow">Name</DIV></U></B></TD>
<TD><B><U><DIV ID=weightB STYLE="color:Yellow">Weight</DIV></U></B></TD>
<TD><B><U><DIV ID=sexB STYLE="color:Yellow">Sex</DIV></U></B></TD>
<TD><B><U><DIV ID=ageB STYLE="color:Yellow">Age</DIV></U></B></TD>
<TD><B><U><DIV ID=discovererB STYLE="color:Yellow">Discovered By
</DIV></U></B></TD>
</TR>
</THEAD>
<TBODY>
<TR>
<TD><I><DIV DATAFLD="Name"></DIV></I></TD>
<TD><SPAN DATAFLD="Weight"></SPAN></TD>
<TD><DIV DATAFLD="Sex"></DIV></TD>
<TD><DIV DATAFLD="Age"></DIV></TD>
<TD><DIV DATAFLD="Discoverer"></DIV></TD>
</TR>
</TBODY></TABLE>
</DIV>
<DIV ID=DivC
 STYLE="position:absolute;top:1200;left:20;width:320px;height:320px">
<TABLE BORDER="1" ID="elemtblC" DATASRC="#groupClist">
<THEAD>
<TR>
<TD><B><U><DIV ID=nameC STYLE="color:Yellow">Name</DIV></U></B></TD>
<TD><B><U><DIV ID=weightC STYLE="color:Yellow">Weight</DIV></U></B></TD>
<TD><B><U><DIV ID=sexC STYLE="color:Yellow">Sex</DIV></U></B></TD>
<TD><B><U><DIV ID=ageC STYLE="color:Yellow">Age</DIV></U></B></TD>
```

12

```
<TD><B><U><DIV ID=discovererC STYLE="color:Yellow">Discovered By
</DIV></U></B></TD>
</TR>
</THEAD>
<TBODY>
<TR>
<TD><I><DIV DATAFLD="Name"></DIV></I></TD>
<TD><SPAN DATAFLD="Weight"></SPAN></TD>
<TD><DIV DATAFLD="Sex"></DIV></TD>
<TD><DIV DATAFLD="Age"></DIV></TD>
<TD><DIV DATAFLD="Discoverer"></DIV></TD>
</TR>
</TBODY></TABLE>
</DIV>
<SCRIPT LANGUAGE="JavaScript">
function A() {
  GA.style.color="Yellow";
  GB.style.color="White";
  GC.style.color="White";
  DivA.style.top = "100px";
  DivB.style.top = "800px";
  DivC.style.top = "800px";
}

function B() {
  GA.style.color="White";
  GB.style.color="Yellow";
  GC.style.color="White";
  DivA.style.top = "800px";
  DivB.style.top = "100px";
  DivC.style.top = "800px";
}

function C() {
  GA.style.color="White";
  GB.style.color="White";
  GC.style.color="Yellow";
  DivA.style.top = "800px";
  DivB.style.top = "800px";
  DivC.style.top = "100px";
}

function nameAClick() {
  groupAlist.Sort = "Name";
  groupAlist.Reset();
}

nameA.onclick = nameAClick;

function weightAClick() {
  groupAlist.Sort = "Weight";
  groupAlist.Reset();
}

weightA.onclick = weightAClick;
```

continues

Listing 12.6. continued

```
function ageAClick() {
  groupAlist.Sort = "Age";
  groupAlist.Reset();
}

ageA.onclick = ageAClick;

function sexAClick() {
  groupAlist.Sort = "Sex";
  groupAlist.Reset();
}

sexA.onclick = sexAClick;

function nameBClick() {
  groupBlist.Sort = "Name";
  groupBlist.Reset();
}

nameB.onclick = nameBClick;

function weightBClick() {
  groupBlist.Sort = "Weight";
  groupBlist.Reset();
}

weightB.onclick = weightBClick;

function ageBClick() {
  groupBlist.Sort = "Age";
  groupBlist.Reset();
}

ageB.onclick = ageBClick;

function sexBClick() {
  groupBlist.Sort = "Sex";
  groupBlist.Reset();
}

sexB.onclick = sexBClick;

function nameCClick() {
  groupClist.Sort = "Name";
  groupClist.Reset();
}

nameC.onclick = nameCClick;

function weightCClick() {
  groupClist.Sort = "Weight";
  groupClist.Reset();
}

weightC.onclick = weightCClick;
```

```
function ageCClick() {
  groupClist.Sort = "Age";
  groupClist.Reset();
}

ageC.onclick = ageCClick;

function sexCClick() {
  groupAlist.Sort = "Sex";
  groupAlist.Reset();
}

sexC.onclick = sexCClick;

</SCRIPT>
</BODY>
</HTML>
```

I captured Figure 12.4 after clicking on the Group C family name near the top of the page. I did not dynamically sort the table.

Figure 12.4.

The Get to Know Our Blind Giant Squid Families Web page.

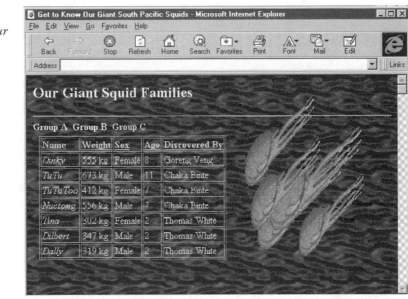

DAY 7

Advanced Issues

Day 7

Chapter 13

Integrating Other Languages and Objects into Dynamic HTML

This chapter contrasts Dynamic HTML with other Web page technologies. By the time you finish this chapter, you will have a significant understanding of some other technologies Web authors use to create interactive Web pages. As you read about other technologies that provide interactivity on a Web page, consider how you would integrate additional technologies with Dynamic HTML. You can try to integrate other Web page technologies yourself by following the examples here.

In this chapter, you'll learn about the following:

- ☐ VBScript
- ☐ ActiveX
- ☐ An example using ActiveX
- ☐ Java

☐ An example using Java

☐ Other Web page technologies

VBScript

Back on Day 3, "The Role of Scripting in Dynamic HTML," you learned about the JavaScript scripting language. Since that point in this book, you have seen Web page scripting examples using both the JavaScript and VBScript scripting languages. JavaScript is a scripting language that closely follows the syntax structure of the Java programming language. VBScript is a scripting language that closely follows the syntax structure of the Visual Basic programming language. Keep in mind that you can use both scripting languages on the same Web page by enclosing each script function in a separate <SCRIPT></SCRIPT> tag pair with the appropriate LANGUAGE attribute.

Visual Basic itself traces its roots back to the BASIC programming language. Programmers have been using BASIC extensively for decades. In fact, BASIC is a language engineers use to program machine control systems such as the machines on a beverage bottling assembly line.

Microsoft uses Visual Basic extensively when it is programming office technology solutions that contain word processing documents, database tables, forms, spreadsheets, presentation slides, and e-mail messages. Supposedly, Visual Basic is an easy language to learn for office workers to use to write office process automation programs.

When you are familiar with Visual Basic, or perhaps even only with BASIC, VBScript is very easy to understand and use within Web page scripting logic. I believe that VBScript is also easy to learn if you understand JavaScript. Some of the Dynamic HTML examples in this book use VBScript instead of JavaScript to provide the functions you need to add interactivity to your Web pages. In most cases, you must make only simple syntax changes to convert a JavaScript script function to a VBScript script function. In other cases, the JavaScript language or VBScript language is easier to implement than the other.

In many cases, you can use scripting language routines without understanding them completely. Just cut and paste them from one Web page to another and change a few variable names and values. I hope you take that attitude toward scripting when you are playing around with new scripts. You really must understand the code in detail only if you need to dissect it or make it work with additional functionality.

As a quick overview to differences in basic syntax between JavaScript and VBScript, consider the following points about VBScript:

☐ VBScript does not use semicolons to indicate the end of a line of code. Instead, VBScript uses end-of-line characters that you usually create on a keyboard with the Enter key. End-of-line characters are white space in most text editors.

13

☐ VBScript uses more keywords than JavaScript. With VBScript, you set a variable by using the set keyword. You also explicitly end if statement control blocks with an end if statement. You use the word next at the end of a while control block.

☐ VBScript uses a single equal sign for an equality comparison, not two equal signs.

☐ VBScript is often more forgiving of *case* than JavaScript. Case refers to the capitalization of text. VBScript often treats an uppercase character and a lowercase character as though they were the same character.

If you want to learn more, visit your neighborhood bookstore. Visual Basic books are plentiful.

Similar to the discussion in Chapter 11, "Data Bound Form Fields," VBScript functionality, like data-awareness, has been easy for Microsoft to add to its Internet Explorer Web browser. Microsoft had been in the data-awareness and Visual Basic businesses for a long time before it turned its attention to Web browsers. Keep in mind that currently VBScript is foreign to Netscape's Navigator Web browser. Netscape would prefer that you script using JavaScript.

So, why do I spend time including a section here on VBScript? First, I thought a little background information would be helpful for you. You might already know everything you need to know about VBScript. Second, discussion about VBScript leads you into the next topic, ActiveX. As you will see shortly, most current implementations of the ActiveX technology contain VBScript scripts.

ActiveX

ActiveX is an integration technology devised by Microsoft to add new features to the Internet Explorer Web browser. You might ask, "What is an integration technology?" You might think "integration technology" sounds pretty vague. To truly understand Microsoft's full intent for providing ActiveX, you must think about ActiveX in a few different ways.

First and foremost, ActiveX technology was rolled out with Internet Explorer 3.0, a full version release before Dynamic HTML. ActiveX could be considered Microsoft's response to Netscape's plug-in architecture capability: Both enable a programmer to extend Web browser functionality with the programmer's own code. Microsoft has spent as many hours creating complex, component-based applications as any other software development company. Both the Windows 95 and NT operating system applications contain many different functions, controls, and processes, combined to provide a whole on which programmers can rely when creating applications that run on top of the operating system. Programmers write programs that rely on the operating system to provide services that make their programs run.

Try to think about a Web browser as a new kind of operating system for a minute. Programmers would love to extend a Web browser to provide new features to their audiences on the Web. ActiveX is the technology Microsoft created to enable programmers to extend

13

the Internet Explorer Web browser efficiently to handle new functionality. To make ActiveX even more tempting, Microsoft created an ActiveX plug-in that adds ActiveX features to Netscape Navigator.

ActiveX incrementally increases the capabilities of a reader's Web browser. A Web user can download ActiveX components similar to plug-in applications. In fact, ActiveX components autoload if you let them. Yet, Microsoft expects ActiveX components to be smaller and more reusable than plug-in applications. If you are familiar with Microsoft's Component Object Model (COM) through using Object Linking and Embedding (OLE), you have a good picture of what ActiveX does for a Web browser. ActiveX uses the same COM as OLE, but is optimized more for size and speed than usability.

NOTE
A Web browser user controls whether an ActiveX component downloads automatically when he or she encounters one on the Web. After the component is downloaded, a certificate of authenticity presents the user with a dialog box with security information. The user then confirms whether he or she wants to run the downloaded logic. A user can also choose to bypass all certificates if he or she prefers.

So, you are thinking to yourself, "What components make up ActiveX technology?" Currently, Microsoft promotes the following as key ActiveX components:

- □ *ActiveX Controls* are the objects on a Web page that provide interactive and user-controllable functions.

- □ *ActiveX Document filtering* enables users to view non-HTML documents, such as Excel or Word files, through a Web browser.

- □ *Active Scripting* controls the integrated behavior of several ActiveX controls or Java applets from the browser or server.

- □ *ActiveX Server Framework* provides several Web server-based functions such as security, database access, and others.

ActiveX components can be developed using a variety of programming languages, including Visual Basic, C, C++, and Java. ActiveX defines how the component coexists with the Web page, not the specific syntax used to create the component. ActiveX integrates new objects with the Web browser.

NOTE Remember that C and C++ programs are compiled for use with a specific operating system. To use the same control on multiple operating systems, the control must be compiled several times for each specific operating system. For Visual Basic and Java, a different interpreter must be available for each operating system on which the control is to run. Java interpreters are already included with different versions of the most popular Web browsers.

Remember Chapters 11, "Data-Bound Form Fields" and 12, "Dynamic Table Generation and Expansion," in which you created data-aware Web pages using Microsoft's data-awareness ActiveX control. The data-awareness control is included in the Internet Explorer 4.0 Web browser. Already more than 1,000 other reusable controls are available in the market. You can download many of the available controls for free and use them with ActiveX technology. You will see an example in this chapter after a few more introductory words about ActiveX.

ActiveX has been used successfully by Web authors who have been using Microsoft's development tools and strategies for a long time. ActiveX is a Web development approach you would expect from Microsoft. However, if you have not been indoctrinated into the Microsoft way of doing things, should you bet your time on ActiveX? No one can make that decision for you, but I can give you some additional points about ActiveX to consider, straight from Microsoft's ActiveX Web pages.

- [ ] Microsoft has announced that it will transfer ActiveX to an appropriate industry standards body.
- [ ] Microsoft continues to build ActiveX Web server functionality. Using ActiveX technology, Web servers are able to capture preferences from each Web visitor, create individual profiles for each user, and then tailor Web page content so that each user receives only the information of interest to him or her.
- [ ] Microsoft supports Authenticode code-signing security to certify ActiveX components before a Web user downloads them on his or her computer.

NOTE At the time I wrote this chapter, Microsoft provided much useful information about ActiveX in its http://www.microsoft.com/ activeplatform/ directory on its Web site. Microsoft included a warning that the pages were scheduled to be deleted because third-party Web sites were to take over the information dissemination responsibility.

13

An Example Using ActiveX

Keep in mind that ActiveX is an integration technology. You must see many different examples of ActiveX in action before you fully understand the full intent of ActiveX technology. The example in this chapter emphasizes how you can find an ActiveX control on the Web and reuse it for your own purposes.

In this section, you learn how to implement a cascading menu control using ActiveX that I found on the Web. I downloaded the Web page, read the code to understand the different pieces, and then changed some of the variables to make the control work for my content.

There is a Web site with the URL `http://www.activex.com/` that Microsoft recommends you use to download ActiveX controls. When you visit the ActiveX Web site, a cascading menu appears on the home page. A reader can use the cascading menu to go to other Web pages of interest. Because the cascading menu is an ActiveX control, I decided to use it to create my own cascading menu.

NOTE

Visit the ActiveX Web site at `http://www.activex.com/` to review and download ActiveX controls, many of which are free.

Cascading menus are popular because they save precious screen real estate. A cascading menu is a hierarchy of multiple menus in which a submenu opens, depending on where a reader clicks on its parent menu. Submenu options do not take up screen space until a user summons the submenu with a mouse click. Some cascading menus now do not require a mouse click but, instead, open when the user passes the mouse over the parent menu.

The cascading menu in this example requires a mouse click to activate a submenu. If you are still unsure of what a cascading menu is, look ahead to Figure 13.1. Listing 13.1 implements an ActiveX cascading menu control. I used the ActiveX cascading menu control to create a simple menu with two submenus. The first submenu includes links to the home pages for the five universities at which I have attended classes in my lifetime. The second submenu includes links to the home pages for the five companies at which I have worked the longest in my lifetime.

The scripting in this example is more rigorous and lengthy than other examples in this book. You do not need to understand everything to use the control. The explanation that follows the listing points out the most important parts of Listing 13.1. Look at Listing 13.1 in its entirety and then continue reading for an explanation.

Listing 13.1. Implementation of an ActiveX cascading menu control.

```
<HTML>
<HEAD>
<TITLE>Cascading Menus</TITLE>
</HEAD>
<BODY BGCOLOR="#FFFFFF" TEXT="#000000" LINK="#054BBB" VLINK="#054BBB">
<A NAME=#top>
<TABLE WIDTH=600 BORDER=0 CELLPADDING=0 CELLSPACING=0>
<TR><TD WIDTH=180 VALIGN=top ALIGN=left>
<P>
<!-- CASCADING MENU CONTROL -->
<OBJECT ID="TheMenu" WIDTH=0  HEIGHT=0
CLASSID="CLSID:8AF24F88-E71E-11CF-B9E3-080009D9611D"
CODEBASE="http://www.activex.com/Activetoolbar/
➥SmartControls.CAB#Version=1,0,0,0">
    <PARAM NAME="ForeColor" VALUE="0">
    <PARAM NAME="BackColor" VALUE=" 49407">
    <PARAM NAME="SelectedBackColor" VALUE="79985">
    <PARAM NAME="SelectedForeColor" VALUE="16777215">
    <PARAM NAME="ItemHeight" VALUE="20">
    <PARAM NAME="ItemWidth" VALUE="160">
    <PARAM NAME="ItemLeftMargin" VALUE="5">
</OBJECT>
<!-- PARAMETERS FOR CASCADING MENUS: MENU ITEMS AND URLS -->
<SCRIPT LANGUAGE="VBScript">
<!--
sub OpenScript()
    document.writeln "<SCR" & "IPT>"
end sub

sub CloseScript()
    document.writeln "</SC" & "RIPT>"
end sub

' Build the menu
sub BuildMenu(Button, Parent, Title, URL, Status, Icon, Handles)
    ' Walk arrays
    if (MenuUp) then exit sub
    MenuUp = true
    call Button.FreezeImage(2)
    last = UBound(Parent)
    for i = 0 to last
      pindex = Parent(i)
      if pindex = -1 then
          pindex = 0
      else
          pindex = Handles(pindex)
      end if
      Handles(i) = TheMenu.AddItem(pindex,Title(i),URL(i),Status(i), Icon(i))
    next
    call TheMenu.ShowMenu(Button.hWnd, 2, 0, 0, 0)
    call TheMenu.RemoveAll()
    call Button.FreezeImage(-1)
```

13

continues

Listing 13.1. continued

```
     MenuUp = false
     call Button.CancelMouseAction()
   end sub

' Used to generate mouse event routines
sub GenMouseEventSub(n)
   document.open
   call OpenScript()
   document.writeln "sub SmartButton" & n & "_MouseDown(Button, Shift, x, y)"
   document.writeln "call BuildMenu(SmartButton" & n & ", Parent" & n &
   ➥", Title" & n & ", URL" & n & ", Icon" & n & ", Status" & n &
   ➥", Handles" & n & ")"
   document.writeln "end sub"
    call CloseScript()
    document.close
   end sub

sub GenObject(n, Upimage, Downimage, Overimage)
   document.open
   ' Create OBJECT
   document.writeln "<OBJECT ID=""SmartButton" & n & """ WIDTH=150 HEIGHT=24"
   document.writeln "CLASSID=""CLSID:8AF24F84-E71E-11CF-B9E3-080009D9611D"""
   document.writeln "CODEBASE=""" & "http://www.activex.com/Activetoolbar/
   ➥SmartControls.CAB#Version=1,0,8,0" & """>"
   document.writeln "<PARAM NAME=""UpImage"" VALUE=""" & Upimage & """>"
   document.writeln "</OBJECT>"
   ' Set mouseover (or potentially mousedown) images after page is loaded
   call OpenScript()
   document.writeln "sub SmartButton" & n & "_SetImages()"
   document.writeln "SmartButton" & n & ".MouseoverImage = """ &
   ➥OverImage & """"
   document.writeln "end sub"
   call CloseScript()

   document.close

   end sub

sub MakeMenu(n, Upimage, Downimage, Overimage)
    call GenMouseEventSub(n)
    call GenObject(n, Upimage, Downimage, Overimage)
   end sub

' Here's where we build the menu descriptions
' For each top-level menu, there are 4 arrays, as follows
' (where n indicates the index of the menu
'
'   Parentn: integer index of parent (-1 means root menu)
'   Titlen:  string title of this menu item
'   URLn:    string URL for this item (NULL if not a leaf item)
' &&& author specific changes start here
' Universities menu
dim Parent0(4), Title0(4), URL0(4), Status0(4), Icon0(4), Handles0(4)
        Parent0(0)   = -1
        Title0(0)    = "Univ of Wisconsin-Madison"
        URL0(0)      = "http://www.wisc.edu/"
```

```
        Parent0(1)   = -1
        Title0(1)    = "University of Delaware"
        URL0(1)      = "http://www.udel.edu/"

        Parent0(2)   = -1
        Title0(2)    = "Renssaeler-Hartford"
        URL0(2)      = "http://www.hgc.edu/"

        Parent0(3)   = -1
        Title0(3)    = "The University of Connecticut"
        URL0(3)      = "http://www.uconn.edu/"

        Parent0(4)   = -1
        Title0(4)    = "The University of Washington"
        URL0(4)      = "http://www.washington.edu/"

        ' Make the menu
        call MakeMenu(0,"http://www.hitl.washington.edu/people/bdc/univs1.htm",
    ➥"http://www.hitl.washington.edu/people/bdc/univs2.htm",
    ➥"http://www.hitl.washington.edu/people/bdc/univs2.htm")

' Companies menu
dim Parent1(4), Title1(4), URL1(4), Status1(4), Icon1(4), Handles1(4)
        Parent1(0)   = -1
        Title1(0)    = "Ernst & Young"
        URL1(0)      = "http://www.ey.com/"

        Parent1(1)   = -1
        Title1(1)    = "Labatts"
        URL1(1)      = "http://www.labatt.com/"

        Parent1(2)   = -1
        Title1(2)    = "Catapult"
        URL1(2)      = "http://www.pbt.com/"
        Parent1(3)   = -1
        Title1(3)    = "Travelers"
        URL1(3)      = "http://www.travelers.com/"
        Parent1(4)   = -1
        Title1(4)    = "Marshall & Illsley"
        URL1(4)      = "http://www.micorp.com/"
        ' Make the menu
        call MakeMenu(1, "http://www.hitl.washington.edu/people/bdc/corps1.htm",
    ➥"http://www.hitl.washington.edu/people/bdc/corps2.htm",
    ➥"http://www.hitl.washington.edu/people/bdc/corps2.htm")
' &&& author specific changes end here
-->
</SCRIPT>

<!-- INDIVIDUAL CASCADING MENU OBJECTS -->
<SCRIPT LANGUAGE="VBScript">
<!--
    dim MenuUp

    Sub TheMenu_ItemSelect(SelectedItem, StringData)
        window.location = StringData
    end sub
```

continues

13

Listing 13.1. continued

```
Sub TheMenu_ItemHighlight(SelectedItem, StatusText)

    'set the status bar of the main frame to match the menu
    if (Len(StatusText) <= 1) then
        window.status = ""
        exit sub
    end if

    window.status = StatusText

end sub

document.write "<" & "!--"
-->
</SCRIPT>
<SCRIPT LANGUAGE="VBScript">
<!--
    document.write "--" & ">"
-->
</SCRIPT>
</TD>
<TD>
<PRE>
</PRE>
<H2>Active X Cascading Menu Test</H2>
</TD>
</TR>
</TABLE>
</BODY>
</HTML>
```

Figure 13.1 shows the cascading menu after you click the Universities menu item.

Figure 13.2 shows the cascading menu after you click the Companies menu item and move the mouse over Marshall & Illsley.

To simplify how you think about Listing 13.1, consider the HTML tags. Listing 13.1 contains an <OBJECT></OBJECT> tag pair and three <SCRIPT></SCRIPT> tag pairs. The complexity is contained mainly in the first <SCRIPT></SCRIPT> tag pair, which contains six script subfunctions: OpenScript(), CloseScript(), BuildMenu(), GenMouseEventSub(), GenObject(), and MakeMenu().

These six functions work together to create the tags necessary to embed a cascading menu on the Web page. The script functions extensively use the document.writeln function available in VBScript to produce the syntax for the HTML tags and script functions.

The OpenScript() subfunction simply creates an open <SCRIPT> tag. The CloseScript() subfunction simply creates a closing </SCRIPT> tag. Other script functions call the OpenScript() and CloseScript() subfunctions frequently.

Figure 13.1.

The cascading menu after you click Universities.

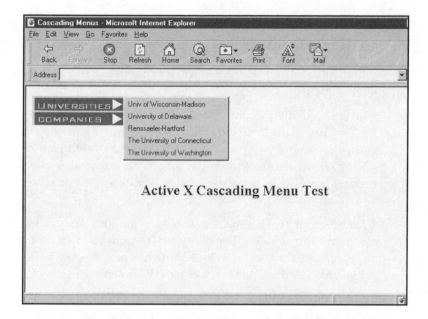

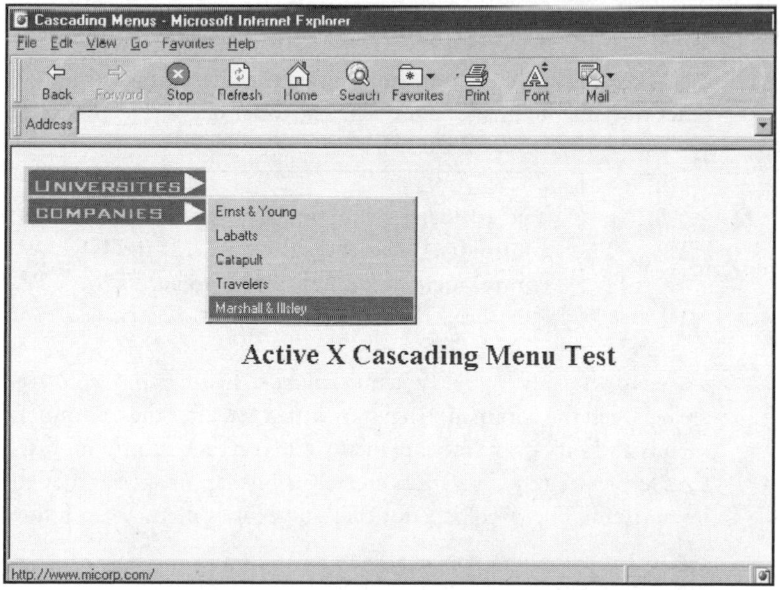

Figure 13.2.

The cascading menu after you click Companies.

The BuildMenu() subfunction creates a submenu when a user clicks its parent. The BuildMenu() subfunction is generic enough to accept any submenu as its parameters. The GenMouseEventSub() subfunction creates a mouse event for each parent menu that triggers the building of the appropriate submenu. The GenObject() subfunction creates a menu item on the high-level cascading menu. Each high-level menu is not active without the appropriate ActiveX control that provides the functionality. Therefore, GenObject() creates the appropriate <OBJECT></OBJECT> tag pair to handle each menu item. Finally, the MakeMenu() subfunction calls the GenMouseEventSub() and GenObject() subfunctions to create each high-level menu item.

I did not need to change any of these subfunctions. I could have just cut and pasted them into my Web page. I did make some changes to make it a more straightforward example, but the changes were unnecessary. My time was spent creating the menu items themselves. In Listing 13.1, after the six subfunctions, I changed the menu array values to create my cascading menu. I decided to create two menu items on my cascading menu: Universities and Companies.

Each submenu item is associated with the appropriate array elements. For example, for the company Ernst & Young, I set the Parent1(0) variable to -1, the Title1(0) variable to Ernst & Young, and the URL1(0) variable to http://www.ey.com/. The title will appear on the submenu and will access the respective URL when a reader clicks the title.

For each high-level menu item, the MakeMenu() subfunction is called and passed three URLs: The first parameter contains an absolute URL to a simple Web page that contains the image to use when a reader has not yet clicked that menu item. The second parameter contains an absolute URL to a simple Web page that contains the image to use when a reader clicks that menu item. The third parameter contains an alternative absolute URL to a simple Web page that contains the image to use when a reader clicks that menu item.

> **NOTE**
>
> The MakeMenu() function requires absolute URLs because the ActiveX control itself references the URLs. If the URLs were relative, the control logic might not be able to access the URL from its location.

To recap, the only changes you must make to Listing 13.1 to create your own cascading menu are between the comments that start with a &&& after the ' comment mark. You can add more menus and vary the number of menu items on each submenu. Just be sure to change the array sizes appropriately. You must create the bitmap images and Web pages for each high-level menu item. The Web page for the Universities menu item follows:

```
<BODY leftmargin=0 topmargin=0>
<img src="univs.jpg" width="150" height="24">
</BODY>
```

The <OBJECT></OBJECT> tag pair near the beginning of Listing 13.1 contains all the information to connect with the ActiveX cascading menu control. You can change the color and size parameters to make changes to the appearance of the submenus, but such changes are not necessary. As you cruise the Web and look at Web page source code, you should now be able to recognize the use of an ActiveX control. To understand more, you must brush up on your VBScript syntax. To learn more about JavaScript syntax, consider the following section on Java.

Java

Java is a programming language. As you just read, ActiveX is an integration technology. Java, on the other hand, is an Internet language. There is a big difference, yet with both you can produce similar results on a Web page.

Java is a programming language, just as BASIC, COBOL, C, Ada, Modula, FORTRAN, PL/1, and C++ are programming languages. In fact, in terms of syntax and development strategy, Java is quite similar to C++, but without some of the programming complexities associated with memory management and pointer flexibility. Java programming is best done following an object-oriented development strategy. As an Internet Java programmer, you create classes, instantiate objects, and then pass messages between objects to bring them to life on a Web page. However, Sun Microsystems did not create Java initially for the Internet. Instead, Sun developed Java as a programming language that was an efficient intermediary between the existing popular operating systems being used around the world: UNIX, Windows, and Macintosh.

To enable Java programs to be run on any computer, Sun developed the Java virtual machine. When, as a programmer, you compile Java code, you create an intermediate bytecode file. A helper application on each computer interprets the bytecode to run the program on top of the native operating system for that computer.

Think of the opportunity Sun had with Java. Other programming languages have been around for years. A team of computer scientists and mathematicians could get together to try to take the best of each existing language and put them together in a new language. When you program in a language over time, your compiled programs become different, even for the same source code. Compiler developers update their compiler applications to perform better and better optimizations. Just as word processor applications tend to all get the same features over time, compilers and operating systems also converge toward a best solution. People worldwide have been working with operating systems and compilers for a long time, and both applications are maturing. The time was ripe for implementing a new language such as Java.

You might be thinking, "This sounds great. Teach me how to use Java and I will never need anything else." Some days I feel that way. Yet, all kinds of great code and features are already available on the market that do not use Java. Some of the available programs have been optimized beyond what you could do currently with Java. There are days when I get sick of programming and just want to use someone else's code, but I might not be able to do that if he or she is trying to earn a living from his or her programs.

13

Enter into the picture an integration technology. With an integration technology, you can use different programs from different producers and tie them together in the same application, such as an application that extends a Web browser. Now, reconsider what ActiveX is. ActiveX is an integration technology that tries to tie different components together on a Web page. In effect, ActiveX should not compete with Java, but instead should help Java communicate with other Web page components.

You are getting close to seeing an example of how to present a Java-based program on a Web page. But, you should fully understand why you would want to use Java instead of another option, such as Dynamic HTML. I believe that the learning curve for Java is much steeper than the learning curve for Dynamic HTML. I also believe that the learning curve for ActiveX is somewhere in between, especially for someone who learned traditional procedural programming in a high school or college course. Perhaps the learning curve for Java could be traveled faster than ActiveX by people who think a certain way. I like to think about object-based development (OOD), but I had already learned traditional procedural programming when I was introduced to OOD.

Anyway, Dynamic HTML is coming on the scene to hide other steeper learning curves from a Web author. With Dynamic HTML, the Web browser developer does all the sophisticated programming (in C, C++, or Java, usually) to include functionality in the Web browser that a Web author can use by writing HTML files (as you have done in Chapters 7 through 12). With Dynamic HTML, the Web author passes some control over to the Web browser developer. Because the browser developer is usually Microsoft or Netscape, you might feel quite confident in handing over that control. I certainly do, which is why I am excited about Dynamic HTML.

NOTE

From the standpoint of society as a whole, it is very efficient for a team of 20 or 30 programming specialists in one organization to write code for a certain Web page feature and spend the time testing and optimizing that code—much more efficient than programmers all around the world independently trying to create that same functionality from scratch. Unfortunately, independent programmers do not use the Web to create teams that collaboratively build new Web functionality. We are not used to working that way.

The bottom line is that there is a trade-off here: quick learning and adequate Web page functionality versus longer learning and substantial Web page functionality. Dynamic HTML is a technology characterized by the first option, and Java represents the latter. I expect both to evolve quickly and often. Competition is really great sometimes.

At this point, you should be able to make a clear distinction among Dynamic HTML, ActiveX, and Java. They represent three different strategies for creating Web page content to be read on a computer. There is a similar distinction for creating 3D virtual worlds to be experienced on a computer: VRML 2, Living Worlds, and Java (with a 3D API). The same trade-offs are encountered by a technologist in a corporation who is trying to use the computer to get work done.

I mentioned that Java has a steep learning curve. Still, you should have a taste of how to use Java on a Web page. You will create the Old Shell Game using Java. You have a choice between using Dynamic HTML or Java to create the Old Shell Game, but use Dynamic HTML because you will agree it is easier. Save your Java skills to create interactions on your Web page that are not currently possible with Dynamic HTML. Or, use Java when someone else has given you most of the code already and you are in a hurry.

An Example Using Java

To use Java on a Web page, you must compile your Java code as an *applet*. Applets are Java programs that include the capability to exist within a Web page.

NEW TERM An *applet* is a Java-based program that requires a Web browser to function. Applets are embedded in Web pages using the HTML <EMBED> tag.

To compile a Java program as an applet, create the main class as an extension of the Applet class. In object-oriented terms, Applet is a base class of your new class that extends the basic applet capabilities. Listing 13.2 creates the class OldShellGame as a Web browser applet. Figure 13.3 shows the Old Shell Game in a Web browser before a reader starts the animation. Look at Listing 13.2 and Figure 13.3, and continue reading to review the details.

INPUT **Listing 13.2. The Java implementation of the Old Shell Game.**

```java
import java.awt.*;
import java.awt.image.*;
import java.net.*;
import java.applet.*;
public class OldShellGame extends Applet {
    static int time=50;        // Number of timing loops between key frames
    static int numframes=8;    // Number of key frames in the animation
    boolean running=false;     // Switch to turn animation on and off
    /**  The keyframe locations of images */
    static int  movesX0[] = {0,0,0,284,0,142,284,142,142};
    static int  movesY0[] = {50,50,50,176,50,176,50,176,50};
    static int  movesX1[] = {142,142,142,142,284,0,0,0,284};
    static int  movesY1[] = {50,50,50,176,50,176,50,176,50};
    static int  movesX2[] = {284,126,284,0,142,284,142,284,0};
```

continues

13

Listing 13.2. continued

```
static int  movesY2[] = {50,176,50,176,50,176,50,176,50};
static int  movesX3[] = {142,142,300,16,158,300,158,300,16};
static int  movesY3[] = {192,192,66,192,66,192,66,192,66};
/**  The current location of images */
int  left[] = {0,142,284,142};
int  top[] = {50,50,50,192};
/** The images for the shell game */
Image shell;
Image stone;
/** Initialize the applet. Resize and load images. */
public void init() {
stone = getImage(getCodeBase(), "gem.gif");
shell = getImage(getCodeBase(), "walnut.gif");
}
/** Paint it. */
public void paint(Graphics g) {
    int count = 0;
    int curframe = 1;
    Dimension d = size();
    g.fillRect(0,0,d.width,d.height);
    g.drawImage(stone, left[3], top[3], this);
    g.drawImage(shell, left[0], top[0], this);
    g.drawImage(shell, left[1], top[1], this);
    g.drawImage(shell, left[2], top[2], this);
    if(running) {
      while(count < time*numframes) {
        left[0] = movesX0[curframe-1] +
           ((movesX0[curframe]-movesX0[curframe-1])*(count % time)/time);
        top[0]=movesY0[curframe-1] +
           ((movesY0[curframe]-movesY0[curframe-1])*(count % time)/time);
        left[1]=movesX1[curframe-1] +
           ((movesX1[curframe]-movesX1[curframe-1])*(count % time)/time);
        top[1]=movesY1[curframe-1] +
           ((movesY1[curframe]-movesY1[curframe-1])*(count % time)/time);
        left[2]=movesX2[curframe-1] +
           ((movesX2[curframe]-movesX2[curframe-1])*(count % time)/time);
        top[2]=movesY2[curframe-1] +
           ((movesY2[curframe]-movesY2[curframe-1])*(count % time)/time);
        left[3]=movesX3[curframe-1] +
           ((movesX3[curframe]-movesX3[curframe-1])*(count % time)/time);
        top[3]=movesY3[curframe-1] +
           ((movesY3[curframe]-movesY3[curframe-1])*(count % time)/time);
        g.fillRect(0,0,d.width,d.height);
        if(count<time || count>=time*numframes) {
                g.drawImage(stone, left[3], top[3], this);
        }
        g.drawImage(shell, left[0], top[0], this);
        g.drawImage(shell, left[1], top[1], this);
        g.drawImage(shell, left[2], top[2], this);
        count++;
        if(count%time==0 && curframe<numframes) {
                curframe++;
```

```
            }
            Delay(200,count);
        }
    }
    running=false;
}
/** The user has clicked in the applet. Start the animation  */
public boolean mouseUp(Event evt, int x, int y) {
        running=true;
        left[3] = 142;
        top[3] = 192;
        repaint();
        return true;
}
public void Delay(long d,int count) {
        long x=0,y=0;
        for(x=0;x<d;x++) {
                y++;
        }
    }
}
```

With Java, you must explicitly import the base classes and interfaces you will extend within your code. The first four lines of Listing 13.2 import everything you need for the Old Shell Game. Basically, in the OldShellGame class, you declare and initialize variables, create the init() and paint() methods that an Applet class expects, establish a mouse-up handling routine, and then add a delay method to slow things down for faster computers.

The variables used are similar to the variables used in Chapter 10, "Dynamically Altering the Placement of Elements." You declare a time variable (called an attribute in object-oriented lingo) and initialize it with the number of times you want to draw each image between key frames. You declare a numframes variable and initialize it with the number of key frames in the animation (not counting the initial key frame). You declare a Boolean variable named running that is set initially to false. You do not want the animation to run initially when the Web page is loaded.

You declare eight move arrays to hold the key frame values for the animation. You declare left and top arrays to hold the current location of each image in the animation. Finally, you declare two Image type variables, shell and stone, to be used in the animation.

An Applet class calls an init() method as soon as the applet has finished loading on the Web page. There is not much you need to initialize except to load the image variables with their appropriate image bitmap files. An Applet class also calls a paint() method when loading to draw any graphics or text to the screen. Because the animation is not running at load time, only the first few lines of the paint() method are run at load time.

The Applet class also enables you to set up many different potential events associated with the keyboard or mouse. In Listing 13.2, only the MouseUp() method is used. The MouseUp()

method passes the event, mouse x location, and mouse y location as parameters whenever the user releases the left mouse button. You do not care about the mouse's specific position at any time. You set the shell image to its initial position, set the running variable to true, and call the repaint() method. The repaint() call triggers the paint() method to run again.

Whenever running is set to true, all the lines in the paint() function run. In the paint() function, a count variable is declared to keep track of which step in the animation loop the Web browser is currently displaying. You set a curframe variable to 1, the first key frame. Within the animation loop, you interpolate each image's location on the Web page and then draw it to the screen. Finally, you add a delay that makes for a smooth animation on, say, a 90 MHz Pentium 586 computer. Without the delay, the animation is just a flash on the computer screen.

So you see that, with Java, you have more control over the Web page logic than with Dynamic HTML. You could alter the interpolation process to provide acceleration between key frames or provide some form of curve between key frames instead of the linear interpolation Dynamic HTML uses. You can also easily overlook important considerations. Your delay logic should be different, depending on which system you run the Web page animation. With Dynamic HTML, that logic is already part of the Web browser. You might have to work hard and perform many tests to get similar logic to work for yourself.

Figure 13.3 is a screen capture of the Old Shell Game loaded in a Web browser.

Figure 13.3.

The Old Shell Game Java implementation.

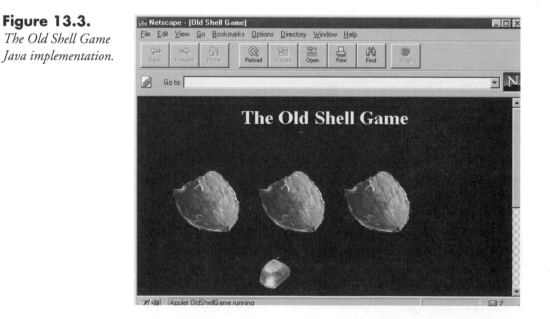

Listing 13.3 provides the HTML tags you use to embed a Java animation in a Web page.

.3. HTML tags to embed a Java animation.

```
ne</TITLE>

)0 TEXT=#FFFFFF>
Shell Game</H1></CENTER>

ellGame.class" BORDER=0 HEIGHT="500" WIDTH="500">
```

n to a Web page, use an `<EMBED> </EMBED>` tag pair with a `CODE` attribute
ir `Applet` class. The name of the applet Java file, `OldShellGame.java`,
class name itself. Then, `OldShellGame.java` becomes `OldShellGame.class`
file with a Java compiler. You can download a compiler free from Sun's
w.`javasoft.com`. You control how large the animation will appear on
IGHT and WIDTH attributes.

3C currently recommends that the `<EMBED>` tag be replaced with
JECT> tag to embed objects on a Web page. The `<OBJECT>` tag
n designed to be very flexible in adding all kinds of external
 to a Web page.

Page Technologies

b page technologies are made available from the Netscape plug-in
t has also implemented in the Internet Explorer Web browser. Plug-ins
an communicate with a Web browser to add functionality to the Web
, the Shockwave plug-in by Macromedia adds multimedia applications
e a plug-in application when you author a Web page, you usually use
t saves your content in an appropriate file format. For example, the
ia authoring tool enables you to save your content as a Shockwave-

ee plug-in content, they must download the appropriate plug-in from
er installs a plug-in, the plug-in installation routine registers the new
Web browser. Then, each time such a file format is encountered on a
riate plug-in application loads and presents the file's contents.

13

The plug-in capability is rather easy for a programmer to implement in an application, yet it is beyond the skill of a typical Web content author. Therefore, as an author, you rarely will create new plug-ins. Instead, you will use plug-ins that are available on the Web and write for the plug-in application.

Popular plug-in applications include Shockwave by Macromedia (`http://www.macromedia.com/`), VRML 2 by Silicon Graphics (`http://vrml.sgi.com`), and QuickTime by Apple (`http://quickTime.apple.com/dev/devweb.html`). For an extensive list of other third-party plug-in applications, see Netscape's Navigator Components Web page at `http://www.netscape.com/comprod/mirror/navcomponents_download.html`.

As you play with plug-in applications, consider whether you could create the same content with Dynamic HTML. If so, do your audience a favor and use Dynamic HTML. Then, they will not have to download an additional plug-in application to see your content.

Summary

Dynamic HTML simplifies how you add interactivity to a Web page. However, because Dynamic HTML provides only a limited set of interactions, you might still want to use other technologies on the Web pages you author. Both ActiveX and Java are Web technologies you can use to extend the functionality of a Web browser. ActiveX is an integration technology you use to tie together Web page features that were created using a variety of programming languages. Most prevalent are ActiveX controls that you can download from the Web and add to your Web pages with VBScript scripting.

Java, on the other hand, is an object-oriented programming (OOP) language. With Java, you can add new functionality by programming any logic in a class that extends the `Applet` base class. The more Dynamic HTML evolves to meet your Web page functionality needs, the less you will resort to integrating other technologies on the Web pages you author. Dynamic HTML is designed to be used by authors with very little formal programming knowledge. In fact, if Dynamic HTML realizes its potential, expect to see many drag-and-drop Web page editing tools that hide the Dynamic HTML code generation from an author. Typically, the tools do not lag too far behind the standard-setting process.

Q&A

Q If I compare your ActiveX example in this chapter with the data-awareness examples in Chapters 11 and 12, I do not see much of a difference in terms of implementation steps. Can Dynamic HTML be considered an extension of ActiveX?

A Great question. There will be much debate as to what exactly constitutes Dynamic HTML. Microsoft includes data-awareness as a Dynamic HTML feature. Netscape certainly does not yet. The key difference is that the ActiveX example requires an external control found on the Web, whereas the data-awareness examples use a control that is provided by the Internet Explorer 4.0 Web browser. Otherwise, you can consider data-awareness an ActiveX technology because VBScript integrates data-awareness on your Web pages.

Q I know the promise of object-oriented programming is the capability to quickly put together classes to reuse code. Are there Java public classes I can download on the Web?

A Yes. The Java classes are there if you look for them. Sun has some classes referenced at its Javasoft site (`http://www.javasoft.com/`), and you can find third-party providers as well. One day, I wanted to find some classes that contained the physics of bouncing balls. It took me about 30 minutes to find the classes I needed on the Web and about three hours to incorporate them into my Web pages. I consider that excellent on a development efficiency scale. I have been re-engineering those classes ever since to add new features.

Quiz

Take the following quiz to see how much you've learned in this chapter.

Questions

1. Which scripting language do you use with ActiveX?
2. Which tag pair do you use to embed an ActiveX control in a Web page?
3. Traditionally, which tag pair do you use to embed a Java applet in a Web page?
4. Which other programming language does Java syntax most resemble?
5. When you create an applet in Java, which method runs right at the beginning?

Answers

1. VBScript.
2. The `<OBJECT></OBJECT>` tag pair.
3. The `<EMBED></EMBED>` tag pair.
4. C++, because you can consider Java to be a subset of C++ for many Java language features.
5. The `init()` method is available to contain initial programming logic.

13

Workshop

Because you completed the squid research Web site in Chapter 12, in this workshop, I want you to take the liberty of working on content that is of your own choosing. Go ahead and think of an interesting feature you would like to add to a Web page. If you want, you can add it to any page you have created so far.

Create a Java applet that provides the feature you want. For example, create a Java applet that produces a dancing squid. Add the applet to your Web page with the appropriate HTML tags. If you are new to Java, surf the Web and find an applet that shows you its source code. Spend the time here learning about alternative technologies. Go to Netscape's Plug-ins page at

`http://www.netscape.com/comprod/mirror/navcomponents_download.html`

download a plug-in, and then find an authoring tool to create content for that particular plug-in technology.

As an example, I decided to download the VRML 2 browser by Silicon Graphics from its Web page (`http://vrml.sgi.com`). VRML 2 enables you to add 3D models to a Web page with which your user can interact. I then created a Web page that uses the VRML file format (which uses a `.wrl` extension). My simple Web page is a 3D red sphere that appears in Listing 13.4. The simple `.wrl` file that creates the 3D sphere appears in Listing 13.5. A picture of my sphere Web page appears in Figure 13.4.

INPUT **Listing 13.4. A simple Web page that uses the VRML 2 plug-in.**

```
<HTML>
<HEAD>
<TITLE>A Sphere</TITLE>
</HEAD>
<BODY BGCOLOR=#000000>
<CENTER>
<EMBED SRC="sphere.wrl" BORDER=0 HEIGHT="500" WIDTH="500">
</CENTER>
</BODY>
</HTML>
```

INPUT **Listing 13.5. The VRML 2 file named `sphere.wrl`.**

```
#VRML V2.0 utf8

DEF sphereview Viewpoint {
    position        0 0 2
    orientation     0 0 1 0
    description     "Sphereview"
```

```
}
Transform {
    children
        Shape {
            appearance Appearance {
                material Material { diffuseColor 1 0 0}
            }
            geometry Sphere {radius .3}
        }
    translation 0 0 0
}
```

Figure 13.4.

A red sphere Web page.

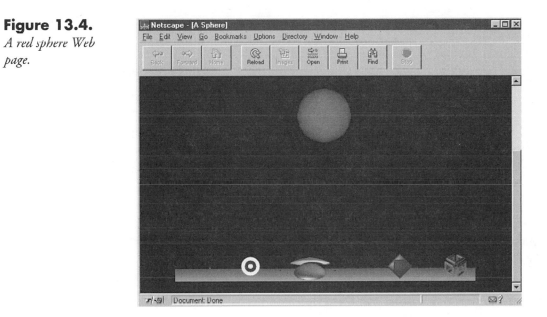

NOTE

As of press time, VRML 2 plug-in applications did not work reliably with Internet Explorer 4.0 beta 2.

13

Day 7

Chapter 14

Intelligent Dynamic Design

It is time you take an opportunity to step back and consider Dynamic HTML from a high level. You have mastered the technical skills required of Dynamic HTML. You have created some fun and interactive Web pages. This chapter goes over design considerations for your Web pages and the future of Dynamic HTML. You also are asked to define when more dynamic interaction is too much. Finally, I try to convince you that HTML is an open standard in which you can participate in its evolution.

In this chapter, you'll learn about the following:

- ☐ Designing dynamic pages
- ☐ How much dynamic is too much?
- ☐ More on data delivery strategies
- ☐ Other future considerations

Designing Dynamic Pages

In Chapter 13, "Integrating Other Languages and Objects into Dynamic HTML," you learned how you can integrate other Web page technologies with Dynamic HTML. No matter how you add your interactive features, you still are confronted by overall design decisions for your pages and your Web site. Many of the design considerations are the same whether you create a dynamic or static Web site. You might ask the following questions about any Web site, dynamic or not:

☐ How busy should each page be?

☐ Should I add frames to help my readers navigate within my site?

☐ Should I create a few long pages or many shorter ones?

☐ How many different browsers should I use to test my content?

☐ After I create a design I really like, how can I shorten the process of creating the next site using that design?

However, when you create dynamic pages, an additional important question should come to mind:

☐ How do I entice a reader to interact with my site?

You will spend some time learning about each of these questions in the following sections. Consider the implications for the Web sites you author.

How Busy Should Each Page Be?

The standard answer to this question is: Only as busy as your audience can technologically handle. Keep in mind that the scripts you have created using Dynamic HTML correspond to longer download times than static HTML files. Keep in mind that the animations you add to your Web pages require Web browser processing that uses computing resources. And, finally, keep in mind that the more interactive Web pages get, the more click-happy your readers become. As readers become used to clicking, you can be sure they will get used to clicking off your page before they barely read anything on it.

If your message is very important, keep it on a simple page. The advertising community learned the keep-it-simple lesson long ago. Remember "Just do it," "Got Milk?" and "We try harder" when you design your pages. As an example, consider Figure 14.1, which shows Silicon Graphics' introductory VRML page.

Only when you're sure your audience has come to read the whole page should you get very fancy. Or, maybe what's even more significant, add more features when you think your audience will print or download the page as a reference.

Figure 14.1.
A Web page with a simple message.

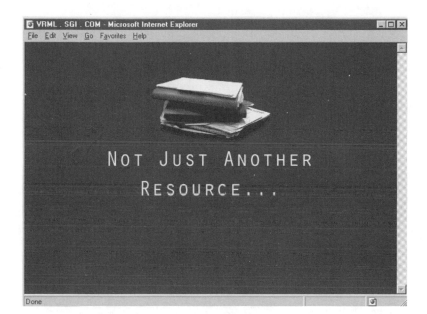

Should I Add Frames to Help My Readers Navigate Within My Site?

Frames are an innovation that I find quite helpful when visiting substantial Web sites. Although the W3C has been slow to incorporate frames into the standard HTML specification, waiting until HTML 4 to do so, frames have been used liberally by Web authors to create multiple independent information areas on a Web page. With frames, a reader is less likely to get lost on any particular Web page within your site if you provide the appropriate controls on the other frames. However, with frames, a reader is more likely to get lost across all the sites he or she visits. Look at Figure 14.2 for an example of frames from a tutorial on building virtual worlds.

In Figure 14.2, a reader is never lost within the left frame because an index is always available in the right frame. Also, a reader is more apt to jump directly to where he or she wants to go if all the options are always readily available. An index's location in a frame is fixed.

Currently, frames do not work very well with a Web browser's bookmarking feature. I have found that you help yourself by providing frames to your audience if you expect them to have high-resolution monitors and a frames-capable browser. Occasionally, though, you might not have helped your reader when he or she wants to bookmark your site. I have noticed that many of the large technology companies have recently eliminated frames from their Web sites. Sun, Lotus, and SGI at one time all used frames heavily, but no longer do so on their home pages.

14

Figure 14.2.
A Web site using frames.

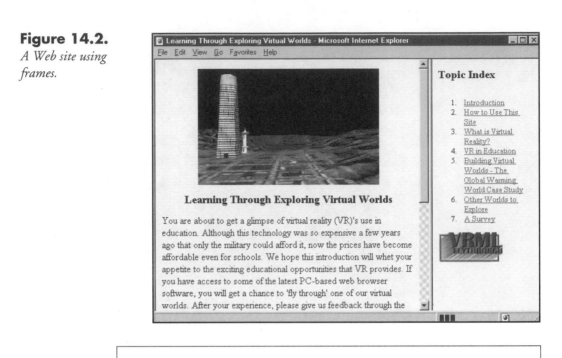

NOTE As Dynamic HTML makes its impact on Web pages felt, authors might rely even less on the capabilities of frames. With Dynamic HTML you have style sheets and dynamic events that can control how different areas (or layers) on a Web page behave. Using multiple style sheets with the event model on a single Web page, you can easily grow or shrink an area on the page in the same way you would use frames to entice the reader to jump from frame to frame. When you use Dynamic HTML, a page index can remain visible to the reader at all times.

You will learn to add frames to your giant squid Web pages in the "Workshop" section of this chapter. If you do a decent job of adding the frames, I think you will agree they are quite appropriate for the giant squid Web site.

Should I Create a Few Long Pages or Many Shorter Ones?

The page organization question really does not change much with the advent of Dynamic HTML. Yet, you might want to shorten pages even more to break interactions to one a page.

14

You can think about this question more intelligently now that you understand data delivery strategies. Web page size and data delivery strategy have many parallel considerations. If you provide smaller pieces, the Web server must perform more tasks. If you provide longer pages, your reader must wait for a longer download time before the page is fully loaded.

Long pages can be easier for a single Web author to administer because fewer files are involved. Yet, shorter pages can be easier for a Web authoring team to administer because each person on the team can be responsible for whole pages instead of co-authoring longer pages.

If you must use many shorter pages, try to limit how often you place the same scripting logic on multiple pages. Use external style sheet files.

How Many Different Browsers Should I Use to Test My Content?

Today, because you are working at a time when new browsers are just being produced, you probably want to test your pages in a minimum of four browsers. Try browsing your pages using Internet Explorer 3.0 and 4.0 as well as Netscape Navigator 3.0 and 4.0.

TIP

> Consider your Macintosh- and UNIX-based readers as well if you want public schoolchildren and university researchers to visit your site.

I agree that it seems as if a lot of testing is necessary to do a good job. Keep an ear out for a good lint routine for Dynamic HTML. A *lint routine* is one you access on the Web to run your HTML file and to tell you where you deviate from a standard. A Dynamic HTML lint routine might be far off today, but you can see the time-saving potential.

Shortening the Process of Creating the Next Site

One of the greatest features of today's office technology applications, such as word processors and spreadsheets, is the *template*. A template is a partially created computer file that contains the structure of what a completed file should look like. For example, an invoice template contains the formatting of an invoice. If you want to invoice a client for a service you have provided, you open the invoice template in your word processor, which already contains your address information and logo, put the client name in a name field, put the service line items in pre-existing rows, place the prices in a pre-existing price column, and recalculate the total amount and date and number the invoice. Save and print the invoice, and the template stays clean for the next time you want to invoice a client.

14

NOTE

> One distinguishing feature I compare when making a purchase decision
> between two software applications is which templates come free with
> my purchase. I am also very hopeful that technologists will use the Web
> to make their templates publicly available for others. No doubt,
> templates will continue to get better over time as you purchase Web
> page authoring tools.

Think in terms of templates when you create the Web site of your dreams. After you build
your wondersite, make a copy of your HTML files, eliminate all the Web site-specific
information from the HTML files, and save the simplified version in a safe place. For your
next Web site, copy your simplified template versions to new filenames, and add the specific
information for that site.

Look at a simple example of the template process. Return for a moment to the Web page you
created in the "Workshop" section for Chapter 7, "Changing Text Attributes." To make the
giant squid home page a template, you would make the changes you see in Listing 14.1. Look
at those changes, and then continue reading for an explanation.

INPUT **Listing 14.1. An example of an HTML template.**

```
<HTML>
<HEAD>
<TITLE>@Titlebar Title@</TITLE>
</HEAD>
<BODY BACKGROUND="@dark.jpg@" TEXT=#FFFFFF LINK=FFFF22 VLINK=FF22FF>
<H2>@Page Header@</H2>
<IMG SRC="@picture.jpg@" ALIGN=RIGHT>
@body text@
<P>
<TABLE BORDER=1>
<TR>
<TD WIDTH=360><CENTER><I>CHOOSE A HYPERLINK</I></CENTER></TD>
</TR><TR>
<TD WIDTH=320><CENTER><I><A HREF="@firstlink@.htm">@LinkText@</A>
</I></CENTER></TD></TR><TR>
<TD WIDTH=320><CENTER><I><A HREF="@secondlink@.htm">@LinkText@</A>
</I></CENTER></TD></TR><TR>

<TD WIDTH=320><CENTER><I><A HREF="@thirdlink@.htm">@LinkText@</A>
</I></CENTER></TD></TR><TR>
<TD WIDTH=320><CENTER><I><A HREF="@fourthlink@.htm">@LinkText@</A>
</I></CENTER></TD></TR><TR>
<TD WIDTH=320><CENTER><I><A HREF="@fourthlink@.htm">@LinkText@</A>
</I></CENTER></TD></TR><TR>
</TR><TR>
</TR>
</TABLE>
</BODY>
</HTML>
```

 14

In Listing 14.1, you replace all giant squid-specific information with generic text strings enclosed in @ signs. You then save the listing in an HTML file. The next time you want to create a page similar to the page in the Chapter 7 workshop, make a copy of this template file, open a word processor, and search and replace for all strings that begin and end with an @ sign. You save a lot of time by not having to reproduce work you did before.

You can look at your templates in a Web browser if you are reviewing different Web page styles you have created over time. Figure 14.3 shows the template from Listing 14.1 loaded in a Web browser. The basic layout of the template is evident when you load the template in a Web browser.

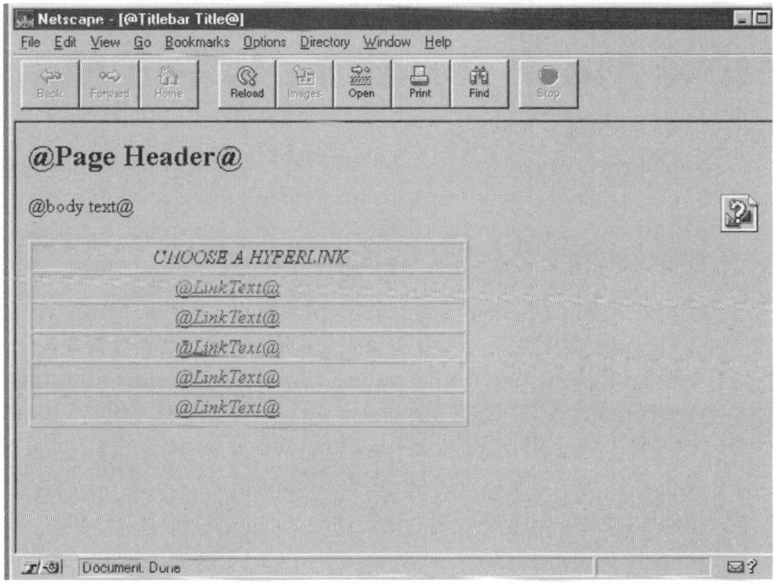

Figure 14.3.
The Web site template.

How Do I Entice a Reader to Interact with My Site?

After you spend the time to add new dynamic features to your Web pages, you probably would like your readers to see your features in action. Dynamic HTML events usually are triggered by the mouse or keyboard. A reader must use the mouse or keyboard to bring the page to life, and you must entice your readers to make the right moves.

You always can use the straightforward approach of adding new Click Here buttons to your pages. Or, you can add text to your pages that explains what interaction is possible. Ideally, if Dynamic HTML catches on and is standardized as part of HTML 4, your readers should come to expect interactivity and will be clicking and passing the mouse over the entire page searching for possible dynamic features. Don't be surprised if Microsoft and Netscape provide "This Page Uses Dynamic HTML" images for you to add to your pages in the future.

14

You can always run a quick animation that demonstrates a feature of a Web page when the page initially loads. Run the animation once, and then hide the images so you do not insult your audience's intelligence.

Perhaps, initially, dynamic Web authors should rely more on scripting to trigger timed effects. Using a timer, you can change the content of a page every 10 seconds or so. However, if you can find a design that naturally attracts a reader to the dynamic features of your page, by all means, use that approach; just do not expect your readers to be automatically moving the mouse around on your page. Dynamic HTML is hot off the press.

How Much Dynamic Is Too Much?

The standard HTML specifications cover the syntax and appropriate use of HTML. The standard contains virtually no limits on how much use of any language feature you add to a Web page. A Web browser can enforce some limits. For example, Netscape Navigator permits layers to go only 10 deep. Beyond the browser, you, the Web page author, are the final decision maker in saying how much functionality is too much.

I can remember being frustrated when I set up my first Mosaic 1.0 browser and a 9600 baud modem on a 20 MHz, 4MB RAM, 386-based computer running the Windows 3.1 operating system. Web surfing would come down to Web puddle jumping when I visited a Web site that contained 10 or 20 graphical images per page. Sure, I spent hours patiently waiting because it was all so new and exciting, but at some point, it was no longer fun.

Now I connect to the Web with a 28.8 modem on a 90 MHz, 16MB RAM, 586-based computer running Windows 95. I like to go to all the science education sites around the country and interact with Web pages that let me interactively discover the physics behind everyday events. Usually, I can go to a site and wait a minute for download and presentation and then enjoy that page for 10 or 15 minutes before needing to download the next page.

NOTE As of July 1, 1997, some 36 million homes have access to the Web. No doubt, there will be new and different ways to connect from home, such as WebTV and sound-based connections for the sight impaired.

During a Web surfing session, I always seem to encounter the occasional page that tries to do too much. Perhaps a page has three or four Java applets running simultaneously, or perhaps I must click through too many graphics to get to the interactive part. These Web sites are just too high-tech for my home setup. Sure, here in Seattle, I can write down a URL and run to the laboratory where I work or zip down to an Internet cafe and load the same site under better conditions. The bottom line is that I am less apt to do so. In most cases, I quickly see an alternative design that would have provided the same content but with a better organization.

Figure 14.4 shows a typical home page for a high-tech computer company. From Figure 14.4, you get a sense of a high-end Web page that I consider acceptable for my home technology. I captured Figure 14.4 from Sun Microsystems' home page (http://www.sun.com/) on July 1, 1997.

Figure 14.4.

A not-too-busy busy Web page.

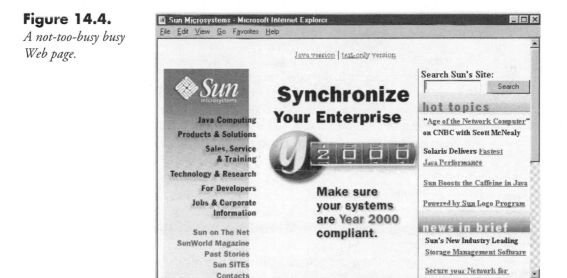

I especially like the two links that appear top-center in Figure 14.4. Sun provides a link to a more sophisticated page and a link to a simplified page. Sun is giving the reader control of how much technology to use in browsing its home page. You can see Sun trying to manage the delicate balance between too much information and not enough. For me, Sun's page is very close to stepping over the line toward too much information, so I suspect it does cross the line to being too busy for some readers.

I am sure that as sites get upgraded to take advantage of new dynamic features such as Dynamic HTML, I will be at even more risk of running into a site that is doing too much for my home-based technology. I can see the scientific simulations of the future in my head right now. They will be more interesting not so much for their new look and feel but for the access to live data I will have at my disposal. I do not see the need for more interactivity than is provided in this book. Instead, I see the need to have access to more data.

14

I hope that, from home, I will not only review the wonderful results scientists from around the world write up in research papers online, but I will watch events as they happen, sending data right onto my screen in meaningful ways. Consider the fictitious giant squid in the South Pacific. Would it not be great if you could actually watch the live tracking of them right on a Web page?

Imagine the roving vehicles Earthlings have sent to Mars. Supposedly, they are amazing works of rugged robot technology. Because of the vast distance between Earth and Mars, the latest robot to be set loose on Mars, the Pathfinder, has the capability to choose its own course of travel on Mars' surface. Sending messages back and forth from Earth just takes too long. It would be thrilling to be able to follow a roving vehicle's progress at the same time the scientists themselves receive update transmissions.

The Web page I would like to use to follow a Mars-based robot has quite a simple presentation: a nice attractive background image, a single interactive area with a dynamic map that shows the robot's trail colored bright yellow, and another smaller area where you could get a picture of any section of the Mars landscape by clicking on the interactive map. Add a few links that let you go back in time and a few links to background information on robotics, Mars, and the research teams, and you would be very happy.

NOTE

I believe, as do a lot of other technologists, that the world is ripe for another experience like the first man landing on the moon. The moon landing brought the world together as families watched from their black-and-white television sets. The Pathfinder mission reached the imagination of millions as a true Internet phenomenon. Imagine the improvements home technology will offer for the next worldwide event of interest.

Here in Seattle, there exists a great Web site that tracks highway traffic flow. Again, the presentation is very simple, but the data is real-time data. On the Web page, you can see a simple colored map on which each color represents a certain density of cars and average velocity (at the extremes, green is very good and red is very bad). About every mile, a small black camera is on the map. If you click the camera, you open a Web page with a picture of that span of the road that is updated about every five minutes. The site has created quite a stir in Seattle. The live data probably is what gets everyone excited. No one to whom I have talked about the site has complained about the traffic images being black and white.

A Web surfer probably will consider a Web page too dynamic when the page itself interferes with a reader's ability to focus on any data being presented. Moving text can be fun initially, but it certainly gets old quickly if you read it for any length of time. Think of how you feel trying to read all the credits at the end of a movie to get the name of an actor you liked, a song you heard, or a location you saw in the film.

You and I need Dynamic HTML, Java, ActiveX, VRML, and other new Web technologies to bring the state-of-the-art in computer applications to the Web. Many Web authors want to compete with CD-ROM titles and bring their content to the Web. Dynamic HTML is a huge step in satisfying Web author needs by making authoring simpler. Continue to keep your audience in mind at all times while you put your Web pages together. Be critical of each new and exciting feature you add to a page; ask yourself if the next feature you add is one too many.

More on Data Delivery Strategies

You thought a lot about data delivery strategies in Chapters 11, "Data-Bound Form Fields," and 12, "Dynamic Table Generation and Expansion," when you learned about data-awareness in Internet Explorer 4.0. The data you learned in Chapters 11 and 12 are traditional relational database data. Relational data contain records that contain fields that are represented with characters and are usually limited to fewer than 255 characters per field. You can perform a lot of analysis on relational data using filtering, sorting, and mathematical computations.

Relational data are also great because they are so compactly represented in computer file space relative to other forms of data, such as sound and image data. Over the Web, I could send you information about 200 new hospital births you could review in the Web page you created in Chapter 12. For the same file size, I could send you a couple seconds' worth of sound of one baby's first cry or a small picture of a single baby. But besides the fact it is more compact, I like relational data because they let me think more.

A baby's first cry and first picture are very literal. As you consume sound and images, they both go straight into your mind's memory. As you consume relational data, you interpret the data before you build your own images of what the data represents to you. You might sort the data by sex and see a picture in your mind of 133 female babies and 67 male babies. You might filter the data by date of birth and see the hospital staff overworked on a Tuesday when 14 babies were born. In other words, you play with the information to exercise your mind.

Delivering sound, pictures, and video is a different problem to solve than delivering text-based data. Technologists invent some really impressive solutions to compress and decompress sound and video. Compression makes file sizes as small as possible by using computing algorithms. *Streaming* technology is impressive, as well. With streaming, files are sent over the Internet and played by the receiver while the file continues to be sent. Streaming works for sound and video because those data types can afford to lose bits in the transmission. Errors appear as snaps, crackles, and blips to the Web surfer, but the main message is not drastically

14

affected. Text-based data, on the other hand, cannot afford the same treatment as streaming data. With text, a simple error in transmission can change a baby's name from Stanlay to Satan.

Perhaps by now you are thinking you should be able to stream sound, images, and video while you continue to acknowledge text transmissions. That sounds great, but it is not the way the HyperText Transport Protocol (HTTP) works today. You use the HTTP whenever you send an HTML file to a reader. Today, streaming just is not available to a reader who uses a simple Web browser.

My point is that the nature of pure text will continue to be significantly different from multimedia for both storage and consumption. You might always want to consider providing both to your audience for their choosing. To do so, you will need to consider data delivery strategies carefully as they mature. Understanding data-awareness is just the tip of the Web content delivery iceberg.

As I look at the Internet today, I think there is still a tremendous opportunity to deliver multimedia content via the CD-ROM or, better still, by some of the new, higher density disk-based technologies. However, CD-ROM content need no longer be limited by the disk itself. You can still deliver your initial sounds, pictures, images, and 3D worlds to your audience via disk, CD-ROM, or even an initial compressed file downloaded from the Internet. After the multimedia content is delivered once to your audience, you can refer to it for years to come in new Web pages that are changing, dynamic, and interactive. Imagine the possibilities for a company such as Disney to deliver all of its characters' images and sounds on a single CD-ROM and then provide content on the Web for years that use those characters and sounds.

If the Internet is not bogged down and clogged up from data transmission, it can be used for communication. A CD-ROM alone cannot connect two people in the world together. The Internet can connect people. Six people can all enjoy the same CD-ROM title together by using the Web as the connecting communication vehicle.

Even text-based data can benefit from a CD-ROM. For example, a census agency could deliver the last 100 years' worth of census information on a single CD-ROM and then provide a dynamic Web site that enabled a reader to download the latest information. The Web browser could then enable a reader to perform trend analysis across the new data and the old.

If you take this mixed delivery strategy to the extreme, you get to the point at which the information on the CD-ROM is able to create new sounds, images, and pictures by combining components on the CD-ROM with just a few bits coming from the server. I like that thought. Using that strategy, Internet traffic stays minimal, and more people can use the available bandwidth without frustration. But, certainly, more bandwidth will always be coming. More bandwidth is the easy solution, but a cost is associated with providing new bandwidth.

14

Data delivery strategies become more important to me now that Dynamic HTML is on its way to making interactivity easier. I want access to real-time data, as I suspect many other people do. I want to do my own weather forecasting, predict when the next earthquake is going to hit, and determine whether the next super-duper, subatomic particle collider should be built. If data continues to be delivered uncompressed via the current hypertext transport protocol, I am sure I will be back to a state of frustration sitting here at home and connecting to the Web. At the other end, the Web servers will be overworked and underpaid.

Other Future Considerations

Enough of data delivery issues. There are other issues for you as a Web author to consider. The other issues are related to where Dynamic HTML goes from here. Although I have not had time to think about everything related to the so-called browser war between Microsoft and Netscape, I still think I want Dynamic HTML to become a standard part of HTML 4. I do not think the W3C needs to accept Dynamic HTML wholesale as part of the HTML 4 standard, but I would rather hear and see Web page authors refer to their pages as HTML 4-compliant than Dynamic HTML-compliant. The HTML standard is a big success so far.

Much of what I understand about the Web technology standards setting process comes from following the Virtual Reality Modeling Language (VRML) standard setting process. The VRML standard setting process is a tribute to online collaboration and interorganizational cooperation. If I apply VRML's standards development model to HTML, the HTML standard could continue to evolve as follows:

1. The HTML community votes electronically to accept a proposal for an HTML specification. The W3C documents the standard and makes it readily available online on the Internet for anyone to access and read.

2. Web browser developers work hard to implement the complete HTML standard along with their own special features. Any questions regarding implementation are answered in online chat forums, mailing lists, and usenets.

3. Third-party software developers work to create Web page authoring tools that make standard HTML page development easier. Tool creation proceeds with much online feedback from special beta partner Web authors who try out iterative beta versions of the software.

4. Web authors work with the tools to create standard pages and then use other technologies such as Java, ActiveX, and plug-ins to extend the capabilities of the Web page beyond the latest HTML specification.

14

5. New innovative features that work are submitted to the W3C and HTML community for review as possible candidates for inclusion in the next standard specification. The feature innovator is given credit for the innovation. The W3C works to find the best way of translating the new feature into HTML syntax.

6. Working with the W3C, HTML community, and feature innovators, one or more potential new HTML specifications are considered as the next version (HTML 5, for example).

7. The process returns to step 1.

I believe such a progression works wonderfully if enough people are dedicated to making it work. The HTML standard setting process would work much better if innovators were fairly monetarily rewarded for their contributions to the standard. It would be even better if the name recognition alone brought its just reward to an innovator. I believe name recognition has its own monetary rewards today.

Even if the HTML standard setting process is not quite working as I have outlined in steps 1 through 7 now, you can consider Dynamic HTML to be in step 1 right now.

You and I as Web authors have a new proposal at our fingertips: Dynamic HTML. You can vote on whether it should be standardized by using it or not using it. You can become involved in Netscape's and Microsoft's online forums to provide feedback on their Dynamic HTML Web browser implementations. You can work hard to get wind of an authoring tool provider, use its beta software, and provide critical feedback. You can extend Dynamic HTML's features by using Java or ActiveX and work hard to get recognition for your efforts. Publish a paper on the Web about your Web page innovations. Finally, you can go to the W3C's Web site at `http://www.w3.org/MarkUp/` to read the technical recommendations associated with HTML. Usually, the author of the recommendation provides an e-mail address to which you can send questions or comments.

NOTE

If you are unsure of what I mean by a Web authoring tool, look at Kinetix's Hyperwire tool or Elemental Software's Drumbeat tool. Kinetix's Web page URL is `http://www.ktx.com/hyperwire/`. Elemental Software's URL is `http://www.elementalsoftware.com`. Both these authoring tools allow for drag-and-drop, visual Web page authoring of Web pages. Both provide trial versions you can download for free. Although neither creates Dynamic HTML output, both give you a flavor of how simple Web page authoring should be in the future.

14

The great part of standardization is the fact that Web page authoring becomes easier for everyone because everyone comes together to play a part in its development. A standardization process such as the one previously outlined breeds competition, making the technology better. Without an interorganizational process, software development is restricted to one or a few large providers who ultimately provide market barriers to entry and obtain great wealth. So far, I have yet to see where wealth has not bred complacency in the long run.

I suspect many exciting new technologies will come to the Internet through HTML, but perhaps new technologies will come to the Internet through completely new innovations. Understanding how Dynamic HTML started, how it is currently implemented, how it is treated in the HTML standardization process, and where it goes from here will help you understand the process for future Internet technologies. Because you have a voice through your Internet connection, you can make a difference in how technology is implemented and, maybe even more directly, how it is used.

In a nutshell, the issues related to HTML always reflect the best way to deliver content over the Web. You, as a content developer, drive the standard by the way you want to present your pages and how you want your audience to interact with your pages. If all Web authors wanted to deliver 3D Web pages, HTML would either become more involved with 3D representations or be superseded by another technology. Remember that the technologists ultimately fail if Web authors do not use the technology. I see that realization dawning on my peers daily.

I hope you are committed to using Web technologies for purposes you believe in. I hope the Web pages you create speak words you believe in. I hope you are excited to add Dynamic HTML to your Web pages to make experiencing your pages more fun for your readers. I hope you do not stop there but will keep up with new, breaking technologies and voice an opinion.

Summary

In this chapter, you considered the impact of Dynamic HTML on traditional Web page design decisions. You also investigated the question of where HTML goes from here. Perhaps your mind is spinning when you realize how much there is for a Web author to think about when he or she creates a simple Web page.

In this chapter, I come to the conclusion that Dynamic HTML provides enough interactivity to last for a while. After you master Dynamic HTML and roll your dynamic Web pages out to a Web audience, your next focus should be on making the Web participatory. Web users already have traditional applications that present information on their computer monitors. The Web provides the capability to access real-time data and communicate with others from home. Figure out how to create a Web page that establishes a community. Figure out how people can meet at your Web site. Use Dynamic HTML to make your Web pages fun and interactive.

14

Q&A

Q Why do you suppose technology companies are moving away from using frames on their Web pages?

A I think everyone is slowly realizing the fact that smaller Web pages are better for everyone. Basically, Web pages must be pretty compact to fit on a single television screen or computer monitor window. If you make your pages small enough, you do not need frames because there is no risk of your indexes scrolling off the screen. I am hopeful as well that technologists are not using frames because the W3C has not blessed them wholeheartedly, but that might be a naive assumption. Also note that the new <DIV> and <SPAN> tags replace some of the need for frames because they enable you to create independent Web page areas.

Q Are there technologies I can use to make the template process easier?

A Yes. Try using a form generation package with which you can build a form to enter variable information. Create a form as a front end to your templates. With a form, you enter the variable information in fields next to form labels, and an automated process does the string replacement for you. For example, you can use Word Basic to create a front-end form in your word processor.

Q Doesn't that sound a lot like the data form concept from Chapter 11?

A It does. You could create forms in HTML and then write a script that would process the form data and create your Web pages from the respective templates. You have much flexibility in creating a form-handling script using available Web technologies, but you will have some learning to do to get the process started. Often, an available form generation package or word processor capability would be easier to learn from scratch.

Quiz

Take the following quiz to see how much you've learned in this chapter.

Questions

1. How busy should a Web page be?
2. What HTML feature enables you to load two or more Web pages in a Web browser window at the same time?
3. What do you call a generic version of a Web page or Web site?
4. Which generally leaves a larger file footprint—text or images?
5. What do you call the process of making a file smaller by applying a computer algorithm?

14

Answers

1. Only as busy as your audience can technologically handle.
2. Frames
3. A Web page or Web site template
4. Images, by far
5. Compression

Workshop

In this workshop, you add frames to your giant squid Web site to aid your readers with the navigation process. Frames are maturing on the Web, and your readers probably know how to use them by now. But in this workshop, I want you to provide an alternative page for those readers who are using Web browsers that do not support frames.

To add frames to your Web site, you first must create a frame definition document. The frame definition document is an HTML file that creates the frames for a Web site and assigns Web pages to each frame. You create a frame definition document in Listing 14.2. You use the <FRAMESET></FRAMESET> tag pair to break the Web browser window into multiple independent areas.

The <FRAMESET> tag includes an attribute that defines in which direction you split the window. The COLS attribute is available to split the window vertically. The ROWS attribute is available to split the window horizontally. You can subdivide a frame in a frameset by embedding a second <FRAMESET></FRAMESET> tag pair inside the first one. Keep in mind that your readers will have to wait for Web pages to load in each frame. The more frames, the longer they wait. Add <FRAME> tags, one per frame, to place Web content in each frame. Finally, you can add a <NOFRAMES></NOFRAMES> tag pair to provide an alternative page for your readers who are using browsers that do not support frames.

In Listing 14.2, the frames are divided vertically. The left frame contains six buttons that link to the six pages in the Web site. Each time a user clicks a button in the left frame, the appropriate link is opened in the right frame. Look at Listing 14.2 and Figure 14.5, and then continue reading for more details.

INPUT **Listing 14.2. A frame definition document for my Web site.**

```
<HTML>
<HEAD>
<TITLE>Giant Blind South Pacific Squid</TITLE>
<NOFRAMES>
```

14

continues

Listing 14.2. continued

```
<HTML>
<HEAD>
<TITLE>Giant Blind South Pacific Squid Welcome Page</TITLE>
</HEAD>
<BODY BACKGROUND="water.jpg" TEXT=#FFFFFF LINK=FFFF22 VLINK=FF22FF>
<H2>Welcome To The Giant Blind South Pacific Squid Research Page</H2>
<IMG SRC="giant.gif" ALIGN=RIGHT>
We hope you will visit this page often to follow the research of the world
re-knowned <FONT COLOR=#FFFF00><I>Giant Squid Marine Biology Team</I>
</FONT> and keep up with their amazing discoveries as they happen.
Go ahead and bookmark this page.  You won't regret that you have.
We all can learn a lot from blind giant squid in the South Pacific.
<P>
<TABLE BORDER=1>
<TR>
<TD WIDTH=360><CENTER><I>CHOOSE A HYPERLINK</I></CENTER></TD>
</TR><TR>
<TD WIDTH=320><CENTER><I><A HREF="dyn08wrk.htm">What is a Squid?</A>
</I></CENTER></TD>
</TR><TR>
<TD WIDTH=320><CENTER><I><A HREF="dyn09wrk.htm">Who Researches Squid?</A>
</I></CENTER></TD>
</TR><TR>
<TD WIDTH=320><CENTER><I><A HREF="dyn10wrk.htm">How Do We Track
Giant Squid? </A>
</I></CENTER></TD>
</TR><TR>
<TD WIDTH=320><CENTER><I><A HREF="dyn11wrk.htm">How Diverse Are Squid?</A>
</I></CENTER></TD>
</TR><TR>
<TD WIDTH=320><CENTER><I><A HREF="dyn12wrk.htm">Get To Know Our Blind Giant
Squid Families</A></I></CENTER></TD>
</TR>
</TABLE>
</BODY>
</HTML>
</NOFRAMES>
<FRAMESET COLS="120,*">
<FRAME SRC="index.htm" NAME="INDEX" FRAMEBORDER=0 FRAMESPACING=0 SCROLLING=NO>
<FRAME SRC="dyn07wrk.htm" NAME="DESC" FRAMEBORDER=0 FRAMESPACING=0>
</FRAMESET>
</HEAD>
</HTML>
```

Figure 14.5 shows the giant squid Web site implemented with frames. I captured the screen shot in Figure 14.5 immediately after loading the Web site for the first time.

The first frame-related tag you encounter in Listing 14.2 is the <NOFRAMES> tag. Between the opening tag and the </NOFRAMES> end tag, you see the complete Web page created in the Workshop of Chapter 7, "Changing Text Attributes." Your readers who do not have the ability to load frames in their Web browsers will not be affected by the frames.

14

Figure 14.5.

The final giant squid Web site.

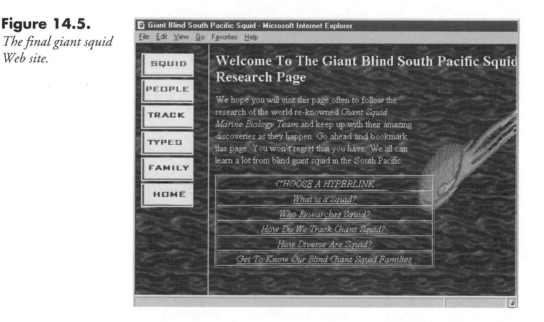

The first <FRAMESET> created divides the Web browser window vertically. The COLS="120,*" attribute divides the Web browser window into a left frame with width of 120 pixels and a right frame that fills the balance of the window. Always include an asterisk as one value in the list of frameset dimensions to give the Web browser the flexibility to present your frames on monitors with different resolutions and windows of different dimensions. The * is a wildcard value that tells the browser to fill the rest of the window with this frame.

NOTE

If you prefer to place your site index in a frame that lays out horizontally along the bottom of the Web browser window, you can use the ROWS attribute instead of the COLS attribute. You cannot use both. To create four separate frames across a Web browser window, you would use an attribute such as COLS="200,150,*,100". You define one value per frame in the attribute value list.

The top <FRAME> tag fills the leftmost frame. The left frame is named INDEX with a NAME attribute. The index.htm file is loaded in the left frame with the SRC attribute. FRAMEBORDER=0 prevents a border from appearing around the frame. FRAMESPACING=0 eliminates the gap between frames. Finally, the SCROLLING attribute is set to NO because Internet Explorer 3.0 was placing a vertical scroll bar in the frame when none was necessary.

14

The bottom <FRAME> tag fills the right frame. The right frame is named DESC with a NAME attribute. The dyn07wrk.htm file is loaded in the right frame with the SRC attribute. The dyn07wrk.htm file is the Web page from Chapter 7's workshop. Again, FRAMEBORDER=0 prevents a border from appearing around the frame, and FRAMESPACING=0 eliminates the gap between frames. This frame should scroll when necessary. Frames scroll when necessary by default.

After defining all the frames, close the </FRAMESET> tag pair. Listing 14.3 provides the index.htm HTML file used to create the navigation index for the left frame.

INPUT   **Listing 14.3. The Web site navigation index.htm file.**

```
<HTML>
<HEAD>
<TITLE>Giant Blind South Pacific Squid</TITLE>
</HEAD>
<BODY BACKGROUND="water.jpg" TEXT=#FFFFFF LINK=FFFF22 VLINK=FF22FF>
<A HREF="dyn08wrk.htm" TARGET="DESC"><IMG SRC="button1.jpg"></A>
<A HREF="dyn09wrk.htm" TARGET="DESC"><IMG SRC="button2.jpg"></A>
<A HREF="dyn10wrk.htm" TARGET="DESC"><IMG SRC="button3.jpg"></A>
<A HREF="dyn11wrk.htm" TARGET="DESC"><IMG SRC="button4.jpg"></A>
<A HREF="dyn12wrk.htm" TARGET="DESC"><IMG SRC="button5.jpg"></A>
<A HREF="dyn07wrk.htm" TARGET="DESC"><IMG SRC="button6.jpg"></A>
</BODY>
</HTML>
```

Listing 14.3 is all standard HTML tags. You create six button images and embed them in the appropriate links. The anchor tags you use to create the links include a TARGET attribute. The TARGET attribute contains the value of a frame name—in Listing 14.3's case, the DESC frame. When a reader clicks the link image, the associated Web page opens in the DESC frame instead of opening in the index frame. Do not forget to add the appropriate targets to your links.

Appendixes

HTML 4.0 Quick Reference

by Bob Correll

HTML 4.0 is an ambitious attempt to meet the needs of Web developers worldwide, both casual and professional. This appendix provides a quick reference to all the elements and attributes of the language.

NOTE

This appendix is based on the information provided in the *HTML 4.0 Specification W3C Working Draft 8-July-1997*, which can be found at http://www.w3.org/TR/WD-html40/.

In order to make the information readliy accessible, this appendix organizes HTML elements by their function in the following order:

- ☐ Structure
- ☐ Text phrases and paragraphs
- ☐ Text formatting elements
- ☐ Lists
- ☐ Links
- ☐ Tables
- ☐ Frames
- ☐ Embedded content
- ☐ Style
- ☐ Forms
- ☐ Scripts

Within each section the elements are listed alphabetically and the following information is presented:

- ☐ Usage—A general description of the element
- ☐ Start/End Tag—Indicates whether these tags are required, optional, or illegal
- ☐ Attributes—Lists the attributes of the element with a short description of their effects
- ☐ Empty—Indicates whether the element can be empty
- ☐ Notes—Relates any special considerations when using the element and indicates whether the element is new, deprecated, or obsolete

NOTE   Several elements and attributes have been *deprecated*, which means they have been outdated by the current HTML version, and you should avoid using them. The same or similar functionality is provided using new features.

NOTE   HTML 4.0 introduces several new attributes that apply to a significant number of elements. These are referred to as %coreattrs, %i18n, and %events and are explained in the last section of the appendix.

A

Following this, the common attributes (those with a % in front of them) and intrinsic events are summarized.

Structure

HTML relies upon several elements to provide structure to a document (as opposed to structuring the text within) as well as provide information that is used by the browser or search engines.

<BDO>...</BDO>

Usage	The bidirectional algorithm element is used to selectively turn off the default text direction.
Start/End Tag	Required/Required
Attributes	lang="..."— The language of the document.
	dir="..."—The text direction (ltr, rtl).
Empty	No
Notes	The dir attribute is mandatory.

<BODY>...</BODY>

Usage	Contains the content of the document.
Start/End Tag	Optional/Optional
Attributes	%coreattrs, %i18n, %events
	background="..."—Deprecated. URL for the background image.
	bgcolor="..."—Deprecated. Sets background color.
	text="..."—Deprecated. Text color.
	link="..."—Deprecated. Link color.
	vlink="..."—Deprecated. Visited link color.
	alink="..."—Deprecated. Active link color.
	onload="..."—Intrinsic event triggered when the document loads.
	onunload="..."—Intrinsic event triggered when document unloads.
Empty	No
Notes	There can be only one BODY and it must follow the HEAD. The BODY element can be replaced by a FRAMESET element. The presentational attributes are deprecated in favor of setting these values with style sheets.

Comments `<!-- ... -->`

Usage	Used to insert notes or scripts that are not displayed by the browser.
Start/End Tag	Required/Required
Attributes	None.
Empty	Yes
Notes	Comments are not restricted to one line and can be any length. The end tag is not required to be on the same line as the start tag.

`<DIV>...</DIV>`

Usage	The division element is used to add structure to a block of text.
Start/End Tag	Required/Required
Attributes	%coreattrs, %i18n, %events
	align="..."—Deprecated. Controls alignment (left, center, right, justify).
Empty	No
Notes	Cannot be used within a P element. The align attribute is deprecated in favor of controlling alignment through style sheets.

`<!DOCTYPE...>`

Usage	Version information appears on the first line of an HTML document and is a Standard Generalized Markup Language (SGML) declaration rather than an element.

`<H1>...</H1>` through `<H6>...</H6>`

Usage	The six headings (H1 is the uppermost, or most important) are used in the BODY to structure information in a hierarchical fashion.
Start/End Tag	Required/Required
Attributes	%coreattrs, %i18n, %events
	align="..."—Deprecated. Controls alignment (left, center, right, justify).
Empty	No
Notes	Visual browsers will display the size of the headings in relation to their importance, with H1 being the largest and H6 the smallest. The align attribute is deprecated in favor of controlling alignment through style sheets.

A

\<HEAD> . . . \</HEAD>

Usage	This is the document header, and it contains other elements that provide information to users and search engines.
Start/End Tag	Optional/Optional
Attributes	%i18n
	profile="..."—URL specifying the location of META data.
Empty	No
Notes	There can be only one HEAD per document. It must follow the opening HTML tag and precede the BODY.

\<HR>

Usage	Horizontal rules are used to separate sections of a Web page.
Start/End Tag	Required/Illegal
Attributes	%coreattrs, %events
	align="..."—Deprecated. Controls alignment (left, center, right, justify).
	noshade="..."—Displays the rule as a solid color.
	size="..." —Deprecated. The size of the rule.
	width="..."—Deprecated. The width of the rule.
Empty	Yes

\<HTML> . . . \</HTML>

Usage	The HTML element contains the entire document.
Start/End Tag	Optional/Optional
Attributes	%i18n
	version="..."—URL of the document type definition specifying the HTML version used to create the document.
Empty	No
Notes	The version information is duplicated in the <!DOCTYPE...> declaration and therefore is not essential.

\<META>

Usage	Provides information about the document.
Start/End Tag	Required/Illegal

Attributes	`%i18n`
	`http-equiv="..."`—HTTP response header name.
	`name="..."`—Name of the meta information.
	`content="..."`—Content of the meta information.
	`scheme="..."`—Assigns a scheme to interpret the meta data.
Empty	Yes

<SPAN>...</SPAN>

Usage	Organizes the document by defining a span of text.
Start/End Tag	Required/Required
Attributes	`%coreattrs, %i18n, %events`
Empty	No

<TITLE>...</TITLE>

Usage	This is the name you give your Web page. The TITLE element is located in the HEAD element and is displayed in the browser window title bar.
Start/End Tag	Required/Required
Attributes	`%i18n`
Empty	No
Notes	Only one title allowed per document.

Text Phrases and Paragraphs

Text phrases (or blocks) can be structured to suit a specific purpose, such as creating a paragraph. This should not be confused with modifying the formatting of the text.

<ACRONYM>...</ACRONYM>

Usage	Used to define acronyms.
Start/End Tag	Required/Required
Attributes	`%coreattrs, %i18n, %events`
Empty	No

<ADDRESS>...</ADDRESS>

Usage	Provides a special format for author or contact information.
Start/End Tag	Required/Required

Attributes	%coreattrs, %i18n, %events
Empty	No
Notes	The BR element is commonly used inside the ADDRESS element to break the lines of an address.

`<BLOCKQUOTE>...</BLOCKQUOTE>`

Usage	Used to display long quotations.
Start/End Tag	Required/Required
Attributes	%coreattrs, %i18n, %events
	cite="..."—The URL of the quoted text.
Empty	No

`<BR>`

Usage	Forces a line break.
Start/End Tag	Required/Illegal
Attributes	%coreattrs, %i18n, %events
	clear-"..."—Sets the location where the next line begins after a floating object (none, left, right, all).
Empty	Yes

`<CITE>...</CITE>`

Usage	Cites a reference.
Start/End Tag	Required/Required
Attributes	%coreattrs, %i18n, %events
Empty	No

`<CODE>...</CODE>`

Usage	Identifies a code fragment for display.
Start/End Tag	Required/Required
Attributes	%coreattrs, %i18n, %events
Empty	No

`<DEL>...</DEL>`

| Usage | Shows text as having been deleted from the document since the last change. |
| Start/End Tag | Required/Required |

Attributes	%coreattrs, %i18n, %events
	cite="..."—The URL of the source document.
	datetime="..."—Indicates the date and time of the change.
Empty	No
Notes	New element in HTML 4.0.

<DFN>...</DFN>

Usage	Defines an enclosed term.
Start/End Tag	Required/Required
Attributes	%coreattrs, %i18n, %events
Empty	No

<EM>...</EM>

Usage	Emphasized text.
Start/End Tag	Required/Required
Attributes	%coreattrs, %i18n, %events
Empty	No

<INS>...</INS>

Usage	Shows text as having been inserted in the document since the last change.
Start/End Tag	Required/Required
Attributes	%coreattrs, %i18n, %events
	cite="..."—The URL of the source document.
	datetime="..."—Indicates the date and time of the change.
Empty	No
Notes	New element in HTML 4.0.

<KBD>...</KBD>

Usage	Indicates text a user would type.
Start/End Tag	Required/Required
Attributes	%coreattrs, %i18n, %events
Empty	No

A

`<P>...</P>`

Usage	Defines a paragraph.
Start/End Tag	Required/Optional
Attributes	`%coreattrs, %i18n, %events`
	`align="..."`—Deprecated. Controls alignment (`left`, `center`, `right`, `justify`).
Empty	No

`<PRE>...</PRE>`

Usage	Displays preformatted text.
Start/End Tag	Required/Required
Attributes	`%coreattrs, %i18n, %events`
	`width="..."`—The width of the formatted text.
Empty	No

`<Q>...</Q>`

Usage	Used to display short quotations that do not require paragraph breaks.
Start/End Tag	Required/Required
Attributes	`%coreattrs, %i18n, %events`
	`cite="..."`—The URL of the quoted text.
Empty	No
Notes	New element in HTML 4.0.

`<SAMP>...</SAMP>`

Usage	Identifies sample output.
Start/End Tag	Required/Required
Attributes	`%coreattrs, %i18n, %events`
Empty	No

`<STRONG>...</STRONG>`

Usage	Stronger emphasis.
Start/End Tag	Required/Required
Attributes	`%coreattrs, %i18n, %events`
Empty	No

_{...}

Usage	Creates subscript.
Start/End Tag	Required/Required
Attributes	%coreattrs, %i18n, %events
Empty	No

^{...}

Usage	Creates superscript.
Start/End Tag	Required/Required
Attributes	%coreattrs, %i18n, %events
Empty	No

<VAR>...</VAR>

Usage	A variable.
Start/End Tag	Required/Required
Attributes	%coreattrs, %i18n, %events
Empty	No

Text Formatting Elements

Text characteristics such as the size, weight, and style can be modified using these elements, but the HTML 4.0 specification encourages you to use style instead.

<B>...</B>

Usage	Bold text.
Start/End Tag	Required/Required
Attributes	%coreattrs, %i18n, %events
Empty	No

<BASEFONT>

Usage	Sets the base font size.
Start/End Tag	Required/Illegal
Attributes	size="..."—The font size (1–7 or relative, that is +3).
	color="..."—The font color.
	face="..."—The font type.

Empty	Yes
Notes	Deprecated in favor of style sheets.

`<BIG>...</BIG>`

Usage	Large text.
Start/End Tag	Required/Required
Attributes	%coreattrs, %i18n, %events
Empty	No

`<FONT>...</FONT>`

Usage	Changes the font size and color.
Start/End Tag	Required/Required
Attributes	size="..."—The font size (1–7 or relative, that is, +3).
	color="..."—The font color.
	face="..."—The font type.
Empty	No
Notes	Deprecated in favor of style sheets.

`<I>...</I>`

Usage	Italicized text.
Start/End Tag	Required/Required
Attributes	%coreattrs, %i18n, %events
Empty	No

`<S>...</S>`

Usage	Strikethrough text.
Start/End Tag	Required/Required
Attributes	%coreattrs, %i18n, %events
Empty	No
Notes	Deprecated.

`<SMALL>...</SMALL>`

Usage	Small text.
Start/End Tag	Required/Required
Attributes	%coreattrs, %i18n, %events
Empty	No

<STRIKE>...</STRIKE>

Usage	Strikethrough text.
Start/End Tag	Required/Required
Attributes	%coreattrs, %i18n, %events
Empty	No
Notes	Deprecated.

<TT>...</TT>

Usage	Teletype (or monospaced) text.
Start/End Tag	Required/Required
Attributes	%coreattrs, %i18n, %events
Empty	No

<U>...</U>

Usage	Underlined text.
Start/End Tag	Required/Required
Attributes	%coreattrs, %i18n, %events
Empty	No
Notes	Deprecated.

Lists

You can organize text into a more structured outline by creating lists. Lists can be nested.

<DD>...</DD>

Usage	The definition description used in a DL (definition list) element.
Start/End Tag	Required/Optional
Attributes	%coreattrs, %i18n, %events
Empty	No
Notes	Can contain block-level content, such as the <P> element.

<DIR>...</DIR>

Usage	Creates a multi-column directory list.
Start/End Tag	Required/Required
Attributes	%coreattrs, %i18n, %events
	compact—Deprecated. Compacts the displayed list.

A

Empty	No
Notes	Must contain at least one list item. This element is deprecated in favor of the UL (unordered list) element.

`<DL>...</DL>`

Usage	Creates a definition list.
Start/End Tag	Required/Required
Attributes	%coreattrs, %i18n, %events
	compact—Deprecated. Compacts the displayed list.
Empty	No
Notes	Must contain at least one `<DT>` or `<DD>` element in any order.

`<DT>...</DT>`

Usage	The definition term (or label) used within a DL (definition list) element.
Start/End Tag	Required/Optional
Attributes	%coreattrs, %i18n, %events
Empty	No
Notes	Must contain text (which can be modified by text markup elements).

`<LI>...</LI>`

Usage	Defines a list item within a list.
Start/End Tag	Required/Optional
Attributes	%coreattrs, %i18n, %events
	type="..."—Changes the numbering style (1, a, A, i, I), ordered lists, or bullet style (disc, square, circle) in unordered lists.
	value="..."—Sets the numbering to the given integer beginning with the current list item.
Empty	No

`<MENU>...</MENU>`

Usage	Creates a single-column menu list.
Start/End Tag	Required/Required
Attributes	%coreattrs, %i18n, %events
	compact—Deprecated. Compacts the displayed list.

Empty   No

Notes   Must contain at least one list item. This element is deprecated in
                favor of the UL (unordered list) element.

<OL>...</OL>

Usage   Creates an ordered list.

Start/End Tag   Required/Required

Attributes   %coreattrs, %i18n, %events

                type="..."—Sets the numbering style (1, a, A, i, I).

                compact—Deprecated. Compacts the displayed list.

                start="..."—Sets the starting number to the chosen integer.

Empty   No

Notes   Must contain at least one list item.

<UL>...</UL>

Usage   Creates an unordered list.

Start/End Tag   Required/Required

Attributes   %coreattrs, %i18n, %events

                type="..."—Sets the bullet style (disc, square, circle).

                compact—Deprecated. Compacts the displayed list.

Empty   No

Notes   Must contain at least one list item.

Links

Hyperlinking is fundamental to HTML. These elements enable you to link to other
documents.

<A>...</A>

Usage   Used to define links and anchors.

Start/End Tag   Required/Required

Attributes   %coreattrs, %i18n, %events

                charset="..."—Character encoding of the resource.

                name="..."—Defines an anchor.

                href="..."—The URL of the linked resource.

target="..."—Determines where the resource will be displayed (user-defined name, _blank, _parent, _self, _top).

rel="..."—Forward link types.

rev="..."—Reverse link types.

accesskey="..."—Assigns a hotkey to this element.

shape="..."—Enables you to define client-side imagemaps using defined shapes (default, rect, circle, poly).

coords="..."—Sets the size of the shape using pixel or percentage lengths.

tabindex="..."—Sets the tabbing order between elements with a defined tabindex.

Empty	No

\<BASE>

Usage	All other URLs in the document are resolved against this location.
Start/End Tag	Required/Illegal
Attributes	href="..."—The URL of the linked resource.
	target="..."—Determines where the resource will be displayed (user-defined name, _blank, _parent, _self, _top).
Empty	Yes
Notes	Located in the document HEAD.

\<LINK>

Usage	Defines the relationship between a link and a resource.
Start/End Tag	Required/Illegal
Attributes	%coreattrs, %i18n, %events
	href="..."—The URL of the resource.
	rel="..."—The forward link types.
	rev="..."—The reverse link types.
	type="..."—The Internet content type.
	media="..."—Defines the destination medium (screen, print, projection, braille, speech, all).
	target="..."—Determines where the resource will be displayed (user-defined name, _blank, _parent, _self, _top).
Empty	Yes
Notes	Located in the document HEAD.

Tables

Tables are meant to display data in a tabular format. Before the introduction of HTML 4.0, tables were widely used for page layout purposes, but with the advent of style sheets this is being discouraged by the W3C.

<CAPTION>...</CAPTION>

Usage	Displays a table caption.
Start/End Tag	Required/Required
Attributes	%coreattrs, %i18n, %events
	align="..."—Deprecated. Controls alignment (left, center, right, justify).
Empty	No
Notes	Optional.

<COL>

Usage	Groups columns within column groups in order to share attribute values.
Start/End Tag	Required/Illegal
Attributes	%coreattrs, %i18n, %events
	span="..."—The number of columns the group contains.
	width="..."—The column width as a percentage, pixel value, or minimum value.
	align="..."—Horizontally aligns the contents of cells (left, center, right, justify, char).
	char="..."—Sets a character on which the column aligns.
	charoff="..."—Offset to the first alignment character on a line.
	valign="..."—Vertically aligns the contents of a cell (top, middle, bottom, baseline).
Empty	Yes

<COLGROUP>...</COLGROUP>

Usage	Defines a column group.
Start/End Tag	Required/Optional
Attributes	%coreattrs, %i18n, %events
	span="..."—The number of columns in a group.

A

width="..."—The width of the columns.

align="..."—Horizontally aligns the contents of cells (left, center, right, justify, char).

char="..."—Sets a character on which the column aligns.

charoff="..."—Offset to the first alignment character on a line.

valign="..."—Vertically aligns the contents of a cell (top, middle, bottom, baseline).

Empty	No

<TABLE>...</TABLE>

Usage	Creates a table.
Start/End Tag	Required/Required
Attributes	%coreattrs, %i18n, %events

align="..."—Deprecated. Controls alignment (left, center, right, justify).

bgcolor="..."—Deprecated. Sets the background color.

width="..."—Table width.

cols="..."—The number of columns.

border="..."—The width in pixels of a border around the table.

frame="..."—Sets the visible sides of a table (void, above, below, hsides, lhs, rhs, vsides, box, border).

rules="..."—Sets the visible rules within a table (none, groups, rows, cols, all).

cellspacing="..."—Spacing between cells.

cellpadding="..."—Spacing in cells.

Empty	No

<TBODY>...</TBODY>

Usage	Defines the table body.
Start/End Tag	Optional/Optional
Attributes	%coreattrs, %i18n, %events

align="..."—Horizontally aligns the contents of cells (left, center, right, justify, char).

char="..."—Sets a character on which the column aligns.

charoff="..."—Offset to the first alignment character on a line.

valign="..."—Vertically aligns the contents of cells (top, middle, bottom, baseline).

Empty   No

`<TD>...</TD>`

Usage	Defines a cell's contents.
Start/End Tag	Required/Optional
Attributes	%coreattrs, %i18n, %events

axis="..."—Abbreviated name.

axes="..."—axis names listing row and column headers pertaining to the cell.

nowrap="..."—Deprecated. Turns off text wrapping in a cell.

bgcolor="..."—Deprecated. Sets the background color.

rowspan="..."—The number of rows spanned by a cell.

colspan="..."—The number of columns spanned by a cell.

align="..."—Horizontally aligns the contents of cells (left, center, right, justify, char).

char="..."—Sets a character on which the column aligns.

charoff="..."—Offset to the first alignment character on a line.

valign="..."—Vertically aligns the contents of cells (top, middle, bottom, baseline).

Empty   No

`<TFOOT>...</TFOOT>`

Usage	Defines the table footer.
Start/End Tag	Required/Optional
Attributes	%coreattrs, %i18n, %events

align="..."—Horizontally aligns the contents of cells (left, center, right, justify, char).

char="..."—Sets a character on which the column aligns.

charoff="..."—Offset to the first alignment character on a line.

valign="..."—Vertically aligns the contents of cells (top, middle, bottom, baseline).

Empty   No

<TH>...</TH>

Usage	Defines the cell contents of the table header.
Start/End Tag	Required/Optional
Attributes	%coreattrs, %i18n, %events

axis="..."—Abbreviated name.

axes="..."—axis names listing row and column headers pertaining to the cell.

nowrap="..."—Deprecated. Turns off text wrapping in a cell.

bgcolor="..."—Deprecated. Sets the background color.

rowspan="..."—The number of rows spanned by a cell.

colspan="..."—The number of columns spanned by a cell.

align="..."—Horizontally aligns the contents of cells (left, center, right, justify, char).

char="..."—Sets a character on which the column aligns.

charoff="..."—Offset to the first alignment character on a line.

valign="..."—Vertically aligns the contents of cells (top, middle, bottom, baseline).

Empty	No

<THEAD>...</THEAD>

Usage	Defines the table header.
Start/End Tag	Required/Optional
Attributes	%coreattrs, %i18n, %events

align="..."—Horizontally aligns the contents of cells (left, center, right, justify, char).

char="..."—Sets a character on which the column aligns.

charoff="..."—Offset to the first alignment character on a line.

valign="..."—Vertically aligns the contents of cells (top, middle, bottom, baseline).

Empty	No

<TR>...</TR>

Usage	Defines a row of table cells.
Start/End Tag	Required/Optional

Attributes   %coreattrs, %i18n, %events

align="..."—Horizontally aligns the contents of cells (left, center, right, justify, char).

char="..."—Sets a character on which the column aligns.

charoff="..."—Offset to the first alignment character on a line.

valign="..."—Vertically aligns the contents of cells (top, middle, bottom, baseline).

bgcolor="..."—Deprecated. Sets the background color.

Empty   No

Frames

Frames create new "panels" in the Web browser window that are used to display content from different source documents.

<FRAME>

Usage   Defines a frame.

Start/End Tag   Required/Illegal

Attributes   name="..."—The name of a frame.

src="..."—The source to be displayed in a frame.

frameborder="..."—Toggles the border between frames (0, 1).

marginwidth="..."—Sets the space between frame the border and content.

marginheight="..."—Sets the space between the frame border and content.

noresize—Disables sizing.

scrolling="..."—Determines scrollbar presence (auto, yes, no).

Empty   Yes

<FRAMESET>...</FRAMESET>

Usage   Defines the layout of FRAMES within a window.

Start/End Tag   Required/Required

Attributes   rows="..."—The number of rows.

cols="..."—The number of columns.

onload="..."—The intrinsic event triggered when the document loads.

onunload="..."—The intrinsic event triggered when the document unloads.

Empty	No
Notes	FRAMESETs can be nested.

<IFRAME>...</IFRAME>

Usage	Creates an inline frame.
Start/End Tag	Required/Required
Attributes	name="..."—The name of the frame.

src="..."—The source to be displayed in a frame.

frameborder="..."—Toggles the border between frames (0, 1).

marginwidth="..."—Sets the space between the frame border and content.

marginheight="..."—Sets the space between the frame border and content.

scrolling="..."—Determines scrollbar presence (auto, yes, no).

align="..."—Deprecated. Controls alignment (left, center, right, justify).

height="..."—Height.

width="..."—Width.

Empty	No

<NOFRAMES>...</NOFRAMES>

Usage	Alternative content when frames are not supported.
Start/End Tag	Required/Required
Attributes	None.
Empty	No

Embedded Content

Also called inclusions, embedded content applies to Java applets, imagemaps, and other multimedia or programattical content that is placed in a Web page to provide additional functionality.

\<APPLET>...\</APPLET>

Usage	Includes a Java applet.
Start/End Tag	Required/Required
Attributes	`codebase="..."`—The URL base for the applet.
	`archive="..."`—Identifies the resources to be preloaded.
	`code="..."`—The applet class file.
	`object="..."`—The serialized applet file.
	`alt="..."`—Displays text while loading.
	`name="..."`—The name of the applet.
	`width="..."`—The height of the displayed applet.
	`height="..."`—The width of the displayed applet.
	`align="..."`—Deprecated. Controls alignment (`left`, `center`, `right`, `justify`).
	`hspace="..."`—The horizontal space separating the image from other content.
	`vspace="..."`—The vertical space separating the image from other content.
Empty	No
Notes	Applet is deprecated in favor of the `OBJECT` element.

\<AREA>

Usage	The `AREA` element is used to define links and anchors.
Start/End Tag	Required/Illegal
Attributes	`shape="..."`—Enables you to define client-side imagemaps using defined shapes (`default`, `rect`, `circle`, `poly`).
	`coords="..."`—Sets the size of the shape using pixel or percentage lengths.
	`href="..."`—The URL of the linked resource.
	`target="..."`—Determines where the resource will be displayed (user-defined name, `_blank`, `_parent`, `_self`, `_top`).
	`nohref="..."`—Indicates that the region has no action.
	`alt="..."`—Displays alternative text.
	`tabindex="..."`—Sets the tabbing order between elements with a defined `tabindex`.
Empty	Yes

`<IMG>`

Usage	Uncludes an image in the document.
Start/End Tag	Required/Illegal
Attributes	`%coreattrs`, `%i18n`, `%events`
	`src="..."`—The URL of the image.
	`alt="..."`—Alternative text to display.
	`align="..."`—Deprecated. Controls alignment (`left`, `center`, `right`, `justify`).
	`height="..."`—The height of the image.
	`width="..."`—The width of the image.
	`border="..."`—Border width.
	`hspace="..."`—The horizontal space separating the image from other content.
	`vspace="..."`—The vertical space separating the image from other content.
	`usemap="..."`—The URL to a client-side imagemap.
	`ismap`—Identifies a server-side imagemap.
Empty	Yes

`<MAP>...</MAP>`

Usage	When used with the AREA element, creates a client-side imagemap.
Start/End Tag	Required/Required
Attributes	`%coreattrs`
	`name="..."`—The name of the imagemap to be created.
Empty	No

`<OBJECT>...</OBJECT>`

Usage	Includes an object.
Start/End Tag	Required/Required
Attributes	`%coreattrs`, `%i18n`, `%events`
	`declare`—A flag that declares but doesn't create an object.
	`classid="..."`—The URL of the object's location.
	`codebase="..."`—The URL for resolving URLs specified by other attributes.

data="..."—The URL to the object's data.

type="..."—The Internet content type for data.

codetype="..."—The Internet content type for the code.

standby="..."—Show message while loading.

align="..."—Deprecated. Controls alignment (left, center, right, justify).

height="..."—The height of the object.

width="..."—The width of the object.

border="..."—Displays the border around an object.

hspace="..."—The space between the sides of the object and other page content.

vspace="..."—The space between the top and bottom of the object and other page content.

usemap="..."—The URL to an imagemap.

shapes=—Enables you to define areas to search for hyperlinks if the object is an image.

name="..."—The URL to submit as part of a form.

tabindex="..."—Sets the tabbing order between elements with a defined tabindex.

Empty	No

<PARAM>

Usage	Initializes an object.
Start/End Tag	Required/Illegal
Attributes	name="..."—Defines the parameter name.
	value="..."—The value of the object parameter.
	valuetype="..."—Defines the value type (data, ref, object).
	type="..."—The Internet media type.
Empty	Yes

Style

Style sheets (both inline and external) are incorporated into an HTML document through the use of the STYLE element.

\<STYLE>...\</STYLE>

Usage	Creates an internal style sheet.
Start/End Tag	Required/Required
Attributes	`%i18n`

`type="..."`—The Internet content type.

`media="..."`—Defines the destination medium (`screen`, `print`, `projection`, `braille`, `speech`, `all`).

`title="..."`—The title of the style.

Empty	No
Notes	Located in the `HEAD` element.

Forms

Forms create an interface for the user to select options and submit data back to the Web server.

\<BUTTON>...\</BUTTON>

Usage	Creates a button.
Start/End Tag	Required/Required
Attributes	`%coreattrs, %i18n, %events`

`name="..."`—The button name.

`value="..."`—The value of the button.

`type="..."`—The button type (`button`, `submit`, `reset`).

`disabled="..."`—Sets the button state to disabled.

`tabindex="..."`—Sets the tabbing order between elements with a defined `tabindex`.

`onfocus="..."`—The event that occurs when the element receives focus.

`onblur="..."`—The event that occurs when the element loses focus.

Empty	No

\<FIELDSET>...\</FIELDSET>

Usage	Groups related controls.
Start/End Tag	Required/Required
Attributes	`%coreattrs, %i18n, %events`
Empty	No

\<FORM\>...\</FORM\>

Usage	Creates a form that holds controls for user input.
Start/End Tag	Required/Required
Attributes	`%coreattrs`, `%i18n`, `%events`
	`action="..."`—The URL for the server action.
	`method="..."`—The HTTP method (`get`, `post`). `get` is deprecated.
	`enctype="..."`—Specifies the MIME (Internet media type).
	`onsubmit="..."`—The intrinsic event that occurs when the form is submitted.
	`onreset="..."`—The intrinsic event that occurs when the form is reset.
	`target="..."`—Determines where the resource will be displayed (user-defined name, `_blank`, `_parent`, `_self`, `_top`).
	`accept-charset="..."`—The list of character encodings.
Empty	No

\<INPUT\>

Usage	Defines controls used in forms.
Start/End Tag	Required/Illegal
Attributes	`%coreattrs`, `%i18n`, `%events`
	`type="..."`—The type of input control (`text`, `password`, `checkbox`, `radio`, `submit`, `reset`, `file`, `hidden`, `image`, `button`).
	`name="..."`—The name of the control (required except for `submit` and `reset`).
	`value="..."`—The initial value of the control (required for `radio` and checkboxes).
	`checked="..."`—Sets the radio buttons to a checked state.
	`disabled="..."`—Disables the control.
	`readonly="..."`—For text password types.
	`size="..."`—The width of the control in pixels except for text and password controls, which are specified in number of characters.
	`maxlength="..."`—The maximum number of characters that can be entered.
	`src="..."`—The URL to an image control type.
	`alt="..."`—An alternative text description.

usemap="..."—The URL to a client-side imagemap.

align="..."—Deprecated. Controls alignment (left, center, right, justify).

tabindex="..."—Sets the tabbing order between elements with a defined tabindex.

onfocus="..."—The event that occurs when the element receives focus.

onblur="..."—The event that occurs when the element loses focus.

onselect="..."—Intrinsic event that occurs when the control is selected.

onchange="..."—Intrinsic event that occurs when the control is changed.

accept="..."—File types allowed for upload.

Empty	Yes

\<ISINDEX>

Usage	Prompts the user for unput.
Start/End Tag	Required/Illegal
Attributes	%coreattrs, %i18n
	prompt="..."—Provides a prompt string for the input field.
Empty	Yes
Notes	Deprecated.

\<LABEL>...\</LABEL>

Usage	Labels a control.
Start/End Tag	Required/Required
Attributes	%coreattrs, %i18n, %events
	for="..."—Associates a label with an identified control.
	disabled="..."—Disables a control.
	accesskey="..."—Assigns a hotkey to this element.
	onfocus="..."—The event that occurs when the element receives focus.
	onblur="..."—The event that occurs when the element loses focus.
Empty	No

<LEGEND>...</LEGEND>

Usage	Assigns a caption to a FIELDSET.
Start/End Tag	Required/Required
Attributes	%coreattrs, %i18n, %events
	align="..."—Deprecated. Controls alignment (left, center, right, justify).
	accesskey="..."—Assigns a hotkey to this element.
Empty	No

<OPTION>...</OPTION>

Usage	Specifies choices in a SELECT element.
Start/End Tag	Required/Optional
Attributes	%coreattrs, %i18n, %events
	selected="..."—Specifies whether the option is selected.
	disabled="..."—Disables control.
	value="..."—The value submitted if a control is submitted.
Empty	No

<SELECT>...</SELECT>

Usage	Creates choices for the user to select.
Start/End Tag	Required/Required
Attributes	%coreattrs, %i18n, %events
	name="..."—The name of the element.
	size="..."—The width in number of rows.
	multiple—Allows multiple selections.
	disabled="..."—Disables the control.
	tabindex="..."—Sets the tabbing order between elements with a defined tabindex.
	onfocus="..."—The event that occurs when the element receives focus.
	onblur="..."—The event that occurs when the element loses focus.
	onselect="..."—Intrinsic event that occurs when the control is selected.
	onchange="..."—Intrinsic event that occurs when the control is changed.
Empty	No

\<TEXTAREA\>...\</TEXTAREA\>

Usage	Creates an area for user input with multiple lines.
Start/End Tag	Required/Required
Attributes	%coreattrs, %i18n, %events
	name="..."—The name of the control.
	rows="..."—The width in number of rows.
	cols="..."—The height in number of columns.
	disabled="..."—Disables the control.
	readonly="..."—Sets the displayed text to read-only status.
	tabindex="..."—Sets the tabbing order between elements with a defined tabindex.
	onfocus="..."—The event that occurs when the element receives focus.
	onblur="..."—The event that occurs when the element loses focus.
	onselect="..."—Intrinsic event that occurs when the control is selected.
	onchange="..."—Intrinsic event that occurs when the control is changed.
Empty	No
Notes	Text to be displayed is placed within the start and end tags.

Scripts

Scripting language is made available to process data and perform other dynamic events through the SCRIPT element.

\<SCRIPT\>...\</SCRIPT\>

Usage	The SCRIPT element contains client-side scripts that are executed by the browser.
Start/End Tag	Required/Required
Attributes	type="..."—Script-language Internet content type.
	language="..."—Deprecated. The scripting language, deprecated in favor of the type attribute.
	src="..."—The URL for the external script.
Empty	No
Notes	You can set the default scripting language in the META element.

`<NOSCRIPT>...</NOSCRIPT>`

Usage	The NOSCRIPT element provides alternative content for browsers unable to execute a script.
Start/End Tag	Required/Required
Attributes	None
Empty	No

Common Attributes and Events

Four attributes are abbreviated as `%coreattrs` in the preceding sections. They are

- ☐ `id="..."`—A global identifier.
- ☐ `class="..."`—A list of classes separated by spaces.
- ☐ `style="..."`—Style information.
- ☐ `title="..."`—Provides more information for a specific element, as opposed to the TITLE element, which entitles the entire Web page.

Two attributes for internationalization (i18n) are abbreviated as `%i18n`:

- ☐ `lang="..."`—The language identifier.
- ☐ `dir="..."`—The text direction (`ltr`, `rtl`).

The following intrinsic events are abbreviated `%events`:

- ☐ `onclick="..."`—A pointing device (such as a mouse) was single-clicked.
- ☐ `ondblclick="..."`—A pointing device (such as a mouse) was double-clicked.
- ☐ `onmousedown="..."`—A mouse button was clicked and held down.
- ☐ `onmouseup="..."`—A mouse button that was clicked and held down was released.
- ☐ `onmouseover="..."`—A mouse moved the cursor over an object.
- ☐ `onmousemove="..."`—The mouse was moved.
- ☐ `onmouseout="..."`—A mouse moved the cursor off an object.
- ☐ `onkeypress="..."`—A key was pressed and released.
- ☐ `onkeydown="..."`—A key was pressed and held down.
- ☐ `onkeyup="..."`—A key that was pressed has been released.

APPENDIX

B

JavaScript Language Reference

The first part of this reference is organized by object, with properties and methods listed by the object to which they apply. The second part covers independent functions in JavaScript not connected with a particular object, as well as operators in JavaScript.

A Note About JavaScript 1.2

JavaScript 1.2 is designed to interface seamlessly with Netscape Navigator 4.0. New features have been introduced in various areas of the language model, including but not limited to

- ☐ Events
- ☐ Objects
- ☐ Properties
- ☐ Methods

Netscape Navigator 4.0 has been coded to support these new features, but earlier versions of Navigator have not. Backward compatibility is therefore an issue.

In this appendix, techniques that work only in Netscape Navigator 4.0 and above are clearly marked. At each heading, the words "Navigator 4.0 Only" will appear.

Finally, note that in development, you should now clearly identify which version of JavaScript you are using. If you fail to do so, your scripts might not work. You do this by using the LANGUAGE attribute within the <SCRIPT> tag. The following are some examples:

```
<Script Language = "JavaScript"> - Compatible with 2.0 and above

<Script Language = "JavaScript 1.1"> - Compatible with 3.0 and above

<Script Language = "JavaScript 1.2"> - Compatible with 4.0 and above
```

The following codes are used to indicate where objects, methods, properties, and event handlers are implemented:

- ☐ C—Client JavaScript (Server JavaScript is not covered in this appendix)
- ☐ 2—Netscape Navigator 2
- ☐ 3—Netscape Navigator 3
- ☐ 4—Netscape Navigator 4 only (this is not to say Navigator 4 will work with these items only, Navigator 4 will handle all implementations)
- ☐ I—Microsoft Internet Explorer 3

The anchor **Object [C|2|3|4|I]**

The anchor object reflects an HTML anchor.

Properties

- ☐ name—A string value indicating the name of the anchor. (Not 2|3)

The applet **Object [C|3]**

The applet object reflects a Java applet included in a Web page with the APPLET tag.

Properties

- ☐ name—A string reflecting the NAME attribute of the APPLET tag.

The area **Object [C|3]**

The area object reflects a clickable area defined in an imagemap. area objects appear as entries in the links array of the document object.

Properties

- [ ] **hash**—A string value indicating an anchor name from the URL.
- [ ] **host**—A string value reflecting the host and domain name portion of the URL.
- [ ] **hostname**—A string value indicating the host, domain name, and port number from the URL.
- [ ] **href**—A string value reflecting the entire URL.
- [ ] **pathname**—A string value reflecting the path portion of the URL (excluding the host, domain name, port number, and protocol).
- [ ] **port**—A string value indicating the port number from the URL.
- [ ] **protocol**—A string value indicating the protocol portion of the URL, including the trailing colon.
- [ ] **search**—A string value specifying the query portion of the URL (after the question mark).
- [ ] **target**—A string value reflecting the TARGET attribute of the AREA tag.

Methods

- [ ] **getSelection**—Gets the current selection and returns this value as a string.

Event Handlers

- [ ] **onDblClick** —Specifies JavaScript code to execute when the user double-clicks the area. (Not implemented on Macintosh.) Netscape Navigator 4.0 Only.
- [ ] **onMouseOut** —Specifies JavaScript code to execute when the mouse moves outside the area specified in the AREA tag.

New Properties with JavaScript 1.2

type	Indicates a MouseOut event.
target	Indicates the object to which the event was sent.
layer[n]	Where [n] represents X or Y, used (in conjunction with page[n] and screen[n]) to describe the cursor location when the MouseOut event occurred.
page[n]	Where [n] represents X or Y, used (in conjunction with layer[n] and screen[n]) to describe the cursor location when the MouseOut event occurred.
screen[n]	Where [n] represents X or Y, used (in conjunction with layer[n] and page[n]) to describe the cursor location when the MouseOut event occurred.

B

☐ **onMouseOver** —Specifies JavaScript code to execute when the mouse enters the area specified in the AREA tag.

New Properties with JavaScript 1.2

type	Indicates a MouseOver event.
target	Indicates the object to which the event was sent.
layer[n]	Where [n] represents X or Y, used (in conjunction with page[n] and screen[n]) to describe the cursor location when the MouseOver event occurred.
page[n]	Where [n] represents X or Y, used (in conjunction with layer[n] and screen[n]) to describe the cursor location when the MouseOver event occurred.
screen[n]	Where [n] represents X or Y, used (in conjunction with layer[n] and page[n]) to describe the cursor location when the MouseOver event occurred.

The Array Object [C│3│I]

The Array object provides a mechanism for creating arrays and working with them. New arrays are created with *arrayName* = new Array() or *arrayName* = new Array(*arrayLength*).

Properties

☐ **length**—An integer value reflecting the number of elements in an array.

☐ **prototype**—Provides a mechanism to add properties to an Array object.

Methods

☐ **concat(*arrayname*)**—Combines elements of two arrays and returns a third, one level deep, without altering either of the derivative arrays. Netscape Navigator 4.0 Only.

☐ **join(*string*)**—Returns a string containing each element of the array separated by *string*. (Not I)

☐ **reverse()**—Reverses the order of an array. (Not I)

☐ **slice(arrayName, beginSlice, endSlice)**—Extracts a portion of some array and derives a new array from it. The beginSlice and endSlice parameters specify the target elements at which to begin and end the slice. (Netscape Navigator 4.0 Only.)

☐ **sort(*function*)**—Sorts an array based on function which indicates a *function* defining the sort order. *function* can be omitted, in which case the sort defaults to dictionary order. Note: sort now works on all platforms.

The button **Object** [C|2|3|I]

The button object reflects a pushbutton from an HTML form in JavaScript.

Properties

- ☐ **enabled**—A Boolean value indicating whether the button is enabled. (Not 2|3)
- ☐ **form**—A reference to the form object containing the button. (Not 2|3)
- ☐ **name**—A string value containing the name of the button element.
- ☐ **type**—A string value reflecting the TYPE attribute of the INPUT tag. (Not 2|I)
- ☐ **value**—A string value containing the value of the button element.

Methods

- ☐ **click()**—Emulates the action of clicking the button.
- ☐ **focus()**—Gives focus to the button. (Not 2|3)

Event Handlers

- ☐ **onMouseDown**—Specifies JavaScript code to execute when a user presses a mouse button.
- ☐ **onMouseUp**—Specifies JavaScript code to execute when the user releases a mouse button.
- ☐ **onClick**—Specifies JavaScript code to execute when the button is clicked.
- ☐ **onFocus**—Specifies JavaScript code to execute when the button receives focus. (Not 2|3)

The checkbox **Object** [c|2|3|I]

The checkbox object makes a checkbox in an HTML form available in JavaScript.

Properties

- ☐ **checked**—A Boolean value indicating whether the checkbox element is checked.
- ☐ **defaultChecked**—A Boolean value indicating whether the checkbox element was checked by default (that is, it reflects the CHECKED attribute).
- ☐ **enabled**—A Boolean value indicating whether the checkbox is enabled. (Not 2|3)
- ☐ **form**—A reference to the form object containing the checkbox. (Not 2|3)
- ☐ **name**—A string value containing the name of the checkbox element.
- ☐ **type**—A string value reflecting the TYPE attribute of the INPUT tag. (Not 2|I)
- ☐ **value**—A string value containing the value of the checkbox element.

Methods

☐ **click()**—Emulates the action of clicking the checkbox.

☐ **focus()**—Gives focus to the checkbox. (Not 2|3)

Event Handlers

☐ **onClick**—Specifies JavaScript code to execute when the checkbox is clicked.

☐ **onFocus**—Specifies JavaScript code to execute when the checkbox receives focus. (Not 2|3)

The combo Object [C|I]

The combo object reflects a combo field in JavaScript.

Properties

☐ **enabled**—A Boolean value indicating whether the combo box is enabled. (Not 2|3)

☐ **form**—A reference to the form object containing the combo box. (Not 2|3)

☐ **listCount**—An integer reflecting the number of elements in the list.

☐ **listIndex**—An integer reflecting the index of the selected element in the list.

☐ **multiSelect**—A Boolean value indicating whether the combo field is in multiselect mode.

☐ **name**—A string value reflecting the name of the combo field.

☐ **value**—A string containing the value of the combo field.

Methods

☐ **addItem(*index*)**—Adds an item to the combo field before the item at *index*.

☐ **click()**—Simulates a click on the combo field.

☐ **clear()**—Clears the contents of the combo field.

☐ **focus()**—Gives focus to the combo field.

☐ **removeItem(*index*)**—Removes the item at *index* from the combo field.

Event Handlers

☐ **onClick**—Specifies JavaScript code to execute when the mouse clicks the combo field.

☐ **onFocus**—Specifies JavaScript code to execute when the combo field receives focus.

The Date Object [C | 2 | 3 | 1]

The Date object provides mechanisms for working with dates and times in JavaScript. Instances of the object can be created with the following syntax:

newObjectName = new Date(*dateInfo*)

Where *dateInfo* is an optional specification of a particular date and can be one of the following:

"*month day, year hours:minutes:seconds*"

year, month, day

year, month, day, hours, minutes, seconds

where the later two options represent integer values.

If no *dateInfo* is specified, the new object will represent the current date and time.

Properties

☐ **prototype**—Provides a mechanism for adding properties to a Date object. (Not 2)

Methods

☐ **getDate()**—Returns the day of the month for the current Date object as an integer from 1 to 31.

☐ **getDay()**—Returns the day of the week for the current Date object as an integer from 0 to 6 (where 0 is Sunday, 1 is Monday, and so on).

☐ **getHours()**—Returns the hour from the time in the current Date object as an integer from 0 to 23.

☐ **getMinutes()**—Returns the minutes from the time in the current Date object as an integer from 0 to 59.

☐ **getMonth()**—Returns the month for the current Date object as an integer from 0 to 11 (where 0 is January, 1 is February, and so on).

☐ **getSeconds()**—Returns the seconds from the time in the current Date object as an integer from 0 to 59.

☐ **getTime()**—Returns the time of the current Date object as an integer representing the number of milliseconds since 1 January 1970 at 00:00:00.

☐ **getTimezoneOffset()**—Returns the difference between the local time and GMT as an integer representing the number of minutes.

☐ **getYear()**—Returns the year for the current Date object as a two-digit integer representing the year less 1900.

☐ **parse(*dateString*)**—Returns the number of milliseconds between January 1, 1970 at 00:00:00 and the date specified in *dateString*. *dateString* should take the following format: (Not I)

Day, DD Mon YYYY HH:MM:SS TZN

Mon DD, YYYY

☐ **setDate(*dateValue*)**—Sets the day of the month for the current Date object. *dateValue* is an integer from 1 to 31.

☐ **setHours(*hoursValue*)**—Sets the hours for the time for the current Date object. *hoursValue* is an integer from 0 to 23.

☐ **setMinutes(*minutesValue*)**—Sets the minutes for the time for the current Date object. *minutesValue* is an integer from 0 to 59.

☐ **setMonth(*monthValue*)**—Sets the month for the current Date object. *monthValue* is an integer from 0 to 11 (where 0 is January, 1 is February, and so on).

☐ **setSeconds(*secondsValue*)**—Sets the seconds for the time for the current Date object. *secondsValue* is an integer from 0 to 59.

☐ **setTime(*timeValue*)**—Sets the value for the current Date object. *timeValue* is an integer representing the number of milliseconds since January 1, 1970 at 00:00:00.

☐ **setYear(*yearValue*)**—Sets the year for the current Date object. *yearValue* is an integer greater than 1900.

☐ **toGMTString()**—Returns the value of the current Date object in GMT as a string using Internet conventions in the form

Day, DD Mon YYYY HH:MM:SS GMT

☐ **toLocaleString()**—Returns the value of the current Date object in the local time using local conventions.

☐ **UTC(*yearValue, monthValue, dateValue, hoursValue, minutesValue, secondsValue*)**—Returns the number of milliseconds since January 1, 1970 at 00:00:00 GMT. *yearValue* is an integer greater than 1900. *monthValue* is an integer from 0 to 11. *dateValue* is an integer from 1 to 31. *hoursValue* is an integer from 0 to 23. *minutesValue* and *secondsValue* are integers from 0 to 59. *hoursValue*, *minutesValue*, and *secondsValue* are optional. (Not I)

The document Object [C|2|3|I]

The document object reflects attributes of an HTML document in JavaScript.

Properties

- [ ] **alinkColor**—The color of active links as a string or a hexadecimal triplet.
- [ ] **anchors**—Array of anchor objects in the order they appear in the HTML document. Use anchors.length to get the number of anchors in a document.
- [ ] **applets**—Array of applet objects in the order they appear in the HTML document. Use applets.length to get the number of applets in a document. (Not 2)
- [ ] **bgColor**—The color of the document's background.
- [ ] **cookie**—A string value containing cookie values for the current document.
- [ ] **embeds**—Array of plugin objects in the order they appear in the HTML document. Use embeds.length to get the number of plug-ins in a document. (Not 2|I)
- [ ] **fgColor**—The color of the document's foreground.
- [ ] **forms**—Array of form objects in the order the forms appear in the HTML file. Use forms.length to get the number of forms in a document.
- [ ] **images**—Array of image objects in the order they appear in the HTML document. Use images.length to get the number of images in a document. (Not 2|I)
- [ ] **lastModified**—String value containing the last date of modification of the document.
- [ ] **linkColor**—The color of links as a string or a hexadecimal triplet.
- [ ] **links**—Array of link objects in the order the hypertext links appear in the HTML document. Use links.length to get the number of links in a document.
- [ ] **location**—A string containing the URL of the current document. Use document.URL instead of document.location. This property is expected to disappear in a future release.
- [ ] **referrer**—A string value containing the URL of the calling document when the user follows a link.
- [ ] **title**—A string containing the title of the current document.
- [ ] **URL**—A string reflecting the URL of the current document. Use instead of document.location. (Not I)
- [ ] **vlinkColor**—The color of followed links as a string or a hexadecimal triplet.

Event Handlers

- [ ] **onMouseDown**—Specifies JavaScript code to execute when a user presses a mouse button.
- [ ] **onMouseUp**—Specifies JavaScript code to execute when the user releases a mouse button.

B

☐ **onKeyUp**—Specifies JavaScript code to execute when the user releases a specific key. (Netscape Navigator 4.0 Only.)

☐ **onKeyPress**—Specifies JavaScript code to execute when the user holds down a specific key. (Netscape Navigator 4.0 Only.)

☐ **onKeyDown**—Specifies JavaScript code to execute when the user presses a specific key. (Netscape Navigator 4.0 Only.)

☐ **onDblClick**—Specifies JavaScript code to execute when the user double-clicks the area. (Not implemented on Macintosh; Netscape Navigator 4.0 Only.)

Methods

☐ **captureEvents()**—Used in a window with frames (in conjunction with `enableExternalCapture`), this specifies that the window will capture all specified events. New in JavaScript 1.2.

☐ **clear()**—Clears the document window. (Not I)

☐ **close()**—Closes the current output stream.

☐ **open(*mimeType*)**—Opens a stream that allows `write()` and `writeln()` methods to write to the document window. *mimeType* is an optional string that specifies a document type supported by Navigator or a plug-in (for example, `text/html` or `image/gif`).

☐ **releaseEvents(*eventType*)**—Specifies that the current window must release events (as opposed to capture them) so that these events can be passed to other objects, perhaps further on in the event hierarchy. New in JavaScript 1.2.

☐ **routeEvent(event)**—Sends or routes an event through the normal event hierarchy.

☐ **write()**—Writes text and HTML to the specified document.

☐ **writeln()**—Writes text and HTML to the specified document followed by a newline character.

The `FileUpload` Object [C|3]

Reflects a file upload element in an HTML form.

Properties

☐ **name**—A string value reflecting the name of the file upload element.

☐ **value**—A string value reflecting the file upload element's field.

The form **Object [C|2|3|I]**

The form object reflects an HTML form in JavaScript. Each HTML form in a document is reflected by a distinct instance of the form object.

Properties

☐ **action**—A string value specifying the URL to which the form data is submitted.

☐ **elements**—Array of objects for each form element in the order in which they appear in the form.

☐ **encoding**—String containing the MIME encoding of the form as specified in the ENCTYPE attribute.

☐ **method**—A string value containing the method of submission of form data to the server.

☐ **target**—A string value containing the name of the window to which responses to form submissions are directed.

Methods

☐ **reset()**—Resets the form. (Not 2|I)

☐ **submit()**—Submits the form.

Event Handlers

☐ **onReset**—Specifies JavaScript code to execute when the form is reset. (Not 2|I)

☐ **onSubmit**—Specifies JavaScript code to execute when the form is submitted. The code should return a true value to enable the form to be submitted. A false value prevents the form from being submitted.

The frame **Object [C|2|3|I]**

The frame object reflects a frame window in JavaScript.

Properties

☐ **frames**—An array of objects for each frame in a window. Frames appear in the array in the order in which they appear in the HTML source code.

☐ **onblur**—A string reflecting the onBlur event handler for the frame. New values can be assigned to this property to change the event handler. (Not 2)

☐ **onfocus**—A string reflecting the onFocus event handler for the frame. New values can be assigned to this property to change the event handler. (Not 2)

B

- **parent**—A string indicating the name of the window containing the frameset.
- **self**—An alternative for the name of the current window.
- **top**—An alternative for the name of the top-most window.
- **window**—An alternative for the name of the current window.

Methods

- **alert(*message*)**—Displays *message* in a dialog box.
- **blur()**—Removes focus from the frame. (Not 2)
- **clearInterval(*intervalID*)**—Cancels time outs that are created with the setInterval method. New in JavaScript 1.2.
- **close()**—Closes the window.
- **confirm(*message*)**—Displays *message* in a dialog box with OK and Cancel buttons. Returns true or false based on the button clicked by the user.
- **focus()**—Gives focus to the frame. (Not 2)
- **open(*url*,*name*,*features*)**—Opens *url* in a window named *name*. If *name* doesn't exist, a new window is created with that name. *features* is an optional string argument containing a list of features for the new window. The feature list contains any of the following name-value pairs separated by commas and without additional spaces:

toolbar=[yes,no,1,0]	Indicates whether the window should have a toolbar
location=[yes,no,1,0]	Indicates whether the window should have a location field
directories=[yes,no,1,0]	Indicates whether the window should have directory buttons
status=[yes,no,1,0]	Indicates whether the window should have a status bar
menubar=[yes,no,1,0]	Indicates whether the window should have menus
scrollbars=[yes,no,1,0]	Indicates whether the window should have scrollbars
resizable=[yes,no,1,0]	Indicates whether the window should be resizable
width=*pixels*	Indicates the width of the window in pixels
height=*pixels*	Indicates the height of the window in pixels

- **print()**—Prints the contents of a frame or window. This is the equivalent of the user pressing the Print button in Netscape Navigator. New in JavaScript 1.2.

☐ **prompt(*message,response*)**—Displays *message* in a dialog box with a text entry field with the default value of *response*. The user's response in the text-entry field is returned as a string.

☐ **setInterval(*function*, msec, [args])**—Repeatedly calls a function after the period specified by the msec parameter. New in JavaScript 1.2.

☐ **setInterval(*expression*, msec)**—Evaluates *expression* after the period specified by the msec parameter. New in JavaScript 1.2.

☐ **setTimeout(*expression,time*)**—Evaluates *expression* after *time* where *time* is a value in milliseconds. The time out can be named with the following structure:

name = setTimeOut(*expression,time*)

☐ **clearTimeout(*name*)**—Cancels the time out with the name *name*.

Event Handlers

☐ **onBlur**—Specifies JavaScript code to execute when focus is removed from a frame. (Not 2)

☐ **onFocus**—Specifies JavaScript code to execute when focus is removed from a frame. (Not 2)

☐ **onMove**—Specifies JavaScript code to execute when the user moves a frame. (Netscape Navigator 4.0 Only.)

☐ **onResize**—Specifies JavaScript code to execute when a user resizes the frame. (Netscape Navigator 4.0 Only.)

The Function Object [C|3]

The Function object provides a mechanism for indicating JavaScript code to compile as a function. The syntax to use the Function object is:

functionName = new Function(*arg1*, *arg2*, *arg3*, ..., *functionCode*)

This is similar to

```
function functionName(arg1, arg2, arg3, ...) {
   functionCode
}
```

except that in the former *functionName* is a variable with a reference to the function, and the function is evaluated each time it is used rather than being compiled once.

Properties

☐ **arguments**—An integer reflecting the number of arguments in a function.

☐ **prototype**—Provides a mechanism for adding properties to a Function object.

The hidden Object [C | 2 | 3 | I]

The hidden object reflects a hidden field from an HTML form in JavaScript.

Properties

- ☐ **name**—A string value containing the name of the hidden element.
- ☐ **type**—A string value reflecting the TYPE property of the INPUT tag. (Not 2|I)
- ☐ **value**—A string value containing the value of the hidden text element.

The history Object [C | 2 | 3 | I]

The history object enables a script to work with the Navigator browser's history list in JavaScript. For security and privacy reasons, the actual content of the list is not reflected into JavaScript.

Properties

- ☐ **length**—An integer representing the number of items on the history list. (Not I)

Methods

- ☐ **back()**—Goes back to the previous document in the history list. (Not I)
- ☐ **forward()**—Goes forward to the next document in the history list. (Not I)
- ☐ **go(*location*)**—Goes to the document in the history list specified by *location*. *location* can be a string or integer value. If it is a string, it represents all or part of a URL in the history list. If it is an integer, *location* represents the relative position of the document on the history list. As an integer, *location* can be positive or negative. (Not I)

The Image Object [C | 3]

The Image object reflects an image included in an HTML document.

Properties

- ☐ **border**—An integer value reflecting the width of the image's border in pixels.
- ☐ **complete**—A Boolean value indicating whether the image has finished loading.
- ☐ **height**—An integer value reflecting the height of an image in pixels.
- ☐ **hspace**—An integer value reflecting the HSPACE attribute of the IMG tag.
- ☐ **lowsrc**—A string value containing the URL of the low-resolution version of the image to load.

☐ **name**—A string value indicating the name of the Image object.

☐ **prototype**—Provides a mechanism for adding properties as an Image object.

☐ **src**—A string value indicating the URL of the image.

☐ **vspace**—An integer value reflecting the VSPACE attribute of the IMG tag.

☐ **width**—An integer value indicating the width of an image in pixels.

Event Handlers

☐ **onKeyUp**—Specifies JavaScript code to execute when the user releases a specific key. (Netscape Navigator 4.0 Only.)

☐ **onKeyPress**—Specifies JavaScript code to execute when the user holds down a specific key. (Netscape Navigator 4.0 Only.)

☐ **onKeyDown**—Specifies JavaScript code to execute when the user presses a specific key. (Netscape Navigator 4.0 Only.)

☐ **onAbort**—Specifies JavaScript code to execute if the attempt to load the image is aborted. (Not 2)

☐ **onError**—Specifies JavaScript code to execute if there is an error while loading the image. Setting this event handler to null suppresses error messages if an error occurs while loading. (Not 2)

☐ **onLoad**—Specifies JavaScript code to execute when the image finishes loading. (Not 2)

The Layer Object [4] Netscape Navigator 4.0 Only

The Layer object is used to embed layers of content within a page. These can be hidden or not. Either type is accessible through JavaScript code. The most common use for layers is in the development of Dynamic, or DHTML. Layers enable you to create animations or other dynamic content on a page by cycling through the layers you have defined.

Properties

☐ **above**—Places a layer on top of a newly created layer.

☐ **background**—Used to specify a tiled background image of the layer.

☐ **below**—Places a layer below a newly created layer.

☐ **bgColor**—Sets the background color of the layer.

☐ **clip(left, top, right, bottom)**—Specifies the visible boundaries of the layer.

- □ **height**—Specifies the height of the layer, expressed in pixels (integer) or by a percentage of the instant layer.
- □ **ID**—Previously called NAME. Used to name the layer so that it can be referred to by name and accessed by other JavaScript code.
- □ **left**—Specifies the horizontal positioning of the top-left corner of the layer. Used in conjunction with the Top property.
- □ **page[n]**—Where [n] is X or Y. Specifies the horizontal (X) or vertical (Y) positioning of the top-left corner of the layer, relative to the overall, enclosing document. (Note: This is different than the Left and Top properties.)
- □ **parentLayer**—Specifies the layer object that contains the present layer.
- □ **SRC**—Specifies HTML source to be displayed with the target layer. (This source can also include JavaScript within it.)
- □ **siblingAbove**—Specifies the layer object immediately above the present one.
- □ **siblingBelow**—Specifies the layer object immediately below the present one.
- □ **top**—Specifies the vertical positioning of the top-left corner of the layer. (Used in conjunction with the Left property.)
- □ **visibility**—Specifies the visibility of the layer. There are three choices: show (it is visible), hidden (it is not visible), and inherit (the layer inherits the properties of its parent).
- □ **width**—Specifies the width of the layer. Used for wrapping procedures; that is, the width denotes the boundary after which the contents wrap inside the layer.
- □ **z-index**—Specifies the Z-order (or stacking order) of the layer. Used to set the layer's position within the overall rotational order of all layers. Expressed as an integer. (Used where there are many layers.)

Events

- □ **onBlur**—Specifies JavaScript code to execute when the layer loses focus.
- □ **onFocus**—Specifies JavaScript code to execute when the layer gains focus.
- □ **onLoad**—Specifies JavaScript code to execute when a layer is loaded.
- □ **onMouseOut**—Specifies JavaScript code to execute when the mouse cursor moves off the layer.

New Properties	
type	Indicates a MouseOut event.
target	Indicates the object to which the event was sent.
layer[n]	Where [n] represents X or Y, used (in conjunction with page[n] and screen[n]) to describe the cursor location when the MouseOut event occurred.

New Properties

page[n]	Where [n] represents X or Y, used (in conjunction with layer[n] and screen[n]) to describe the cursor location when the MouseOut event occurred.
screen[n]	Where [n] represents X or Y, used (in conjunction with layer[n] and page[n]) to describe the cursor location when the MouseOut event occurred.

☐ **onMouseover**—Specifies the JavaScript code to execute when the mouse cursor enters the layer.

New Properties with JavaScript 1.2

type	Indicates a MouseOver event.
target	Indicates the object to which the event was sent.
layer[n]	Where [n] represents X or Y, used (in conjunction with page[n] and screen[n]) to describe the cursor location when the MouseOver event occurred.
page[n]	Where [n] represents X or Y, used (in conjunction with layer[n] and screen[n]) to describe the cursor location when the MouseOver event occurred.
screen[n]	Where [n] represents X or Y, used (in conjunction with layer[n] and page[n]) to describe the cursor location when the MouseOver event occurred.

Methods

☐ **captureEvents()**—Used in a window with frames (in conjunction with enableExternalCapture), this specifies that the window shall capture all specified events. New in JavaScript 1.2.

☐ **load(*source*, *width*)**—Alters the source of the layer by replacing it with HTML (or JavaScript) from the file specified in *source*. Using this method, you can also pass a width value (in pixels) to accommodate the new content.

☐ **moveAbove(*layer*)**—Places the layer above *layer* in the stack.

☐ **moveBelow(layer)**—Places the layer below *layer* in the stack.

☐ **moveBy(x,y)**—Alters the position of the layer by the specified values, expressed in pixels.

☐ **moveTo(x,y)**—Alters the position of the layer (within the containing layer) to the specified coordinates, expressed in pixels.

☐ **moveToAbsolute(x,y)**—Alters the position of the layer (within the page) to the specified coordinates, expressed in pixels.

- ☐ `releaseEvents(eventType)`—Specifies that the current window should release events instead of capturing them so that these events can be passed to other objects, perhaps further on in the event hierarchy. New in JavaScript 1.2.

- ☐ `resizeBy(width,height)`—Resizes the layer by the specified values, expressed in pixels.

- ☐ `resizeTo(width,height)`—Resizes the layer to the specified height and size, expressed in pixels.

- ☐ `routeEvent(event)`—Sends or routes an event through the normal event hierarchy.

The `link` Object [C|2|3|I]

The `link` object reflects a hypertext link in the body of a document.

Properties

- ☐ `hash`—A string value containing the anchor name in the URL.

- ☐ `host`—A string value containing the host name and port number from the URL.

- ☐ `hostname`—A string value containing the domain name (or numerical IP address) from the URL.

- ☐ `href`—A string value containing the entire URL.

- ☐ `pathname`—A string value specifying the path portion of the URL.

- ☐ `port`—A string value containing the port number from the URL.

- ☐ `protocol`—A string value containing the protocol from the URL (including the colon, but not the slashes).

- ☐ `search`—A string value containing any information passed to a GET CGI-BIN call (such as any information after the question mark).

- ☐ `target`—A string value containing the name of the window or frame specified in the TARGET attribute.

Event Handlers

- ☐ `onMouseDown`—Specifies JavaScript code to execute when a user presses a mouse button. (JavaScript 1.2 and Netscape Navigator 4.0 only.)

- ☐ `onMouseOut`—Specifies JavaScript code to execute when the user moves the mouse cursor out of an object. (JavaScript 1.2 and Netscape Navigator 4.0 only.)

New Properties with JavaScript 1.2

type	Indicates a MouseOut event.
target	Indicates the object to which the event was sent.

New Properties with JavaScript 1.2

`layer[n]`	Where `[n]` represents X or Y, used (in conjunction with `page[n]` and `screen[n]`) to describe the cursor location when the `MouseOut` event occurred.
`page[n]`	Where `[n]` represents X or Y, used (in conjunction with `layer[n]` and `screen[n]`) to describe the cursor location when the `MouseOut` event occurred.
`screen[n]`	Where `[n]` represents X or Y, used (in conjunction with `layer[n]` and `page[n]`) to describe the cursor location when the `MouseOut` event occurred.

☐ **onMouseUp**—Specifies the JavaScript code to execute when the user releases a mouse button.

☐ **onKeyUp**—Specifies the JavaScript code to execute when the user releases a specific key. (Netscape Navigator 4.0 Only.)

☐ **onKeyPress**—Specifies the JavaScript code to execute when the user holds down a specific key. (Netscape Navigator 4.0 Only.)

☐ **onKeyDown**—Specifies the JavaScript code to execute when the user presses a specific key. (Netscape Navigator 4.0 Only.)

☐ **onDblClick**—Specifies the JavaScript code to execute when the user double-clicks the area. (Not implemented on Macintosh.) (Netscape Navigator 4.0 Only.)

☐ **moveMouse**—Specifies the JavaScript code to execute when the mouse pointer moves over the link. (Not 2|3)

☐ **onClick**—Specifies the JavaScript code to execute when the link is clicked.

☐ **onMouseOver**—Specifies the JavaScript code to execute when the mouse pointer moves over the hypertext link.

New Properties with JavaScript 1.2

`type`	Indicates a `MouseOver` event.
`target`	Indicates the object to which the event was sent.
`layer[n]`	Where `[n]` represents X or Y, used (in conjunction with `page[n]` and `screen[n]`) to describe the cursor location when the `MouseOver` event occurred.
`page[n]`	Where `[n]` represents X or Y, used (in conjunction with `layer[n]` and `screen[n]`) to describe the cursor location when the `MouseOver` event occurred.
`screen[n]`	Where `[n]` represents X or Y, used (in conjunction with `layer[n]` and `page[n]`) to describe the cursor location when the `MouseOver` event occurred.

B

The `location` Object [C | 2 | 3 | I]

The `location` object reflects information about the current URL.

Properties

☐ **hash**—A string value containing the anchor name in the URL.

☐ **host**—A string value containing the host name and port number from the URL.

☐ **hostname**—A string value containing the domain name (or numerical IP address) from the URL.

☐ **href**—A string value containing the entire URL.

☐ **pathname**—A string value specifying the path portion of the URL.

☐ **port**—A string value containing the port number from the URL.

☐ **protocol**—A string value containing the protocol from the URL (including the colon, but not the slashes).

☐ **search**—A string value containing any information passed to a GET CGI-BIN call (such as information after the question mark).

Methods

☐ **reload()**—Reloads the current document. (Not 2|I)

☐ **replace(url)**—Loads *url* over the current entry in the history list, making it impossible to navigate back to the previous URL with the back button. (Not 2|I)

The `Math` Object [C | 2 | 3 | I]

The `Math` object provides properties and methods for advanced mathematical calculations.

Properties

☐ **E**—The value of Euler's constant (roughly 2.718) used as the base for natural logarithms.

☐ **LN10**—The value of the natural logarithm of 10 (roughly 2.302).

☐ **LN2**—The value of the natural logarithm of 2 (roughly 0.693).

☐ **LOG10E**—The value of the base 10 logarithm of e (roughly 0.434).

☐ **x**—The value of the base 2 logarithm of e (roughly 1.442).

☐ **PI**—The value of PI; used to calculate the circumference and area of circles (roughly 3.1415).

☐ **SQRT1_2**—The value of the square root of one-half (roughly 0.707).

☐ **SQRT2**—The value of the square root of two (roughly 1.414).

Methods

☐ **abs(*number*)**—Returns the absolute value of *number*. The absolute value is the value of a number with its sign ignored so abs(4) and abs(-4) both return 4.

☐ **acos(*number*)**—Returns the arccosine of *number* in radians.

☐ **asin(*number*)**—Returns the arcsine of *number* in radians.

☐ **atan(*number*)**—Returns the arctangent of *number* in radians.

☐ **atan2(*number1*,*number2*)**—Returns the angle of the polar coordinate corresponding to the Cartesian coordinate (*number1*,*number2*). (Not I)

☐ **ceil(*number*)**—Returns the next integer greater than *number*—in other words, rounds up to the next integer.

☐ **cos(*number*)**—Returns the cosine of *number*, where *number* represents an angle in radians.

☐ **exp(*number*)**—Returns the value of E to the power of *number*.

☐ **floor(*number*)**—Returns the next integer less than *number*—in other words, rounds down to the nearest integer.

☐ **log(*number*)**—Returns the natural logarithm of *number*.

☐ **max(*number1*,*number2*)**—Returns the greater of *number1* and *number2*.

☐ **min(*number1*,*number2*)**—Returns the smaller of *number1* and *number2*.

☐ **pow(*number1*,*number2*)**—Returns the value of *number1* to the power of *number2*.

☐ **random()**—Returns a random number between 0 and 1 (at press time, this method was available only on UNIX versions of Navigator 2.0).

☐ **round(*number*)**—Returns the closest integer to *number*—in other words, rounds to the closest integer.

☐ **sin(*number*)**—Returns the sine of *number*, where *number* represents an angle in radians.

☐ **sqrt(*number*)**—Returns the square root of *number*.

☐ **tan(*number*)**—Returns the tangent of *number*, where *number* represents an angle in radians.

The mimeType **Object [C|3]**

The mimeType object reflects a MIME type supported by the client browser.

Properties

☐ **type**—A string value reflecting the MIME type.

☐ **description**—A string containing a description of the MIME type.

☐ **enabledPlugin**—A reference to `plugin` object for the plug-in supporting the MIME type.

☐ **suffixes**—A string containing a comma-separated list of file suffixes for the MIME type.

The `navigator` Object [C | 2 | 3 | I]

The `navigator` object reflects information about the version of Navigator being used.

Properties

☐ **appCodeName**—A string value containing the code name of the client (for example, "Mozilla" for Netscape Navigator).

☐ **appName**—A string value containing the name of the client (for example, "Netscape" for Netscape Navigator).

☐ **appVersion**—A string value containing the version information for the client in the form

   `versionNumber (platform; country)`

   For example, Navigator 2.0, beta 6 for Windows 95 (international version), would have an `appVersion` property with the value `"2.0b6 (Win32; I)"`.

☐ **language**—Specifies the translation of Navigator. (A read-only property.) New in JavaScript 1.2.

☐ **mimeTypes**—An array of `mimeType` objects reflecting the MIME types supported by the client browser. (Not 2|I)

☐ **platform**—Specifies the platform for which Navigator was compiled. (For example, Win32, MacPPC, UNIX.) New in JavaScript 1.2.

☐ **plugins**—An array of `plugin` objects reflecting the plug-ins in a document in the order of their appearance in the HTML document. (Not 2|I)

☐ **userAgent**—A string containing the complete value of the user-agent header sent in the HTTP request. This contains all the information in `appCodeName` and `appVersion`:

   `Mozilla/2.0b6 (Win32; I)`

Methods

☐ **javaEnabled()**—Returns a Boolean value indicating whether Java is enabled in the browser. (Not 2|I)

☐ **preference(*preference.Name*, setValue)**—In signed scripts, this method enables the developer to set certain browser preferences. Preferences reachable with this method are

`general.always_load_images`	`true`/`false` value that sets whether images are automatically loaded.
`security.enable_java`	`true`/`false` value that sets whether Java is enabled.
`javascript.enabled`	`true`/`false` value that sets whether JavaScript is enabled.
`browser.enable_style_sheets`	`true`/`false` value that sets whether style sheets are enabled.
`autoupdate.enabled`	`true`/`false` value that sets whether `autoinstall` is enabled.
`network.cookie.cookieBehavior`	`(0,1,2)` Value that sets the manner in which cookies are handled. There are three parameters. `0` accepts all cookies; `1` accepts only those that are forwarded to the originating server; `2` denies all cookies.
`network.cookie.warnAboutCookies`	`true`/`false` value that sets whether the browser will warn on accepting cookies.

The `Option` Object [C|3]

The `Option` object is used to create entries in a select list using the syntax

optionName = new Option(*optionText*, *optionValue*, *defaultSelected*, *selected*)

and then

selectName.options[index] = *optionName*.

Properties

- [ ] `defaultSelected`—A Boolean value specifying whether the option is selected by default.
- [ ] `index`—An integer value specifying the option's index in the select list.
- [ ] `prototype`—Provides a mechanism to add properties to an `Option` object.
- [ ] `selected`—A Boolean value indicating whether the option is currently selected.
- [ ] `text`—A string value reflecting the text displayed for the option.
- [ ] `value`—A string value indicating the value submitted to the server when the form is submitted.

The password **Object [C | 2 | 3 | I]**

The password object reflects a password text field from an HTML form in JavaScript.

Properties

- ☐ **defaultValue**—A string value containing the default value of the password element (such as the value of the VALUE attribute).
- ☐ **enabled**—A Boolean value indicating whether the password field is enabled. (Not 2|3)
- ☐ **form**—A reference to the form object containing the password field. (Not 2|3)
- ☐ **name**—A string value containing the name of the password element.
- ☐ **value**—A string value containing the value of the password element.

Methods

- ☐ **focus()**—Emulates the action of focusing in the password field.
- ☐ **blur()**—Emulates the action of removing focus from the password field.
- ☐ **select()**—Emulates the action of selecting the text in the password field.

Event Handlers

- ☐ **onBlur**—Specifies JavaScript code to execute when the password field loses focus. (Not 2|3)
- ☐ **onFocus**—Specifies JavaScript code to execute when the password field receives focus. (Not 2|3)

The plugin **Object**

The plugin object reflects a plug-in supported by the browser.

Properties

- ☐ **name**—A string value reflecting the name of the plug-in.
- ☐ **filename**—A string value reflecting the filename of the plug-in on the system's disk.
- ☐ **description**—A string value containing the description supplied by the plug-in.

The radio **Object [C | 2 | 3 | I]**

The radio object reflects a set of radio buttons from an HTML form in JavaScript. To access individual radio buttons, use numeric indexes starting at zero. For example, individual buttons in a set of radio buttons named `testRadio` could be referenced by `testRadio[0]`, `testRadio[1]`, and so on.

Properties

- [ ] `checked`—A Boolean value indicating whether a specific button is checked. Can be used to select or deselect a button.
- [ ] `defaultChecked`—A Boolean value indicating whether a specific button was checked by default (that is, it reflects the CHECKED attribute). (Not I)
- [ ] `enabled`—A Boolean value indicating whether the radio button is enabled. (Not 2|3)
- [ ] `form`—A reference to the form object containing the radio button. (Not 2|3)
- [ ] `length`—An integer value indicating the number of radio buttons in the set. (Not I)
- [ ] `name`—A string value containing the name of the set of radio buttons.
- [ ] `value`—A string value containing the value of a specific radio button in a set (that is, it reflects the VALUE attribute).

Methods

- [ ] `click()`—Emulates the action of clicking a radio button.
- [ ] `focus()`—Gives focus to the radio button. (Not 2|3)

Event Handlers

- [ ] `onClick`—Specifies the JavaScript code to execute when a radio button is clicked.
- [ ] `onFocus`—Specifies the JavaScript code to execute when a radio button receives focus. (Not 2|3)

The RegExp Object

The `RegExp` object is relevant to searching for regular expressions. Its properties are set before or after a search is performed. These do not generally exercise control over the search itself, but instead articulate a series of values that can be accessed throughout the search.

Properties

- [ ] `input`—The string against which a regular expression is matched. New in JavaScript 1.2.
- [ ] `multiline [true, false]`—Sets whether the search continues beyond line breaks on multiple lines (`true`) or not (`false`). New in JavaScript 1.2.

- [ ] **lastMatch**—Property that indicates the characters last matched. New in JavaScript 1.2.
- [ ] **lastParen**—Property that indicates the last matched string that appeared in parentheses. New in JavaScript 1.2.
- [ ] **leftContext**—Property that indicates the string just before the most recently matched regular expression. New in JavaScript 1.2.
- [ ] **rightContext**—Property that indicates the remainder of the string, beyond the most recently matched regular expression. New in JavaScript 1.2.
- [ ] **$1,..$9**—Property that indicates the last nine substrings in a match, where those substrings are enclosed in parentheses. New in JavaScript 1.2.

The Regular Expression Object

The Regular Expression object contains the pattern of a regular expression.

Parameters

- [ ] **regexp**—Parameter that specifies the name of the regular expression object. New in JavaScript 1.2.
- [ ] **pattern**—Parameter that specifies the text of the regular expression. New in JavaScript 1.2.

Flags

- [ ] **i**—Option that specifies that during the regular expression search, case is ignored (that is, the search is not case sensitive).
- [ ] **g**—Option that specifies that during the regular expression search, the match (and search) should be global.
- [ ] **gi**—Option that specifies that during the regular expression search, case is ignored and the match (and search) should be global.

Properties

- [ ] **global [true,false]**—A property that sets the g flag value in code, for example, whether the search is global (true) or not (false). New in JavaScript 1.2.
- [ ] **ignoreCase [true,false]**—A property that sets the i flag value in code, for example, whether the search is case sensitive (true) or not (false). New in JavaScript 1.2.

□ **lastIndex**—A property (integer value) that indicates the index position at which to start the next matching procedure (for example, lastIndex == 2). New in JavaScript 1.2.

□ **source**—A property (read-only) that contains the pattern's text. New in JavaScript 1.2.

Methods

□ **compile**—Compiles the regular expression. This method is usually invoked at script startup, when the regular expression is already known and will remain constant. New in JavaScript 1.2.

□ **exec(str)**—Executes a search for a regular expression within the specified string (str). New in JavaScript 1.2. Note: This uses the same properties as the RegExr object.

□ **test(str)**—Executes a search for a regular expression and a specified string (str). New in JavaScript 1.2. Note: This uses the same properties as the RegExr object.

The reset Object [C|2|3||]

The reset object reflects a reset button from an HTML form in JavaScript.

Properties

□ **enabled**—A Boolean value indicating whether the reset button is enabled. (Not 2|3)

□ **form**—A reference to the form object containing the reset button. (Not 2|3)

□ **name**—A string value containing the name of the reset element.

□ **value**—A string value containing the value of the reset element.

Methods

□ **click()**—Emulates the action of clicking the reset button.

□ **focus()**—Specifies the JavaScript code to execute when the reset button receives focus. (Not 2|3)

Event Handlers

□ **onClick**—Specifies the JavaScript code to execute when the reset button is clicked.

□ **onFocus**—Specifies the JavaScript code to execute when the reset button receives focus. (Not 2|3)

The Screen Object (New in JavaScript 1.2)

The Screen object describes (or specifies) the characteristics of the current screen.

Properties

☐ **availHeight**—Property that specifies the height of the screen in pixels. (Minus static display constraints set forth by the operating system.) New in JavaScript 1.2.

☐ **availWidth**—Property that specifies the width of the current screen in pixels. (Minus static display constraints set forth by the operating system.) New in JavaScript 1.2.

☐ **height**—Property that specifies the height of the current screen in pixels. New in JavaScript 1.2.

☐ **width**—Property that specifies the width of the current screen in pixels. New in JavaScript 1.2.

☐ **pixelDepth**—Property that specifies the number of bits (per pixel) in the current screen. New in JavaScript 1.2.

☐ **colorDepth**—Property that specifies the number of possible colors to display in the current screen. New in JavaScript 1.2.

The select Object [C|2|3]

The select object reflects a selection list from an HTML form in JavaScript.

Properties

☐ **length**—An integer value containing the number of options in the selection list.

☐ **name**—A string value containing the name of the selection list.

☐ **options**—An array reflecting each of the options in the selection list in the order they appear. The options property has its own properties:

defaultSelected	A Boolean value indicating whether an option was selected by default (that is, it reflects the SELECTED attribute).
index	An integer value reflecting the index of an option.
length	An integer value reflecting the number of options in the selection list.
name	A string value containing the name of the selection list.
selected	A Boolean value indicating whether the option is selected. Can be used to select or deselect an option.

selectedIndex	An integer value containing the index of the currently selected option.
text	A string value containing the text displayed in the selection list for a particular option.
value	A string value indicating the value for the specified option (that is, reflects the VALUE attribute).

☐ **selectedIndex**—Reflects the index of the currently selected option in the selection list.

Methods

☐ **blur()**—Removes focus from the selection list. (Not 2|3)

☐ **focus()**—Gives focus to the selection list. (Not 2|3)

Event Handlers

☐ **onBlur**—Specifies the JavaScript code to execute when the selection list loses focus.

☐ **onFocus**—Specifies the JavaScript code to execute when focus is given to the selection list.

☐ **onChange**—Specifies the JavaScript code to execute when the selected option in the list changes.

The String Object [C|2|3|I]

The String object provides properties and methods for working with string literals and variables.

Properties

☐ **length**—An integer value containing the length of the string expressed as the number of characters in the string.

☐ **prototype**—Provides a mechanism for adding properties to a String object. (Not 2)

Methods

☐ **anchor(name)**—Returns a string containing the value of the string object surrounded by an A container tag with the NAME attribute set to name.

☐ **big()**—Returns a string containing the value of the string object surrounded by a BIG container tag.

☐ **blink()**—Returns a string containing the value of the string object surrounded by a BLINK container tag.

☐ **bold()**—Returns a string containing the value of the string object surrounded by a B container tag.

☐ **charAt(_index_)**—Returns the character at the location specified by _index_.

☐ **charCodeAt(_index_)**—Returns a number representing an ISO-Latin-1 codeset value at the instant _index_. (Netscape Navigator 4.0 and above only.)

☐ **concat(_string2_)**—Combines two strings and derives a third, new string. (Netscape Navigator 4.0 and above only.)

☐ **fixed()**—Returns a string containing the value of the string object surrounded by a FIXED container tag.

☐ **fontColor(_color_)**—Returns a string containing the value of the string object surrounded by a FONT container tag with the COLOR attribute set to _color_, where _color_ is a color name or an RGB triplet. (Not I)

☐ **fontSize(_size_)**—Returns a string containing the value of the string object surrounded by a FONTSIZE container tag with the size set to _size_. (Not I)

☐ **fromCharCode(_num1_, _num2_, ...)**—Returns a string constructed of ISO-Latin-1 characters. Those characters are specified by their codeset values, which are expressed as _num1_, _num2_, and so on.

☐ **indexOf(_findString_,_startingIndex_)**—Returns the index of the first occurrence of _findString_, starting the search at _startingIndex_, where _startingIndex_ is optional—if it is not provided, the search starts at the start of the string.

☐ **italics()**—Returns a string containing the value of the string object surrounded by an I container tag.

☐ **lastIndexOf(_findString_,_startingIndex_)**—Returns the index of the last occurrence of _findString_. This is done by searching backward from _startingIndex_. _startingIndex_ is optional and is assumed to be the last character in the string if no value is provided.

☐ **link(_href_)**—Returns a string containing the value of the string object surrounded by an A container tag with the HREF attribute set to _href_.

☐ **match(_regular_expression_)**—Matches a regular expression to a string. The parameter _regular_expression_ is the name of the regular expression, expressed either as a variable or a literal.

☐ **replace(_regular_expression_, newSubStr)**—Find and replace _regular_expression_ with newSubStr.

☐ **search(_regular_expression_)**—Find _regular_expression_ and match it to some string.

☐ **slice(*beginSlice*, [*endSlice*])**—Extract a portion of a given string and derive a new string from that excerpt. *beginSlice* and *endSlice* are both zero-based indexes that can be used to grab the first, second, and third character, and so on.

☐ **small()**—Returns a string containing the value of the string object surrounded by a SMALL container tag.

☐ **split(*separator*)**—Returns an array of strings created by splitting the string at every occurrence of *separator*. (Not 2||) split has additional functionality in JavaScript 1.2 and for Navigator 4.0 and above. That new functionality includes the following elements:

Regex and fixed string splitting	One can now split the string string by both regular expression argument and fixed string.
Limit Count	One can now add a limit count to prevent the inclusion of empty elements within the string.
White Space Splitting	The capability to split on white space (including any white space, such as space, tab, newline, and so forth).

☐ **strike()**—Returns a string containing the value of the string object surrounded by a STRIKE container tag.

☐ **sub()**—Returns a string containing the value of the string object surrounded by a SUB container tag.

☐ **substr(*start*, [*length*])**—Used to extract a set number (length) of characters within a string. Use *start* to specify the location at which to begin this extraction process. New in JavaScript 1.2.

☐ **substring(*firstIndex*,*lastIndex*)**—Returns a string equivalent to the substring beginning at *firstIndex* and ending at the character before *lastIndex*. If *firstIndex* is greater than *lastIndex*, the string starts at *lastIndex* and ends at the character before *firstIndex*. Note: In JavaScript 1.2, X and Y are no longer swapped. To obtain this result, you must specify JavaScript 1.2 with the language attribute within the <SCRIPT> tag.

☐ **sup()**—Returns a string containing the value of the string object surrounded by a SUP container tag.

☐ **toLowerCase()**—Returns a string containing the value of the string object with all characters converted to lowercase.

☐ **toUpperCase()**—Returns a string containing the value of the string object with all characters converted to uppercase.

The submit Object [C|2|3|I]

The submit object reflects a submit button from an HTML form in JavaScript.

Properties

- ☐ **enabled**—A Boolean value indicating whether the submit button is enabled. (Not 2|3)
- ☐ **form**—A reference to the form object containing the submit button. (Not 2|3)
- ☐ **name**—A string value containing the name of the submit button element.
- ☐ **type**—A string value reflecting the TYPE attribute of the INPUT tag. (Not 2|I)
- ☐ **value**—A string value containing the value of the submit button element.

Methods

- ☐ **click()**—Emulates the action of clicking the submit button.
- ☐ **focus()**—Gives focus to the submit button. (Not 2|3)

Event Handlers

- ☐ **onClick**—Specifies the JavaScript code to execute when the submit button is clicked.
- ☐ **onFocus**—Specifies the JavaScript code to execute when the submit button receives focus. (Not 2|3)

The text Object [C|2|3|I]

The text object reflects a text field from an HTML form in JavaScript.

Properties

- ☐ **defaultValue**—A string value containing the default value of the text element (that is, the value of the VALUE attribute).
- ☐ **enabled**—A Boolean value indicating whether the text field is enabled. (Not 2|3)
- ☐ **form**—A reference to the form object containing the text field. (Not 2|3)
- ☐ **name**—A string value containing the name of the text element.
- ☐ **type**—A string value reflecting the TYPE attribute of the INPUT tag. (Not 2|I)
- ☐ **value**—A string value containing the value of the text element.

Methods

- [ ] `focus()`—Emulates the action of focusing in the text field.
- [ ] `blur()`—Emulates the action of removing focus from the text field.
- [ ] `select()`—Emulates the action of selecting the text in the text field.

Event Handlers

- [ ] `onBlur`—Specifies the JavaScript code to execute when focus is removed from the field.
- [ ] `onChange`—Specifies the JavaScript code to execute when the content of the field is changed.
- [ ] `onFocus`—Specifies the JavaScript code to execute when focus is given to the field.
- [ ] `onSelect`—Specifies the JavaScript code to execute when the user selects some or all of the text in the field.

The `textarea` Object [C|2|3|I]

The `textarea` object reflects a multiline text field from an HTML form in JavaScript.

Properties

- [ ] `defaultValue`—A string value containing the default value of the textarea element (that is, the value of the VALUE attribute).
- [ ] `enabled`—A Boolean value indicating whether the textarea field is enabled. (Not 2|3)
- [ ] `form`—A reference to the `form` object containing the textarea field. (Not 2|3)
- [ ] `name`—A string value containing the name of the textarea element.
- [ ] `type` A string value reflecting the type of the textarea object. (Not 2|I)
- [ ] `value`—A string value containing the value of the textarea element.

Methods

- [ ] `focus()`—Emulates the action of focusing in the textarea field.
- [ ] `blur()`—Emulates the action of removing focus from the textarea field.
- [ ] `select()`—Emulates the action of selecting the text in the textarea field.

Event Handlers

- ☐ **onKeyUp**—Specifies the JavaScript code to execute when the user releases a specific key. (Netscape Navigator 4.0 Only.)

- ☐ **onKeyPress**—Specifies the JavaScript code to execute when the user holds down a specific key. (Netscape Navigator 4.0 Only.)

- ☐ **onKeyDown**—Specifies the JavaScript code to execute when the user presses a specific key. (Netscape Navigator 4.0 Only.)

- ☐ **onBlur**—Specifies the JavaScript code to execute when focus is removed from the field.

- ☐ **onChange**—Specifies the JavaScript code to execute when the content of the field is changed.

- ☐ **onFocus**—Specifies the JavaScript code to execute when focus is given to the field.

- ☐ **onSelect**—Specifies the JavaScript code to execute when the user selects some or all of the text in the field.

The window Object [C|2|3|I]

The window object is the top-level object for each window or frame and is the parent object for the document, location, and history objects.

Properties

- ☐ **defaultStatus**—A string value containing the default value displayed in the status bar.

- ☐ **frames**—An array of objects for each frame in a window. Frames appear in the array in the order in which they appear in the HTML source code.

- ☐ **innerHeight()**—Specifies the vertical size of the content area (in pixels). New in JavaScript 1.2.

- ☐ **innerWidth()**—Specifies the horizontal size of the content area (in pixels). New in JavaScript 1.2.

- ☐ **length**—An integer value indicating the number of frames in a parent window. (Not I)

- ☐ **name**—A string value containing the name of the window or frame.

- ☐ **opener**—A reference to the window object containing the open() method used to open the current window. (Not 2|I)

- ☐ **pageXOffset**—Specifies the current X position of the viewable window area (expressed in pixels). New in JavaScript 1.2.

- [ ] **pageYOffset**—Specifies the current Y position of the viewable window area (expressed in pixels). New in JavaScript 1.2.
- [ ] **parent**—A string indicating the name of the window containing the frameset.
- [ ] **personalbar [visible=true,false]**—Represents the Directories bar in Netscape Navigator and whether it is visible. New in JavaScript 1.2.
- [ ] **scrollbars [visible=true,false]**—Represents the scrollbars of the instant window and whether they are visible. New in JavaScript 1.2.
- [ ] **self**—An alternative for the name of the current window.
- [ ] **status**—Used to display a message in the status bar—this is done by assigning values to this property.
- [ ] **statusbar=[true,false,1,0]**—Specifies whether the status bar of the target window is visible.
- [ ] **toolbar=[true,false,1,0]**—Specifies whether the toolbar of the target window is visible.
- [ ] **top**—An alternative for the name of the top-most window.
- [ ] **window**—An alternative for the name of the current window.

Methods

- [ ] **alert(*message*)**—Displays *message* in a dialog box.
- [ ] **back()**—Sends the user back to the previous URL stored in the history list. (Simulates a click on the Back button in Navigator.) New in JavaScript 1.2.
- [ ] **blur()**—Removes focus from the window. On many systems, this sends the window to the background. (Not 2|I)
- [ ] **captureEvents()**—Used in a window with frames (in conjunction with enableExternalCapture), this specifies that the window will capture all specified events.
- [ ] **clearInterval(*intervalID*)**—Cancels time outs that are created with the setInterval method. New in JavaScript 1.2.
- [ ] **close()**—Closes the window. (Not I)
- [ ] **confirm(*message*)**—Displays *message* in a dialog box with OK and Cancel buttons. Returns true or false based on the button clicked by the user.
- [ ] **disableExternalCapture()**—Prevents the instant window with frames from capturing events occurring in pages loaded from a different location. New in JavaScript 1.2.
- [ ] **enableExternalCapture()**—Enables the instant window (with frames) to capture events occurring in pages loaded from a different location. New in JavaScript 1.2.

B

☐ **find([string], [true, false], [true, false])**—Finds string within the target window. There are two true/false parameters: the first specifies the Boolean state of case sensitivity in the search; the second specifies whether the search is performed backward. New in JavaScript 1.2.

☐ **focus()**—Gives focus to the window. On many systems, this brings the window to the front. (Not 2|I)

☐ **forward()**—Sends the user to the next URL in the history list. (Simulates a user clicking the Forward button in Navigator.) New in JavaScript 1.2.

☐ **home()**—Sends the user to the user's Home Page URL. (Example: In a default configuration of Netscape Navigator, this will send the user to http://home.netscape.com.) New in JavaScript 1.2.

☐ **moveBy(horizontal, vertical)**—Moves the window according to the specified horizontal and vertical values. New in JavaScript 1.2.

☐ **moveTo(x, y)**—Moves the top-left corner of the window to the specified location, where *x* and *y* are screen coordinates. New in JavaScript 1.2.

☐ **navigator(url)**—Loads url in the window. (Not 2|3)

☐ **open(url,name,features)**—Opens url in a window named name. If name doesn't exist, a new window is created with that name. features is an optional string argument containing a list of features for the new window. The feature list contains any of the following name-value pairs separated by commas and without additional spaces. (Not I)

toolbar=[yes,no,1,0]	Indicates whether the window should have a toolbar.
location=[yes,no,1,0]	Indicates whether the window should have a location field.
directories=[yes,no,1,0]	Indicates whether the window should have directory buttons.
status=[yes,no,1,0]	Indicates whether the window should have a status bar.
menubar=[yes,no,1,0]	Indicates whether the window should have menus.
scrollbars=[yes,no,1,0]	Indicates whether the window should have scrollbars.
resizable=[yes,no,1,0]	Indicates whether the window should be resizable.
width=pixels	Indicates the width of the window in pixels.

`alwaysLowered=[yes,no,1,2]`	Indicates (if true) that the window should remain below all other windows. (This feature has varying results on varying window systems.) New in JavaScript 1.2. Note: The script must be signed to use this feature.
`alwaysRaised=[yes,no,1,2]`	Indicates (if true) that the window should always remain the top-level window. (This feature has varying results on varying window systems.) New in JavaScript 1.2. Note: The script must be signed to use this feature.
`dependent[yes,no,1,2]`	Indicates that the current child window will die (or close) when the parent window does. New in JavaScript 1.2.
`hotkeys=[yes,no,1,2]`	Indicates (if true) that most hotkeys are disabled within the instant window. New in JavaScript 1.2.
`innerWidth=pixels`	Indicates the width (in pixels) of the instant window's content area. New in JavaScript 1.2.
`innerHeight=pixels`	Indicates the height (in pixels) of the instant window's content area. New in JavaScript 1.2.
`outerWidth=pixels`	Indicates the instant window's horizontal outside width boundary. New in JavaScript 1.2.
`outerHeight=pixels`	Indicates the instant window's horizontal outside height boundary. New in JavaScript 1.2.
`screenX=pixels`	Indicates the distance that the new window is placed from the left side of the screen (horizontally). New in JavaScript 1.2.
`screenY=pixels`	Indicates the distance that the new window is placed from the top of the screen (vertically). New in JavaScript 1.2.

B

`z-lock=[yes,no,1,2]`   Indicates that the instant window does not move through the cycling of the Z-order; that is, it does not rise above other windows, even if activated. New in JavaScript 1.2. Note: The script must be signed for this feature to work.

`height=pixels`   Indicates the height of the window in pixels.

- `print()`—Prints the contents of a frame or window. This is the equivalent of the user pressing the Print button in Netscape Navigator. New in JavaScript 1.2.

- `prompt(message,response)`—Displays *message* in a dialog box with a text-entry field with the default value of *response*. The user's response in the text-entry field is returned as a string.

- `releaseEvents(eventType)`—Specifies that the current window should release events instead of capturing them so that these events can be passed to other objects, perhaps further on in the event hierarchy. New in JavaScript 1.2.

- `resizeBy(horizontal, vertical)`—Resizes the window, moving from the bottom-right corner. New in JavaScript 1.2.

- `resizeTo(outerWidth, outerHeight)`—Resizes the window utilizing `outerWidth` and `outerHeight` properties. New in JavaScript 1.2.

- `routeEvent(event)`—Sends or routes an event through the normal event hierarchy. New in JavaScript 1.2.

- `scrollBy(horizontal, vertical)`—Scrolls the viewing area of the current window by the specified amount. New in JavaScript 1.2.

- `scrollTo(x, y)`—Scrolls the current window to the specified position, calculated in X and Y coordinates, starting at the top-left corner of the window. New in JavaScript 1.2.

- `setInterval(function, msec, [args])`—Repeatedly calls a function after the period specified by the `msec` parameter. New in JavaScript 1.2.

- `setInterval(expression, msec)`—Evaluates *expression* after the period specified by the `msec` parameter. New in JavaScript 1.2.

- `setTimeout(expression,time)`—Evaluates *expression* after *time*, where *time* is a value in milliseconds. The time out can be named with the structure

  `name = setTimeOut(expression,time)`

- `scrollTo(x,y)`—Scrolls the window to the coordinate *x,y*. (Not 2II)

- `stop()`—Stops the current download. This is the equivalent of the user pressing the Stop button in Netscape Navigator.

- `clearTimeout(name)`—Cancels the time out with the name *name*.

Event Handlers

- [ ] **onDragDrop**—Specifies the JavaScript code to execute when the user drops an object onto the window. (Netscape Navigator 4.0 and Above Only.)

- [ ] **onBlur**—Specifies the JavaScript code to execute when focus is removed from a window. (Not 2|I)

- [ ] **onError**—Specifies the JavaScript code to execute when a JavaScript error occurs while loading a document. This can be used to intercept JavaScript errors. Setting this event handler to null effectively prevents JavaScript errors from being displayed to the user. (Not 2|I)

- [ ] **onFocus**—Specifies the JavaScript code to execute when the window receives focus. (Not 2|I)

- [ ] **onLoad**—Specifies the JavaScript code to execute when the window or frame finishes loading.

- [ ] **onMove**—Specifies the JavaScript code to execute when the user moves a window. (Netscape Navigator 4.0 Only.)

- [ ] **onResize**—Specifies the JavaScript code to execute when a user resizes the window.

- [ ] **onUnload**—Specifies the JavaScript code to execute when the document in the window or frame is exited.

Independent Functions, Operators, Variables, and Literals

Independent Functions

- [ ] **cooapc(*oharaotor*)** Returns a string containing the ASCII encoding of *character* in the form %xx, where xx is the numeric encoding of the character. (C|2|3|I)

- [ ] **eval(*expression*)**—Returns the result of evaluating *expression*, where *expression* is an arithmetic expression. (C|2|3|I)

- [ ] **isNaN(*value*)**—Evaluates *value* to see if it is NaN. Returns a Boolean value. (C|2|3|I) (On UNIX platforms, not 2.)

- [ ] **parseFloat(*string*)**—Converts *string* to a floating-point number and returns the value. It continues to convert until it hits a non-numeric character and then returns the result. If the first character cannot be converted to a number, the function returns NaN (zero on Windows platforms). (C|2|3|I)

- [ ] **parseInt(*string*,*base*)**—Converts *string* to an integer of base *base* and returns the value. It continues to convert until it hits a non-numeric character and then returns the result. If the first character cannot be converted to a number, the function returns NaN (zero on Windows platforms). (C|2|3|I)

☐ **taint(*propertyName*)**—Adds tainting to *propertyName*. (C|3)

☐ **toString()**—This is a method of all objects. It returns the object as a string or returns "[object *type*]" if no string representation exists for the object. (C|2|3) Note: In JavaScript 1.2, this will convert objects and strings to literals.

☐ **unescape(*string*)**—Returns a character based on the ASCII encoding contained in *string*. The ASCII encoding should take the form "%integer" or "hexadecimalValue". (C|2|3|I)

☐ **untaint(*propertyName*)**—Removes tainting from *propertyName*. (C|3)

Statements

☐ **break**—Terminates a while or for loop and passes program control to the first statement following the loop. (2|3|4) Note: In JavaScript 1.2, break has the added functionality of being able to break out of labeled statements.

☐ **comment**—Used to add a comment within the script. This comment is ignored by Navigator. Comments in JavaScript work similar to those in C. These are enclosed in a /* (start), */ (end) structure. (2|3|4)

☐ **continue**—Terminates execution of statements within a while or for loop and continues iteration of the loop. (2|3|4) Note: In JavaScript 1.2, continue has added functionality that enables you to continue within labeled statements.

☐ **do while** —Sets up a loop that continues to execute statements and code until the condition evaluates to false. New in JavaScript 1.2.

☐ **export**—Used in conjunction with the import statement. In secure, signed scripts, this enables the developer to export all properties, functions, and variables to another script. New in JavaScript 1.2.

☐ **for([*initial-expression*]; [*condition*]; [*incremental-expression*];))**— Specifies the opening of a for loop. The arguments are these: initialize a variable (*initial-expression*), create a condition to test for (*condition*), and specify an incrementation scheme (*incremental-expression*). (2|3|4)

☐ **for..in**—Imposes a variable to all properties of an object and executes a block of code for each. (2|3|4)

☐ **function [*name*]()**—Declares a function so that it can be referred to or reached by event handlers (or other processes). (2|3|4)

☐ **if..else**—A structure used to test whether a certain condition is true. If..else blocks can contain nested statements and functions (and call these) if a condition is either true or false. (2|3|4)

☐ **import**—Used in conjunction with the export statement. In secure, signed scripts, this enables the developer to import all properties, functions, and variables from another script. New in JavaScript 1.2.

- ☐ **label (labeled statements)**—Statement that creates a label or pointer to code elsewhere in the script. By calling this label, you redirect the script to the labeled statement.

- ☐ **new**—Creates an instance of a user-defined object. (new can also be used to create an instance of built-in objects, inherent to JavaScript, such as new Date.) (2|3|4)

- ☐ **return [value]**—Specifies a value to be returned by a given function. For example, return x returns the variable value associated with x. (2|3|4)

- ☐ **switch**—Evaluates an expression and attempts to match it to a case pattern or label. If the expression matches the case, trailing statements associated with that label are executed. New in JavaScript 1.2. (Operates in a similar fashion to the switch statement in C Shell syntax.)

- ☐ **this**—A statement used to refer to a specific object (2|3|4). For example,

  ```
  onClick = 'javascript:my_function(this.form)'
  ```

- ☐ **var [name]**—Declares a variable by name. (2|3|4)

- ☐ **while**—Statement that begins a while loop. while loops specify that as long as (while) a condition is true, some code should be executed. (2|3|4)

- ☐ **with**—Statement that sets the value for the default object; a method that is similar to creating a global variable with a function. (2|3|4)

Operators

- ☐ **Assignment Operators**—(See Table B.1.) Assignment operators in JavaScript. (C|2|3|1)

Table B.1. Assignment operators.

Operator	Description
=	Assigns the value of the right operand to the left operand
+=	Adds the left and right operands and assigns the result to the left operand
-=	Subtracts the right operand from the left operand and assigns the result to the left operand
*=	Multiplies the two operands and assigns the result to the left operand
/=	Divides the left operand by the right operand and assigns the value to the left operand
%=	Divides the left operand by the right operand and assigns the remainder to the left operand

☐ **Arithmetic Operators**—(See Table B.2.) Arithmetic operators in JavaScript. (C|2|3|I)

Table B.2. Arithmetic operators.

Operator	Description
+	Adds the left and right operands
-	Subtracts the right operand from the left operand
*	Multiplies the two operands
/	Divides the left operand by the right operand
%	Divides the left operand by the right operand and evaluates to the remainder
++	Increments the operand by one (can be used before or after the operand)
- -	Decreases the operand by one (can be used before or after the operand)
-	Changes the sign of the operand

☐ **Bitwise Operators**—Bitwise operators deal with their operands as binary numbers but return JavaScript numerical value (see Table B.3). (C|2|3|I)

Table B.3. Bitwise operators in JavaScript.

Operator	Description
AND (or &)	Converts operands to integers with 32 bits, pairs the corresponding bits, and returns one for each pair of ones. Returns zero for any other combination.
OR (or ¦)	Converts operands to integers with 32 bits, pairs the corresponding bits, and returns one for each pair where one of the two bits is one. Returns zero if both bits are zero.
XOR (or ^)	Converts operands to integer with 32 bits, pairs the corresponding bits, and returns one for each pair where only one bit is one. Returns zero for any other combination.
<<	Converts the left operand to an integer with 32 bits and shifts bits to the left the number of bits indicated by the right operand. Bits shifted off to the left are discarded and zeros are shifted in from the right.
>>>	Converts the left operand to an integer with 32 bits and shifts bits to the right the number of bits indicated by the right operand. Bits shifted off to the right are discarded and zeros are shifted in from the left.

Operator	Description
>>	Converts the left operand to an integer with 32 bits and shifts bits to the right the number of bits indicated by the right operand. Bits shifted off to the right are discarded and copies of the leftmost bit are shifted in from the left.

☐ **Logical Operators**—(See Table B.4.) Logical operators in JavaScript. (C|2|3|I)

Table B.4. Logical operators.

Operator	Description
&&	Logical AND. Returns `true` when both operands are true, otherwise it returns `false`.
||	Logical OR. Returns `true` if either operand is true. It returns `false` only when both operands are false.
!	Logical NOT. Returns `true` if the operand is false and `false` if the operand is true. This is a unary operator, and it precedes the operand.

☐ **Comparison Operators**—(See Table B.5.) Comparison operators in JavaScript. [C|2|3|I]

Table B.5. Logical (comparison) operators.

Operator	Description
==	Returns `true` if the operands are equal.
!=	Returns `true` if the operands are not equal.
>	Returns `true` if the left operand is greater than the right operand.
<	Returns `true` if the left operand is less than the right operand.
>=	Returns `true` if the left operand is greater than or equal to the right operand.
<=	Returns `true` if the left operand is less than or equal to the right operand.

☐ **Conditional Operators**—Conditional expressions take one form:

```
(condition) ? val1 : val2
```

If `condition` is true, the expression evaluates to `val1`, otherwise it evaluates to `val2`. (C|2|3|I)

☐ **String Operators**—The concatenation operator (+) is one of two string operators. It evaluates to a string combining the left and right operands. The concatenation assignment operator (+=) is also available. (C|2|3|I)

☐ **The typeof Operator**—The typeof operator returns the type of its single operand. Possible types are object, string, number, boolean, function, and undefined. (C|3|I)

☐ **The void Operator**—The void operator takes an expression as an operand but returns no value. (C|3)

☐ **Operator Precedence**—JavaScript applies the rules of operator precedence as follows (from lowest to highest precedence):

    Comma (,)
    Assignment operators (=, +=, -=, *=, /=, %=)
    Conditional (? :)
    Logical OR (¦¦)
    Logical AND (&&)
    Bitwise OR (¦)
    Bitwise XOR (^)
    Bitwise AND (&)
    Equality (==, !=)
    Relational (<, <=, >, >=)
    Shift (<<, >>, >>>)
    Addition/subtraction (+, -)
    Multiply/divide/modulus (*, /, %)
    Negation/increment (!, -, ++, --)
    Call, member ((), [])

APPENDIX

C

VBScript Language Reference

This appendix summarizes the statements, functions, and operators used in the Visual Basic Scripting Edition.

Category/ Keyword	Type	Usage
Arithmetic		
Atn	Function	Returns the arctangent of a number Atn(*number*)
Cos	Function	Returns the cosine of an angle Cos(*number*)
Exp	Function	Returns a number raised to a power Exp(*number*)
Log	Function	Returns the logarithm of a number Log(*number*)
Randomize	Statement	Primes the internal random number generator Randomize
Rnd	Function	Returns a random number Rnd
Sin	Function	Returns the sine of an angle Sin(*number*)
Sqr	Function	Returns the square root of a number Sqr(*number*)
Tan	Function	Returns the tangent of an angle Tan(*number*)
Array Handling		
Dim	Statement	Declares an array Dim *arrayname([subscripts])*
Erase	Statement	Clears the contents of an array Erase *arrayname*
IsArray	Function	Returns True if *var* is an array, and False if not IsArray(*var*)
LBound	Function	In VBScript, always returns 0 Lbound(*arrayname*)

Category/ Keyword	Type	Usage
Preserve	Statement	Copies the contents of a dynamic array to a resized dynamic array
		`Redim Preserve arrayname(subscripts)`
ReDim	Statement	Declares a dynamic array or redimensions a dynamic array (see Preserve)
		`ReDim arrayname()`
		or
		`ReDim arrayname([subscripts])`
UBound	Statement	Returns the largest subscript of an array
		`Ubound(arrayname)`

Assignment

-	Operator	Assigns a value to a variable or property
		`variable = value`
Set	Statement	Assigns an object reference to a variable
		`Set variable - object`

Comment

Rem	Statement	Declares the following line as a comment to be ignored by the language engine
		`Rem comment_text`

Constants/Literals

Empty	Literal	Declares a special uninitialized variable value
		`variable = Empty`
False	Constant	A Boolean value representing 0
		`variable = False`
Nothing	Literal	Used to disassociate an object reference from a variable; used in conjunction with Set
		`Set variable = Nothing`

C

Category/ Keyword	Type	Usage
Null	Literal	Represents no valid data
		`variable = Null`
True	Constant	Boolean value representing -1
		`variable = True`

Conversions

Keyword	Type	Usage
Abs	Function	Returns the unsigned (absolute) value of a number
		`Abs(number)`
Asc	Function	Returns the ANSI/ASCII code of a character
		`Asc(string)`
CBool	Function	Returns a Boolean subtype Variant value from any valid expression
		`CBool(expression)`
CByte	Function	Returns a Byte subtype Variant value from any valid expression
		`CByte(expression)`
CDate	Function	Returns a Date subtype Variant value from any valid date expression
		`CDate(expression)`
CDbl	Function	Returns a Double Precision subtype Variant value from any valid numeric expression
		`CDbl(expression)`
Chr	Function	Returns the character corresponding to the ANSI or ASCII code
		`Chr(number)`
CInt	Function	Returns an Integer subtype Variant value from any valid numeric expression
		`CInt(expression)`
CLng	Function	Returns a Long Integer subtype Variant value from any valid numeric expression
		`CLng(expression)`

Category/ Keyword	Type	Usage
CSng	Function	Returns a Single Precision subtype Variant value from any valid numeric expression
		CSng(*expression*)
CStr	Function	Returns a String subtype Variant value from any valid expression
		CStr(*expression*)
DateSerial	Function	Returns a date subtype Variant from valid year, month, and day values
		DateSerial(*year*,*month*,*day*)
DateValue	Function	Returns a Date subtype Variant value from any valid date expression
		DateValue(*expression*)
Hex	Function	Returns a string subtype Variant representing the hexadecimal value of a number
		Hex(*number*)
Int	Function	Returns an Integer subtype Variant rounded down from the number supplied
		Int(*number*)
Fix	Function	Returns an Integer subtype Variant rounded up from the number supplied
		Fix(*number*)
Oct	Function	Returns a string subtype Variant representing the octal value of a number
		Oct(*number*)
Sgn	Function	Returns an integer subtype Variant representing the sign of a number
		Sgn(*number*)
		values > 0 return 1
		values = 0 return 0
		values < 0 return -1

C

Category/Keyword	Type	Usage
TimeSerial	Function	Returns a Date subtype Variant from valid hour, minute, and second values
		`TimeSerial(hour,minute,second)`
TimeValue	Function	Returns a Date subtype Variant value from any valid time expression
		`TimeValue(expression)`

Dates and Times

Category/Keyword	Type	Usage
Date	Function	Returns the current system date
		`Date()`
DateSerial	Function	Returns a Date subtype Variant from valid year, month, and day values
		`DateSerial(year,month,day)`
DateValue	Function	Returns a Date subtype Variant value from any valid date expression
		`DateValue(expression)`
Day	Function	Returns an Integer subtype Variant representing the day (1-31) from a valid date expression
		`Day(dateexpression)`
Hour	Function	Returns an Integer subtype Variant representing the hour (0-23) from a valid time expression
		`Hour(timeexpression)`
Minute	Function	Returns an Integer subtype Variant representing the minute (0-60) from a valid time expression
		`Minute(timeexpression)`
Month	Function	Returns an Integer subtype Variant representing the month (1-12) from a valid date expression
		`Month(dateexpression)`
Now	Function	Returns the current date and time of the system
		`Now()`
Second	Function	Returns an Integer subtype Variant representing the second (0-60) from a valid time expression
		`Second(timeexpression)`

Category/ Keyword	Type	Usage
Time	Function	Returns the current system time
		`Time()`
TimeSerial	Function	Returns a Date subtype `Variant` from valid hour, minute, and second values
		`TimeSerial(hour,minute,second)`
TimeValue	Function	Returns a Date subtype `Variant` value from any valid time expression
		`TimeValue(expression)`
Weekday	Function	Returns an Integer subtype `Variant` between 1 and 7 representing the day of the week, starting at Sunday, from a date expression
		`Weekday(dateexpression)`
Year	Function	Returns an Integer subtype `Variant` representing the year from a valid date expression
		`Year(dateexpression)`

Declarations

Dim	Statement	Declares a variable
		`Dim variable`
End	Statement	Declares the end of a `Sub` procedure or function
		`End Sub`
		`End Function`
Exit	Statement	Use with `Do`, `For`, `Function`, or `Sub` to prematurely exit the routine
		`Exit Do/For/Function/Sub`
Function	Statement	Declares a function and the argument list passed into the function, and declares the end of a function; also used with `Exit` to prematurely end a function
		`Function functionname(argumentlist)`
		`Exit Function`
		`End Function`
		`Public variable`

C

Category/ Keyword	Type	Usage

Sub	Statement	Declares a custom procedure or event handler and the argument list, if any, and declares the end of a custom procedure or event handler; also used with Exit to prematurely end a custom procedure or event handler
		
		`Sub subroutinename([argumentlist])`
		
		`Exit Sub`
		
		`End Sub`

Error Handling

Category/Keyword	Type	Usage
Clear	Method	A method of the Err object to reset the Err.Number property to 0 `Err.Clear`
Description	Property	A property of the Err object that contains a description of the last error as specified in the Err.Number property `Err.Description`
Err	Object	An object containing information about the last error `Err.property¦method`
On Error	Statement	Used in conjunction with Resume Next to continue execution with the line directly following the line in which the error occurred `On Error Resume Next`
Raise	Method	A method of the Err object used to simulate the occurrence of an error specified by number `Err.Raise(errornumber)`
Number	Property	A property of the Err object that contains the error code for the last error, or 0 if no error has occurred `Err.Number`
Source	Property	Returns the name of the object or application that raised the error `Err.Source`

Category/ Keyword	Type	Usage
Input/Output		
InputBox	Function	Displays a dialog box to allow user input
		`InputBox(caption[,title][,value][, x][,y])`
MsgBox	Function	Displays a dialog box
		`MsgBox(prompt[, definition][, title])`
Operators		
+	Operator	Addition of two numerical expressions
		`result = expr1 + expr2`
AND	Operator	Logical conjunction operator
		`If expression AND expression Then`
/	Operator	Division operator
		`result = expression / expression`
=	Operator	Equality operator
		`If expression = expression Then`
Eqv	Operator	Logical equivalence operator
		`If expression Eqv expression Then`
^	Operator	Exponentiation operator
		`result = expression ^ expression`
>	Operator	Greater-than comparison
		`If expression > expression Then`
>=	Operator	Greater-than or equal-to comparison
		`If expression >= expression Then`
Imp	Operator	Logical implication
		`If expression Imp expression Then`
<>	Operator	Inequality comparison
		`If expression <> expression Then`
\	Operator	Integer division operator
		`result = expression \ expression`

C

Category/ Keyword	Type	Usage
<	Operator	Less-than comparison `If expression < expression Then`
<=	Operator	Less-than or equal-to comparison `If expression <= expression Then`
Mod	Operator	Modulus arithmetic; returns only the remainder of a division of two numbers `result = expression mod expression`
*	Operator	Multiplication `result = expression * expression`
-	Operator	Subtraction `result = expression - expression`
Or	Operator	Logical disjunction `If expression Or expression Then`
&	Operator	Concatenation of two string values `result = string & string`
Xor	Operator	Logical exclusion `If expression Xor expression Then`

Options

Option Explicit	Statement	Forces a compile-time error if an undeclared variable is found `Option Explicit`

Program Flow

Call	Statement	Passes execution to a subroutine or event handler; also can be used to replicate the actions of the user
		`Call myroutine()`
		`Call cmdbutton_OnClick()`

Category/ Keyword	Type	Usage

Do...Loop	Statement	Repeats code while a condition is met or a until a condition is met
		
		`Do While condition`
		`...`
		`Loop`
		
		or
		
		`Do Until condition`
		`...`
		`Loop`
		
		or
		
		`Do`
		`...`
		`Loop While condition`
		
		or
		
		`Do`
		`...`
		`Loop Until condition`

For...Next	Statement	Repeats a block of code until the counter reaches a given number
		
		`For counter = lower to upper [step]`
		`...`
		`Next`

If...Then...Else	Statement	Conditional execution of code
		
		`If condition Then`
		`  ... (if condition met)`
		`Else`
		`  ... (if condition not met)`
		`End If`

Select Case	Statement	Selective execution of code, where *testexpression* must match *expression*
		
		`Select Case testexpression`
		`Case expression`
		`...`
		`Case expression`
		`...`
		`Case Else`
		`End Select`

Category/ Keyword	Type	Usage

While...Wend	Statement	Execution of a code block while a condition is met
		`While expression`
		`...`
		`Wend`

Strings

InStr	Function	Returns the starting point of one string within another string, or `0` if not found `result = InStr(start,searched,sought)`
LCase	Function	Converts a string to lowercase `result = LCase(string)`
Left	Function	Returns the *n* leftmost characters of a string `result = Left(string, length)`
Len	Function	Returns the length of a string `result = Len(string)`
LTrim	Function	Removes all leading spaces `result = LTrim(string)`
Mid	Function	Returns a string of length *L*, starting at *S* within `string` `result = Mid(string, S, L)`
Right	Function	Returns the rightmost *n* characters `result = Right(string, n)`
RTrim	Function	Removes all trailing spaces from a string `result = RTrim(string)`
Space	Function	Returns a string consisting of *n* spaces `result = Space(n)`

StrComp	Function	Returns an `integer` subtype `Variant` representing the result of a comparison of two strings
		`result = StrComp(string1, string2)`
		`string1 < string2 returns -1`
		`string1 < string2 returns 0`
		`string1 < string2 returns 1`

Category/ Keyword	Type	Usage
String	Function	Returns a string consisting of character C, of length L
		`result = String(L, C)`
Trim	Function	Removes both leading and trailing spaces
		`result = Trim(string)`
UCase	Function	Returns a string as uppercase alphabetical characters
		`result = UCase(string)`

Variants

IsArray	Function	Returns True (-1) if *expression* is an array, and False (0) if not
		`result = IsArray(expression)`
IsDate	Function	Returns True (-1) if *expression* is a valid date and False (0) if not
		`result = IsDate(expression)`
IsEmpty	Function	Returns True (-1) if *expression* equates to an Empty subtype and False (0) if not
		`result = IsEmpty(expression)`
IsNull	Function	Returns True (-1) if *expression* equates to a Null subtype and False (0) if not
		`result = IsNull(expression)`
IsNumeric	Function	Returns True (-1) if *expression* is a valid numeric expression and False (0) if not
		`result = IsNumeric(expression)`
VarType	Function	Returns an integer representing the sub data type of a Variant
		`result = VarType(expression)`

APPENDIX

D

CSS1 Quick Reference

This appendix provides an overview of the attributes with which you can control the appearance of your HTML documents through style sheets. The World Wide Web Consortium (W3C) set the current standard for style sheets as Cascading Style Sheets 1 (CSS1). W3C's complete recommendation for CSS is located at the W3C Web site at http://www.w3.org/pub/WWW/TR/REC-CSS1.

Basic Syntax

All styles within a style sheet definition follow the same basic syntax. You'll notice that there are a lot of opportunities to add other attributes or members of a group:

```
SELECTOR[.class] [,SELECTOR2[.class2]] ...
{ attribute1: value1  [;
  attribute2: value2] [;
  ... ]                [;
  attributen: valuen] }
```

The SELECTOR is how the style is referenced within the rest of the HTML page. It uses one of the existing HTML tags, such as <CODE> or <P>, along with an optional class to create additional substyles. A class is a subset of a selector, allowing the same element to have a variety of styles. For example, you could color code block quotes to identify sources or speakers.

In addition to the standard HTML tags, you can use two other values for a selector: first-line and first-letter. The first-line value sets the style for the first line of text in a document or several passages within a document, such as paragraph or block quote. The first-letter value creates drop caps and other special effects on the first letter in a document or passage.

Groups of selectors and their classes are separated by commas. Any member of the group receives the same style as any other member in the group. For example, if you wanted all headings to be displayed in red, you could list H1 through H6 with the attributes to set the color to red. All other tag attributes, such as size, would remain unaffected.

Another option is contextual selectors, which tell the browser what to do with a certain tag when found nested within the parent tag.

```
OUTER_SELECTOR INNER_SELECTOR {attribute:value}
```

This means that when the INNER_SELECTOR is used within the OUTER_SELECTOR, the style is used. Otherwise, other occurrences of INNER_SELECTOR are handled according to browser default.

After making all of the selector and group definitions, use a curly bracket along with a series of attributes and their values. Mate each attribute and its value with a colon and separate each pair from the next pair by a semicolon. The values within a definition, such as the name of a typeface or a color value, are not case-sensitive. For example, for font-family, you can have Garamond, garamond, or GARAMOND, and it will all work out the same in the browser.

As with all good syntax, you can place style definitions in three ways within a document: with an embedded style sheet, with a linked style sheet, and with an inline style sheet.

Embedded Style Sheet

The <STYLE> tags contain an embedded style sheet. As a matter of structure, the format of an HTML page with an embedded style sheet is as follows:

```
<HTML>
<HEAD>...</HEAD>
<STYLE>...</STYLE>
<BODY>...</BODY>
</HTML>
```

The <STYLE> tags contain the list of selectors and styles.

Linked Style Sheet

The linked style sheet is a .css file that contains nothing but a set of <STYLE> tags and their contents. Identify the style file within an HTML document using the <LINK> tag in the head:

```
<HEAD>
<LINK rel=stylesheet href="filename.css" type="text/css">
</HEAD>
```

At runtime, the browser will load the style in the .css file and use it to format the document. If the HTML page also includes an embedded style sheet that conflicts with the linked style sheet, the embedded version also takes precedence.

Inline Style Sheet

The last option, inline style sheets, uses style sheet syntax, although it's technically not a style sheet implementation. This option uses the style sheet nomenclature to customize single incidents of tags within the document:

```
<TAG style="attribute1:value1; ...">
```

Essentially, this is a way to customize HTML tags on a case-by-case basis. When you use all three forms of syntax, they occur in a cascading form of precedence. The highest priority is inline, followed by embedded, then linked.

Style Attributes

Several classes of attributes are used within the definition for a selector. The following sections cover each of the attributes within a class.

Fonts

There are no current standards for typefaces and their use on different user machines, so you'll need to choose carefully and include several options to achieve the desired effect for the user.

The font-family Attribute

The font-family attribute lists font families in order of preference, separated by commas. Two types of variables are used: family name and generic family.

```
BODY {font-family: Garamond, Palatino, Serif}
```

A family name is the name of a specific typeface such as Helvetica, Garamond, Palatino, or Optima. Enclose font names with spaces in quotes, such as "Gil Sans". The generic family is one of five choices that classifies the typeface by its style and is recommended as the last option in a font-family list:

☐ Serif: Fonts with accents at the tips of the lines (for example, Times)

☐ Sans serif: Fonts without finishing accents (for example, Helvetica)

- ☐ Cursive: Scripts that more closely resemble hand-drawn calligraphy (for example, Zapf Chancery)
- ☐ Fancy: Special-use decorative fonts (for example, Comic Book Sans)
- ☐ Monospace: Fonts that maintain uniform spacing despite letter width (for example, Courier)

The `font-style` Attribute

This attribute specifies the type of treatment a font receives and is represented by the values `normal`, `italic`, or `oblique`. The `normal` value is also referred to as Roman in some typeface references. The `oblique` value is similar to `italic` except that it is usually slanted manually by the system rather than by a separate style of the font, like italic.

```
BODY {font-style: italic}
```

The `font-variant` Attribute

Similar to `font-style`, this attribute sets small caps. Its two values are `normal` and `small-caps`.

```
BODY {font-variant: small-caps}
```

If there is no true small caps version of the typeface, the system will attempt to scale the capital letters to a smaller size for lowercase letters. As a last resort, the text will appear in all capitals.

The `font-weight` Attribute

A number of values for this attribute set the darkness or lightness of a typeface. The primary values are `normal` and `bold`. You can substitute these values with one of a list of values from `100` to `900`. If a typeface includes a "medium" weight, it will correspond to `500`. Bold is represented by `700`.

```
BODY {font-weight: bold}
```

Two additional values are `bolder` and `lighter`, which increase the weight from the current parent weight by one level, such as 200 to 300 for bolder or 700 to 600 for lighter.

The `font-size` Attribute

Four methods can define the size of a font in a style—absolute size, relative size, length, or percentage.

- ☐ Absolute size: This method is represented in several ways. The first is with a value that represents its size relative to other sizes within the family (`xx-small`, `x-small`, `small`, `medium`, `large`, `x-large`, `xx-large`). You can also use a numerical value, such as `12pt` (12 points).

  ```
  BODY {font-size: 18pt}
  ```

- ☐ Relative size: This method sets the size relative to the parent style. It can be one of two values, `smaller` or `larger`, and it adjusts the size up or down the scale of sizes.

If a font doesn't include a mapping to size names, a scaling of 1.5 is recommended between sizes. For example, a 10pt font would be scaled larger to 15pt or smaller to 7pt.

```
P {font-size: smaller}
```

☐ Length: This method is another form of relative size that sets the size by the scale factor of the width of an em, such as `1.5em`.

```
P {font-size: 2em}
```

☐ Percentage: This method is also a relative specification that multiplies the size of the parent font by the percentage value to achieve the new size, such as `150%`.

```
H3 {font-size: 300%}
```

The `font` Attribute

This attribute provides a shorthand for setting all of the previous attributes under one umbrella. The order of the attributes should be `font-style`, `font-variant`, `font-weight`, `font-size`, `line-height`, `font-family`. Place no commas between each of the attribute values, except for listed font families:

```
BODY {font: small-caps bold 14pt garamond, palatino, serif}
```

Color and Background

These elements set the color values for the text (foreground) and the area behind the text (background). In addition to setting a background color, you can also define a background image. All color values are defined using the same methods as the `color` attribute.

The `color` Attribute

This attribute defines the color of the text element and is specified using one of the color keywords (such as `red`). You can also define the color using a hexadecimal triplet, denoting the mix of red, green, and blue (such as `rgb(255,0,0)`).

```
BLOCKQUOTE {color: rgb(0,255,255)}
```

The `background-color` Attribute

This attribute sets the background color for a style. You can set this attribute independently of a background color for the document to enable you to highlight text in a different manner.

```
BLOCKQUOTE {background-color: blue}
```

The `background-image` Attribute

This attribute specifies a background image for a style element. Use it in conjunction with `background-color` to ensure a substitute effect if the image becomes unavailable. If the image is available, it will display on top of the background color.

```
BLOCKQUOTE {background-image: url(logo.gif)}
```

D

The `background-repeat` Attribute

If the background image should be repeated (tiled), use this attribute to define how. Its values include `repeat`, `repeat-x`, and `repeat-y`. The `repeat` value indicates that the image should be tiled normally. The `repeat-x` value repeats the image in a single horizontal line, and the `repeat-y` value repeats the image in a vertical line.

```
BLOCKQUOTE {background-image: url(logo.gif);
           background-repeat: repeat-x}
```

The `background-attachment` Attribute

This attribute, an extended feature of background images not seen in HTML before, sets whether the background image is attached to the foreground text (`scroll`) or anchored to the background (`fixed`). This feature is apparent only when the user scrolls across a selection of text.

```
BLOCKQUOTE {background-image: url(logo.gif);
           background-attachment: repeat-x}
```

The `background-position` Attribute

When you use a background image through normal HTML, the starting point is always the top left of the screen. With a style sheet, you can specify a starting point anywhere within the box that contains the style content.

You can specify the image's starting position in three ways. The first way is with keyword locations. For horizontal placement, your choices are `left`, `center`, or `right`. For vertical placement, your choices are `top`, `center`, or `bottom`. Alternatively, you can represent the position as a percentage of the available area, with `0% 0%` being the top left (default) and `100% 100%` being the bottom right. The last option is to specify an actual measurement in centimeters or inches.

If only one value for the placement is given, it's used as the horizontal position. If both values are given, the first is evaluated as horizontal and the second as vertical.

```
BLOCKQUOTE {background-image: url(logo.gif);
           Background-repeat: repeat-y;
           background-position: right top; }
```

The `background` Attribute

This shorthand attribute, similar to `font`, enables you to define a set of values for the background in one stop. The order is `background-color`, `background-image`, `background-repeat`, `background-attachment`, and `background-position`.

```
P { background: black url(logo.gif) repeat-y fixed right top }
```

Text

This set of style attributes covers the values that can affect the appearance of text, but not by directly changing the typeface. This includes values for spacing, underlining, blinking and strike-through. It also supports some of the positioning attributes, including left and right justification and indents.

The word-spacing **Attribute**

This attribute indicates an addition to the default amount of space between individual words and is specified in *ems*. An *em* is the space occupied by the letter "m" and is the baseline for determining widths within a font. To return the value to its default, use 0em or normal.

```
BODY { word-spacing: 1em }
```

The letter-spacing **Attribute**

The letter-spacing attribute is similar to word-spacing, except that letter-spacing adds an extra bit of spacing between individual letters. In addition to the default method the browser uses to determine spacing, additional letter spacing is also affected by text alignment.

```
BODY { letter-spacing: 0.2em }
```

The text-decoration **Attribute**

This attribute is more closely related to its cousins in the font family. It specifies extra text flourishes, such as underline, strike-through, and blinking. The four values are none, underline, overline, line-through, and blink.

```
STR.blink { text-decoration: underline blink }
```

The vertical-align **Attribute**

This attribute sets the vertical position of the text either to an absolute reference or in relation to the parent element. It supports a range of values and keywords:

- ☐ Baseline: Aligns the baseline of the style with the baseline of the parent element
- ☐ Sub: Assigns the style to a subscript relative to the parent element
- ☐ Super: Assigns the style to a superscript relative to the parent element
- ☐ Text-top: Aligns the top of the text with the top of the parent's text
- ☐ Text-bottom: Aligns the bottom of the text with the bottom of the parent's text
- ☐ Middle: Aligns the vertical halfway point of the element with the baseline of the parent plus half of the x-height of the parent (x-height is the height of the lowercase x of the font)
- ☐ Top: Aligns the top of the element with the tallest element on the current line

☐ Bottom: Aligns the bottom of the element with the lowest element on the current line

☐ (Percentage): Using a positive or negative percentage value, raises or lowers the element beyond the baseline of the parent

```
SUB { vertical-align: -10% }
```

The text-transform Attribute

This attribute sets the capitalization of the affected text to one of four choices: capitalize (first letter of every word), uppercase (all letters in capitals), lowercase (all letters in lowercase), and none.

```
STR.caps { text-transform: uppercase }
```

The text-align Attribute

This attribute moves beyond the standard HTML left-right-center alignment to provide full justification (justify left and right). If a browser doesn't support justify, it will typically substitute left.

```
BLOCKQUOTE { text-align: justify }
```

The text-indent Attribute

The text-indent attribute, specified in an absolute value measured in ems or inches, defines the amount of space that is added before the first line.

```
P { text-indent: 5em }
```

The line-height Attribute

This attribute sets the distance between adjacent baselines using a length (in ems), multiplication factor, or percentage. Factors are indicated without any units, such as 1.5. When you use this method, the child inherits the factor, not the resulting value.

```
DIV { line-height: 1.5; font-size: 12pt }
```

In this instance, the line height becomes 18 points and the font size remains at 12 points.

Margins, Padding, and Borders

Each element created in a style sheet is presented in its own "box." All of the styles from the element inside the box are applied, although the box itself can have its own properties that define how it relates to adjoining elements on the page. Length is specified in inches (in), centimeters (cm), ems (em), points (pt), or pixels (px).

Box properties are divided into three basic categories. Margin properties set the border around the outside of the box, padding properties determine how much space to insert between the border and the content, and border properties define graphical lines around an element.

Additional properties of the box include its width, height, and physical position.

The `margin-top, margin-bottom, margin-right,` **and** `margin-left` Attributes

These four attributes set the amount of space between the element and adjoining elements, whether defined by length or percentage of parent text width or handled automatically.

```
BLOCKQUOTE { margin-top: 4em;
             Margin-bottom: auto }
```

The `margin` **Attribute**

The `margin` attribute provides a shorthand method for setting the four margin values.

When you specify the four values, they are applied, in order, to the top, right, bottom, and left. If you provide only one value, it applies to all sides. If you use two or three values, the missing values are copied from the opposite sides.

```
BLOCKQUOTE {margin: 4em 2em}
```

The `padding-top, padding-bottom, padding-right,` **and** `padding-left` Attributes

These attributes set the distance between the boundaries of the box and the elements inside the box. It can use any of the physical measurements or a percentage of the parent's width.

```
BLOCKQUOTE {padding-top: 110%; padding-bottom: 115%}
```

The `padding` **Attribute**

The `padding` attribute provides a shorthand method for setting the four padding values.

When you specify the four values, they are applied, in order, to the top, right, bottom, and left. If you provide only one value, it applies to all sides. If you use two or three values, the missing values are copied from the opposite sides.

```
BLOCKQUOTE {padding: 10pt 12pt}
```

The `border-top, border-bottom, border-right,` **and** `border-left` Attributes

These four attributes set the style and color of each border around an element. Specify styles with one of the border style keywords: `none, dotted, dashed, solid, double, groove, ridge, inset,` and `outset`. For more information on these, see the information on `border-style` later in this chapter.

Specify colors using a color keyword. For more information, see the `border-color` later in this chapter.

```
BLOCKQUOTE {border-left: solid red}
```

The `border-top-width`, `border-bottom-width`, `border-right-width`, and `border-left-width` Attributes

These attributes define a physical border around the box, similar to the border used for HTML tables. In addition to defining a specific width in ems, you can also use the keywords `thin`, `medium`, and `thick`. Using a measurement in ems results in a border whose width changes in relation to the size of the current font.

```
STR {border-right-width: 2pt;
     border-left-width: 2pt }
```

The `border-width` Attribute

The `border-width` attribute provides a shorthand method for setting the width of the four borders.

When you specify the four values, they are applied, in order, to the top, right, bottom, and left. If you provide only one value, it applies to all sides. If you use two or three values, the missing values are copied from the opposite sides.

```
BLOCKQUOTE {border-width: medium 0pt 0pt thick}
```

The `border-color` Attribute

This attribute sets the color of all four borders and uses one color keyword as its value. You cannot set the color of each side independently.

```
BLOCKQUOTE {border-color: yellow}
```

The `border-style` Attribute

The border's appearance can take on several different settings, represented by `none`, `dotted`, `dashed`, `solid`, `double`, `groove`, `ridge`, `inset`, and `outset`. The last four values are represented in 3D, if the browser supports it. Alternatively, the browser also can present all of the variations as a solid line, except `none`.

Like `border-color`, the style is applied uniformly to all four sides.

```
BLOCKQUOTE {border-style: groove}
```

The `border` Attribute

The `border` attribute provides a shorthand method for setting all of the border variables, including width, style, and color. It sets the values for all four sides at the same time, overriding any individual settings that may have been set previously for the same element.

```
BLOCKQUOTE {border: 1.5pt double black}
```

The `height` Attribute

This attribute sets the overall height of the bounding box that contains either the text or image element. If the content is text, scrollbars are added as needed so that all of the material is still available to the user. If the content is an image, it's scaled to fit inside the area. You can set a physical value or use auto to let the browser allocate space as needed.

```
BLOCKQUOTE {height: 100px}
```

The width **Attribute**

Similar to height, the width attribute sets the overall width of the bounding box that contains the element. If the content is text, scrollbars are added as needed so that all of the material is still available for the user. If both elements are used with an image and the value of one element is auto, the aspect ratio for the image is maintained.

```
BLOCKQUOTE {width: auto}
```

The float **Attribute**

This attribute sets a value similar to the align attribute used in HTML. The three possible values are left, right, and none. The none value allows the element to fall where it may, and the other two values force the element to the left or right of the screen with text wrapping around the opposite side.

```
BLOCKQUOTE {float: right}
```

The clear **Attribute**

This attribute mimics the clear attribute used with the HTML <BR> tag and uses the same keywords as float. If you use it with right or left, elements will move below any floating element on that respective side. If you set it to none, floating elements are allowed on both sides.

```
BLOCKQUOTE {clear: left right}
```

Classification

These attributes control the general behavior of other elements more than actually specifying an appearance. In addition, classification includes the attributes for list items, identified in HTML with the <LI> tag.

The display **Attribute**

This attribute identifies when and if a style element should be used. Four keywords determine its behavior:

- [ ] Inline: A new box is created within the same line as adjoining text items and is formatted according to the size and amount of content within its borders, such as an image (IMG) or text (STR).

- [ ] Block: A new box is created relative to the surrounding elements. This is common with elements such as H1 and P.

D

☐ List-item: Similar to block, only list item markers, which behave more like inline content, are added.

☐ None: Turns off the display of the element in any situation, including for children of the element.

```
IMG {display: inline}
BLOCKQUOTE {display: block}
```

The white-space Attribute

The name of this attribute is a bit misleading because it relates to how spaces and line breaks are handled. The choices are normal (in which extra spaces are ignored), pre (as in preformatted HTML text), and nowrap (in which lines are broken only with <BR>).

```
BLOCKQUOTE {white-space: pre}
```

The list-style-type Attribute

This element sets the type of markers used for a list. Your choices are disc, circle, square, decimal, lower-roman, upper-roman, lower-alpha, upper-alpha, and none. For more information on how each of these is represented onscreen, see Chapter 9, "Dynamically Changing Content."

```
LI.outline1 {list-style-type: upper-roman}
LI.outline2 {list-style-type: upper-alpha}
LI.outline3 {list-style-type: decimal}
```

The list-style-image Attribute

In lieu of a text marker for the list item, you can also specify the URL of an image to use. If the image is unavailable, the text marker is used as default.

```
LI.general {list-style-image: url(bullet.jpg)}
```

The list-style-position Attribute

The two values for this attribute, inside and outside, determine the formatting of text following the list item marker. The outside value, the default value, lines up the additional lines of text beyond the first line with the first character in the first line. If you use the inside value, the second and following lines are justified with the list item marker.

```
LI {list-style-position: inside}
```

The list-style Attribute

This attribute is a shorthand element for the list-style-type, list-style-image, and list-style-position attributes.

```
OL {list-style: lower-alpha outside}
UL {list-style: square url(bullet.jpg) inside}
```

INDEX

U

U.S. Census Web site, 304
<U> tag, 398
UBound statement, 463
UCase function, 473
<UL> tag, 400
underlined text, HTML markup, 398
unescape() function, 456
unload events, 158-160
unordered lists, HTML markup, 400
user agents, 227
user-generated events, 265-266
user_agent attribute, 49
UTC() method, 424

V

validating forms
blur event, 168-169
focus event, 169
var statement, 457
<VAR> tag, 396
variables
HTML markup, 396
JavaScript, 110
VarType function, 473
VBScript (Visual Basic Scripting Edition), 46, 342-343
case sensitivity, 343
constants, 463
error handling, 468
functions
Abs, 464
Asc, 464
Atn, 462
CBool, 464
CByte, 464
CDate, 464
CDbl, 464
Chr, 464
CInt, 464
CLng, 464
Cos, 462
CSng, 465
CStr, 465
Date, 466

DateSerial, 465-466
DateValue, 465-466
Day, 466
Exp, 462
Fix, 465
Hex, 465
Hour, 466
InputBox, 469
InStr, 472
Int, 465
IsArray, 462, 473
IsDate, 473
IsEmpty, 473
IsNull, 473
IsNumeric, 473
LBound, 462
LCase, 472
Left, 472
Len, 472
Log, 462
LTrim, 472
Mid, 472
Minute, 466
Month, 466
MsgBox, 469
Now, 466
Oct, 465
Right, 472
Rnd, 462
RTrim, 472
Second, 466
Sgn, 465
Sin, 462
Space, 472
Sqr, 462
StrComp, 472
String, 473
Tan, 462
Time, 467
TimeSerial, 466-467
TimeValue, 466-467
Trim, 473
UCase, 473
VarType, 473
Weekday, 467
Year, 467
JavaScript, compared, 342-343
literals, 463
operators, 469-470
set keyword, 343

statements
Call, 470
Dim, 462-463, 467
Do...Loop, 471
End, 467
Erase, 462
Exit, 467
For...Next, 471
Function, 467
If...Then...Else, 471
Option Explicit, 470
Preserve, 463
Randomize, 462
Rem, 463
Select Case, 471
Set, 463
Sub, 468
UBound, 463
While...Wend, 472
vector format, 11
vertical-align attribute, 481-482
baseline value, 481
bottom value, 482
capitalize value, 482
lowercase value, 482
middle value, 481
sub value, 481
super value, 481
text-bottom value, 481
text-top value, 481
top value, 481
uppercase value, 482
viewing templates, 371
virtual environments, 247
visibility attribute, 129
Visual Basic Scripting Edition, see VBScript
VRML Web site, 362

W

W3C (World Wide Web Consortium), 24-25
DHTML standards, 25-30
browser information, 29
content manipulation, 29
document manipulation, 28
DOM, 28
event model, 29
GUI, 28

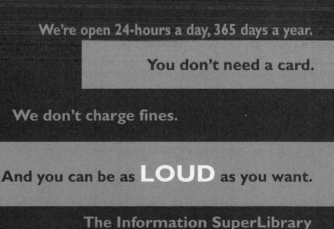

Teach Yourself Web Publishing with HTML 4 in a Week, Fourth Edition

—Laura LeMay

Teach Yourself Web Publishing with HTML in a Week, Fourth Edition is a thoroughly revised version of the shorter, beginner's soft cover edition of the best-selling book that started the whole HTML/Web publishing craze. This book now covers the new HTML Cougar specifications, plus the Netscape Communicator and Microsoft Internet Explorer 4 environments, as well as style sheets, Dynamic HTML, and XML. This book teaches Web publishing in a clear, step-by-step manner with lots of practical examples of Web pages. It's still the best HTML tutorial on the market.

Price: $29.99 US/$42.95 CDN   *User Level: New–Casual*
ISBN: 1-57521-336-2   *720 pages*

HTML Unleashed

—Rick Darnell, Michael Larson, et al.

A comprehensive guide and reference to the foundation language of the World Wide Web, *HTML Unleashed* provides an exhaustive resource devoted to the language of Web development. The Web's explosive growth continues to give us an expanding market of Web authors ranging from casual home hobbyists to the professional Web developer. *HTML Unleashed* gives you the information you need to grow with an ever-changing technology. It covers all the latest proprietary extensions, including Microsoft's Active HTML and Netscape's JavaScript Stylesheets, and includes information on integrating HTML with other technologies such as Java and ActiveX. It details new HTML technologies such as the experimental "Cougar" specification, cascading style sheets, and Extensible Markup Language (XML).

The CD-ROM contains a wide variety of HTML development tools, a collection of examples from the authors, and two electronic books in HTML format.

Price: $49.99 USA/$70.95 CAN   *User level: Accomplished–Expert*
ISBN: 1-57521-299-4   *1,080 pages*

Laura Lemay's Web Workshop: Designing with Style Sheets, Tables, and Frames

—Molly Holzschlag

Web page designers have long complained that HTML is too primitive a language to give them the same control over the layout and design of their Web pages that they're used to in a desktop publishing environment. *Laura Lemay's Web Workshop: Designing with Style Sheets, Tables, and Frames* gives intermediate to experienced Web authors a practical, example-rich guide to controlling the appearance and layout of Web pages. It provides a clear, hands-on guide to designing and creating sophisticated Web page layout with style sheets, tables, and frames.

The CD-ROM includes a hand-picked selection of the best Web publishing tools and utilities, including custom-designed style sheets and page layout templates.

Price: $39.99 USA/$56.95 CAN
ISBN: 1-57521-249-8

User level: Casual–Accomplished
607 pages

Teach Yourself Web Publishing with HTML 4 in 14 Days, Second Professional Reference Edition

—Laura Lemay and Arman Danesh

A thoroughly revised version of the best-selling book that started the whole HTML/Web publishing phenomenon, *Teach Yourself Web Publishing with HTML 4 in 14 Days, Second Professional Reference Edition* is easy enough for the beginner yet comprehensive enough that even experienced Web authors will find it indispensable for reference. It includes 16 more chapters than the softcover edition, plus a 300-page HTML reference section. It covers the new "Cougar" specification for the next version of HTML and the new Netscape and Microsoft technologies such as style sheets, absolute positioning, and dynamic HTML.

The CD-ROM includes an electronic version of the reference section, plus additional Web publishing tools for Windows and Macintosh platforms.

Price: $59.99 USA/$84.95 CAN
ISBN: 1-57521-305-2

User level: New–Casual–Accomplished
Price: 1,176   pages

Add to Your Sams.net Library Today
with the Best Books for Internet Technologies

ISBN	Quantity	Description of Item	Unit Cost	Total Cost
1-57521-336-2		Teach Yourself Web Publishing with HTML 4 in a Week, 4E	$29.99	
1-57521-299-4		HTML Unleashed	$49.99	
1-57521-249-8		Laura Lemay's Web Workshop: Designing with Style Sheets, Tables, and Frames	$39.99	
1-57521-305-2		Teach Yourself Web Publishing with HTML 4 in 14 Days, Second PRE	$59.99	
		Shipping and Handling: See information below.		
		TOTAL		

Shipping and Handling: $4.00 for the first book, and $1.75 for each additional book. If you need to have it NOW, we can ship product to you in 24 hours for an additional charge of approximately $18.00, and you will receive your item overnight or in two days. Overseas shipping and handling adds $2.00. Prices subject to change. Call between 9:00 a.m. and 5:00 p.m. EST for availability and pricing information on latest editions.

201 W. 103rd Street, Indianapolis, Indiana 46290

1-800-428-5331 — Orders   1-800-835-3202 — FAX   1-800-858-7674 — Customer Service

Book ISBN 1-57521-335-4

MACMILLAN COMPUTER PUBLISHING USA

A VIACOM COMPANY

Technical

Support:

If you need assistance with the information in this book or with a CD/Disk
accompanying the book, please access the Knowledge Base on our Web
site at **http://www.superlibrary.com/general/support**. Our most
Frequently Asked Questions are answered there. If you do not find the
answer to your questions on our Web site, you may contact Macmillan
Technical Support **(317) 581-3833** or e-mail us at **support@mcp.com**.

What's on the Companion Web Page

The companion Web page for this book contains more details about this title as well as any source code or examples that the author outlined in the chapters. This source code is available for download from our site for you to use in conjunction with this book. You may access these files by visiting the Sams Publishing web site at

```
http://www.mcp.com/info/1-57521/1-57521-335-4
```

These code examples and/or templates are available in a self-extracting file for your convenience. To review the latest information about these files and the book, select the README document included in the self-extracting file.

Technical Support

If you need assistance with the information in this book or with the code associated with this book, please access the Knowledge Base on our Web site at

```
http://www.mcp.com/
```

Our most Frequently Asked Questions are answered there. If the answer to your question cannot be found in our Knowledge Base, you can e-mail us at support@mcp.com.